ANIMAL

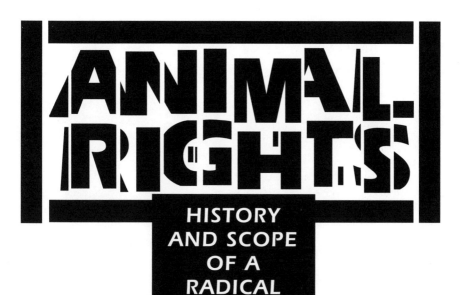

ANIMAL RIGHTS

HISTORY AND SCOPE OF A RADICAL SOCIAL MOVEMENT

Harold D. Guither

Southern Illinois University Press
Carbondale and Edwardsville

Library of Congress Cataloging-in-Publication Data
Guither, Harold D.
    Animal rights : history and scope of a radical social movement /
    Harold D. Guither.
        p. cm.
    Includes bibliographical references and index.
    1. Animal rights. 2. Animal welfare—Moral and ethical aspects.
    I. Title.
    HV4708.G85   1998
    179'.3—dc21   97-23656
                                   CIP
    ISBN 0-8093-2158-0
    ISBN 0-8093-2199-8 pbk.

The paper used in this publication meets the minimum requirements
of American National Standard for Information Services—Permanence
of Paper for Printed Library Materials, ANSI Z 39.48-1984. ∞

Contents

Appendixes

Tables

Preface

Radical social movements are not new in American history. Abolition of slavery, women's suffrage, prohibition (and repeal), and, in recent years, the civil rights movement and anti-Vietnam war protests were launched by radical thinkers who eventually amassed public support and achieved their goals.

Now in the past decade, as philosopher Bernard Rollin points out, we have "witnessed a major revolution in social concern with animal welfare and moral status of animals." [1]

The animal rights movement has emerged from old ideas but with new philosophies emphasizing moral and ethical standards for how humans should treat animals. This emerging social movement has received literary attention from its advocates and opponents. This book attempts to describe and document the movement from the middle of the road. Such a goal, if not impossible, is not easy. Most philosophers in this field present ideas that appear to be reasonable and plausible. But in the real world, confusion, suspicion, misunderstanding, and mistrust exist about the activists and the opponents in the movement, their true character, objectives, and beliefs.

On the one side are those who resist reform, are concerned about the consequences of radical change in handling and treating animals, and are ready to defend their business, property rights, position, and beliefs. On the other side, activists who accept the new philosophies are determined to convince others of their beliefs.

So in this work, my goal is to present a brief history of animal protection and the emergence of animal rights, describe the scope of the movement, and identify some of the major players and organizations.

To develop a useful reference for students, animal owners, users, and other interested persons is a formidable task. My purpose is not to answer why the movement has reached its current status but rather to document what is happening in the 1990s and the possible consequences for those who own, use, or enjoy animals in entertainment and leisure pursuits.

This publication should be most useful as a text and reference for students in animal sciences, veterinary medicine, philosophy, and public policy. Animal owners, practitioners, and professionals engaged in animal and biomedical research, animal protection, education, and public policy making and implementation, and those manufacturing and distributing animal equipment and supplies should find this work a useful reference.

Organizations and movement participants have changed and will continue to change. Comments and quotes from individuals may be misunderstood or taken out of context as the reader or listener applies his or her own values or knowledge to what is said.

In researching the literature, reports, and documents, one can find lots of philosophical doctrine and opinions, mixed with limited supporting data and objective scientific evidence. In this setting, I have tried to report the situation without condemning any organization or individual but still presenting a broad perspective of the animal rights movement in the 1990s.

I hope that by presenting the many facets of animal and human relationships that you, the reader, can decide who to believe or to follow in this often controversial arena.

President Eisenhower once observed, "It takes much more courage to walk alone down the middle of the road being stoned from both sides than to walk down either side in the comparative shelter of your extremist friends."

Acknowledgments

This book could not have been written without extensive assistance and support of many people and organizations. Grateful appreciation is due to many organizations that provided annual reports, brochures, and other literature to show their activities and programs.

Research grants from the University of Illinois Campus Research Board, the Illinois Pork Producers, and the US Department of Agriculture Office of International Cooperation and Development enabled me to travel to conferences and gather data. I attended lectures presented by Andrew Rowan, Bernard Rollin, Tom Regan, Jim Mason, and Ingrid Newkirk that provided enlightening insights into the philosophy and character of these thought leaders in the animal rights and animal welfare movements.

At the University of Illinois, the library staffs in the Agriculture, Veterinary Medicine, Law, History and Philosophy, Education, Newspaper, and Undergraduate departmental libraries were most helpful. The Institute of Government and Public Affairs assisted in early stages of data collection.

The university approved a six-month sabbatical leave for the author in 1993, which provided time to complete research and writing of an early draft. David L. Chicoine, the former head of the Department of Agricultural Economics and now dean of the College of Agricultural, Consumer, and Environmental Sciences, supported and encouraged my efforts.

Wesley Jamison at Oregon State University, now at the University of Arkansas, conducted research and wrote chapter 5 and made suggestions on other chapters. William Lunch in the Department of Political Science at Oregon State University also participated in parts of this research.

Personal interviews and conversations with John Hoyt, Kathleen Marquardt, John Boyce, Adele Douglass, Hugh Johnson, Steve Kopperud, Stephen Zawistowski, Bradley Miller, Jenny Woods, Peter Wood, and Gene Bauston provided special insights into their organization's perspectives. Frank Leguen de Lacroix and Andrew John Wilson at the Commission of the European Communities provided special insights into the animal welfare work at the Commission for the European Communities. Two unnamed reviewers made constructive suggestions that helped in many ways to build the manuscript into its final form.

Colleagues at the University of Illinois at Urbana-Champaign, Gilbert Hollis, James Corbin, Leroy Biehl, David Purnell, Ken Koelkebeck, and Michael Hutjens deserve special thanks for answering questions and providing information during the writing process. Research and library search assistance from Michelle Lenkaitis, Jeff Beavers, and Aaron Perkinson was invaluable. And a special note of thanks is due to my secretary Pat Roosevelt who provided assistance in numerous ways. My wife, Lois, deserves special recognition as she provided a pleasant home environment and endured many hours alone so that this project could be completed.

Acronyms

The following acronyms are used for organizations and agencies mentioned throughout this book:

AAALAC	American Association for Accreditation of Laboratory Animal Care	AWI	Animal Welfare Institute
AALAS	American Association of Laboratory Animal Science	BUAV	British Union for the Abolition of Vivisection
AAMC	Association of American Medical Colleges	CDFG	California Department of Fish and Game
AAVS	American Anti-Vivisection Society	CEASE	Coalition to End Animal Suffering and Exploitation
ABR	Association for Biomedical Research	CITES	Convention on International Trade in Endangered Species
AFAAR	American Fund for Alternatives to Animal Research	CSC	Congressional Sportsmen's Caucus
AFBF	American Farm Bureau Federation	DDAL	Doris Day Animal League
AHA	American Humane Association	DIIAAR	Disabled and Incurably Ill for Alternatives to Animal Research
AIF	Animal Industry Foundation	DNR	(Minnesota) Department of Natural Resources
ALDF	Animal Legal Defense Fund		
ALF	Animal Liberation Front	EC	European Economic Community
ALRM	Animal Liberation/Rights Movement	EU	European Union
		FACT	Food Animal Concerns Trust
AMA	American Medical Association	FAR	Feminists for Animal Rights
APA	American Psychological Association	FARM	Farm Animal Reform Movement
		FAWC	Farm Animal Welfare Coalition (US)
API	Animal Protection Institute		
ARI	Animal Rights International		Farm Animal Welfare Council (UK)
ARM!	Animal Rights Mobilization!		
ASPCA	American Society for the Prevention of Cruelty to Animals	FBI	Federal Bureau of Investigation
		FBR	Foundation for Biomedical Research
AVAR	Association of Veterinarians for Animal Rights		
		FDA	Food and Drug Administration
AVMA	American Veterinary Medical Association	FFA	Fund for Animals
		FOA	Friends of Animals

FWS	Fish and Wildlife Service	NIDA	National Institute on Drug Abuse
HARE	Humans Against Rabbit Exploitation	NIH	National Institutes of Health
		NPPC	National Pork Producers Council
HFA	Humane Farming Association	NPS	National Park Service
HHS	Department of Health and Human Services	NRA	National Rifle Association
		NSF	National Science Foundation
HSUS	Humane Society of the United States	OSU	Oregon State University
		PAWS	Performing Animal Welfare Society
IBR	Institute for Behavioral Research	PCRM	Physicians Committee for Responsible Medicine
IDA	In Defense of Animals		
IIFAR	Incurably Ill for Animal Research		
ISAR	International Society for Animal Rights	PETA	People for the Ethical Treatment of Animals
LCI	Livestock Conservation Institute	PPF	Putting People First
MAFF	Ministry of Agriculture, Fisheries and Food (UK)	PsyETA	Psychologists for the Ethical Treatment of Animals
MLPF	Mountain Lion Preservation Foundation	PTN	PETA Teachers' Network
		RSPCA	Royal Society for the Prevention of Cruelty to Animals
MSPCA	Massachusetts Society for the Prevention of Cruelty to Animals	SCAW	Scientists Center for Animal Welfare
NABR	National Association for Biomedical Research	UAA	United Action for Animals
		UEP	United Egg Producers
NAIA	National Animal Interest Alliance	UK	United Kingdom (England, Scotland, Wales, Northern Ireland)
NAS	National Academy of Science		
NAVS	National Anti-Vivisection Society		
NCBA	National Cattlemen's Beef Association	UPC	United Poultry Concerns
		USDA	United States Department of Agriculture
NCIB	National Charities Information Bureau		
		USU	Utah State University
NEAVS	New England Anti-Vivisection Society	YNP	Yellowstone National Park
NFU	National Farmers Union		
NHES	National Humane Education Society		

1

The Evolution of Animal Welfare and Animal Rights

Organized efforts to improve humane treatment of animals began in the nineteenth century in England and the United States. The early goals were to prevent cruelty and oppose experiments on animals. The first US animal rights organizations originated in the 1970s. Their actions and activities were much broader and included both political and social objectives.

The close ties between humans and animals go back many centuries. Keith Thomas describes the close associations in England where animals and families shared living quarters, where pets providing companionship were often fed better than servants, and where horses were so valuable for work and transportation that no custom of eating their meat developed.[1]

By the beginning of the eighteenth century, writers began to discuss animal feelings of pain and suffering, vivisection (the surgical operations performed upon live animals during experiments), cruel treatment of animals raised and slaughtered for food, and the religious teachings that influenced humane treatment of both humans and animals. This new emphasis upon animals' feelings of sensation in the eighteenth century brought growing criticism of some forms of cruelty. Doubts about the ethics of castrating domestic animals were raised as early as 1714.[2]

Humane Societies: The Beginning of Animal Welfare

It is not surprising that the pressure to change methods of treating animals did not come from the owners, the grooms, servants, and cab drivers. Educated country clergymen and well-to-do townsmen remote from agricultural operations first expressed this new sentiment toward animals.[3]

However, the age-old association of hunting linked to class privilege made some of the upper class resistant to the new sentiments about animal treatment.[4] And the pressure to eliminate the cruel sports such as cock fighting stemmed from a desire to discipline the new working class into more industrious work habits.[5]

After several unsuccessful attempts, the first society for the prevention of cruelty to animals was founded in London in 1824. It later became the Royal Society for the Prevention of Cruelty to Animals. Its objectives were to attack animal cruelty and promote kindness to animals in support of prevailing social and religious values, support enforcement of existing laws, and pass new ones.[6]

Public policy establishing the animal welfare movement began in Great Britain with the passage of an act in 1835 to "consolidate and amend the several laws relating to the cruelty and improper treatment of animals." In 1911, Parliament passed the *Protection of Animals Act*, which is still in force. Established on the principle that while humans are free to subjugate animals, it is wrong for people to cause them to suffer unnecessarily.[7]

Ruth Harrison initiated much of the public concern for the welfare of farm animals under modern production methods when her book *Animal Machines* was published in England in 1964. Among animal activists, her influence in stimulating concerns and public actions about how humans treat animals has been compared to Rachel Carson who stimulated interest and public policies in the US environmental movement.

Harrison is believed to be the first to label confinement livestock and poultry production as factory farming. She criticized the practices by which farm animals

> are being taken off the fields and the old lichen covered barns are being replaced by dawky, industrial type buildings into which the animals are put, immobilized through density of stocking and often automatically fed and watered. Mechanical cleaning reduces still further the time the stockman has to spend with them, and the sense of unity with his stock which characterizes the traditional farmer is condemned as being uneconomic and sentimental. Life in the factory farm revolves entirely around profits, and animals are assessed purely for their ability to convert food into flesh, or saleable products.[8]

Harrison concluded that the modern methods by which farm animals were being reared were cruel. The more she studied the subject, the deeper her conviction that other issues were involved. She believes that the issue is less one of animal rights versus human rights than one of human responsibilities. She opposes activism that involves breaking of laws that she feels to be destructive of the very cause these people purport to help.[9]

The Brambell Report

Following the publication of Ruth Harrison's *Animal Machines* in 1964, the British Parliament called for an investigation. In 1965, the Brambell Committee, a group of scientists and concerned citizens, issued their report that set the stage for animal welfare and animal rights groups to criticize and work for improvements in the modern production systems used for food animals and poultry.[10]

The report recommended certain mandatory standards that would conform to good husbandry. In addition, it called for certain statutory provisions that would define suffering to enable the government to establish regulations for particular animals. The act and regulations would be enforced by the State Veterinary Service, and an advisory committee was to be set up to advise the government.

Specific practices recommended for poultry included these: Cages for laying hens were not to contain more than three birds, should measure at least 20 inches wide and 17 inches deep, and have an average height of 18 inches. The floor of the cage should consist of rectangular metal mesh not finer than number 10 gauge. Deep litter laying birds should have at least 3 square feet of floor space per bird. Loose housing of poultry on wire floors or slats should be prohibited. Broilers above six weeks should have at least 1 square foot of floor space. Poultry houses should be provided with lighting bright enough for all birds to be seen clearly for routine inspection. Debeaking of battery birds and broilers should be prohibited.

Recommended practices for pigs included the following: Housed pigs between 150 and 210 pounds should have a minimum of 8 square feet of floor space per animal. For those above 210 pounds, the minimum should be 10 square feet. Pig houses should be provided with lighting bright enough for all animals to be seen clearly for routine inspection. Docking should be prohibited except as remedial treatment by a veterinary surgeon. Pregnant sows should not be kept without daily exercise in quarters that do not permit them to turn around, and they should not be tethered indoors.

For cattle, the report recommended these practices: Milk substitute or other manufactured diets for calves should be so reinforced with iron in a suitable form to ensure that the normal intake of the animal is in no way deficient in this element. All calves should be provided with palatable roughage daily at all ages from a week after birth. Yoking or close tethering of calves, except for short periods and for specific purposes, should be prohibited. Individual pens for calves should be sufficient to allow the calf freedom of movement including the ability to turn around, and for calves from 200 to 300 pounds, the pen should measure at least 5 feet by 3 feet 6 inches, and the sides should not be solid above 2 feet from the floor. Pens for more than one calf should not allow less than 12 square feet per animal. Calves should be provided with sufficient clean straw or other bedding on which to lie down. The restraint by prolonged or permanent short tethering or yoking of animals being fattened for beef should be prohibited. Housed cattle of more than 500 pounds should each have a minimum space of 25 square feet. Bedding should be provided for animals kept in houses or yards.

For turkeys, the report called for 1.5 square feet of floor space up to 8 weeks, 25 square feet from 8 to 12 weeks, and 4 square feet above 12 weeks. Wire floors should meet the specification suggested for caged poultry. Although the report did not make recommendations for statutory standards for sheep or rabbits, it called for a review of husbandry practices by the Farm Animal Welfare Standing Advisory Committee.

The Brambell report is cited frequently as the landmark standard for farm animal welfare. It set the stage for animal welfare reform in the United Kingdom and other northern European countries. In the United States, efforts to establish husbandry standards under state or federal law have not succeeded. But pressures to establish standards along the lines of the Brambell report are expected to continue.

Animal Welfare in the United States

The social and cultural evolution of animal protection in Europe led to change in the United States. The formation of local humane societies to care for abandoned and stray animals also dates back to the nineteenth century. Founding of these national and state societies indicate a growing concern for animal welfare:

- The American Society for the Prevention of Cruelty to Animals, 1866
- The Massachusetts Society for the Prevention of Cruelty to Animals, 1868
- The Washington (D.C.) Humane Society for the Prevention of Cruelty to Animals, 1870
- The American Humane Association, 1877 [11]
- The Humane Society for the Promotion of Animal Welfare, 1883 (no longer in existence)
- The Humane Society for Promotion of Animal Welfare, Grand Rapids, Michigan, 1883
- The Animal Rescue League of Boston, 1889
- The Anti-Cruelty Society (Society for the Prevention of Cruelty to Animals of Illinois), 1899

Antivivisection efforts also trace back to the nineteenth century:

- The American Anti-Vivisection Society, 1883
- The New England Anti-Vivisection Society, 1895

Throughout the twentieth century, local humane societies have continued to emphasize prevention of cruelty to animals, provided shelters, and worked to encourage proper care and treatment.

The Emergence of the Animal Rights Movement

Although the animal rights concept originated in nineteenth-century England, the serious social and political movement in the United States emerged in the 1970s. Its aims are distinct from the traditional humane societies that still work to stop people from treating animals cruelly or the early antivivisection groups that opposed scientific experimental work with animals. In its ideological values and its ethical assumptions, the modern animal rights movement is radically different. Concern for protecting animal welfare was eclipsed by the philosophical imperative that animals, like humans, possess certain fundamental and inalienable rights, and therefore should be treated as moral equals. Often comparing the use of animals in research and industry to slavery, many advocates of animal rights oppose all ways in which animals are confined and utilized by humans, whether it be for food, clothing, servitude, or household pets. [12] The new animal rightists "embrace the idea of animal equality—a philosophy that contains a strain of Eastern religions and carries 'cultural relativism' to its ultimate extreme." [13]

Many new organizations have emerged, focusing on specific aspects of animal welfare and animal rights. Departing from the traditional emphasis on animal welfare and humane treatment, many of these groups actively oppose use of animals for any purpose and speak out against biomedical research, confinement livestock and poultry production, and use of animals in product testing, for pleasure and leisure activities.

Other organizations conduct campaigns and demonstrations against the production and use of animals for fur; they also oppose trapping and hunting, whaling, and the killing of dolphins in the fishing industry or capture for display in zoos and aquariums. Some groups engaged in these activities fit the abolitionist category mentioned later in this chapter.

One private study reported, "The animal rights movement today is the successor to the antiwar and human rights crusades of the 1960s and 1970s. After decades of being 'on the fringe,' animal rights advocacy has become a mainstream grassroots movement. Some of these organizations do not deny the necessity of using animals in humane tests for medical purposes, but many do, and virtually all decry animal testing related to beauty and household products." [14]

Several groups have emphasized the need to find alternatives to animals for both research and testing purposes. Others advocate more emphasis on preventive education and less for animal research (see chapter 6).

Farm animal welfare has become a new priority for activists. Nationwide, various groups publicize what they see as unacceptable conditions for farm animals and lobby for legislation to set stricter standards for their shelter, management, and treatment (see chapter 7).

The political influence of the animal industry probably explains why the federal government so far has notably avoided regulation of animal care on farms despite several bills brought before Congress. However, efforts to force changes in management practices in livestock and poultry production are likely to continue.

Violence by animal rights activists began in England, home to the world's oldest animal welfare tradition. The Hunt Saboteurs Association, Band of Mercy, and Animal Liberation Front have engaged in disrupting hunts, destroying shooting ranges, and targeting the fur, food, and animal research industry. Similar movements have cropped up in other nations, including the United States in 1977 and Canada in 1979 (see chapter 4 and appendix 6).

Political and Social Dimensions

The political dimension of the animal rights movement involves individual and group efforts supporting or opposing specific issues. The methods include campaigns to influence legislation through letter writing and other direct contacts; seminars and media events to influence members of Congress and public opinion; demonstrations to draw public attention to what activists see as improper treatment of animals; inviting sympathetic members of Congress and other government officials to speak or receive awards at annual meetings and other special events; and securing sponsorship of bills in Congress. The activists participating in these activities may be reformists or abolitionists.

The social dimension involves longer range goals and objectives to change attitudes and gain public favor and sympathy for animal rights principles and goals. Several organizations provide special publications and classroom materials to influence children. Some organizations assist students who object to dissecting dead animals in laboratory class exercises. One organization schedules seminars at key locations across the country to educate and indoctrinate new converts and interested persons to animal rights activities. On college campuses, student animal rights organizations are encouraged and given support. Prominent animal rights activists give lectures to influence college students and gain support for various activities where activists and demonstrators are needed.

The animal rights movement of the 1990s, that has built upon earlier anticruelty and animal welfare efforts, covers many issues from many different perspectives. Speaking before the 1994 International Animal Rights Symposium, Kenneth Shapiro identified four phases of the animal rights movement.[15]

1. Identifying the problems of animal mistreatment. For example, various groups condemn laboratory animal research, intensive farming methods, fur farming and trapping, hunting, capture and exhibition of marine mammals, face branding of cattle imported from Mexico, and poisoning of predatory wild animals.

2. Developing appropriate ideology to cover the principles and concerns in human and nonhuman animal relationships. A single ideology cannot cover the full range of animal issues. Some programs and campaigns have elements of both reformist and abolitionist goals. Animal activists are asked to respect each other's efforts. For example, Richard Ryder identifies three main doctrines of the animal rights movement in the 1990s: (1) the animal rights philosophy of inherent value, opposition to abuse of animals in any way, and concern for each animal as an individual, most closely associated with Tom Regan; (2) the utilitarian doctrine that asserts that causing pain is wrong unless it outweighs the benefits and is necessary for human benefit, most closely associated with Peter Singer; and (3) the concept of pain in which Ryder claims it is wrong to inflict pain on individual animals regardless of their species.[16]

3. Understanding how change occurs. To bring about change, activists are advised to recognize certain stages of change in attitudes, study the tactics that bring about progressive social changes, develop a critical mass of opinion on an issue, and work together to influence changes in public policy and private decisions.

4. Developing explicit standards of ethics for advocacy. The acts of animal extremists have hurt the public image of the animal rights movement (see chapter 13). Although none of the more than three hundred identified actions in the Department of Jus-

tice report involved personal injury or nonviolent loss of life, Shapiro asserts that activists cannot do evil deeds to get good results. He suggests a "summit for animals" in which activist groups could discuss ethical restraints openly and advocate honesty, fairness, and nonviolent practices.

Shapiro believes that the animal rights movement is doing well on identifying the problems and developing ideology, but it is not doing so well on understanding change or setting ethical standards for advocacy.

Goals and Strategies

Although Phillip Martin's study for Harvard University centered on the movement as it affected biomedical research, he identified strategies and goals that apply to most aspects of animal rights. In the early years, antivivisectionists relied primarily on emotion and sentimentality. Since this approach yielded only limited success, today's animal rights activists are using these strategies:

• Attack the validity of biomedical research as it is now conducted and assert that the use of animals in research is not only cruel and immoral but unnecessary for the advancement of medicine and science since valid alternatives exist or can be created (see chapter 6).

• Continue efforts to establish legal rights for animals. Through court decisions in recent years, a body of law has emerged that recognizes and protects the rights of animals (see chapter 14).

• Recruit scholars such as philosophers, veterinarians, physicians, and scientists into the animal rights movement. The strategy has met with some success, and the presence of these professionals on the lecture circuit and on college campuses has increased the awareness of the movement and the believability of its arguments (see chapter 10).

• Launch a major public education or propaganda campaign that uses a variety of communication vehicles, including paid advertising, the news media, and written material for members and the general public. Also, hold public meetings and demonstrations to attract large crowds.

• Develop classroom teaching materials at the elementary level where teachers can make lasting impressions with young children (see chapter 8).

The long-established humane societies rely heavily on letter-writing campaigns and the legislative process. The more liberal animal rights groups rely on demonstrations, celebrity endorsements, and testimony to enhance their credibility and organize media campaigns. However, in the political process to achieve their objective, animal rights activists tend to be reluctant to moderate their demands or actions. Some believe they are morally correct; thus, they feel it would be immoral to compromise and accept only partial solutions.[17]

The Animal Rights Power Cluster

Daniel Ogden, a political scientist sees public policy making as segmented and decentralized through various "power clusters." He characterizes such policy making through the use of a system of power clusters, organized around broad subject areas including agriculture and food, natural resources, health, education, defense, transportation, justice and law enforcement, and others that operate in relative isolation from one another.

Within each power cluster, the federal government's executive agencies, congressional committees, organized interest groups, professionals, certain special individuals, and an attentive public interact to identify problems, arrive at acceptable solutions, and provide the resources to carry out the decisions.[18] Although participants in the power cluster do not always agree, they share common interests and concerns. The power cluster, described by Ogden, applies to the animal rights movement: government agencies responsible for enforcing legislation dealing with humane treatment of animals; members of Congress who have special interests in animals; animal organizations organized as interest groups; the professionals from philosophy, medicine, psychology, veterinary medicine, sociology, and law; certain individuals; thought leaders identified in earlier and later chapters; and a large population of public supporters who contribute millions of dollars to support the animal protection groups.

The animal rights community as a power cluster is less than fifteen years old—in its relative infancy compared with the longer established power clusters mentioned above. To reach many of their objectives, the animal rights power cluster must compete at different times and in different ways with the clusters encompassing food and agriculture, biomedical research, companion animals, fur, hunting and outdoor sportsmen and -women, horse racing, dog racing, zoos, and aquariums. Consequently, some animal rights organizations concentrate their legislative, educational, and fund-raising efforts on a few specific concerns, rather than cover the whole range of animal related issues.

Another feature of power clusters can be identified in the animal rights movement: the movement of persons from one part of the cluster to another; yet they continue to work and network with the different parts of the power cluster. The list of persons in "Who's Who in Animal Rights and Animal Welfare" identifies a number of persons who have worked with more than one organization or serve one organization along with board, committee, or advisory roles in other groups (see appendix 1). Some of the most recent shifts and connections that illustrate this personnel interaction and movement within the animal rights power cluster: Kim Stallwood from PETA to editor of *Animals' Agenda*; Merritt Clifton from news editor of *Animals' Agenda* to editor, *Animal People*; Kim Bartlett from editor, *Animals' Agenda*, to publisher, *Animal People*; Wayne Pacelle from Fund for Animals to Humane Society of the United States; Cleveland Amory from board member of Humane Society of the United States to founder, Fund for Animals, and president, New England Anti-Vivisection Society; Neal Bernard, president of Physicians for Responsible Medicine and board member, New England Anti-Vivisection Society, former board member, Animal Rights Network; Alex Pacheco, cofounder of PETA and vice-president, New England Anti-Vivisection Society; Ingrid Newkirk, cofounder, PETA, and board member, New England Anti-Vivisection Society.

As a power cluster, although not formally organized as such, animal rights organizations, their leaders, and related government agencies can work together as a force to influence public policy, provide oversight on laws and regulations, and advance their principles and objectives.

Defining the Terms

It is difficult if not impossible to classify different organizations and individuals into a single group according to their beliefs, values, and activities related to animals.

Animal protection refers to all efforts to prevent cruelty, improve humane treatment, reduce stress and strain, and monitor research with animals. Animal protection also involves individuals and groups with many variations of philosophy and ethical values and with economic and professional interests in all kinds of animals.

Animal welfare generally describes those who support the humane treatment of all animals without concern for their ultimate use. An "animal welfarist" believes that humans have the right to use animals, as long as suffering is reduced or eliminated. Those who believe in animal welfare work for the reform of cruel or abusive situations to alleviate animal suffering. Animal scientists and agricultural engineers have conducted extensive research on animal treatment, the production environment, and design of facilities. Farmers have historically been perceived as strong supporters of animal welfare because they believe that animals raised under humane conditions and practices will be the most productive and profitable.

Gary Francione and Tom Regan view animal welfare as a contradiction of animal rights. Francione asserts, "What you do when you merely ameliorate the conditions of enslavement is that you perpetuate the enslavement." Regan views the efforts of animal welfarists as efforts "to improve the corrupt system of exploitation" and "prolong injustice." [19]

The animal rights philosophy (encompassing animal liberation) includes some fundamental differences from animal welfare. It involves the idea that nonhuman animals are sentient beings—that they have the capacity to experience pain and pleasure. And accompanying this belief is the idea that animals have certain inalienable moral rights, which humans should not violate. Like animal welfarists, most animals rights activists work to abolish cruel or abusive situations, thus eliminating animal suffering. However, some animal rights advocates believe that nonhuman animals have the right not to be used for any purpose by humans—that animals are "not ours to eat, wear or experiment on." [20] To implement this philosophy means the elimination of all uses of animals for food, clothing, leisure, or research purposes. People would adopt vegetarian diets; eliminate wool, leather, feathers, and fur for clothing or ornamental purposes; and abolish use of animals for leisure activities, such as in hunting, horse and dog racing, zoos, circuses, or aquariums.

Reformist or abolitionist? Rowan suggests that indiscriminate and careless use of animal rights terminology tends to confuse rather than clarify issues. He believes a more useful way would be to distinguish between different categories of how people relate to animals: (1) those groups that have been unwilling to depart from traditional animal sheltering and cruelty investigations; (2) those that have broadened their concerns to include farm animals and research animals but who tend to work within the system; and (3) those who have resorted to high-profile activist campaigns to confront and challenge the establishment and call for a radical change in the way we treat animals.[21]

Even this modified scale may be too simple. Rowan suggests a more accurate way of distinguishing different groups campaigning on behalf of animals would be to separate groups on the basis of their philosophy on treatment and humane use of animals and also on their political approach from dialogue to illegal activities.[22] Animal rights in the political context can mean almost anything from a campaign to achieve the liberation of all animals, including pets, to much more limited goals pursued via standard political tactics including horse trading and compromise.[23]

Following Rowan's suggestion, a clearer understanding of animal activists in the 1990s may be gained by identifying individuals or groups as reformists or abolitionists. The reformists usually include those who have read and believe in the works of philosophers, such as Singer and Regan, but who want to work within the system to improve the conditions under which animals are treated. The abolitionists work to eliminate all uses of animals that they see as causing pain and suffering. Efforts to destroy the fur apparel industry, eliminate veal production, stop laboratory animal research and product testing, promote vegetarian diets, and ban hunting are a few goals of abolitionists in the animal rights (or liberation) movement.

However, as new people join the animal rights movement, the movement and the views of its followers become more diverse.[24] Most animal welfare advocates can probably be classed as reformists. But some animal rights advocates might also support reform in the short run hoping to achieve abolition of animal usage in the long run.

Current Assessments

The interests in animal protection have evolved through three types of organizations: (1) local humane societies and societies for the prevention of cruelty to animals (SPCAs), (2) national organizations with a range of objectives and differing degrees of reformist and abolitionist goals, and (3) grassroots activist organizations encouraged by the leading animal rights and animal welfare groups. The largest and most active groups, their leadership, objectives, and finances are described in later chapters (see chapters 4 and 15).

Within the movement, different people have different ideas about how humans should treat animals. Those who believe in animal welfare may want to bring about reform or maintain the status quo. Those who advocate animal rights embrace a different philosophy. Unlike the old-line antivivisectionists opposed to animal experimentation, the new animal rightists embrace the philosophy of ethical treatment and want to abolish all utilization of animals by humans.

Francione expresses the most definitive animal rights position. He believes that any attempt to balance human and animal interests with laws that prohibit inhumane treatment or unnecessary suffering will be futile. He sees property rights as the most valued human right and believes that most human-animal conflicts occur because humans seek to exploit their animal property. So his proposed strategy is to get laws and regulations that prohibit, not regulate, animal use and reflect and recognize that animal interests are not subject to being sacrificed or traded away for certain reasons. In addition, the interest of animals should be consistent with the inherent value of the animal and not as human property.[25]

The animal rights movement attracts thousands of financial supporters and appears to be growing. In 1994 and 1995, seventeen organizations had total support and revenues of over $1 million; three had over $15 million. Some groups are well endowed while others operate on very limited resources and volunteers (see chapter 15).

While the size of the movement and the wealth of some groups makes the movement a potentially powerful political force, deep divisions within the movement remain. In the larger organizations, some staff members lean more to the animal rights philosophy while others advocate reform but still believe in moderate animal welfare policy. Some animal activists are also sympathetic and supportive of activists in the environmental, wildlife preservation, feminist, and other social action groups. Among the recognized animal rights organizations, some follow strict abolitionist animal rights doctrine but are willing to compromise and support reforms because they realize that abolition cannot take place all at once.

To further public awareness and gain public support, the National Alliance for Animals sponsored the March for Animals in June 1990 and a second march in June 1996 in Washington, D.C. The National Park Service estimated a crowd of 24,000 at the 1990 march, although the sponsors claimed from 50,000 to 75,000 participants (see chapter 5 for a study of participants).

The National Park Service estimated that three thousand participated in the 1996 march. Several months before the march, some leading animal activists expressed concern about who should be invited to participate. Close observers labeled the June 1996 event "a public failure" and were questioning how the money donated to fund the march had been spent.[26]

The groups targeted by animal rights campaigns have begun actions to counter the campaigns against them. During the 1996 March for Animals, animal rights opponents staged media sessions to present their position on animal research and the benefits of biomedical research. It was estimated that 65 percent of the media coverage was negative to the animal rights movement.[27]

Through their past achievements, educational efforts, and contacts with government agencies and members of Congress, animal industries and organizations have a backlog of goodwill and strong sympathetic support.

Robert Charrow, a former deputy general counsel in the US Department of Health and Human Services, explains the movement's success this way: "The yuppified animal rights movement was born in a courtroom and has generated much of its more legitimate publicity as a result of lawsuits. This trend is not surprising. Litigation has long been the tool of single-issue special interest groups. The courtroom provides a unique forum for those who advocate extreme positions, who champion causes of minimal social utility, or feel spurned by government decision-makers." [28]

Bernard Rollin assesses the animal rights movement from his philosophical viewpoint: "Anyone with any historical perspective on the United States knows full well not only that we have never had a social and moral revolution that was not incremental, but also that one cannot hold back these revolutions." [29]

2

A Changing Philosophy for Human and Animal Relationships

The animal rights movement has emerged in the late twentieth century as a result of the writings of philosophers and critics concerning how animals are treated. The philosophers and activists do not completely agree on how humans should interact with animals, but all support more humane treatment. These concerns have ignited a social movement that is not likely to go away since the arguments are based on reason, not emotion. If enough people accept these ideas, major changes in the use and treatment of animals will take place.

The writings of philosophers and the actions of their converts have sparked innovative and controversial ethical standards for human relationships toward animals. Since the 1970s, their writings have activated the latent support of millions of citizens, stimulated new movements, driven the development of new organizations, and generated intense political activity.

For philosophers, debate about the moral status of animals is not new. They frequently quote works of Aristotle, Descartes, Bentham, and Salt in their writings. But in recent years, the volume of literature has greatly expanded from anticruelty discussions to moral and ethical principles. The treatment of animals has emerged as a branch of applied ethics and is being examined, along with such issues as abortion and euthanasia, in philosophy courses and in the schools.[1]

In this new approach, philosophers present different and conflicting ideas about the moral and ethical basis for dealing with animals. However, most agree that changes and improvements are needed.[2]

Philosophical Concepts for the Treatment of Animals

By definition, *philosophy* is the study of the processes governing thought and conduct and a study of human morals, character, and behavior.[3] Now in the last quarter of the twentieth century, philosophers are debating how humans should treat and care for animals. And inspired by their writings, dedicated individuals and groups are building a new social movement and introducing the concepts of animal liberation, animal rights, and animal welfare.

Philosophy, as a field of study, is normally considered complex and difficult to understand for those who have not read extensively and studied the lines of reasoning used by philosophers. However, to understand the relationships between these philosophical writings and the emergence of the animal rights movement, we must try to understand certain terms and concepts.

Animal liberation refers to ending the sacrifice of animals for human benefit. In contrast, anticruelty limits the moral concern to humane handling and treatment but treats animals as resources for human consumption. Peter Singer wrote about animal liberation, but later writers and activists have used the term *animal rights*. He believed that liberation demanded an end to prejudice and discrimination and an expansion of our moral horizons. He compared the emerging concept of animal liberation with movements to liberate slaves in the nineteenth century and the civil rights movement in the twentieth century.

Speciesism is a prejudice or attitude toward the interests of members of one's own species and against those of members of other species.[4] Richard Ryder is credited with originating this term, but Singer picked it up and others have expanded and furthered Singer's views. The objections to racism and sexual prejudice apply equally to speciesism. From the philosopher's ethical perspective, humans and animals are equal whether they stand on two feet, four, or none at all.

However, this concept does not imply that animals have all the same rights as humans. Differences between humans and nonhuman animals also provide a basis for differences in their rights. But the basic principle is one of equality, not necessarily treating animals and humans in the same way, but giving them equal consideration for the abilities that they possess. The speciesist allows the interests of his or her own species to override the interests of those of other species.

Sentient beings are living beings that have the capacity to feel pain, suffer, and experience enjoyment. Under the new moral ethic, animals are considered sentient beings, like human beings. While some early philosophers disagreed with this concept, most people believe that mammals with a nervous system similar to humans do feel pain. This recognition underlies many of the moral and ethical principles of animal liberation and animal rights.

Jeremy Bentham initiated this perception in an often-quoted passage: "But a full grown horse or dog is beyond comparison a more rational as well as a more conversable animal than an infant of a day or a week or even a month old. But suppose they were otherwise. What would it avail? The question is not, can they reason? can they talk? but can they suffer?"[5]

Is there a line between living things and sentient beings? Philosophers usually take the position that plants do not have the same feelings of pain and sufferings as animals. And the presence of sensation in lower life forms, such as cold-blooded animals or insects, is an open question.[6] Most philosophy scholars on human and animal relationships limit the sentient being concept to mammals.

Equal consideration of interests is a moral principle that should guide how humans treat animals. If animals have interests, then they should not be excluded from moral concerns of how they are treated. But a major question among philosophers is whether animals, not being able to talk, have the ability to communicate and reveal what their interests really are. Nevertheless in Singer's view, and many others who follow his principles, animals should not be killed for food, experimented upon if the same experiment would not be performed on a human, raised or hunted for their fur, or caused to suffer pain in any other way. However, all interests of humans and animals need not be given equal weight. But where they have similar interests such as avoiding physical pain, then those interests should be counted equally.[7]

Inherent value is a complex concept that involves the belief that individuals, both human and nonhuman, have equality and value in themselves. Inherent value is considered distinct from intrinsic value, which is related to experiences animals have as individuals. Inherent value means individuals have value in their own right distinct from the experiences that they undergo. In Tom Regan's view, humans have duties to treat animals justly because they are equal in the sense that they have equal inherent value.[8] According to Regan, what we need to know is whether the animals that are routinely eaten, hunted, and used in our laboratories are like us in being subjects of a life. The principle of equal inherent value of animals requires their equal right to be treated with respect. Since in our moral code, we do not justify harming or killing a human being for research, and humans and nonhuman animals have equal moral standing, neither can we justify harming or killing a creature such as a laboratory rat.

Utilitarianism involves basing decisions concerning what is morally right or wrong on the outcome that will bring about the best total consequences for everyone affected, not just the best consequences for the individual who acts. Some philosophers agree with this principle, others do not. Even those who follow utility theory do not always agree.[9]

Singer and Regan definitely disagree on this principle. Singer is considered a utilitarian since he has stated that at times animal experimentation could be justified if it would cure a major disease.[10] He also suggests if a person does not oppose painless killing of animals, he could consciously eat animals that had lived free of suffering and were slaughtered painlessly.[11] So as a utilitarian, Singer is viewed as a liberationist but not really an advocate of animal rights in the same meaning that Regan is. Singer cannot object to the painless killing of animals while Regan claims that animals, like humans, are "subjects of a life" who can be harmed by death.[12]

Justice, as a philosophical principle, requires that we owe animals respectful treatment, neither out of kindness nor because of the sentimental interests of others. This belief that all animals should be treated with respect and as a matter of strict justice implies that respectful treatment is their right.[13] Regan believes that by justifying the independent value and rights of other animals, we have scientifically informed and morally impartial reasons for denying that these animals exist to serve us.

Anthropomorphism is the portrayal of a nonhuman, such as an animal, with the characteristics of humans. Leahy accuses some philosophers of indulging in anthropomorphism in their characterization of animals.[14]

Building a Foundation for Animal Liberation and Animal Rights

The writings of thoughtful philosophers and others have inspired and motivated people to actively support the animal rights (or liberation) movement. Some philosophers who are frequently quoted to further support animal rights concepts and animal protection are identified below.

Henry Salt was not the first to argue for the rights of animals, but some of Salt's ideas have had an enduring effect. Later philosophers recognize that he contributed to a continuing debate. He lived in England most of his life, founded the Humanitarian League, and led campaigns against flesh eating, blood sports, and the captivity of wild animals. His book *Animal Rights* published in 1892 laid the philosophical foundation for animals rights and the opposing arguments that are still around a century later. Later observers credit Salt with establishing the right of domestic animals to be treated with courtesy and fairness.

Peter Singer, a professor of philosophy and director of the Center of Human Bioethics at Monash University in Melbourne, Australia, wrote *Animal Liberation*, published in 1975 and revised in 1990. Some regard it as the bible of the new animal rights movement, since it presents many of the basic philosophical concepts for ethical treatment of animals. Philosophy scholars see some of Salt's ideas in Singer's writings. At least partly as a result, animal liberation (more frequently termed *animals rights* by others) has emerged as an influential and often dominating ethical and moral force to protect animals. For Singer, the animal rights movement is an expansion of our moral horizons beyond our own species and thus a significant stage in the development of human ethics.[15] Although a vegetarian, he is more tolerant of how humans use animals than are some other philosophers.

R. G. Frey presents his case for moral vegetarianism but separates his arguments from the belief that eating meat is wrong. He believes the more serious wrong is the pain and suffering that animals endure in their production, in being killed, and in the violation of their rights.[16] Although he believes that killing is wrong and that farm animals endure painful practices, he suggests that the wrongness of these practices depends on how one values the life of the animal. But evaluating the wrongness of killing an animal is difficult when people do not agree on such issues as abortion, euthanasia, and capital punishment for humans.[17] He criticizes Singer for his utilitarian approach to how humans should treat and use animals, and he believes that one cannot argue for benefits to humans from practices that cause pain and suffering for the animals.

Stephen Clark makes the simple claim that it is wrong to treat animals badly, for the same reasons that it is wrong to treat human beings badly. Since we say that animals are injured, not damaged like an inanimate object, then Clark reasons that animals are proper objects for moral concern.[18] He believes that animals are deserving of respect, even though they cannot be given moral credit for their actions, and must be given greater toleration.[19] So even if animals are without rights in the sense of human rights, he does not believe that we have any right to eat their flesh, command their service, or torment them.[20] He concludes that "there are other sentient creatures all about us, who may lack our verbalizing gifts but who have their lives to live and their own visions of reality to worship. We are not separate from them, and owe them honor. To imagine that their lesser intelligence (whatever that may be) licenses our tyranny is to leave the way open for any human intellectual elite to treat the rest of us as trash." [21] He believes that vegetarianism is a necessary pledge of moral devotion.

Tom Regan, an American philosopher and author, has set forth a more definite animal rights philosophy in contrast to Singer's utilitarian approach. His writings have further expanded interest and support for animal rights. He emphasizes two propositions: first, that animals have certain basic moral rights and, second, that recognition of their rights requires fundamental changes in how we treat them.[22] Regan sees the fundamental wrong as a system that allows us to view animals as our resources, here for us to eat, manipulate surgically, or exploit for sport or money.[23]

Part of the strategy of the animal rights movement is to cite well-known people from the past who supported some phase of animal rights philosophy. Leonardo da Vinci is cited as a vegetarian for moral reasons. Mark Twain is described as an abolitionist regarding use of nonhuman animals in science, for moral reasons.

So Regan explains that a vital part of the animal rights movement's future depends on how well animal advocates identify and support the "gifted hands, voices, and minds who express positive concern for animals in their work, in their painting, theater performances, dance, poetry, legal and moral theory." He views those involved in the struggle for animal rights as part of what is best in the world, not a throwback to what is worst.[24]

Giving farm animals more space, more natural environments, or more companions does not right the fundamental wrong. In Regan's philosophy, only the recognition of the animal's autonomous rights will resolve the moral dilemma. "There are battles to be fought in the classroom and the courts, in places of worship and before government bodies, in the marketplace and in the cafeteria line." [25]

Richard Ryder opposes the use of animals in research. He wonders why scientists accept the basic Darwinian assertion that humans and animals are on the same biological continuum but do not, other than for sentiment, put humans and animals upon the same moral continuum. He believes that humans intellectually accept their biological relationship with other animals without taking the logical step of acknowledging a moral relationship and treating animals for what they really are—our relatives.[26] Ryder uses the term *speciesism* to describe the widespread discrimination that is practiced by humans against the other species. He identified speciesism and racism as forms of prejudice that show a selfish disregard for the interests of others and for their sufferings.[27] In his arguments against animal research, he labeled as nonsense the argument that the pain suffered by conscious creatures of one species is justified by benefits experienced by conscious individuals of another species because the latter species is better than the former.[28] So he reasons, to impose suffering, allegedly in order to reduce it, and to take life, allegedly in order to save it, are self-contradicting claims.

S. F. Sapontzis points out that the most common defense of our exploiting animals—and one that is best supported by our moral tradition—is that we are rational beings, while animals are not.[29] But even if this is a morally important difference, it does not justify our exploiting animals, according to Sapontzis. A recurrent theme in his work is his effort to show that an assumption that human beings are superior to animals is both unreasonable and will not support the weight it is asked to bear.[30] Our everyday moral tradition and concepts, such as our well-established concerns with fairness and minimizing suffering, provide a sufficient basis for that argument.

Mary Midgley analyzes animal and human relationships around what constitutes a person or a nonperson and the division of the world into persons and property. The changing attitudes toward slavery provide an example. As she sees the situation, "What makes creatures our fellow beings, entitled to basic consideration, is not their intellectual capacity but emotional fellowship." The powers that justify a higher claim and bring some creatures nearer to the degree of consideration which is due to humans are sensibility, and social and emotional complexity expressed by deep, subtle, and lasting relationships. In her view of animal rights, a proper understanding of their place cannot be achieved without a much more fundamental critique than conventional moral theories.[31]

Bernard Rollin has raised questions about the morality of animal use in the sciences and has attempted to effect significant change in this area. He sees a growing moral concern for animals and their welfare among the general public that is putting pressure on scientists to investigate animal consciousness and suffering. He believes that if science can study and measure how, when, and to what extent animals feel pain, fear, anxiety, sorrow, boredom, and aggression, then it would be possible to discuss the all-important details of our moral obligations to animals.[32]

Dale Jamieson presents arguments against keeping animals in zoos; he also argues that it is morally wrong to take animals out of their native habitats, transport them great distances, and keep them in alien environments in which their liberty is restricted.[33] If we respect animals' interests, Jamieson argues, it is not in their interest to be taken from the wild. He discredits the perceived benefits of amusement, education, scientific research, and preserving species as reasons for having zoos.

Michael P. T. Leahy disagrees with many philosophers in *Against Liberation—Putting Animals in Perspective*. He supports the British 1986 *Animals Scientific Pro-*

cedures Law and asserts that animals should be treated humanely. But with this provision, they may also be killed, experimented upon, hunted, raced, or petted—legal and defensible actions.[34] He is obviously in a different camp than the advocates for animal liberation and animal rights. "They will see my conclusions as both casting pagan doubt upon the theoretical sub-structure of the movement for animal rights . . . but also as giving aid and comfort to meat eaters, experimental researchers and wearers of fur coats whose behavior they detest." [35]

However, despite the differences and the debate among philosophers on how humans should treat animals, a social movement has emerged from their writings and teaching. While the debate continues, actions have moved into the world of activists, organizations, citizen volunteers, and animals owners and users.

From Moral Principles to Application for Human and Animal Relationships

Singer and Regan, whose works provide widely recognized philosophical analyses, set the stage for the animal liberation (Singer's term) or animal rights movement (Regan's term).[36] Although both are concerned about harm and suffering of animals, they use different arguments to reach their conclusions.

Although Singer is concerned about treatment of animals to avoid pain and suffering and wants species treated equally with respect to infliction of pain, he also advocates the best balance of good and bad consequences for everyone and suggests using animals for certain purposes may be justified. These views are considered "utilitarian." However, Regan criticizes Singer's utilitarian reasoning that emphasizes aggregate concerns, since it does not provide a foundation for the claims of an individual over a group.[37]

Given these principles, the philosophers have established a new code for moral and ethical treatment for animals. Singer called upon his readers to live without inflicting suffering on animals. The biggest examples of speciesism, and almost universally accepted, are animal research and growing of animals for food. Yet Singer advises to temper one's ideals with common sense and suggests that one could oppose research without insisting that all experiments terminate.[38] But research that has no direct or urgent purpose to help human welfare should be stopped immediately. The remaining areas should be phased out as alternative methods for research and testing are developed. As a solution, governments need to change their policies, and people need to change their own lives, Singer concludes.

For Singer, the most practical and effective step to stop the killing of nonhuman animals and the infliction of suffering is to become a vegetarian. He opposes rearing animals for food on a large scale because he believes that the animals suffer from castration, separation of mothers from their young, branding, and crowding during transport. And he firmly believes that psychologically it is not possible to have concern for nonhuman animals and continue to eat them. He feels that people are ignorant of the abuse of living creatures that lies behind the food they eat with all but the end product delicately screened from their eyes.[39]

Vegetarianism would serve as a form of boycott that would affect the number of animals raised. However, Singer believes it is more urgent to stop eating meat and eggs because of the suffering involved in their production. He is less critical of those who continue to eat dairy products. But to have absolute purity in all that one consumes or wears, Singer advises not to eat animal products or wear leather shoes or fur products.[40]

On the vegetarian issue, animal rights activists see a strange paradox: On the one hand, people naturally love animals; on the other, they eat them. So they ask, how is it possible to eat what one loves? To animal rights activists like Regan, "it is not larger, cleaner cages that justice demands in the case of animals used in science, but empty cages; not traditional animal agriculture, but a complete end to all commerce in the flesh of dead animals"; not more humane hunting and trapping, but the total eradication of these practices.[41]

Using animals in research is viewed as a brutal consequence of speciesism. Philosophers usually look at research as causing animal suffering, exploiting animals for questionable purposes or benefit to humans, and, when used for testing products, as unreliable. Their solution is to use alternative testing methods for drugs and other products or do without new and nonessential products. In the view of most animal rights activists, the best, most moral solution that society can reach when considering the use of animals in science is not to use them at all.

Although raising and killing animals for food and using them in research are the most widespread "exploitation," animal rights activists also oppose hunting, fur farming, circuses, rodeos, and capturing wild animals for zoos.

Regan sums up the animal rights movement as committed to three goals: (1) the total abolition of the use of animals in science, (2) the total dissolution of commercial animal agriculture, and (3) the total elimination of commercial and sport hunting and trapping.[42] Two decades after *Animal Liberation* was first published, animal activists can cite the move away from testing cosmetics on animals, a reduction in number of animals used in laboratory experiments, and efforts in Europe to make livestock and poultry production less stressful. Singer believes it is important to see these reforms as stepping stones on the path to further goals, not as the be-all and end-all of the campaign.[43]

Related Philosophies: Religion and the Environment

Most religions have some beliefs or doctrines dealing with the use and treatment of animals. For Christians and Jews, Genesis 1:28 is the Bible verse often cited to justify the use of animals: "Be fruitful and multiply and fill the earth, and subdue it: And have dominion over the fish of the sea, over the birds of the air, and over every living thing that moves on the earth." However, there is a question of whether dominion should be defined as domination over animals or stewardship and responsibility. One interpretation puts moral obligations upon humans to care for animals.

Another interpretation in Genesis 1 : 29 – 30 suggests a mandate for humans to live upon the vegetation of the earth rather than animal flesh. "Behold I have given you every plant yielding seed which is upon the face of all the earth and every tree with seed in its fruit; you shall have them for food. And to every beast of the earth, and to every bird of the air, and to everything that creeps on the earth, everything that has the breath of life, I have given every green plant for food."

Singer points out the influence of the Judeo-Christian insistence on the God-like nature of human beings and the standard Western doctrine of the sanctity of human life: a doctrine that puts the life of the most hopelessly and irreparably brain-damaged human being above the life of a chimpanzee. As Singer explains the difference, the chimpanzee is not a member of our species and the brain-damaged "human vegetable" is biologically human.[44]

Within the traditions of Christianity, Judaism, and other religions are many interpretations of how humans should deal with animals. Leahy faults the world's great religions as "notorious for simultaneously looking in different directions." He criticizes the current attempt to establish an authoritative position for vegetarianism and animals rights within Judaism. He points out that rabbinical writers, whether orthodox or reform, uphold a tradition of not causing distress to living creatures while supporting the eating of meat and the role of the ritual slaughterer in its preparation.[45]

Although papal pronouncements and the writings of some scholars show a sense of concern, the Roman Catholic moral theology denies that humans have direct duties to animals. The writings of St. Thomas Aquinas dominate much of Catholic thinking in which Aquinas approved the use of animals for the good of humans.[46] Three elements distinguished Aquinas's view of the status of animals: (1) Animals are irrational, possessing no mind or reason; (2) they exist to serve human ends; (3) and they have no moral status in themselves except as some human interests are involved.[47] However, Andrew Linzey relates the writings of Humphry Primatt in which he emphasizes the common misery of pain that requires justice and "universal benevolence" toward animals.[48] On the Christian perspective of animal rights, Linzey proposes "theos-rights" for animals, consistent with the idea of reverence and responsibility. Although a complex and debatable concept, Linzey believes that when we speak of animal rights, we conceptualize what is owed to animals as a matter of justice by virtue of their Creator's right.[49]

Linzey admits that we have to recognize that the Gospel records do not supply answers to many contemporary questions we would like to ask of the historical Jesus. On animal rights as with other questions, "we have no alternative but to work from the hints and guesses that are there within the text."[50]

In the environmental area, some philosophers have concluded that the foundations of environmentalism and animal rights are not compatible since environmentalists look at the whole biotic system, while animal rights advocates consider the interests of individual animals.[51] However, some believe that the perspectives of environmentalists and animal rights can also be complementary.[52] Certainly, the animal rights concerns for the needless killing of wildlife and protection of endangered species are compatible. A complete discussion of this debate is beyond the scope of this manuscript.

Awareness and Consequences

The writings and teachings of Singer, Regan, and others to justify the granting of animals a higher moral status have revolutionized the teaching of applied ethics. More importantly, their work has inspired a generation of activists and radicalized a dormant animal protection movement. As a result, animal rights supporters threaten those who have a vested interest in continuing traditional uses and treatment of animals.[53]

Although philosophers introduce new ideas, values, and concepts, will the general public accept them? Andrew Rowan points out that the different approaches of academic philosophers to the proper treatment of animals illustrates how difficult it is to establish any sort of consensus position on the moral status of animals or particular groups of animals.[54] However, animal activists point out that at one time slavery, limited rights for women, and cruelty to animals were accepted as part of the values and culture of the society. Today these values and practices have changed.

Vance has alerted the medical profession by a reasoned assessment of the Animal Liberation/Rights Movement (ALRM): that the movement is based on rational arguments, not emotion; that the movement is careful to distinguish between animals and humans; and that although leaders Singer and Regan have theoretical differences, they agree on the need for a radical change in human attitudes toward and treatment of animals. Vance asserts that at its best ALRM is intelligent, politically astute, and resourceful and urges the medical profession to understand "their most dangerous and sophisticated critics." [55]

Luther Tweeten observes that the animal welfare movement finds allies in the broad alternative agriculture movement and in the even more encompassing counterculture movement. Many animal welfare advocates subscribe to a wider alternative agriculture agenda, including advocacy of small farms, organic or sustainable farming, use of renewable energy, regional and national food self-sufficiency, cooperatives (if not state-owned enterprises), and appropriate technology.[56]

Marlene Halverson may characterize the situation most clearly: "We are mistaken if we believe that social concerns regarding the treatment of animals are going to go away or that they can continue to be answered by denial and resistance. Social judgments regarding the welfare status of animals in agriculture are and will continue to be based not only on the findings of science, but on humans' intuitive beliefs regarding the existence of animal consciousness and on humans' increasing willingness to apply a kind of golden rule that extends outside the human sphere to animals." [57]

The major conflicts of values have arisen between (1) those who follow and advocate acceptance of the ethical teachings and moral values of some specific philosophers and (2) those who own and work with animals in some phase of a business or profession. The future outcome of these conflicting values concerning the use and care of animals will depend on whether a majority of society accepts the "new" animal ethics and it becomes a part of public moral standards and public policy, or whether most members of society retain the more traditional standards and policies for treating and using animals.

Regardless of the status of animals, the movement to recognize and protect animals will continue to grow. The contemporary lifestyles and practices of owners, users, and consumers of animal products and services will continue to be challenged by those who believe that animals are exploited and that new ethical standards for their care and treatment should be followed. Philosophers and others have presented arguments that challenge the traditional morality and its assumption of the superiority of humans and the primacy of human interests. They believe that the traditional morality that assumes fundamental boundaries between species is no longer supportable.[58] In Gary Francione's assessment, "Animal rights, once more people understand the issue, will emerge as the civil rights movement of the twenty-first century." [59]

3

Animal Welfare in Europe

The private and public interest in animal protection that has emerged in Europe since World War II may partly explain the rising tide of activism in the United States. Bernard Rollin points out, "The Atlantic is a shrinking ocean that ideas cross with great speed." [1] Most Western European countries have regulations dealing with food animal production, laboratory animal care, animal transport, animals in zoos, animals in the wild, and pets. Consumers have opportunities to buy meat and poultry products identified as produced under humane conditions.

In Europe, laws dealing with prevention of cruelty to animals date back to the nineteenth century. However, a series of events in Europe since World War II has led to formal policies that promote humane treatment of animals with laws and regulations to implement them (see the chronology listed in appendix 3).

Development of Animal Welfare Policies

In Europe, protection of animals is a matter of political importance. Developing animal welfare policies is a complex process that involves the Council of Europe, the Commission of the European Union (earlier called the European Community) that makes recommendations, the Council of Ministers (the Minister of Agriculture from each member country), which approves them, and the European Parliament, which makes policy recommendations. However, after directives are issued, each member country is responsible for implementing the rules and regulations.

The European Union and Animals in Research

In November 1986, the European Communities Council issued its directive for protection of animals used for "experimental and other scientific purposes." [2] The directive was designed to provide guidelines for uniform laws in the member countries. The objective was to reduce use of animals for experimental purposes to a minimum, insure that they were adequately cared for, and avoid or minimize pain, suffering, distress, or harm.

The directive included research for development and testing of drugs, foodstuffs, and other products; studying diseases of humans, animals, or plants; protecting the environment; preservation of the species; and investigating biomedical issues.[3] According to the directive:

• Animals were to be provided suitable housing, in environments that allowed freedom of movement, adequate food and water, and appropriate care.

• Each member state would designate the authority responsible for verifying that the directive was properly carried out.

• Experiments would be performed by competent authorized persons and would not be performed if another scientifically satisfactory method of obtaining the result was possible.

• The appropriate species and number of animals for the experiment would be carefully considered and justified if necessary.

• Research on animals taken from the wild would not be permitted unless use of other animals would not be satisfactory.

• All experiments must be designed to avoid distress and unnecessary pain and must be carried out under general or local anesthesia, unless the anesthesia would be more traumatic than the experiment itself or incompatible with the experiment.

• If the animal were in pain after anesthesia had worn off, it would be given a painkiller or be killed humanely.

• An animal would be used only once for an experiment if it entailed pain, distress, or suffering.

• Procedures would be established so that authorities within each country would be notified of the research and persons conducting it. The advance notice would also report any research that might involve severe pain, and the authority could take administrative action if not satisfied that the research was sufficiently important to meet the essential needs of humans or animals.

• The government in each member state would keep records on numbers and kinds of animals used in research and the purposes of the experiments. Commercially sensitive information would be kept confidential.

• Persons conducting experiments and caring for research animals would have to have appropriate education and training. A veterinarian would also have to be available to advise on the well-being of the animals.

• Suppliers of animals for research would need to be approved or registered with the government authority and provide animals only from breeding or supplying establishments or animals lawfully imported. Generally, wild or stray animals could not be used, although special exemptions could be granted. Suppliers would have to keep records of the number of animals sold, sources of animals, and numbers dying while in the breeding establishment.

• All animals in breeding and research establishments after reaching weaning age would need an individual identification mark applied in the least-painful manner.

• To avoid duplication of experiments and satisfy health and safety legislation, member countries would have to recognize validity of data generated by other member states.

• The member states would be encouraged to develop and validate alternative techniques to provide needed information but which would involve fewer animals or entail less-painful procedures.

• Member states might adopt stricter measures for protecting animals used in research.

Animals covered by the directive included mice, rats, guinea pigs, golden hamsters, rabbits, nonhuman primates, dogs, cats, and quail.

Farm Animal Welfare in the United Kingdom

The farm animal welfare policies and regulations in the United Kingdom are developed in line with the European Union directives and have often led the way for other European countries. The major issues around which all European animal welfare policies have developed focus on housing, rearing, feeding, transporting, marketing, and killing.[4]

The UK Ministry of Agriculture, Fisheries and Food (MAFF) recognizes that both ethical and scientific issues play a part. For advice and counsel on animal welfare issues, it looks to the Farm Animal Welfare Council (FAWC), comprised of scientists, educators, and producers (and not to be confused with the Farm Animal Welfare Coalition, also known by the acronym FAWC, in the United States).

The FAWC is expected to "identify systems which go beyond the range of acceptability but also to stimulate positive development of systems, whether intensive or extensive, which combine the use of appropriate new technology with efficient use of available resources and adequate provision for the welfare and behavioral needs of animals."[5] The policies and regulations established are primarily welfare oriented with less-noticeable activism for animal rights as observed in the United States.

Extensive codes of practice for the humane treatment of farm animals have been developed following European Community guidelines. The MAFF in its codes of recommendations for the welfare of farm animals includes: comfort and shelter; readily accessible fresh water and a diet to maintain the animals in full health and vigor; freedom of movement; the company of other animals, particularly of like kind; the opportunity to exercise most normal patterns of behavior; light during the hours of daylight; space allowances; flooring that neither harms the animals nor causes undue strain; prevention or rapid diagnosis and treatment of injury or parasitic infestation and disease; the avoidance of unnecessary mutilation; emergency arrangements to cover outbreaks of fire, breakdown of essential mechanical services, and the disruption of supplies; and specific management practices that apply to that species of livestock.[6]

The National Farmers Union (NFU), the largest general farm organization, accepts "a duty to protect the economic viability and competitiveness of our members' livestock enterprises. We also have a moral duty to promote the humane treatment of farm animals. Consumers have a right to expect that the meat and dairy products they buy have been produced humanely." [7]

On trade, the NFU believes that "farmers have a right to expect that they will not be undercut by products coming in from abroad which do not carry a guarantee of the same standards of animal welfare. Equally, consumers have a right to be informed about sources of supply which do not meet our standards."

If this statement were translated into international trade policies of the European Union, American animal products to be exported to the EU market would need to meet the same welfare guidelines that now exist in the European Union countries.

Under the animal welfare regulations, more practices requiring a veterinary surgeon are spelled out. Citizens who believe a livestock owner is not following the welfare guidelines can file a complaint. Then government veterinary inspectors would determine if violations have occurred.

Producers are consulted as new animal welfare regulations are developed, but in their minority position, must accept the final policy decision. Many of the welfare guidelines simply represent good management practices that any considerate producer would follow.

The NFU has agreed that any future welfare strategy can best be founded on existing constraints—both legal and advisory—as drawn up by the FAWC and accepted by the MAFF.

NFU respects the FAWC and its recommendations. Producers are represented and are given the opportunity to comment on proposed regulations. Since they have a chance to cooperate in setting up the regulations, they see no other way but to go along with the final regulations. However, the organization staff recognizes that complying with welfare guidelines will inevitably increase production costs.

Regulations to insure humane treatment of animals are now closely associated with regulations and practices that aim to facilitate production under improved environmental conditions. The goal is to maintain or improve water quality, encourage and enhance wildlife habitat, and prevent soil erosion.

The Scottish Pig Industry Initiative is one example of a plan to produce a quality-controlled product in which producers undertake a production management training program and follow a prescribed production system. This system includes humane handling, high quality feed rations, no castration, limited use of drugs and medicines, sanitary housing, and marketing at around 80 kilograms live weight. Standards are also established for loading and transporting, handling at abattoirs and cutting plants, processing of carcasses, and packaging and labeling.

Individual meat packers have also developed contracts with individual producers to encourage production of pork that will be viewed as humanely produced, be free of undesirable residues, and be a safe and quality product.

The MAFF reported eleven "successful" prosecutions, which also assisted local authorities and the police in bringing sixty-nine successful cases to court. The penalties imposed for some of these cases indicates that welfare matters are being given more serious consideration within the courts. Magistrates now seem more willing to impose heavier fines, lifetime bans from keeping livestock, and, in the most serious cases, prison sentences. Two farmers received life bans from keeping livestock. One of these also received a fine of £2,000 for causing unnecessary suffering to cattle, pigs, and sheep. Another was banned from keeping livestock for five years after being prosecuted for the third time in two years on welfare-related offenses.[8]

UK officials are very conscious that they cannot get too far ahead in their animal welfare regulations, since they do not want to become noncompetitive with other EU countries. In 1992, it appeared that the United Kingdom would be the only country to eliminate gestation stalls. There was concern that all countries should have the same regulation.

Changes in Production Practices

In the United Kingdom, sow tethering in new production units will be banned after 1996. Existing sow-tethering systems must be phased out by 1998.

Due to animal welfare interests, castration of boar pigs is not carried out except when pigs are held to weights above 80 kilograms. The NFU leaflet points out that modern pig management systems that keep boars and gilts apart have given some farmers second thoughts about the need for castration. Such pigs, NFU points out, grow more quickly and produce a higher proportion of lean meat. Yet they also point out that certain sections of the meat trade still prefer carcasses from castrated pigs. Pigs are sold at lighter weight than in the United States.

Generally producers feel there is no need to castrate when the pig's weight at slaughter does not exceed 80 kilograms (approximately 176 pounds). However, when the animal's weight exceeds 80 kilograms, castration is required. It is estimated that 80 percent of pigs in the United Kingdom are slaughtered at 65 to 75 kilograms.

In the United Kingdom, extensive research has been conducted on natural behavior of sows, development of a system to give more space per animal, and building designs to allow more movement and use of bedding have received attention.

In 1991, the FAWC issued its recommendations for humane egg production in a colony system in which the hens are free to move about a laying house. Because of concerns for hens in battery cage egg production systems, the European Union Commission reviewed and made recommendations for improving the cage system in 1992.

But debate remains about the best system for producing eggs. Although egg producers are under strong pressure to improve the welfare of their layers and alternative systems have been developed, the question remains, do they offer a better life for the hens.[9] P. Dun claims that the cage system was adopted initially to overcome the problems with bird health and welfare, not to make more profit for the egg producer. Cages have the welfare advantage of a clean, low-disease risk environment that separates hens from their droppings and minimizes risk of cannibalism.

Further improvements to cages are possible, such as providing access to nests, dust baths, and perches. Dun recommends further research on improving cages along with research into alternative systems.[10]

The FAWC issued its report on the welfare of broiler chickens in 1992. It recommended a maximum stocking density of 34 kilograms per square meter, not be exceeded any time during the growing period. It also stressed environmental comfort considering temperature, ventilation, light, adequate floor litter, availability of feed and water at a maximum distance of four meters, and further research to see if leg problems could be reduced.

Animal Welfare in Other Countries

In Sweden, the *Animal Protection Act of 1988* brought together in one act the most detailed and comprehensive laws dealing with animal welfare in any country. The government through the National Board of Agriculture received extensive authority to establish regulations for the care and treatment of domestic animals and other animals if they are kept in captivity. Following passage of the act, the government issued its *Animal Protection Ordinance* to implement the act: [11]

• Livestock buildings must be "sufficiently spacious" to allow all the animals to lie down at one time and move freely. Premises shall be designed to allow the animals to behave naturally. Buildings must be fitted with windows to let in daylight.

• Buildings designed for horses, cattle, reindeer, pigs, sheep, goats, poultry, or furred animals may not be built, extended, or remodeled without approval of the building with respect to animal protection and animal health. The local county agricultural board must inspect livestock buildings before they are used.

• The National Board of Agriculture must approve new technical systems with regard to animal health and protection.

• Animal housing requirements include the following: Laying hens must not be housed in cages; milk cows must be sent out to pasture in the summer; other cattle must be kept outdoors in summer or sent out to pasture; breeding pigs must be given the opportunity to stay outdoors in summer where possible; pigs shall be housed in loafing barns; equipment to immobilize pigs must be used only temporarily; electric cow trainers are prohibited. The dairy cow pasture requirement is viewed as the most troublesome for many producers.[12]

• Castration of cattle and sheep before the age of two months, pigs before six weeks, dehorning of cattle before one month and goats before two weeks, and lamb docking (tails cut off) before one week is permitted.

• Feeding animals hormones to alter their characteristics for any purpose other than to prevent or cure disease is prohibited.

• Slaughter requires stunning to cause rapid unconsciousness.

• A veterinarian appointed by the National Board of Agriculture, or a county administrative board, must be present at public races involving animals. The national board may also issue directions concerning training of animals and their use in races.

• Strict limits are placed on taking animals on tours and exhibition in menageries. When zoos are established, they must be approved by the National Board of Agriculture. For animals in research, the law requires ethical advisory committees, examinations of proposed experiments to determine whether the experiment can be regarded as being in the public interest, assessment of the amount of suffering inflicted on the animals, anesthesia when surgery is performed, and prior approval for the premises used for laboratory animals.

• Laying cages in use at the time the law was passed must phased out by the end of 1998.

The National Board of Agriculture has authority to grant exemptions and exceptions to the rules and regulations. However, the extensive and detailed regulations accompanying the act place the government in a very close supervisory role in livestock and poultry management and husbandry practices.

In Switzerland, laying cages are being phased out. Veal calves must receive iron and roughage in their rations. Pigs must be provided bedding of straw or other material. Standards are established for lighting, flooring materials, and space. However, in 1992, Swiss voters defeated a referendum that would have limited animal experiments only to those deemed essential for medical research.

In the Netherlands, pregnant sows must not be kept in gestation crates.

Conclusions about European Animal Welfare Regulations

In countries of the European Union, the guidelines for animal welfare regulations are developed by the EU Commission in Brussels and approved by the Council of Ministers. For example, in 1996, the EU Commission proposed that French, Italian, and Dutch farmers could continue to use crates for raising veal calves until the year 2008. However, new crates will be banned after 1998.

Each country has an obligation to establish regulations to implement EU regulations. Each member country realizes that it must not get very far out of line with EU guidelines. Each country wants to keep a competitive position yet comply with animal welfare regulations that could increase costs or reduce efficiency.

Producers are subject to certain regulations put in place by those concerned for the welfare of the animals. Specified housing space requirements are coming. Guidelines for transport of live hogs and other farm animals have been recommended. New guidelines have been issued for handling animals before and at the time of slaughter.

To develop and implement regulations, a major bureaucracy to implement and enforce welfare policies has emerged. Some reorganization has taken place to carry out animal welfare policies.

Differences within the European Union exist on animal welfare policies. The northern countries are more sympathetic to welfare policies than the southern countries. Eastern countries are in transition, and animal welfare policies have much lower priority than other economic and social concerns.

Producers' attitudes toward animal welfare regulations have changed over the last fifteen to twenty years. Many now recognize that public opinion cannot be ignored if they are to maintain a market for their products.

The development of regulations to promote more welfare-oriented production practices is only part of the evolution of government influence on management and husbandry practices. Along with concerns for humane treatment of animals is the concern for quality and safety. Production regulation also involves pollution controls, manure disposal, dead animal disposal, and use of medicines, pharmaceuticals, and feed additives that could affect the safety of the processed animal product.

Consumer Reactions

European consumers seem more concerned about humane treatment than in the United States. A public opinion survey dealing with animal welfare was conducted and a report published by J. R. Hill and D. W. B. Sainsbury at the Cambridge University Center for Animal Health and Welfare in 1990.[13] The purpose was to find out what British citizens understood about animal welfare, if it differed from farm animal welfare, and how they felt animals were treated.

Respondents expressed a compassion for animals but most frequently did not feel fully aware of the factors affecting animal welfare. They generally disapproved of intensive farming systems and associated them as undesirable—practices most frequently associated with caged laying hens, pigs in crowded pens on slatted floors, and sows neck tethered or in farrowing crates. Scientific production methods were often criticized but "stockmanship" was frequently used as the preferred conduct in caring for farm animals. Respondents expressed concern with the handling of livestock and poultry in transport to market.

A majority of respondents felt that animal welfare was important in modern society and the media, especially television, influenced public opinion, sometimes with unbalanced views. Some of those close to animal production were concerned that UK regulations should not be out of line with the rest of the European Union countries. Others thought that regulations were inadequate and animal owners would avoid compliance. The responses suggested more knowledge was needed about the circumstances of housing, feeding, and handling under confinement or relative freedom, as a basis for determining animal welfare.

There is a growing consumer awareness of how food is produced. The number-one concern is food safety. Humane treatment of animals is second with interest growing in this area.[14] The rising profile of welfare in public awareness is contributing to growing demands for food that is labeled as having been produced under certain standards.[15]

Consumer demand for eggs produced in colony systems has resulted in starting a move away from laying cages. In 1991, it was estimated that 10 percent of eggs produced in the United Kingdom were from noncage systems, the majority of these under "free-range" conditions.

A market for "humanely produced" products exists, but consumers must pay higher prices. The supermarkets, even country stores, offer a choice between regular, caged layer–produced eggs, "free-range," and "barn-raised" eggs. Prices for free-range and barn-raised eggs are higher. In one instance, the price of free-range eggs was 38 percent higher than for regular, cage-produced eggs of the same size and quality.

Plans and programs between meat packers and producers are being developed in England and Scotland to provide humanely produced and environmentally sound products to meet the growing market and concern among consumers.

In Germany, some questions arise about whether products from producers highlighting animal welfare management methods will be able to gain shares in the market. The share for higher-priced products, including products with special animal welfare specifications, still shows wide variations.[16]

Citizen Support for Animal Welfare

Animal welfare is a major issue in those European countries with affluence, adequate food supplies, and a population that has active groups concerned with ethical and moral issues in dealing with animals. Concerns for pets and wild animals was the first concern. With capital intensive food animal production, the concern has spread to farm animals as well.[17]

In the United Kingdom, the Royal Society for the Prevention of Cruelty of Animals (RSPCA) carries out a broad program of education, communications, investigations, legislative efforts, and services on behalf of animals' welfare. Income comes from legacies, subscriptions, investments, and departmental services.

The society has supported efforts to ban egg production in battery cages, eliminate sow tethering and gestation crates, promote loose housing for veal calves, stop killing of whales and badgers, ban research with wild-caught primates, and change the rules for transporting livestock.[18]

In Germany, animal welfare organizations are some of the strongest and best organized in Europe. The German Animal Protection League (Deutsches Tierschutzbund) publishes a monthly magazine and carries out educational programs and campaigns on animal welfare issues its members believe need attention. The league has been critical of cage layer egg production, the leg-hold trap, sow tethering, and veal production in individual crates.

Other Western European countries have active animal protection organizations. Their programs promote humane treatment of farm animals, protection of wild animals and birds, and campaigns against use of animals in research.

Eastern European countries have not advanced as much as Western Europe in animal protection, sheltering, and anticruelty laws.[19] Animal suffering based on human apathy and economic exploitation was widespread in the years following World War II. In recent years, a few animal protectors worked against odds to save animals endangered by war in the former Yugoslavia, political upheavals in Romania, and killing of stray animals in Bulgaria.

Poland is making progress in spay-neutering of pets and protecting wild animals. Hungary lacks anticruelty laws. However, with Hungary now a member of the Council of Europe, pressure is mounting to obtain ratification of the conventions on farm animals, transport, slaughter, experimentation, and pet animals.

Although Czechoslovakia had no animal welfare laws, such a law was being prepared. What the outcome of the split into two republics will be remains uncertain. Although zoos lack humane standards, scientists are working to upgrade laboratory animal procedures.

Although Russia passed an anticruelty law in 1988, it is viewed as weak by animal protectors. The dog population is substantial, but there are no real animal shelters.

The European Economic Union, in developing a common market since World War II, has influenced its member countries to follow more uniform policies that include the care and treatment of animals. Citizen-group interest and concern have been translated into laws and regulations to include animals on farms, during transport, in laboratories, in zoos, and in the wild. Many of these concerns have also emerged in the United States.

The comments of a British business executive may reflect a more reformist attitude than exists across the United States: "The issue of animal welfare is a moral one not an economic one. . . . the prime concern is the responsibility not to abuse power over fellow creatures." [20]

Animal Rights, American Style, to Europe

Most animal activism in Europe has been animal welfare and reformist oriented, even though animal extremists carried out illegal incidents (usually associated with animal rights activists) in Great Britain before such actions occurred in the United States. However, Europeans may see more animal rights activism in the future.

In late 1993, People for the Ethical Treatment of Animals (PETA) went international, opening offices in London, Hamburg, and Amsterdam. With legislation in the European Parliament that could affect the American fur trade, PETA believed it was time to recognize the influence of such developments for animals. They hoped to work on international issues and help the animal rights movement abroad to network successfully across borders and oceans.

PETA's International Campaigns Department has demonstrated against the fur trade in Paris, Milan, and Tokyo, against hamburger consumption in Moscow, and animal testing of cosmetics in Paris.[21]

European Experiences Transported to the United States

As Rollin points out, "The Atlantic is a shrinking ocean that ideas cross with great speed." [22] The nineteenth-century traditions and customs for humane treatment of animals, the twentieth-century policies to regulate animal care and treatment, and the illegal actions carried out in protest against alleged mistreatment of animals originated in the United Kingdom and some other Western European countries. Animal welfare philosophies have spread to most Western European countries and are established as public policies with accompanying laws and regulations.

The philosophies and activism of animal rights seem less evident in Europe than in the United States. Nevertheless, the animal welfare and animal rights movement in the United States in the last decade of the twentieth century can trace back to many ideas and philosophies imported from Europe.

4

Reformists and Abolitionists: Organizations and Their Leaders

Whether reformist or abolitionist, the organizations working to improve how humans treat animals vary in their philosophies, activities, and financial resources.[1] Some groups have characteristics of both abolitionists and reformists. Their future success lies with coalitions they can form to achieve their program goals.

In the 1990s, most animal activist organizations have had specific program goals. The reformists identify with the strategies of animal welfare, advocating humane treatment of animals. The abolitionists, sometimes portrayed as radicals, advocate eliminating use of animals for food, apparel, and pleasure purposes. As an intermediate step, they select specific targets to achieve their long-range goals.

The focus of the animal rights and animal welfare groups include advocacy; education; litigation on behalf of animals; stopping vivisection; promoting shelter and sanctuary maintenance; and advocating wildlife preservation and protection. The groups take reformist or abolitionist approaches, and some have activities and programs that relate to both. Some enroll regular members and, in addition, solicit contributions to specific campaigns.

Some groups have over 100,000 members and operate with multimillion-dollar annual budgets. The nineteen major organizations, each with more than $500,000 in total revenue, had total membership or contributors of more than 3,000,000 and total revenues of $243.6 million in the latest years that reports were available. Some individuals may hold membership in more than one group.

American Society for the Prevention of Cruelty to Animals (ASPCA), 1866

When ASPCA was chartered by a special act of the New York legislature as the first private humane society in the United States, its major objective was to provide effective means for the prevention of cruelty to animals throughout the country. Its 1994 membership was reported to be 350,000.[2]

Unlike many organizations, ASPCA operated an animal shelter and an animal control program in New York City until December 31, 1994. However, when its contract expired, ASPCA notified the city that it would not renew the contract. The end of animal shelter and control operations reduced revenue, and the payment for the ASPCA shelter facilities transferred to the City of New York required litigation and negotiation.

In 1993, the society took 60,000 animals into its two shelters. Of those about 9,000 were adopted, 1,300 were returned to their owners, 7,600 were turned in by their owners to be killed, and 34,800 were killed because they were sick, injured, or poor candidates for adoption.[3]

With the shelter and control program removed, the organization planned to place more emphasis on preventing population explosion among urban pets, rather than deal with its effects. It also carries on information and legislative campaigns nationwide. Among its legislative activities, the group has worked to ban the LD-50 test, outlaw the Draize test, pass laws against the steel-jaw leghold trap, regulate factory farming, repeal pound seizure laws, eliminate the hot-iron face branding of cattle, protect America's endangered species, curtail enforcement of no-pet clauses in leases, and improve conditions for carriage horses. In 1996, ASPCA acquired the National Animal Poison Control Center, which responds to emergency inquiries nationwide.

The organization's humane concerns extend to all animals including household pets, farm animals, laboratory rats, and wild animals. Its main programs involve animals as pets, humane education, animals for sport and entertainment, animal industries, and protection of wild animals and endangered species. Through information pamphlets, it has used the veal calf as "fund-raising" animal of the year. It has come out strongly against veal calf factory farming and rodeo cruelty.

The ASPCA opposes the raising of any animal under cruel and inhumane conditions. Practices in their view falling under this definition include veal calf farming when calves are raised in individual crates or stalls, branding the faces of cattle, and intensive food animal production. It also opposes the sacrificial slaughter of animals on religious grounds and the injury or stress to animals used for entertainment or work purposes, including dog fighting and cock fighting. ASPCA has become increasingly abolitionist over the past decade but still has enormous clout based on its traditional reputation.[4] Its *Animal Rights Handbook*, published in 1990, strongly endorses certain animal rights philosophies.[5]

In the early 1990s, ASPCA experienced conflicting views between its board and officers. Roger Caras replaced John Kullberg as president. Views differed on whether the organization should continue as an animal welfare organization or move toward more animal rights advocacy.

Internal problems developed in late 1993 and 1994 over allegations of poor housekeeping conditions at its New York animal shelter and excessive wages for overtime, exceeding by several times the basic pay for those workers. The board fired several top officials to correct these problems. Some observers believed the ASPCA's problems resulted from a board of long-time members who had a tenuous commitment to animal protection or at least seemed out of step with many people in the humane movement.

Massachusetts Society for the Prevention of Cruelty to Animals (MSPCA), 1868

The MSPCA is one of the oldest organizations for protecting and preventing cruelty to animals. It operates eight animal shelters and three animal hospitals and has eleven law enforcement agents to enforce animal cruelty laws. It has also been active in education, legislative lobbying, and emergency rescue programs.

The organization's total revenues and support place it as one of the wealthiest animal protection groups. Substantial salaries are paid to its top management, with six staff members receiving salaries of $100,000 or more in 1994.[6] When operating expenses exceeded revenues in 1990 and 1991, the management dipped into the endowment funds to develop a five-year strategy for cost containment and planned growth.

American Humane Association (AHA), 1877

The American Humane Association is considered the first national organization promoting the welfare of animals and children. It is a national federation of concerned individuals and animal care and control agencies dedicated to the prevention of cruelty, neglect, abuse, and exploitation of animals. It is the parent organization for the American Association of Protecting Children, a child welfare division.

Its Hollywood office works actively with the movie industry to ensure humane treatment of animals used in filmmaking.[7] AHA activities also include legislative advocacy, professional training programs for shelter personnel, the National Hearing Dog Project, saving animals during disasters, ending pet overpopulation, and surveys and research into shelter and animal population statistics. In the mid-nineties, AHA initiated its Campaign Against Violence—a specific effort to address the link between violence to animals and children.

The Standards of Excellence Program is the cornerstone of AHA's national effort to upgrade and improve the care and handling of animals in shelters. It gives shelters criteria to measure and evaluate the effectiveness of their programs and policies by addressing facilities and staff, operational programs, euthanasia, community relations and education, and planning. It also offers professional leadership and management and executive training programs and provides curriculum-oriented, humane teaching materials to teachers in primary, secondary, undergraduate, and graduate education programs.

AHA has joined with other animal welfare organizations to oppose the release of pets in shelters for laboratory experimentation and oppose efforts to weaken laws protecting wild horses and burros. It has been instrumental in the passage of child labor laws, establishing a juvenile court system, advocating the humane treatment of livestock in transit and at the slaughterhouse, and promoting the protection of animals used in the entertainment field.

The Science Advisory Panel composed of scientists, mainly veterinarians, provides background information on farm animal well-being and other scientific and technical issues.

American Anti-Vivisection Society (AAVS), 1882

The major objective of AAVS is to bring about the total abolition of animal experimentation. The group encourages passage of laws mandating alternative research; combats research use of pound animals; and underwrites research that does not use animals. It has a close relationship with the National Anti-Vivisection Society, including mutual sponsorship of the International Foundation for Ethical Research. It publishes *AV Magazine* eleven times a year.

In addition to its ethical concerns, AAVS strongly opposes animal experimentation. It asserts, "During the last decade, the biomedical research industry in the United States has deliberately produced and killed more than 600 million laboratory animals and has spent more than $80 billion of consumer and taxpayer money in the process. What's more terroristic than that?"[8] AAVS conducts nonanimal methods programs to provide support and incentive for the replacement of animals in research, testing, and education.

AAVS participated in the 1990 and 1996 Washington March for Animals. Its leaders described the 1990 march as "heralding the real trends and progress in the animal rights movement: the increasing of public, political and scientific sophistication on the animal rights issues; the development of alternative methodology to the use of live animals in experimental laboratories; the sound philosophical and moral foundation on which the movement has been built; and the promotion of preventive medicine through prudent dietary and exercise programs."[9]

Yet in admitting "some acts of so-called terrorism," AAVS asks, "Can they be called terroristic when no one was injured and the sole purpose was to release thousands of animals from unnecessary pain, torture and death?"[10]

New England Anti-Vivisection Society (NEAVS), 1895

Founded in 1895, NEAVS is one of the oldest and wealthiest antivivisection organizations in the United States. The group has worked for repeal of pound laws in Massachusetts and conducted a town-by-town campaign to repeal pound law ordinances in local communities. The organization awarded the Tufts University School of Medicine a $100,000 grant to develop an alternative to the Draize Eye Test.

NEAVS has promoted boycotts and demonstrations against Gillette and U.S. Surgical because they use animals in research and testing. The group has also proposed state legislation that would give activists standing to sue the government on behalf of animals.

In 1990, NEAVS president Cleveland Amory declared, "Vivisection remains a crime but it has also become a relic of the past. Our ethical argument is now buttressed by scientific and economical fact. . . . Alternatives to vivisection exist now; alternatives that are surer, safer, provide truer applicability for the human species, and make more efficient use of funds." [11] Amory reasons that vivisection persists because of the profits of breeding and experimenting on animals, bureaucratic inertia, and reactionaries whose professional standing is threatened by the new developments in science.

In 1987, PETA staged a successful campaign takeover of the NEAVS board, after failing in its takeover attempt in 1983.[12] Alex Pacheco of PETA raised money for a special fund, outside of PETA's regular accounts, so PETA members could go to Boston and participate in that meeting.[13] Cleveland Amory, president and founder of the Fund for Animals, then took over as president of NEAVS. Alex Pacheco and Ingrid Newkirk, codirectors of PETA, joined the board. Other board members included Dr. Neal Barnard of the Physicians Committee for Responsible Medicine and Theo Capaldo, a member of the NEAVS-funded Psychologists for the Ethical Treatment of Animals. Funds were liberally dispersed to groups and projects aligned with PETA and Fund for Animals after the 1987 contested election.[14]

In 1989, NEAVS held total assets of $8.5 million with nearly $7.6 million in cash and securities. So it not surprising that outside interests would seek to gain control of such a wealthy organization. Substantial losses occurred in 1990 and 1992. As a result, major changes occurred in 1993 when all but two of the staff were laid off due to financial problems. NEAVS has cut back to just two projects, the education and legislative offices. In 1994, assets were $6.3 million.

In September 1995, a group of fifty animal activist leaders from various New England animal protection groups formed the Philip G. Peabody Coalition. In a letter to President Cleveland Amory, they protested what they saw as "the failure of NEAVS to live up to its basic, central concept of abolishing vivisection." Its stated goal was to help NEAVS "recover its purpose and recommit its organization to that purpose." [15] They felt that NEAVS had no direct programs targeting vivisection—the major reason why the organization was formed in the beginning.

Amory defended the ongoing NEAVS program dealing with legislative initiatives, lobbying to reduce budgets for animal experiments, educational programs, press releases, and displays at the Boston Public Library. He also claimed credit for Harvard University no longer using dogs or any animals in their physiology laboratories.

The coalition called for placing trained animal advocates on research oversight committees; exposing Class B dealers and backyard breeding of dogs and cats for research; including birds, rats, mice, and farm animals under the *Animal Welfare Act*; and mobilizing demonstrations at primate centers.

When Cleveland Amory retired as president in 1996, PETA cofounders Alex Pacheco and Ingrid Newkirk, along with Neal Barnard and some other board member activists, contested the selection of Theo Capaldo as the next president, even though the Massachusetts Office of the Attorney General declared he was the legal president-elect and

Irene Cruikshank, the managing director. The dispute was resolved, and Capaldo was accepted as president in 1997.[16]

National Anti-Vivisection Society (NAVS), 1929

NAVS educates the public concerning its views of the problems in using animals in product testing, biomedical research, and education. It concentrates specifically on animals used in research, with the objectives of replacing animal experimentation, both biomedical and psychological, with other forms of testing and eventually eliminating all laboratory experiments involving animals.

Some of its major programs include publishing a quarterly bulletin, publications on animal research and alternatives to research with animals; maintaining a library and compiling statistics on laboratory animals used; identifying cosmetic and household products firms that do and do not undertake animal testing; jointly sponsoring the International Foundation for Ethical Research; and making small grants to support grassroots organizations.

NAVS is a founding member of the National Coalition to Protect Our Pets and works at local and national levels to repeal pound seizure. It has hosted a Cruelty-Free Fair in Chicago and organized protests against cat and macaque research at Northwestern University. It maintains that the pressure tactics it advocates—letter writing and refusing to buy animal-tested products—have induced firms such as Avon and Revlon to discontinue animal testing and others, such as Procter and Gamble, to investigate alternative methods.[17]

NAVS has been criticized for its substantial stock holdings in companies that perform and promote vivisection, including U.S. Surgical, which is reported to underwrite pro-vivisection groups.[18] It has also been targeted in the animal press because the executive director succeeded her father; family members held board seats; the director's husband, an attorney, was paid substantial fees for representing the society; and board members were paid the highest expense allowances of any animal or habitat protection organization.[19]

National Humane Education Society (NHES), 1948

The major programs have been to foster kindness to animals, oppose vivisection, promote research alternatives, eliminate trapping, reform factory farming, and provide food and shelter to stray and homeless animals.

NHES operates Peace Plantation, an animal sanctuary in Walton, New York, and supports education programs to foster responsible pet ownership and reduce the number of unwanted animals. In 1995, operating costs for Peace Plantation totalled $663,838, an average cost of $1443 per animal based on the average daily feline population of 435 and canine population of 25.

After hiring a fund-raising firm in 1986, direct-mail campaigns increased revenue from $852,000 in 1986 to $2.2 million in 1990. Increased revenue enabled the organization to double the number of animals in their care. Reports indicate that the standard of care or the dedication of Anna C. Briggs, founder and president, was not in question.

However, fund-raising expenses have claimed an increasingly large share of the income from 39 percent in 1990 to 48 percent in 1994.[20] Of reported contributions of $3.37 million in 1995, only about 20 percent were used for direct animal care.

Animal Welfare Institute (AWI), 1951

AWI's major focus is the humane treatment of laboratory animals and the development of nonanimal testing methods wherever possible, the preservation of species threatened with extinction, reform of methods of trapping animals, prevention of cruel experiments on animals by untrained persons, and reform of what they see as cruel methods of raising food animals on "factory farms." AWI has carried out a longtime effort to keep whales safe and end their needless slaughter. It has opposed Japan's Southern Ocean whaling operations that Japan labels as "scientific research."

Christine Stevens, AWI's president and director, through her personal lobbying efforts, is credited with considerable impact, most notably the inclusion of animal welfare provisions in the 1985 farm bill. The organization carries out an extensive publications program including films, books, booklets, and a quarterly newsletter and is affiliated with the Society for Animal Protective Legislation, which is viewed as its lobbying arm.

AWI is viewed traditionally as a very personal organization, serving as an outlet for the interests of Christine Stevens. She has significant access on Capitol Hill and is considered the mother of the *Animal Welfare Act* and the *Endangered Species Act*. She takes no salary for her AWI work.

The Humane Society of the United States (HSUS), 1954

HSUS was chartered to prevent suffering and abuse to animals and pursues this objective through education, investigation, litigation and legislation and is considered one of the few "traditional" or "reformist" animal groups. It claims to be the largest animal protection organization in the world with a staff of more than two hundred and a constituency of more than three million persons.

HSUS is not opposed to "legitimate and appropriate" utilization of animals for their meat and leather and wool for wearing apparel. It has opposed use of fur. The crucial question is who decides what is appropriate.

From 1970 to 1991, John Hoyt, as president, moved HSUS to the forefront of the animal welfare movement. In his leadership role, he worked to encourage moderation but showed an optimistic outlook as he addressed his members: "Whereas we were once regarded as little more than a distraction and annoyance, we are now regarded as a force to be reckoned with, unified or not." [21] Before joining HSUS, he was a Presbyterian minister in Fort Wayne, Indiana.

In 1992, Hoyt became chief executive officer and Paul Irwin became president. A staff of eleven vice-presidents carry specific roles covering higher education, youth education, farm animals and bioethics, wildlife and habitat protection, environment, field services, companion animals, laboratory animals, investigations, and senior counsel.

In an address to the California Farm Bureau in December 1990, Hoyt stated the HSUS position this way:

> We are not a vegetarian organization, and as a matter of policy do not consider the utilization of animals for food to be either immoral or inappropriate, a position that as you might expect earns us a great deal of criticism from various animals rights organizations.
>
> We also recognize that livestock and poultry can make significant contribution to ecological farm management. We are, however, fully committed to pursuing reforms within agriculture that are necessary for insuring our goals for the humane treatment of farm animals and an ecologically sound, sustainable farming structure. [22]

Not all the staff of HSUS view animal welfare issues in the same way. Dr. Michael Fox, the vice president for farm animals and bioethics has commented, "There is simply no reason for anyone to regard meat as a dietary staple. To do so is to show flagrant disregard for the enormous waste and now well-recognized environmental and health risks created by a meat-based agricultural system and a meat-centered diet." He is most critical of pork and broiler production, which uses more grain and protein concentrates, and more supportive of beef and sheep production produced with forage crops. [23]

A staff member told a reporter that the organization was "definitely shifting in the direction of animal rights faster than anyone would realize from our literature." [24] Although claiming not to promote vegetarianism, HSUS launched a campaign about conditions on farms at a January 1991 press conference, calling for Americans to protest "inhumane conditions" for farm animals by eating less meat.

In an April 1993 solicitation letter, president Paul Irwin announced a major campaign to deal with what they perceived as abuses in intensive farm animal production and related health and environmental concerns: "Chemically treated crop monoculture and high density livestock and poultry production systems have seriously polluted aquatic ecosystems, demineralized and organically impoverished the soil, contaminated drinking water, and endangered human, wildlife, and farm animal health." [25]

HSUS sponsored a "breakfast of cruelty" campaign against eggs and pork, asking members to boycott these products until production methods changed. One report suggests that HSUS is being influenced by "radical animal rights elements." [26] In 1993, the organization launched "Eating with Conscience," bringing together three themes: promoting human health, saving the environment, and ending animal suffering. President Paul Irwin admits that the initiative is complex but defends the program against the criticism of animal industry groups. While HSUS members have tried to establish common ground and dialogue with the farm animal industry, they have continued to voice concern over what they see as the plight of farm animals and the spread of factory farms and feedlots that blight, pollute, and impoverish the countryside.[27]

Some specific program efforts have included campaigns against blood sports of dog fighting and cock fighting, killing of dolphins when catching tuna fish, inhumane handling of circus animals and surplus zoo animals, trapping and ranch production of fur-bearing animals, use of fur in wearing apparel, uncontrolled pet reproduction, trapping of animals, hunting and commercial trapping on national wildlife refuges, shooting buffalo outside of national parks, and destruction of habitats for wildlife that would lead to endangered species. HSUS has a large and effective investigative force for animals. Its investigators, operating across the country and through Humane Society International in every region of the world, have exposed what they see as cruelty and as destructive practices toward animals.

HSUS has encouraged development of wildlife contraceptives to address problems of overpopulation of white-tailed deer in urban and suburban areas and wild horse herds on public lands. It has protested killing of predators, such as coyotes, to protect the interests of ranchers. It has opposed federal government support for duck hunting. It credits its work for a ban on commercial trade in elephant ivory.

In its education program, HSUS has developed materials for classroom teachers to assist in teaching humane education and in preparation of materials for biology teachers for responsible use of animals and alternatives to dissection. It sponsors an annual Animal Care Expo to bring together the animal care industry with exhibits, seminars, and demonstrations covering contemporary and humane equipment and services.

Although animal industry groups have seen the HSUS as more reformist than abolitionist, some also see a problem of "issue honesty." They see inconsistency in the HSUS positions that in some ways lean more toward the abolitionist animal rights philosophy than the more moderate animal welfare approach. Some see Hoyt as the politician working for support from the animal industry and livestock commodity groups while they see Michael Fox as the philosopher who takes positions that are not consistent with John Hoyt. HSUS was listed as a cosponsor for the June 1996 March for Animals in Washington, D.C.

Personnel changes in recent years illustrate the power cluster theory taking place at HSUS. Newly hired staff included David Ganz, former president of North Shore Animal League; Wayne Pacelle, former national director of Fund for Animals; Aaron Medlock, attorney; and Ohio lobbyist Bill Long, who had represented the Fund for Animals and HSUS. Accusations and denials erupted in late 1995 and early 1996 as the organization's president and a former vice president charged each other with misusing group funds for personal benefit.[28] In 1996, Patricia Forkan assumed authority over domestic operations and Paul Irwin took over as head of Humane Society International while Hoyt was expected to retire.

Friends of Animals (FOA), 1957

Founded by Alice Herrington (deceased 1994), Friends of Animals is an international, nonprofit animal protection organization that works to reduce and eliminate the suffering of animals, both domestic and wild. Its goal is to achieve a humane relationship between people and non-humans. Its major areas of concern include banning of steel-jaw leghold traps; concern for wildlife destruction; boycott of furs; prohibition of lab animal experimentation; and protection of seals and marine animals. It is affiliated with the Committee for Humane Legislation.

FOA investigates areas of what it sees as animal exploitation and focuses on those that are current, critical, and hopeful of solution. The group has used local correspondents to promote the society's objectives through grassroots communications. It has enlisted local volunteer workers and cooperating veterinarians who conduct a nationwide pet animal spaying program.

Early in 1992, FOA used a mail solicitation campaign to report on the destruction of Koala habitats in Australia. Joined by the Australians for Animals, FOA called for donations to fund a koala hospital at the University of Queensland; acquire a sensitive habitat for the koalas to survive and multiply; hire environmental lawyers so a legal case could be mounted to stop koala "mauling" in sanctuaries and zoos; and to stop the export of koalas to overseas zoos.

It has repeatedly protested against the U.S. Surgical Company's use of dogs in teaching demonstrations. FOA places among the top animal rights and welfare organizations in terms of annual budgets. However, no high paid executives are apparently involved.

The International Society for Animal Rights (ISAR), 1957

Started as the National Catholic Society for Animal Rights, ISAR claims to be the first organization dedicated to animal rights. Its goal is to prevent cruelty to animals and eventually end use of all animals in research. In 1987, the society published Tom Regan's book, *The Struggle for Animal Rights*.

ISAR sponsors seminars, organizes demonstrations, prepares educational materials, serves as an information source for media, and drafts legislation. From 1991 to 1995, it provided funding for the Institute for Animal Rights Law at Brooklyn College of Law. It organized, along with In Defense of Animals, the 1989 protest against addiction research at Yale University. Its major efforts in recent years have included launching campaigns against overpopulation of dogs and cats, advocating spay and neuter clinics, encouraging alternatives to the use of animals in research, and promoting development of animal rights law. In recent years, it has promoted candlelight vigils on Homeless Animals Day to call public attention to the plight of homeless animals.

Increasing personnel turnover occurred in 1994 and 1995. In January 1996, the ISAR board removed Helen Jones from office, thirty-seven years after she founded the organization. ISAR filed a lawsuit against Jones for alleged conversion of more than $1 million of assets for her personal use and other alleged misconduct. Contributions dropped by 29 percent in 1994 from the previous year. Susan Altiere, a longtime staff member was named as acting president.[29]

Fund for Animals (FFA), 1967

Fund for Animals was founded by Cleveland Amory, syndicated columnist and well-known author of *The Status Seekers* and *The Cat Who Came for Christmas*. Much of the credibility of the fund is based on the consistency of its message and membership following. The fund's major goal, and focus, is to eliminate cruelty to animals wherever, however, and whenever it occurs. It operates seventeen field offices in the United States, gives awards to media that have increased public awareness of animal issues, publishes the *Fund for Animals Newsletter*, and also distributes bumper stickers and buttons to reflect the theme, "Animals Have Rights, Too."

Its major areas of interest include whales and seals; feral animals such as wild burros, wild horses, and wild goats; wildlife in general; laboratory animals; hunting; and the fur trade. The fund owns the 600-acre Black Beauty Ranch in Texas for abused and unwanted equine animals. The ranch also houses some silver foxes.

The group strives to protect wildlife; save endangered species; prevent slaughter; fight cruelty to animals; oppose sport hunting abuses; protect lab animals; eliminate greyhound racing, dog fighting and bullfighting; and save baby seals and dolphins.[30] Its motto, "We speak for those who can't," and its slogan, "Animals have rights too," are reflected on bumper stickers and buttons. It encourages individuals to become "armchair activists" by writing to lawmakers, signing petitions, reporting neglect and abuse, and donating time, talent, and money.

In 1991, one of its major achievements was an agreement reached with the National Park Service to drop plans to shoot bison in Yellowstone National Park as part of a livestock disease research project.

The fund has actively engaged in antihunting campaigns. In 1989, Heidi Prescott, then national outreach director who later became director, served a maximum fifteen-day sentence in a Maryland jail, with two days off for good behavior, for rustling leaves with her feet in a public wildlife management area on the opening day of the deer hunting season.

Among the group's supporters are well-known personalities such as Angie Dickinson, Dom DeLuise, Doris Day, Gretchen Wyler, Loretta Swit, and Jonathan Winters.

Animal Protection Institute (API), 1968

API was conceived "to bring together those who wish to protect from cruelty and restore to abounding life all animals everywhere."[31] The institute uses humane education, creative communication techniques, including a national quarterly magazine and TV documentaries, plus special investigations, program planning, research, and work of special volunteers to influence animal protection. It conducts education and informational programs to promote humane treatment of animals, with concentration on marine animals, dog and cat population surplus, and leghold traps. Among its humane education publications are *Mainstream* and *A.P.I Vine*.

Animal Rights International (ARI), 1976

ARI, a coalition of more than four hundred organizations with a combined membership in the millions, is described as a nonprofit umbrella organization for activities of Henry Spira, its founder and coordinator. Although Spira operates from an office in his New York City apartment with only one other employee, he has taken a position of negotiating with large companies to reduce animal testing.

Spira's first successful venture began in 1976 when he targeted the American Museum of Natural History in New York, which was conducting tests on cats. He questioned the value of the research, and within a year, the National Institutes of Health pulled funding from this project.[32] His major objectives are to eliminate the use of animals in testing and in confinement production, encourage substitute testing, and promote vegetarianism. Another main focus has been a campaign against Perdue poultry farms.

ARI encourages companies that conduct tests on animals to sponsor research into devising substitute tests of equal or greater accuracy that do not require the use of animals or that use fewer animals and minimize their pain and suffering. Spira has strongly opposed use of the Draize test using rabbits and the LD-50 test to determine the toxicity of a product.

The organization declared in 1990, "While we would of course, prefer that we instantly transform society to a vegetarian lifestyle, we also need to recognize that people's eating habits tend to change slowly. . . . We urge the animal rights movement to relentlessly pressurize industry to develop, promote and implement systems that reduce farm animal pain and suffering, so long as people continue to eat them."[33]

Spira promotes working with companies to reduce exploitation of animals in industry. Some abolitionist animal rights groups have accused Spira as "part of the old humane movement" and "hob-knobbing with the enemy," viewing him as an industry mediator.[34] His main financial backers have been groups such as HSUS and MSPCA, as well as wealthy individuals.

Animal Legal Defense Fund (ALDF), 1978

ALDF is a national association of over 650 attorneys and 55,000 member contributors dedicated to protecting and promoting animal rights. Its stated purpose is to assure that the interests of all animals are recognized and protected under law. Joyce Tischler, is executive director and cofounder, with corporate offices in California and Maryland. Local chapters operate in Washington, D.C., Boston, Chicago, and Seattle. Except for

ALDF's president, attorneys who serve on the board of directors and who assist prosecutors by conducting legal research and writing friend-of-the-court briefs receive no compensation.

Since currently animals have no legal rights, ALDF believes that the remedy is to change our laws through legislation and litigation, to grant legal rights to animals.

The long-range plan calls for comprehensive legal services for the animals and the movement. ALDF sponsors an annual Animals and the Law Conference; maintains an animal rights lawyer's network, with a central listing of attorneys through the country who are available for animal-related legal assistance; and supports a library of decisions from litigation involving cruelty cases, animal rights, and welfare issues.

The fund formed the Special Committee on Animal Protection in the Young Lawyers Division of the American Bar Association. It provides a forum for attorneys to exchange ideas and information about the law in relation to animals and seeks to increase the protection that animals receive under the law.

Its projects have included preparation of resolutions concerning animal rights and protection for American Bar Association ratification; review of proposed legislation affecting animals and preparation of reports with recommendations concerning the legislation; writing articles concerning animals and the law; preparing model animal protection laws; and preparing manuals to consolidate and explain state animal-related laws.

ALDF founded the Students Against Dissection Hotline program in 1989 to lend support to students and teachers who object to animal dissection in high school and college classrooms. It has also filed suit to halt patenting of genetically engineered animals.

Animal Rights Network and *Animals' Agenda* Magazine, 1979

The Animal Rights Network publishes the *Animals' Agenda* magazine six times a year. This nonprofit, educational enterprise is dedicated to the liberation of animals and nature. In discussing animal issues, *Animals' Agenda* seeks to explore their connections to other important social issues, such as feminism, poverty, hunger, peace, and civil rights. In this way, it attempts to broaden the focus of the animal rights movement, while placing its concerns on the agenda of other progressive movements. Founded in 1979, Animal Rights Network earlier published *Animal Rights Network News. Animals' Agenda* circulation declined from 24,665 in September 1991 to 13,438 in September 1994.[35] Publication frequency shifted from ten to six issues per year. Contributions and gifts have been important to maintain the publication. Subscribers have received direct-mail appeals for contributions because subscription and advertising revenue have fallen short of costs.

A major shift in editors occurred in 1992. The board of directors replaced Merritt Clifton, news editor since 1988. His wife, Kim Bartlett, editor since 1986, resigned. Clifton and Bartlett claimed the board did not like their criticism of high salaries paid by large national animal groups. The board explained the shift due to declining circulation of the magazine and a feeling that it had become too much the vehicle of one couple's opinions. The board also felt there were problems from housing of thirty-three feral and stray cats in the office that were present at the time of the board meeting.

Jim Motavalli served as editor until May 1993. Then the board appointed Kim Stallwood as editor-in-chief and relocated the office from Monroe, Connecticut, to Baltimore, Maryland. Stallwood's goal upon taking up his new duties was "to re-establish *Animals' Agenda* as the "preeminent publication in its field."[36] He had previously served as acting general secretary to the British Union for the Abolition of Vivisection and executive director to People for the Ethical Treatment of Animals.

Under Stallwood, the magazine serves as a voice for the animal rights movement. Stories about opposition to animal rights may appear, but dissension within the movement and the developments unfavorable to the movement will seldom if ever be found.

The 1995 board of directors included Ken Shapiro (PsyETA), Evelyn Kimber (NEAVS), Gene Bauston (Farm Sanctuary), Mitchell Fox (Progressive Animal Welfare Society), Peter Gerard (National Alliance for Animals), Simone Patterson, and Doug Stoll. Its advisory board included Cleveland Amory, Jim Mason, Batya Bauman, Andrew Linzey, Jim Motavalli, and Peter Singer. Gerard later replaced Shapiro as chairman.

People for the Ethical Treatment of Animals (PETA), 1980

PETA, founded by Ingrid Newkirk and Alex Pacheco, shows the most rapid growth and influence of any animal rights organization. In the 1990s, it has been viewed as the most visible animal rights organization in the United States with an approximate membership of 300,000. (All contributors are considered to be members.)

After reading Peter Singer's *Animal Liberation*, Newkirk, formerly chief of Animal Disease Control for the District of Columbia, developed her belief that "animals have a worth in and of themselves, that they are not inferior to human beings but rather just different from us and they really don't exist for us nor do they belong to us."[37] She combines active involvement in the animal rights movement as the cofounder of People for the Ethical Treatment of Animals, lecturer, and author of books giving recommendations for activists.

From its beginning, PETA operated from headquarters in Rockville, Maryland, and used a Washington, D.C., post office address. In 1996, the organization moved to Norfolk, Virginia, where its ninety employees would find low-cost living and proximity to major airports and highways. With a worldwide membership of 500,000 and offices in London, Amsterdam, and Stuttgart, Germany, PETA is probably justified in its claim to being the largest animal rights organization.[38]

In *Save the Animals*, Newkirk's philosophy is not a question simply of how animals should be treated within the context of their actual or perceived usefulness, but rather whether people have a right to use them at all.[39]

With this doctrine, Newkirk calls for:

- abandoning animal testing of cosmetics and household products;
- carefully disposing of trash and garbage in ways that will not endanger domestic and wild animals;
- obtaining pets from humane society shelters and not from pet shops, as well as not keeping exotic animals or birds as pets;
- speaking out against meat consumption and use of fur products;
- promotion of vegetarian diets;
- feeding pets vegetarian rations;
- objecting to dissection of animals in school biology classes;
- protecting birds and wildlife by individuals creating wildlife sanctuaries in their backyards;
- supporting local animal shelters;
- monitoring the care of fish in pet and department stores;
- eating sea vegetables (seaweeds) instead of sea animals;
- boycotting aquariums, which serve as "prisons" for fishes and marine mammals;
- encouraging mobile activists with bumper stickers, license plate messages, leaflets and brochures, and telephone answering machine messages;
- neutering and spaying cats and dogs;
- protecting wildlife by thwarting hunters;
- using humane, nonlethal traps for rodents;
- discouraging use of leather, wool, feathers, and silk for clothing and other uses;
- reading labels and avoiding products that contain animal product ingredients;
- avoiding movies suspected to have scenes that harm animals;
- boycotting souvenirs and products that contain ivory, tortoise shells, skins or furs of wild animals, or marine animal products; and
- avoiding giving of gifts that contain animal products or ingredients.

Alex Pacheco, the cofounder, gave up his studies for the Catholic priesthood to devote himself to animal rights in 1980.[40] He had previously picketed rodeos and fur sales and participated in the sinking of a whaling ship. Pacheco achieved national attention for his work as a volunteer in a Silver Spring, Maryland laboratory.

PETA seeks to gain attention through public demonstrations and media coverage. To obtain media attention in 1991, PETA arranged for an animal rights activist wearing a pig costume to hit the Iowa pork queen in the face with a pie during the World Pork Expo.

Another media attraction involved nude models holding a sign, "We'd rather go naked than wear fur." Although these demonstrations drew considerable attention, one of the models, singer Melissa Etheridge, later dissociated herself from PETA because of its staunch opposition to animal research. When she realized that animal rights had many "gray areas" that she could not support, she publicly stated that animals losing their lives to eradicate cancer and AIDS was acceptable to her.[41]

A full-page advertisement was placed in the *Des Moines Register* in August 1991 comparing the slayings committed by confessed murderer Jeffrey Dahmer in Milwaukee to the slaughter of livestock. The ad offended thousands of readers. Although the *Milwaukee Sentinel* rejected the ad, the Des Moines paper ran the ad and defended that decision in an editorial: "People for the Ethical Treatment of Animals are within their rights and within the law in buying an advertisement that many readers consider in bad taste."[42]

The news story before and after the $11,200 ad was run brought national attention to the issues. The *Register* was swamped with calls from angry readers canceling subscriptions and businesses pulling advertisements. One animal industry leader viewed the PETA ad as a gross insult to American farmers, ranchers, and their families, noting its use of the deaths of seventeen people as a publicity stunt.[43]

PETA seeks to educate the public against "speciesism" and human chauvinist attitudes toward animals through documentary films, slides, and pictures. Newkirk has stated "the livestock industry is the single most destructive problem in the U.S. . . . Eventually, if our dream comes true, there will no longer be a livestock industry."[44]

PETA sponsors seminars on activism; it also sponsors rallies and demonstrations, consumer boycotts, student animal rights organizations, and a special publication, *PETA Kids*, for young activists. It markets a wide variety of merchandise to advertise and promote its objectives. The organization has centered much of its activity against animals in research but has also been active in anti-fur campaigns and alternatives to animal products.

In 1985, PETA received videotapes stolen by the Animal Liberation Front from the University of Pennsylvania Head Injury Clinic. From sixty hours of videotape, the group produced a twenty-four-minute edited version, entitled *Unnecessary Fuss*, that was widely distributed among animal rights/welfare organizations and the media and on Capitol Hill. Health and Human Services Secretary Margaret Heckler suspended funding indefinitely for the University of Pennsylvania Head Injury Laboratory based on documented abuses. PETA took credit for this cabinet-level decision.

PETA has served as the news outlet for incidents of vandalism and laboratory break-ins, but none of its members have ever been implicated in any of these actions.

Although PETA has not always met the ethical requirements of the National Charities Information Bureau, it avoids problems with a large board. In 1995, its report to the Illinois secretary of state listed cofounders Ingrid Newkirk and Alex Pacheco, plus two other trusted associates. PETA'S major programs involved international grassroots campaigns, public outreach and education, research investigations, and rescue. Reports indicate no hint of PETA enriching anyone or failing to spend donations consistent with its charitable purpose; and also according to reports, it is efficiently managed with the self-disciplined nature of the individuals involved.[45]

Animal Rights Mobilization! (ARM!), 1981

Founded by Dr. George Cave, ARM! (formerly known as Trans-Species Limited) is composed of animal rights advocates who are dedicated to eliminating animal use and exploitation. Although its original office was in Williamsport, Pennsylvania, it had regional offices in New York, Philadelphia, Chicago, and Harrisburg, Pennsylvania. The headquarters moved to Denver in 1991 and merged with the Rocky Mountain Humane Society. Robin Duxbury, from Rocky Mountain Humane Society, became national director. This group has operated on very limited budgets with expenses exceeding revenue at times.

Its major aims are to develop a comprehensive educational program on animal abuse, expose to the public specific cases of animal abuse, and encourage and engage in direct, militant, but nonviolent action in opposition to the abuse of animals. One project in the 1980s was Humans Against Rabbit Exploitation (HARE), an international coalition of animal protection organizations dedicated to halting the developing commercial rabbit breeding industry.

In 1988, the group sponsored a campaign against nationally recognized barbiturate addiction studies in cats at Cornell University. As a result of the intense campaign, Cornell returned the research grant to the National Institute on Drug Abuse. ARM! has repeatedly protested drug addiction research using monkeys at New York University and medical school animal laboratories.

Its Campaign for a Fur-Free America is designed to eliminate furs from the marketplace. After moving to Denver, the organization campaigned against establishment of Colorado's Ocean Journey, a proposed educational marine park project supported by major corporations and business firms in the Denver area.

Its policy statement declares that

> Aside from inherited homocentric prejudice and simple ignorance, it is unbridled capitalism which today stands in the way of animal rights, just as in the past it has stood in the way of human rights, and been instrumental in the oppression of minority groups.
>
> The first step toward overcoming these obstacles is the recognition that the liberation of non-human animals is demanded by the same ethical principles which prohibit racism and sexism. . . . The ultimate goal of the animal rights movement is the liberation of all animals from exploitation and infliction of unnecessary pain, suffering, and death. . . . The ultimate goal of the animal rights movement demands a radical transformation of human consciousness and the recognition of the moral and ecological foundations of animal rights.[46]

Farm Animal Reform Movement (FARM), 1981

FARM promotes reverence for life to alleviate and eliminate abuses of farm animals and other adverse impacts of animal agriculture on human health, world hunger, and natural resources. Alex Hershaft, president and founder, was formerly employed by the US Environmental Protection Agency and was active in the environmental movement.

As a long-term goal, FARM aims to end all human exploitation of animals for food or any other purposes. For an interim goal, it hopes to improve the conditions of animals raised in US factory farms and to moderate the other destructive impacts of animal agriculture on human health, food resources, and environmental quality.[47]

FARM has cosponsored the Action for Life annual conference on animal rights, Veal Ban Campaign, World Farm Animals Day, and the "Great American Meatout" to encourage Americans to give up meat for a day and to educate the public on consequences of eating meat. It participated in the June 1990 and 1996 Marches for Animals, sponsored the Decade of the Animals Conference in November 1991, and participated in the National Alliance for Animals Conference in July 1994.

The networking among animal rights groups is illustrated by FARM's list of advisers displayed on a 1995 letterhead. These included: Kim Bartlett of *Animal People* and formerly at *Animals' Agenda*; Helen Jones, International Society for Animal Rights; Elliott Katz, In Defense of Animals; Michael Klaper, physician and author; Frances Lappe, author, *Diet for a Small Planet*; Jim Mason, author of animal rights books; Jeremy Rifkin, *Beyond Beef*; John Robbins, EarthSave Foundation; Peter Singer, author and philosopher; and George Wald, Nobel laureate.

Feminists for Animal Rights (FAR), 1982

Feminists for Animal Rights is a group of feminist, vegetarian women, with a vegan orientation, who are dedicated to ending all forms of abuse against women and animals. Since they believe exploitation of animals and women derive from the same patriarchal mentality, FAR attempts to expose the connections between sexism (discrimination against women) and speciesism (discrimination against animals) whenever and wherever it can.

FAR is dedicated to the promotion of vegetarianism because members "concur with the feminist precept that the personal is political." They feel that not eating the flesh of animals is one way of "putting feminism into action." FAR is one of the smallest animal rights groups with less than one thousand members and an annual operating budget in 1991 of $2,500.[48]

In Defense of Animals (IDA), 1983

Founded by Dr. Elliot Katz, a veterinarian, In Defense of Animals was formerly the Californians for Responsible Research. Organized to create an active watchdog organization, IDA "is committed to ending the terror of institutionalized animal abuse and teaching the benefits of a compassionate life-style." [49]

IDA focuses on animals experiencing cruel treatment in research; the killing of animals for their furs; animal drug addiction; and the ivory trade and other similar practices. It targets research and vivisection, as it seeks to eliminate animal experimentation in the name of science, because it considers the practice to be inhumane and unnecessary. The group attempts to apply public pressure and obtain court injunctions to convince researchers of their actions.

Some of its major activities include sponsoring the World Laboratory Animal Liberation Week; freeing military greyhounds; working against the American Medical Association's efforts to maintain the use of animals in laboratory experiments; encouraging the public not to contribute funds to the American Heart Association, the Diabetes Association, the Cerebral Palsy Foundation, Easter Seals, Parkinson Foundation, or the American Cancer Society because these groups support use of animals in the laboratory; encouraging a boycott of Procter and Gamble because it tests its products on animals; encouraging medical students to abolish the dog laboratory; and encouraging all students to refuse to dissect.

IDA's goal has been to see that conditions under which research is conducted are both responsible and nonabusive. It seeks, through legal actions and sustained public pressure, to force researchers to reconsider seriously the morality of imprisoning animals for experimental procedures. IDA has informed the public of alternatives to animal use, researched the National Institutes of Health funded grants and made information available so that citizens can have more informed input on the use of their tax dollars, and monitored current California legislative actions concerning the use of live animals in research.

IDA filed a lawsuit against the US Department of Agriculture resulting in a formal complaint against the University of California for violations of the federal *Animal Welfare Act*. It also filed a suit, along with Berkeley Citizens for a Toxic-free Environment, challenging the construction of a new animal research facility at the University of California at Berkeley on environmental grounds.

IDA created the Animal Activist Defense Fund to provide legal support to animal rights activists and maintain a hotline for animal abuse reports. It says it will "not hesitate to put our bodies on the line in defense of animals" and has been involved in several demonstration projects in which members were arrested. It has received help from ISAR and United Action for Animals to produce fund-raising materials.

Internal problems erupted between president Elliot Katz, the staff, and the board in late 1993. Katz fired development director Raymond Chavez after Chavez tried to set firm policies with personnel to control cash flow problems. Then the board restricted Katz's authority to hire and fire staff. Attorney Marjorie Martis resigned. Remaining board members, Betsy Swart and Joan Briody, were to meet with Katz by telephone once a month. A personnel director was to be hired to take over staff management when the budget would permit.[50]

Humane Farming Association (HFA), 1985

An offshoot of the Buddhists Concerned for Animals, HFA membership is comprised of 55,000 veterinarians, consumer advocates, family farmers, public health specialists, humane society representatives, and others. The group staunchly opposes any confinement of livestock and poultry and specifically targets stall-raised veal and battery cage layers. They are also concerned with conditions in hatcheries and slaughterhouses, genetic engineering, and animal patenting. One of their major goals is to make farmers provide animals with enough room to fulfill physiological and behavioral needs.

HFA sponsors the National Veal Boycott and the Campaign Against Factory Farming. Group members believe that consumer awareness and consumer pressure will eliminate confinement livestock and poultry production or factory farming, and they strive to promote that awareness. They have run advertisements in national magazines telling consumers that animals are treated inhumanely and that meat is tainted with drugs.

Among its activities to increase public awareness and promote more humane farming practices, HFA works with Speak Out for Animals to convince restaurants to remove milk-fed veal from their menus. (Bennigans was responsive to this campaign.) HFA also places advertisements in *Time* magazine noting the inhumanity of raising milk-fed veal calves, promotes the National Veal Boycott Day, publishes a so-called watchdog newsletter and special reports devoted to the evils of factory farming, and campaigns against the egg industry's practice of killing male chicks, leaving hens in cages, and debeaking hens. It claimed major credit for the indictment against the Vitek Supply Corporation for illegal importation, sale, and use of the toxic drug clenbuterol in veal feed formulation.

HFA's key goal is to make farmers provide animals with enough room to fulfill physiological and behavioral needs. The group asserts that the overproduction of egg and dairy products lowers the quality of the products in addition to hurting taxpayers and the industry. It claims to have a "genuine desire" to improve rather than harm agriculture.[51] Among its board members are Dr. Michael Fox (HSUS) and Alex Pacheco (PETA).

Physicians Committee for Responsible Medicine (PCRM), 1985

PCRM, a nationwide group of 3300 physicians addressing the use of animals in medical science, examines the ethical questions raised by this issue and makes information available to the public and to elected representatives. The group believes that as physicians they have an obligation to examine and advocate ethical principles where they have been compromised or neglected.

Dr. Neal Bernard expresses much of the group's philosophy in his writings. "When we expand our compassion to include non-human animals, it is not just the animals who benefit. We do, too. . . . It is not a question of whether we value an animal or a person more, but rather, do we respect each of them enough to save both."[52] Barnard's columns have appeared in *PETA News* and the *Animals' Agenda*.

PCRM has criticized organizations such as the March of Dimes, which provide funds to support research using animals. The American Medical Association has expressed concern about the group's opposition to the use of animals in biomedical research. It has also questioned the name of the organization since less than 10 percent of its members are physicians.[53]

PCRM is reported to have close affiliations with PETA. Both Alex Pacheco and Ingrid Newkirk appear as supporters of the PCRM "Declaration of Concern and Support."

The supporters list includes two nurses, twenty-six medical doctors, and one veterinarian. Among nonmedical supporters are actresses Doris Day and Loretta Swit, actor Mike Farrell, and singer/musicians Howard Jones, Michael Franks, Nina Hagen, and Lene Lovich. Animal rights and animal welfare leaders Tom Regan, Shirley McGreal, Jean Goldenberg, and Bob and Loretta Hirsch are also listed.

Farm Sanctuary, 1986

Located in a rural farming community on 175 acres near Watkins Glenn, New York, Farm Sanctuary has gained increasing support in the early 1990s. Lorri Bauston, who serves as president, and her husband Gene, executive director, opened this sanctuary for abandoned and crippled animals in 1986. In 1992, they cared for three hundred pigs, chickens, cattle, sheep, goats, turkeys, rabbits, ducks, and geese, all formerly abused and neglected.

The Baustons live in a modest apartment on the second floor of a barn that houses some of the animals. Their office is located on the farm to keep overhead costs low. In addition to a small maintenance staff, they recruit student interns for varying periods, who assist in caring for the animals and hosting visitors.

This organization has received considerable attention from its investigations and campaigns against "downer" and abandoned animals. In 1993, Farm Sanctuary opened a visitors center that includes exhibits and a sales room for animal rights literature and merchandise.

A generous gift announced in 1993 made possible the opening of the Farm Sanctuary—West on a three-hundred-acre county farm near Orland, California, about ninety minutes from Sacramento, a location the Baustons considered desirable for contacting state legislators on animal rights and welfare issues.

Some animal activists have criticized Farm Sanctuary leader Gene Bauston for his compromised position on downed animal legislation, which permits slaughter of injured animals.

The Doris Day Animal League, 1987

Although one of the newer animal rights organizations, the DDAL has been successful in raising substantial funds. Actress Doris Day is the founder, and Holly Hazard is the executive director. During its first five years, the league's direct-mail campaign packages filled millions of mailboxes and raised more than $10 million. About 350,000 contributors, called members, have responded. Its major focus is to lobby for laws to protect millions of animals that the group believes are suffering in laboratories and commercial testing facilities.

DDAL is opposed to the use of animals for research, toxicity testing, and fur. The group has organized mass mailings that include a "Petition to the US Congress" urging the enactment of an "Animal Bill of Rights." The organization has been criticized for high solicitation costs although the organization has claimed their mailings also included educational materials.

DDAL is very keen about citizen action. It wants people who care about animals to sign petitions that are then sent along to Congress. The petition drive lends credence to the claim that certain mailing costs are properly allocated to public education. Although the league is a tax-exempt organization, contributions are not tax deductible to donors because DDAL is primarily a lobbying group.[54]

This group is affiliated with People Protecting Primates, an international coalition of animal rights groups, also chaired by Doris Day. The league's executive director is Holly Hazard, who actively lobbies Congress and several state legislatures on animal rights issues. Day herself has little to do with day-to-day operations, her work with the league averaging about one hour per week. Hazard, a member of the law firm of Galvin, Stanley and Hazard received compensation and a contribution to the employees benefit plan in 1994.

United Poultry Concerns (UPC), 1990

Formed by Karen Davis in Montgomery County, Maryland, UPC's motto describes its major objective: "Promoting compassionate and respectful treatment of domestic fowl." UPC is one of the smallest animal activist groups. With about two thousand members, UPC carries out educational efforts and demonstrations against confinement production of eggs, broilers, and turkeys. UPC also promotes vegetarianism.

Animal People, 1992

Merritt Clifton, editor, and Kim Bartlett, publisher, founded this tabloid newspaper in October 1992 after Clifton was removed from his news editor position at *Animals' Agenda* and Kim Bartlett, his wife and *Animals' Agenda* editor, resigned in protest to the firing. The policy of *Animal People* is to report the news about people and organizations in the animal rights movement, without interference and without concern for political correctness as defined by the major animal rights organizations.

The emphasis on practical problem solving and factual news coverage offers a more complete perspective on animal rights and animal welfare than other animal magazines and organization house organs will present.

Animal Liberation Front (ALF)

ALF is not legally recognized as an organization. It has no official office, staff, board of directors, or other features of a regular interest group. It has been described as a "clandestine organization" and traces its origin to England. The first ALF actions in the United States began in 1982 (see chapter 13 and appendix 6). Thousands of animals have been stolen, and millions of dollars worth of damage has been done to facilities and equipment.

This group supports the work of ALF by all lawful means possible and provides a legal defense fund for ALF activists. In the United States, the Animal Liberation Front Support Group claims a membership of ten thousand. PETA has also acted as a public information outlet for ALF and has provided legal support for suspects in ALF raids.[55]

Coalitions to Achieve Animal Protection Goals

In an effort to separate it from the abolitionist approach of the animal rights activist organizations, HSUS, ASPCA, MSPCA, and 101 other state and local groups published a joint resolution in the *New York Times* on January 29, 1991.

This resolution dealt with laboratory, farm, wild, companion, exhibition, and work animals and stated their opposition to "threats and acts of violence against people and willful destruction and theft of property" and their positive efforts "to reduce as rapidly as possible the massive pain and suffering of billions of animals through nonviolent means."[56] The resolution listed detailed policies:

- to back legislation and regulatory action that promote alternatives to the use of laboratory animals in products testing and other research;
- to eliminate the exemption of animals used for food from protection of anti-cruelty statutes;
- to secure enactment of legislation that requires "basic behavioral and physical needs of farm animals be met so that America's farm animals are assured the following minimum standards: the freedom to stand up, lie down, extend their limbs or spread their wings, make other normal postural adjustments, an adequate supply of nutritious food, adequate veterinary care, and an environment that suits their physical and behavioral requirements";
- to educate the public about the cruelty involved with trapping, raising, and hunting of animals for their fur, and to urge the public not to purchase or wear fur;
- to secure legislation to prohibit sport hunting and trapping on national wildlife refuges;
- to ensure that species designated as threatened or endangered receive protection; and
- to limit the breeding of captive wild animals and provide protection to animals used for exhibition or work purposes.

The HSUS joined forces with the ASPCA, Defenders of Wildlife, and the Society for Animal Protective Legislation to form the Coalition to End the Wild Bird Trade.

In 1988, Humane Farming Association was behind legislation in California to outlaw the veal crate, legislation that failed to pass. It also supported federal legislation with the same goal. In this effort, HFA received financial assistance from the FFA, ASPCA, FOA, Society for Animal Protective Legislation, and local groups.

The Foundation for Biomedical Research (FBR), to strengthen its position, helped organize the Incurably Ill for Animal Research (IIFAR). It has lobbied for continued biomedical research on animals by presenting incurably ill patients arguing that they need such research for cures to be found.

To counter this move, a new group organized as the Disabled and Incurably Ill for Alternatives to Animal Research (DIIAAR) at the prompting of IDA, PETA, and others. DIIAAR members have demonstrated to lawmakers, the media, and the public that not all incurably ill are convinced that animal research is needed for their goals to be achieved and that pain, suffering, and death to animals is not morally acceptable. One of DIIAAR's first publicity exploits was a March 21, 1988, demonstration at the Department of Health and Human Services at which demonstrators in wheelchairs were arrested.[57]

The above examples illustrate the practice of several large animal rights groups, which spawn new spin-off groups that share the philosophy but carry out specific legitimizing or supportive activities. Individuals may be connected with several of these groups.[58]

Movement Growth by Division

Energetic and dedicated people often disagree on the best ways to accomplish their common goals. Within the animal rights movement, both organizations and individuals have disagreed on the best courses of action. New organizations have emerged:[59]

Parent Organization	New Organization and Year Started
American SPCA	Animal Welfare Institute (1951)
American Humane Association	Humane Society of the United States (1954)
	Friends of Animals (1957)
Humane Society of the US	International Society for Animal Rights (1957)
	Fund for Animals (1967)
Friends of Animals	Doris Day Animal League (1987)
	Spay USA (1990)
Animal Protection Institute	United Animal Nations (1987)
Animals' Agenda Magazine	*Animals' Voice* (1986)
	Animal People (1992)

On Stage: Actors Playing Mixed Roles

Animal protection involves many actors playing a variety of roles. On one side of the stage stand the traditional animal welfare organizations, well established, well endowed, and attempting to keep the movement centered on humane treatment of animals, providing shelters for homeless animals, and carrying out educational programs to encourage proper care and treatment of pets and protection of wild animals. Most of their programs follow a reformist approach. However, a few programs may include definite abolition tactics, such as opposing hunting, trapping, fur farming, and use of fur apparel. HSUS, ASPCA, AHA, MSPCA, and AWI are the leaders in this group.

Far to the other side of the stage are the most militant animal rights activists, advocating elimination of animals for food, wearing apparel, research or laboratory uses, pleasure, and sport; and promoting vegetarian diets. These organizations represent the abolitionist position on most animal issues. PETA, Farm Sanctuary, ARM!, IDA, and ISAR are major examples in this segment.

In the middle of the stage between the animal welfare reformists and the animal rights abolitionists are most of the remaining groups. Their programs include efforts to improve humane treatment of animals through reform of current practices and also some specific animal rights efforts to abolish animal experimentation, product testing, and intensive livestock production (factory farming). Organizations in this group include FARM, HFA, and FFA.

Within the animal protection movement are a number of organizations who work primarily to save wild animals. They oppose the importing of wild animals and birds; monitor and publicize harmful treatment of wild animals in zoos and circuses; and make numerous appeals for funds to carry out their work. Some of the major groups involved in these efforts are World Wildlife Fund, International Primate Protection League, Marine Mammal Rescue Fund, and Defenders of Wildlife.

Since 1984, leaders of animal rights groups have held a private event, "Summit for the Animals." This annual event has attempted to unite the groups to pursue common political goals. However, disagreements at the 1997 summit raises a question of whether these annual meetings can accomplish much toward united actions or activities.[60]

Any effort to categorize all animal protection organizations is difficult and may be misleading. The future direction for animal activism lies with the coalitions that are formed, its success in pushing policy objectives into federal and state laws, and the amount of money that it can extract from contributors.

5

A Profile of Animal Rights Activists

Wesley Jamison

Animal rights activists are not socially marginal or isolated people. The movement is characterized by distinct types of behavior and activity—the influential, active, attentive, and general. Typically, the animal rights activist is white, college-educated, middle-class urban or suburban background, in his or her middle thirties, and most frequently female.

The animal rights movement is often dismissed by many members of what might be called the American "political class"—legislators, lobbyists, staff, journalists, and policy experts. Likewise, many of the "apolitical class," like farmers, researchers, and entertainers, discard the movement as something less than serious. The agenda of the animal rights movement—getting rid of fur coats and veal, for example—may seem marginal to many citizens. However, the members of the American animal rights movement are serious. They have had considerable mainstream success, and survey data show that the activists are *not* socially marginal or isolated people. Their views, willingness to work in the political system, and level of sophistication should give pause to those inclined to dismiss the movement in which they play a role.

Who are the people involved in the animal rights movement? In this chapter, we will examine the members of the modern movement. A body of research has emerged that paints a picture of the constituency of the modern animal protection movement. Using social science techniques, researchers from Oregon State University, Utah State University, the State University of New York, the University of California at Berkeley, Western Carolina University, Texas Tech University, and elsewhere have begun to illuminate the physical, emotional, and ideological characteristics of those in the movement. In addition, *Animals' Agenda* magazine provides polling results of its readers.

This chapter is divided into three parts: (1) a model that helps to explain the differences between the various levels of animal rights membership; (2) a brief description of the research projects that provide the basis for information presented; and (3) a review of data on animal rights adherents that has been collected since 1980. Since no explicit, objective data exist concerning animal *welfare* believers, the chapter emphasizes the demographic, attitudinal, and behavioral characteristics of animal *rights* believers.

The Stratification of Movement Constituents

When asked about the membership of mass movements, most Americans tend to generalize. Often mass movements, including animal rights, are presented as monolithic and unwavering groups of people who hold monotonously uniform views. From this perspective, mass movements are viewed as consisting only of "true believers" who all hold identical political beliefs, are extremely intense, and are similarly committed. Upon closer examination, mass movements in American society are neither monotonous nor monolithic; they are not characterized by members who hold the same political beliefs or with identical intensity. The animal rights movement is no exception. Rather than being an combination of "typical" people, the movement contains differing levels of activism and interest. Each level within the movement is characterized by distinct types of behavior and activity.

The research projects presented here have examined different levels in the movement. Hence, some way is needed to help differentiate the research. The stratification pyramid is one such model for picturing how the membership of the animal rights movement differs in its ideology, intensity, and political activity (see figure 1). This pyramid, first loosely elaborated by Gabriel Almond in 1950 to examine differentiated levels of public interest in foreign policy, initially described the various strata that occur within American society in response to any particular issue.[1] Since its introduction, the use of the pyramid has expanded and is now used as a general model by some political scientists to examine how interest groups and mass movements are constructed.[2]

The stratification pyramid provides some basic information about membership levels. As you move up the various strata, the stability, intensity, and commitment of the members increases. Indeed, those at the top have political beliefs concerning animal protection that are revealed in diverse ways, are highly stable, and are very intense. Most importantly, as the membership progresses up in the structure, the more sophisticated are the political abilities of the various members. Hence, the top of the pyramid is the focus of policy formulation and determination of the movement's agendas.

Influential members. This first segment includes less than 1 percent of the animal rights movement. Influential members hold advanced philosophical views. They are considerably more purist in their policy positions than other members, and are far less willing to accept political compromise concerning animal protection issues. Their political beliefs are unusually rigid, and they readily associate day-to-day animal usage with abstract concepts such as animal liberation and radical change. The influential members are also the most willing to invest considerable resources to advance the cause of animal rights. This stratum includes philosophers such as Peter Singer and Tom Regan, leaders like Ingrid Newkirk, and politicians such as Congressman Tom Lantos (Democrat, California).

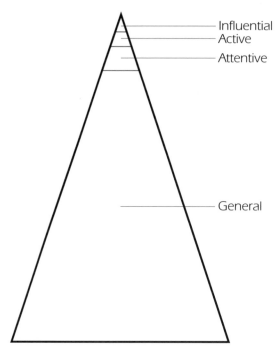

Fig. 1. Stratification of animal activism. Adapted from Almond, *The American People and Foreign Policy*, and Lunch, *Midwives of Democracy*.

Active members. The second stratum is composed of active members and comprises approximately 4 to 5 percent of the animal rights movement. Active members have philosophies that are somewhat less stable and developed than those of the influential members. The active members, however, can be highly emotional for the cause of animal rights. These activists hold very intense views and a willingness to spend large amounts of time and money in forwarding their beliefs; to attend rallies; write their elected representatives; and contribute money on a regular basis. This stratum has younger members than other strata, due to the extraordinary demands on time and physical ability of being actively involved in forwarding the cause. The active members may have lower incomes than the attentive members, but they will make sacrifices as needed for the movement. Most importantly, this strata includes the individuals who participate in protests and direct actions—the individuals that most Americans associate with the animal rights movement.

Attentive members. This third group contains about 10 percent of the members of the animal rights movement. These people have political views that are far less stable and mature than those of the active members and often do not make the distinction between animal rights as opposed to animal welfare. They are more concerned with the protection of innocent animals subjected to useless exploitation, they pay attention to animal protection issues in the media, and they readily identify and empathize with cases of animal cruelty. It usually takes explicit cases of animal exploitation to incense the passions of the attentive members. Nonetheless, they will contribute money on a periodic basis, subscribe to animal rights publications, pay attention to animal welfare and animal rights issues, and also take action when motivated by extreme examples of animal abuse. These members tend to have higher incomes and be older, more established, and more pragmatic in their political agenda.

General members. This final stratum makes up the remaining 85 percent of the movement. These people have highly unstable beliefs. They can identify animal protection issues in the media but have little interest in highly esoteric debates over policy. They are prone to lose interest in animal protection issues, so the animal rights movement must spend significant resources motivating them to send money. These general members are not sure what they are for, but they know what they are against: blatant animal cruelty. So the movement takes great pains to publicize extreme examples of animal cruelty, hoping that the publicity will motivate the general members into action. Ultimately, they contribute to the cause on no more than a sporadic basis.

Viewed through this stratification pyramid, the remaining sections of the chapter will examine the demographic, attitudinal, and behavioral characteristics and refer to these strata. This pyramid helps distinguish between the influential movement leaders who set the agenda, activists who implement animal rights ideas, attentive members who support animal rights, and general members who often belong in name only.

Social Science Research Projects
Oregon State University

Oregon State University (OSU) researchers Wesley Jamison and William Lunch conducted a survey of 426 American animal rights activists at the March for the Animals in Washington, D.C., on June 10, 1990.[3] This event offered an unprecedented opportunity to interview large numbers of activists. The research incorporated face-to-face interviews, which tend to provide accurate information and high response rates. Keep in mind that this research draws from members of the influential and active segments of the movement. So their characteristics and views will differ from the other strata. Before this march, limited numbers of activists had held spontaneous gatherings but nothing like the number that gathered in Washington. The National Park Police estimated that 25,000 animal rights activists attended the march. There had been some prior research into the constituency of the modern animal rights movement, but it was either biased or limited by the number of people interviewed. Much of the data reported in this chapter are drawn from the research conducted at the march in Washington.

Utah State University

In 1990, Utah State University (USU) researchers Rebecca Richards and Richard Krannich conducted a nationwide direct-mail survey of 1,020 subscribers to *Animals'*

Agenda.[4] This magazine is generally recognized as *the* voice of the animal protection movement. The USU survey was drawn from primarily the attentive members of the movement, hence their profile will differ from the activists. Importantly, direct-mail surveys offer the advantages of maximized randomization and coverage for minimal dollars, while having the traditional disadvantages of low-response rate and less accuracy.

Animals' Agenda Magazine

The animal protection movement has been characterized by very loose organization and a lack of a coherent, unified vision. *Animals' Agenda* magazine has emerged as the primary communication mechanism for all the diverse facets of the movement, providing its subscribers with articles, editorials, and news concerning animal issues. In 1984, the magazine surveyed its readers, thus providing a baseline of information for future research.[5] The magazine reported a 1990 circulation of 25,000 subscribers.

Other Information Sources

Both the OSU and USU studies benefited from previous research. During the mid-1980s, Susan Sperling of the University of California at Berkeley conducted perhaps the original anthropological research into the movement. She studied a small sample of San Francisco Bay Area animal rights activists and leaders and uncovered much about the movement. Her research provided the first tentative social science profile of the constituency of the modern movement: Although reliable membership data on demographic categories such as social class, ethnicity, educational level, and sex are not available, the movement's greatest strength is clearly not concentrated among a social elite. Observation suggests that the new activists are typically white, college-educated, from middle-class urban and suburban backgrounds, in their early to middle thirties, and female.[6]

Her research provided a necessary precursor for the research projects that followed. Sperling's work illuminated the foundations of the movement since the literature prior to her study was sparse. So later researchers could focus on the demographic and ideological characteristics of the movement's participants.

Demographic Characteristics

Education. Previous journalistic accounts of the animal rights movement have characterized its activists as well educated. In the OSU survey, 66 percent had received some college or university education; 40.2 percent had a bachelor's degree or less; 7 percent had some graduate education but had not completed an advanced degree; and fully 19 percent had an advanced graduate or professional degree, such as an MS, PhD, or law degree. The USU survey indicated that subscribers to *Animals' Agenda* magazine were also very highly educated. Approximately one-half of the subscribers surveyed had completed some college or had a BS degree, while one-third had completed an advanced, postgraduate college education.

The readership survey conducted in November 1984 by *Animals' Agenda* supports the university research indicating that members of animal protection groups are highly educated. *Animals' Agenda* reports that 84 percent of its readers were college graduates and 25 percent held masters or PhD degrees. These figures are in stark comparison to the US general population where only 20 percent of the population had completed some level of college education.[7]

Race. Anecdotal and ethnographic accounts of the racial composition of the movement suggest that it consists of white activists. This speculation is confirmed by the various research projects. OSU data indicate that 93 percent of respondents were white and 2 percent were black, while American Indians, Hispanic Americans, and Asians each accounted for 1 percent; 2 percent of the respondents reported their race/ethnicity as "other." The USU data likewise point to an overwhelmingly Caucasian movement. White subscribers constituted 97 percent while nonwhites accounted for only 3 percent. The US national population is reported to be 83 percent white and 17 percent nonwhite.[8]

Explanations for the predominantly Caucasian composition of the animal rights movement include socioeconomic differences in income, mobility, education, and time availability of white activists versus minorities. The racial composition of the march in Washington closely mirrored the racial composition of various other social movements in this country. However, Washington, D.C., has a majority African-American population; and the Washington metro area has a large percentage of African-Americans close to the march location. A significant population of middle-class African-Americans live near the site of the march. Yet very few participated. So lack of participation of African-Americans in the contemporary animal rights movement cannot be explained *solely* in terms of socioeconomic factors. An alternative explanation might be that more immediate political concerns thoroughly dominate the political agenda. As a result, issues such as animal rights fade to obscurity in minority communities. While this may indeed be the case, this is only speculation, due to lack of research.

Income. OSU research indicates that activists have annual household incomes, before taxes in 1989, of between $20,000 and $40,000, with a mean income of $37,400 and a median income of $33,000. The USU study shows similar trends: 18 percent of its survey respondents had incomes of less than $20,000, 42 percent had incomes between $20,000 and $50,000, and 39 percent had incomes in excess of $50,000. *Animals' Agenda* reports similar figures from its own survey. The median incomes for its readers in 1984 ranged from $25,000 to $50,000. Compare these figures to the national population. In 1984, the median income for all households in the United States was $25,522, according to the US Department of Commerce.

Gender. Some reports have suggested that most animal rights members are female. This is confirmed by the various research projects. OSU interviews showed 68 percent female; 32 percent were male. The USU study showed that 78 percent of its sample were females, while 22 percent were males. Nationally, 51 percent of the population are females, while 49 percent are males.[9]

Age. In the OSU study, the age of most activists was between 20 and 50 years, with a mean of 29. Interestingly, a large fraction of the marchers were younger. For example, over a third of the activists consisted of people under 30 years of age. Other information shows similar trends. The USU study shows that 23 percent of the surveyed individuals were under 29; 57 percent were between 30 and 40; 20 percent were 50 years old or older.

The *Animals' Agenda* reader survey showed that only 5 percent of its readers were under 21; fully 75 percent reported being between 21 and 49; and 20 percent were 50 years old or older. The US Census of 1980 indicated a much younger population. In the United States, 50 percent were under 29, 24 percent were between 30 and 49, and 26 percent were 50 years old or older.

Employment. Movement members were employed in professional jobs. Forty-four percent of the OSU sample consisted of professionals such as nurses, doctors, architects, lawyers, engineers, professors, and administrators. Respondents were employed in a wide variety of other occupations as well. It has been speculated that many activists do not work outside the home. However, the OSU data showed that 69 percent of the activists classified their current job status as "working for pay," while 14 percent are full-time students. Only 4 percent reported their job status as not working outside the home, and of this 4 percent, only fifteen individuals were homemakers.

The USU study supports these findings. Among the readers surveyed, 60 percent reported their job status as working full-time, while the other 40 percent reported their employment status as "other." The employed included 46 percent in an executive capacity, 28 percent in technical professions or sales, and the remainder worked in a variety of occupations.

Likewise, *Animals' Agenda* reported that fully 80 percent of its readers were businesspeople or worked as professionals. In 1980, the US Census reported that 22 percent of the population worked as executives, 30 percent could be classified as technical/sales, and that all other occupations accounted for 47 percent.

Urban/rural orientation. The OSU data support James Jasper and Dorothy Nelkin's premise, showing that the activists are predominantly from urban areas.[10] Among activists surveyed, 66 percent lived in metropolitan areas, suburbs, or cities with populations of more than 50,000 people; 19 percent lived in towns of between 10,000 and 50,000; 10 percent lived in towns of less than 10,000; and 5 percent did not know or did not answer. The USU study, which reinforced these findings, reported that 73 percent of its sample had an urban orientation, while the remaining 27 percent had a rural orientation.

These figures compared favorably to those of the *Agenda* survey, which reported that 80 percent of its readers had urban orientations. The research conducted by OSU and USU, as well as the survey conducted by *Animals' Agenda*, mirrors the national population at large. In 1980, the US Census reported that 74 percent of the population had an urban orientation while 26 percent lived in rural areas. So the animal protection movement membership is geographically similar to the US population.

Information sources. Some scientists, agriculturalists, and politicians may believe that animal rights activists are acting out of ignorance, but this was not substantiated. The OSU research showed that the activists obtain their information about important public issues from a variety of sources. When asked for their most important source of information about public issues, 27 percent identified newspapers, 22 percent television, and 19 percent magazines.

Some people may also believe that activists rely upon movement magazines or direct mail distributed by the animal rights groups for their animal protection information. The OSU data does not support this contention. Among activists surveyed, 19 percent reported that magazines were their most important source of information, 15 percent reported direct mail, and 6 percent reported other sources such as word of mouths. Over 90 percent reported routine use of more than one source. Use of more than one source of information about public affairs is unusual and indicates a high level of interest. Compared to the general public, these activists show significantly higher interest in public policy and are notably less reliant on television for political information.[11]

Family status. The USU research reported that its respondents tended not to have children—71 percent reported no living children, and 84 percent stated that they had no children (their own children or other's) in the home. The *Animals' Agenda* survey reported that 50 percent of its readers were married, compared to 60 percent of the US population.[12]

Attitudinal and Behavioral Data

Attitudes toward religion. Much of the literature within the movement rejects the view that humanity has dominion over the environment. *Dominion* means that people have religious and ethical authorization to use animals for food, fiber, and as beasts of burden.[13]

While animal rights philosophers sometimes recognize the problem such traditional approaches pose for their position, they clearly reject both religious and secular arguments that rely upon human dominion as justification for animal utilization.[14]

The OSU research measured the extent to which this rejection of human dominion has moved from the movement's opinion leaders outward to activists in general. The survey data, reinforced by informal interviews with movement activists, indicates that rejection of human dominion over the environment is a unifying theme among the divergent animal rights groups. When asked if human dominion caused animal exploitation, 87 percent either agreed or strongly agreed.

In an unrelated 1984 survey, *Animals' Agenda* queried its readers regarding religious beliefs and found that 65 percent reported their religious status as either agnostic or atheist. In the US population, only 13 percent report no affiliation to Protestant, Catholic, or Jewish denominations.

The USU study provides another possible indication of a lack of traditional religious beliefs within the movement. This research provides evidence of the secular nature of the movement: Twenty-two percent of the USU respondents supported school prayer while 54 percent were opposed.

Attitudes toward animal research. During much of this century, research practices were accepted by the general public as a necessary tool of science. Yet protests against animal-based research have intensified over the last fifteen years. The activists were generally opposed to research that utilizes animals, regardless of the degree of harm to the animal or benefit to human beings. However, not *all* animal rights activists are opposed to *all* animal experimentation.

Among activists surveyed, 56 percent either disapproved or strongly disapproved of scientific research that uses animals but does not harm them. In contrast, fully 26 percent of the animal rights activists approved or strongly approved of such research. This approval response suggests that some common ground may exist between animal rights activists and scientists who utilize animals for lab research. But physiological and psychological harm seems to be the turning point for animal activists who may otherwise support animal research. Fully 84 percent disapproved or strongly disapproved of animal research that causes harm to the animals. Those invasive procedures that appear to the activists to be responsible for causing harm to the animal are the focus point of activist opposition to biomedical research.

The USU research showed that the attentive members of the movement are similarly opposed to animal research. On a scale of 1 to 7, where 1 is extremely wrong and 7, not at all wrong, animal use in cosmetic experiments rated a 1. Selling pound dogs for medical experiments also rated a 1, as did animal disease medical experiments.

Attitudes toward pets. Is animal rights activism in part mobilized by highly personal experiences with pets and motivated by concern for petlike animals? The OSU survey sought to measure the activists' emotional attachment to pets. Fully 87 percent either strongly approved or approved of keeping pets at home, 9 percent were neutral about pet ownership, while only 4 percent opposed or strongly opposed keeping pets at home. Intensely emotional experiences with pets were a significant mobilizing force in the activists' lives, based on responses to open-ended questions.

The USU research supports these findings. On the 1-to-7 scale, keeping a dog or cat as a pet scored a 7 ("not at all wrong"). The respondents also believed that it was not at all wrong to neuter a pet. Likewise, the *Animals' Agenda* reader survey reported that fully 89 percent of its readers approve of pet-keeping.

These views are in direct conflict with statements of animal rights opinion leaders. Ingrid Newkirk, cofounder of People for the Ethical Treatment of Animals (PETA), states that pet ownership is an "absolutely abysmal situation brought about by human manipulation."[15] And Peter Singer, in the original introduction to *Animal Liberation*, takes pains to disclaim any sentimentality toward pets or interest in keeping them. This discrepancy regarding the status of pet ownership is significant. But it is not unusual to have internal ideological inconsistencies within interest groups. It is not unusual for leaders of ideologically motivated groups to be conceptually purist and ideologically advanced compared to supporters or even occasional activists. For example, leaders of ideologically motivated groups have been less willing to compromise than their membership and considerably more "purist" than voters who support their agenda.[16]

Attitudes toward occupations and groups. The OSU research identified the feelings of activists toward various occupations and groups by using feeling thermometers—survey instruments that gauge respondents' feelings or values. On an established scale ranging from 0 to 100, a 0 response indicated a very cool or negative response and 100 indicated a very warm or positive response.

Animal rights activists felt most positively toward environmentalists, with a mean score of 88 and a median of 97. Activists also felt favorably disposed towards feminists, with a mean score of 70 and a median of 76. Activists gave veterinarians a mean score of 70 and a median of 74.

A gradual decline-in-feeling thermometer scores from high to low was expected. Instead, a dramatic drop from favored groups to disfavored groups, including scientists and farmers, was indicated. There simply were no middle scores. The activists felt negatively toward scientists, giving them a mean score of 28 and a median score of 21. Politicians, farmers, and businesspeople ranked with scientists as the groups that received the most negative responses. Farmers scored a median of 30 and a mean of 25. The median for politicians was 23, and the mean was 27. Businesspeople brought up the rear with median scores of 20 and mean scores of 25.

Attitudes toward farm animals and their treatment. The OSU research utilized additional feeling thermometers to examine activist feelings of the farm treatment of various farm animals. Activists were given a list of ten animals to score. Again, 100 indicates very positive, 50 indicates neutrality or ambivalence, and 0 indicates very negative. The composite perceptions of agriculture among respondents were negative. Again, a gradual decline in thermometer scores was anticipated.

Instead, all scores were below the neutral/ambivalence score of 50. Horses scored the highest with a median score of 39. Sheep scored 24; dairy cows, 11; beef cows, 1; veal calves, turkeys, broiler chickens, egg-laying hens, pigs, and mink, 0. Analysis indicates that an inverse relationship exists between the perception of highly intense production and activist approval. The greater the perceived intensity and industrialization, the lower the score. Likewise, it is believed that terminal production practices (mink, veal, etc.) may be the cause of negative activist perceptions. However, evidence is indirect and highly speculative.

The USU research measured attitudes that were indirectly related to farm animal production. On the 7-point scale, where 1 is extremely wrong and 7 is not at all wrong, raising cattle for food in a feedlot scored a median of 1. Eating meat scored a median of 2, and using horses for racing also scored a 2. Raising cattle for food on the open range scored somewhat higher, with a median score of 3.

Attitudes toward science. To further measure the activists' perceptions of science, the OSU survey utilized a survey question that the National Science Foundation (NSF) had used. When asked if they felt science does more "good than harm" or more "harm than good", 26 percent of the activists felt that science does more good than harm, while 52 percent believed that science does more harm than good. These data strongly contrast with samples among the general public. In polling conducted by the NSF in 1985 (and in keeping with a consistent pattern over time), 58 percent of the public felt that science does more good than harm, while only 5 percent felt that science does more harm than good.[17]

Attitudes toward animal control. The USU study provides a picture of the animal protection movement's attitudes toward various methods of controlling animals. Using the 7-point scale, the use of leghold traps for wild animals scored a 1. Killing an animal for a fur coat and hunting wild animals with guns also both scored a 1. Keeping animals in zoos scored a 3, while pest control measures scored considerably higher. Killing rats in residential areas scored a 4, while killing cockroaches scored a 6.

The USU survey also measured *Animals' Agenda* readers' attitudes concerning wildlife habitat protection issues. Among all respondents, 96 percent of the readers surveyed agreed that logging techniques should help wildlife even if timber prices consequently rise; 84 percent agreed that cattle and sheep grazing on public land should be limited if plants needed by wildlife are damaged. On the other hand, 94 percent of those surveyed believed that marshes that ducks and wildlife use should not be developed if housing is needed. And 94 percent felt that society should not develop natural resources if wilderness loss reduces wildlife.

Political affiliation. Politically, activists tend to be moderately liberal or liberal. On a scale of 1 to 9, where 1 is the most conservative and 9 is the most liberal, the activists in the OSU study averaged a 6.7. In the OSU study, the marchers gave their political party affiliation as 37 percent independent, 35 percent Democratic, and 14 percent Republican. Interestingly, 11 percent indicated "other," which may indicate the extent of nontraditional political identification within the movement.[18]

The OSU research further clarified party preference by asking respondents who answered independent, if they "leaned" toward the Democratic Party or the Republican Party. The research found that 33 percent leaned toward the Democratic Party, 8 percent toward the Republican Party, and 59 percent did not lean toward either party (true independents).

Voters who describe themselves as independents—and then admit that they lean toward one party—vote for that party more often than voters who identify themselves weakly with the same party to begin with. Thus, the "independent Democrats" vote for Democratic candidates more consistently than self-reported "weak Democrats." The OSU data indicate that most animal rights activists are self-defined liberals with Democratic or independent affiliations and Democratic voting records.

Political behavior. If the animal rights debate can be described as a value-laden political confrontation over the proper relationship between animals and humans, then the political activities of the animal rights movement demonstrate values that are critical of a number of precepts necessary for science. Thus, the most significant potential im-

Table 1. Composite Activist Profile

Characteristic	OSU %	USU %
Sex		
Male	31.6	21.7
Female	68.4	78.3
Age		
29 and under	41.9	23.2
30 to 49	48.0	56.6
50 and over	6.4	20.0
Race		
White	92.9	96.9
Nonwhite	7.1	3.1
Education		
High school diploma, GED, or less	12.3	17.9
Bachelor's degree or some college	40.2	48.4
Some graduate school	7.1	NA
Graduate/professional degree	18.7	33.3
Income		
$19,999 or less	19.0	18.4
$20,000 to $49,999	46.1	42.5
$50,000 or more	18.7	38.9
Residence		
Urban (over 10,000 population)	85.0	73.4
Rural	10.0	26.6
Don't know/Did not answer	5.0	NA
Occupation		
Professional, business, or executive status	44.0	46.0

pact of the animal rights movement on science is reflected in the activists' high level of political activity. Activists are politically active and have both the time and inclination to be involved in politics and social movements. This was illustrated by the extraordinary participation of activists at the March in Washington, D.C.

The OSU study asked activists about various political activities sometimes used to advance the cause of animal rights and in which of these activities they had participated. The responses: Ninety-eight percent strongly approved or approved of contributing money to animal rights groups; 90 percent of the activists had already done so; 99 percent strongly approved or approved of writing to elected representatives about animal rights; and 74 percent had previously contacted their elected representatives on this subject.

Perhaps the most significant dedication is shown by activists' political activity for animal rights candidates. Activists reported that 96 percent strongly approved or approved of campaigning for candidates who favor animal rights, and 38 percent had already done so. Compared to the general public, or even campaign contributors, this level of political activity is truly extraordinary.[19] So the marchers were characterized by profound commitment to the movement and to continued action within the political system. If the marchers in Washington are any indication, American animal rights activists are intense in their views, possess marked political sophistication, and participate in the political process in many ways.

6

The Debate over Animals
in Research, Testing,
and Teaching

Scientists and research workers justify biomedical research using animals on the basis of advancements in medicine, discovery of vaccines for major diseases, and discovering toxic substances. Opponents claim that none of the research has any direct bearing on disease prevention or improved medical care and results may be misleading when drawing conclusions from animals and applying them to humans. The concerns for laboratory animals have led to policies that regulate the care of laboratory animals and has stimulated research on appropriate alternatives to replace animals.

The Setting

Probably the most intense controversy generated by animal rights activists involves the value and benefits of biomedical research. Ten federal government agencies conduct or sponsor laboratory tests with animals including the Departments of Agriculture, Defense, Energy, Interior, and Transportation.[1] The US Department of Agriculture estimated that 106,191 dogs and 33,991 cats were used in registered research facilities in fiscal year 1993.

Andrew Rowan reports that for the six species, dogs, cats, primates, rabbits, hamsters, and guinea pigs, the 1990–1993 average use was 1,228,419. Since 1968, the use of these six species for research has declined about 50 percent. However, rats and mice account for about 80 to 90 percent of the laboratory animal total. The best research community estimates show about two-thirds of the dogs and all of the cats used in research and education are from pounds or shelters rather than bred for research.[2]

According to Bernard Rollin, animals used in research are identified in six categories, although these groups oversimplify very complex activities:

1. Basic biological research with little concern for the practical application.

2. Applied basic biomedical research—the formulation and testing of hypotheses about diseases, dysfunction, genetic defects, new therapies, and treatments.

3. The development of drugs and therapeutic chemicals and biologicals.

4. The testing of various consumer goods for safety, toxicity, irritation, and degree of toxicity. Such testing may include testing of cosmetics, food additives, herbicides, pesticides, and industrial chemicals.

5. The use of animals in educational institutions and elsewhere for demonstration, dissection, surgery practice, induction of disease for demonstration purposes, and high school science projects.

6. The use of animals for extraction of products—serum from horses, musk from civet cats, and other products. This is not strictly research.[3]

Rollin emphasizes that it is important to understand the type of research or testing that may involve animals. Animal activists and organizations may take different positions on these different categories.

The Issues

The issues surrounding animal research focus on these questions:

1. How much regulation should government place on scientists engaged in research with animals?

2. Should proposed research projects be screened for possible benefits before they are undertaken?

3. With the large number of animal research projects and investigators, is the responsible government agency enforcing all applicable rules, regulations, and laws associated with animal research?

4. How should protection of animals from pain and suffering be balanced with the scientific process and hoped-for benefits to humans?

5. Should animals used in research be obtained from licensed dealers and animal shelters or bred and raised specifically for research purposes?

6. Could fewer animals be used in some experiments and obtain reasonably accurate results?

7. Can alternative methods be used to replace the use of animals in research, in testing of drugs and household products, in professional medical or veterinary education, and in other classroom and laboratory teaching?

The Arguments Against Using Animals in Research

The first opposition to use of animals in research dates back to the late nineteenth century with the beginnings of the antivivisection societies. However, the opposition in recent years has emerged as animal activists and antivivisectionists object to causing animals pain and suffering in experiments that they believe have questionable benefit. Biomedical research scientists must now justify what they are doing and the expected benefits from animal research since animal activist opponents, basing their beliefs more on philosophical than scientific reasoning, have attempted to influenced public opinion against their work.

The trial and conviction of Dr. Edward Taub in 1981 alarmed his colleagues in the biomedical community and alerted members of Congress that things were not as they should be in the nation's laboratories.[4] (Taub's conviction was later overturned.) Since 1981, the Silver Spring monkey case has triggered increasing opposition to the use of animals in research from many animal rights and animal welfare organizations.[5]

Animal activists, antivivisectionists, and some scientists are now less willing to accept reassuring statements from scientists that all is well in animal research activities.[6] The opposition to animal research is based on concerns of whether

- some assumptions about animal testing are valid;[7]
- laboratory science can make further contributions;
- basic research in the medical sciences has any direct bearing on preventing diseases or improving medical care;[8]
- improvement in health is likely to come in the future, as in the past, from modification of the conditions that lead to disease, rather than from intervention in the mechanism of disease after it has occurred;[9]
- billions of dollars are being wasted regulating substances that might pose little risk;[10]
- animal research is a perpetuation of cruel and archaic methodology;
- the government should guarantee that animals are treated humanely;
- peer review by scientists assures that only worthwhile and critically important projects are funded;
- animal research is the best way to discover cures and treatments for human diseases;[11]
- money spent on animal experimentation should be made available for preventive measures that could save a far greater number of human lives;[12]
- research results are relevant only to the species under tests and concern for the risk of misleading predictions, since humans and animals often respond quite differently to drugs and disease;
- the choice of species is based on nonscientific considerations such as cost, ease of handling, and laboratory tradition rather than anticipated similarity to people;
- human disease can be studied through animals; in the past, efforts to investigate cholera failed to induce anything similar in animals while contemporary scientists are having the same difficulty with AIDS; and
- animals have certain rights not to be used in ways that would bring pain or suffering.

Research opponents recognize that the knowledge and the health benefits that have arisen out of bioscientific animal abuse cannot be denied or unlearned. But they also argue that spiritually evolving human beings no longer need to proceed in this direction and our inherent fear of death cannot be eliminated but can be spiritually modified.[13]

Those who believe in scientific antivivisectionism feel they have the basis for directly challenging the medical establishment.[14] The real point as they see it is that progress in medicine is not synonymous with improvement in human health. They believe that more lives can be saved through preventive measures than interventive technology. Although these lives may be different lives, they are just as important.[15]

Organizations that oppose the use of animals in research include NAVS, AAVS, PETA, the International Primate Protection League, ALDF, Animal Rights Coalition, ARM!, ARI, CEASE, DDAL, FAR, FOA, FFA, ISAR, NEAVS, and PCRM.

Support for Using Animals in Research

The supporters for using animals in research believe that such research provides many benefits to humans based on scientific evidence. The value of medical research is recognized for extending the scope and precision of hygienic measures, immunization, and therapy and for providing an understanding of the body and its diseases. Strong support for using animals in research comes from those who have the most experience in doing that research and those who have seen the major benefits.

Dr. Michael E. DeBakey, chairman of the Foundation for Biomedical Research, emphasizes, "Not one advancement in the care of patients—advancements that you use and take for granted every day—has been realized without the use of animal research." [16] Major professional groups approving the use animals in research include the National Academy of Sciences Institute of Medicine, the National Association for Biomedical Research, the American Medical Association, and the American Veterinary Medical Association.

The National Academy of Sciences Institute of Medicine (NAS) presents a very personal perspective on animal research benefits: "Animal experiments have provided valuable information on the effects of visual stimulation on brain development, biofeedback techniques, memory loss, programmed instruction in education, aggression, stress, and recovery after strokes or brain injury. We would know much less about these aspects of human life without animal research, and continued animal research is essential if new ways are to be found to cope with behavioral problems." [17]

Of the Nobel prizes awarded in medicine or physiology in the twentieth century, 54 of 76 were based on animal research.[18] Among these have been the prize awarded for the studies using dogs that documented the relationship between cholesterol and heart disease, the studies using chickens that linked viruses and cancer, and the studies using cattle, mice, and chicken embryos that established that a body can be taught to accept tissue from different donors if it is inoculated with different types of tissue prior to birth or during the first year of life, a finding expected to help simplify and advance organ transplants in the future. Studies using animals also resulted in the successful culture of the poliomyelitis virus, the discovery of insulin, and the treatment of diabetes.

Advancements Through Animal Research

John F. Enders, Thomas H. Weller, and Frederick C. Robbins, who received the Nobel prize in 1954, made history for developing the technic of culturing monkey kidney cells in the test tube. Their cell cultures, taken directly from monkey kidneys, made possible the development of the poliomyelitis vaccine by Jonas Salk and Albert Sabin, which has virtually eliminated this dread disease of children. The monkey is the only animal highly susceptible to the polio virus other than man, and thus neither the development of the vaccine nor tests of its effectiveness and safety could have been performed without the use of monkeys in the laboratory.[19]

Research with rhesus monkeys and chimpanzees underlies the recent release of a vaccine for hepatitis B. Rhesus monkeys are also being employed in testing of experimental treatments for Parkinson's disease. Development of revolutionary cancer therapies is heavily dependent upon animal research as well.

Research with animals has brought about the dramatic, almost miraculous, diagnostic and therapeutic advances in cardiovascular research. John Krasney cites the evolution of the thousands of experimental steps necessary before modern heart surgery could be accomplished. One of the most important components in this work has been the dog laboratory where surgeons had to perfect their skills before modern open-heart surgery, the coronary bypass procedures, and the heart transplant could be achieved.[20]

In addition, the use of experimental compounds on animals is regarded as the most reliable alternative to trying the compound on humans. No research method can provide an absolute guarantee of a compound's safety, and animal studies are no exception. Still animal studies provide an eminently reasonable degree of reliability in predicting and characterizing possible adverse effects in people.[21] Testing to discover toxic substances in products has had many critics, yet before the testing of new substances became routine, thousands of people died after taking remedies that turned out to be poisonous.

Scientists are now less concerned with substances that might kill people and more concerned with those that have long-term cumulative effects. The greatest long-term effect is cancer, which usually appears after many years—even decades—of exposure. Because researchers observed that cancer-causing chemicals often caused the same type of cancer in experimental animals as in humans, they learned that human cancer was probably a consequence of exposure to carcinogens. One of the direct results was the enactment of the Delaney Amendment to the *Food, Drug, and Cosmetic Act*, which forbade the use of a food additive of any substance shown by appropriate tests to cause cancer in people or animals.[22] So substances "generally recognized as safe" that might become food additives had to be tested for their carcinogenic potential. The only way of doing this was through animal tests.[23]

The National Association for Biomedical Research argues that companies that claim their products are not tested in animals and therefore are "cruelty-free" mislead consumers since almost all products or the chemical compounds that comprise them were previously tested on animals.[24]

Laboratory Animals in HIV/AIDS Research

In June 1996, the nation's leading AIDS organizations endorsed the use of laboratory animals in HIV/AIDS research. A letter of support highlighted the threat animal activists pose to future breakthroughs in AIDS research. The National Association of People with AIDS expressed the need to use animals and declared that animal studies are a necessary complement to clinical studies in humans. Every drug employed to treat HIV infection and the opportunistic infections that kill most people with HIV were developed using animals. Many compounds that seemed extremely promising in computer models and in vitro were proved in animal models to be extremely toxic. Although AIDS patients support compassionate treatment of animals, they do not want to set research back by shutting down one of the most important avenues to curing this deadly disease.[25]

Animals in Education

Philosophical conflicts from using animals in education have emerged on two fronts: (1) the use of animals in teaching professional medical and veterinary medical students and (2) dissection of animals in teaching biology, both in secondary school and college classes.

Animal use in veterinary medical education has decreased in the late 1980s. Techniques such as videotapes, interactive computer modules, and autotutorials have supplanted much live-animal use. The reasons seem to be based more on the effectiveness of learning and teaching interaction than on ethical or cost considerations. However, ethical concerns have caused many veterinary colleges to offer "alternative" programs in surgery. There are educational, ethical, and, in some cases, legal issues inherent in the evolution of teaching methods that rely less—or not at all—on live animals.[26]

The American Veterinary Medical Association (AVMA) endorses and encourages the humane study of animals in precollege education since the group believes that the use of animals can provide important learning experiences in science and ethics. Such studies should not interfere with an animals's health or well-being or cause it discomfort. The association also emphasizes that supervision should be provided by individuals who are knowledgeable about and experienced with health, husbandry, and the care and handling of the animals species used. Additionally, these individuals need to understand applicable laws, regulations, and policies regarding the use of animals.

Before a school obtains animals for education purposes, AVMA believes that the school needs to develop a plan for their procurement and ultimate disposition.[27] Appropriate care for animals must also be provided daily, including weekend, holidays, and other times when school is not in session.

The Association of Veterinarians for Animal Rights (AVAR) recognizes that the teaching of surgical principles requires the use of live animals. However, AVAR objects to the present system in which animals are used as "disposable commodities" to teach surgical principles to veterinary medical students. The group labels the practice as morally indefensible. Its members believe that veterinary medical students can be trained to perform surgery without resorting to using "practice" animals. AVAR asserts that students should develop basic manual dexterity on inanimate objects. Then students can further their skills by using cadavers of animals who died or were killed for medical reasons. During their clinical training period and with proper supervision, students could begin performing surgery on clients' animals, starting with the most basic operations.

The American Fund for Alternatives to Animal Research (AFAAR) has financed CELLSERV, a laboratory kit for beginning high school and college biology classes, to teach four experiments in cell cultures. These kits are designed to replace some of the animal work now done in beginning biology classes.

AFAAR has also financed summer classes with lab studies in alternatives for high school teachers and pre-med students. Workshops for biology teachers are held to encourage alternative teaching methods to dissection. Topics have included bioethics in the classroom, alternative labs that do not harm animals, and legislation and policies on the use of animals in education.

Dissection in biology classes has emerged as another crucial issue for those concerned with animal protection. Some animal activists question whether students should be forced to participate in such exercises if they do not want to. They believe that grades should not be affected if students refuse to take part in dissection exercises. From an animal rights perspective, this is a clear instance of teaching that human interests take priority over those of nonhuman animals and that science takes priority over nature.[28] Animal activists have worked to develop alternatives to animal dissection using videotapes, plastic models, and other methods that would reduce the need for using animals.

Use of animals in high school science fairs has also drawn criticism from animal protection groups. Animals have sometimes been injured or abused in such demonstrations that involved surgery or feeding of toxic substances.

Gradually, standards have been set by the National Science Teachers Association prohibiting the use of vertebrate animals in experimental procedures that result in pain or discomfort to the animals. Surgery as well as the use of toxic substances, ionizing radiation, aversive stimuli, and deficient diets are specifically prohibited.[29]

In 1994, the National Association of Biology Teachers withdrew its monograph, *The Responsible Use of Animals in Biology Classrooms*, because of ethical concerns about the classroom exercises and unequal representation of animals rights and biomedical research groups in the resource list. A new statement supports alternatives to dissection wherever possible, encourages teachers to be sensitive to student objections to dissection, acknowledges that no alternative can substitute for the actual experience of dissection, and urges teachers to be aware of the limitations of alternatives.[30]

Despite efforts to discourage use of live animals in education, a 1992–1993 study reported in *Academic Medicine* found that most students considered their live-animal laboratory experience useful. Seventy-four percent of the students participating in hands-on studies using dogs thought the method helped them understand the actions of drugs, was preferable to nonanimal alternatives, and did not involve an immoral use of animals. A 1994 study showed that 62 percent of 125 responding medical schools used live animals in one or more courses, but this use is likely to decline.[31]

Alternatives to Animal Research

Finding alternatives for animals in research is not a simple process. The Johns Hopkins Center for Alternatives to Animal Testing has received generous grants and gifts to sponsor research dealing with alternatives. Andrew Rowan of Tufts University concludes, "Scientific interest in the topic of alternatives has been marked by legislative initiatives and campaigns by animal advocates against animal testing. However, the topic is also marked by rhetoric that has served to confuse the public and others."[32]

Within the animal rights movement, the debate over research tends to focus on three exclusive methods: (1) regulating the use of animals through legislation; (2) abolishing the use of animals altogether; and (3) searching for alternatives to the use of animals.

Alternatives research is a relatively new approach and may not give immediate or spectacular results. In the short run, the search for replacements may eliminate fewer animals than regulation would. But over a longer period of time, the replacement approach should eliminate many more animals in research. Supporters of alternatives suggest a step-by-step process in which the need for animals is first reduced and then possibly eliminated in many scientific areas. But to replace animals in various tests, valid alternatives to the use of animals must be found.

The Food and Drug Administration (FDA) points out that many procedures intended to replace animal tests are still in various stages of development. Ultimately, testing must progress to a whole, intact living system, an animal. Not using animal tests when necessary would subject humans and other animals to unreasonable risks.[33]

In many areas of biologic and medical research, the NABR insists that there are no substitutes for the study of living animals. "Many of the processes that occur within the human body remain too complex to be simulated by a computer or cell culture. We face too many terrible health problems—like cancer, AIDS, heart disease, Alzheimer's disease, birth defects and mental illness—to eliminate the animal research that has been responsible for so many advances in medical care."[34]

David Weibers, speaking before members of HSUS, emphasized, "We should not be under any false illusions that all of the findings of animal research can be reproduced in a computer model or tissue culture given our current level of technology and understanding."[35]

Carl Cohen also dismissed as a serious error the thought that alternative techniques could soon be used in most research now using live-animal subjects. He emphasizes that no other methods now on the horizon, or perhaps ever to be available, can fully replace the testing of a drug, a procedure, or a vaccine, in live organisms.[36]

AFAAR attempts to foster interest among scientists through grants to fund research in alternatives. However, validating alternatives to animals in research takes time, personnel, and money. Most researchers generally hold that nonanimal experiments are adjuncts rather than alternatives to animal experiments. Studies that do not use animals can produce much valuable information, but they cannot completely replace the information gained from animal experiments, they believe.[37]

The 1985 amendments to the *Animal Welfare Act* established responsibilities of the principal investigator and of the institutional animal care and use committee in considering alternative methods and unnecessary duplication of research. Each institution engaged in research using animals must have an animal care and use committee. The committee's responsibility is to determine that the investigator has provided written assurance that the activities do not unnecessarily duplicate previous experiments. However, teaching experiments are not considered duplicative because each time a procedure is performed for a new group of students or new audience, new knowledge is gained.

The Procter and Gamble Company and Marrow-Tech announced that they are collaborating on research to adapt Marrow-Tech's cultured human skin for use in Procter and Gamble's ongoing program to replace animals in safety testing. The Marrow-Tech proprietary kits contain living human skin cells arranged three-dimensionally in layers of both dermis and epidermis. The goal is to modify the kits for use in evaluating eye and skin safety. Procter and Gamble announced that it is committed to reducing the use of animals in research as rapidly as possible without jeopardizing the safety of products that it sells. Preliminary studies suggested that the human skin culture system would have potentially broad application in evaluating skin irritation.

The public basically agrees with the argument that animal research is necessary. But many are not entirely comfortable with the feeling that their health depends on practices that often cause death and possible distress of animals. The Scientists Committee for Animal Welfare stresses that if an effective debate on animal research and alternatives is to develop, then the question is not whether animals should be used at all but how both animal distress and the number of animals used in the laboratory might be reduced.[38]

Three R's for Animal Research

British scientists have argued that animal researchers should follow the principle of the "three R's"—replacement, reduction, and refinement. *Replacement* refers to situations in which nonanimal techniques may be substituted for techniques using research animals. For example, rabbits are no longer used in pregnancy tests. Using mice to test the potency of yellow fever vaccine was long ago replaced by a cell culture test.

Reduction refers to cases where the number of animals required for a particular activity or project can be reduced. Most toxicologists now agree that it is not necessary to use from sixty to two hundred rodents to generate a statistically precise lethal dose when perfectly adequate lethal dose data can be obtained using ten to twenty animals. The National Cancer Institute now uses cell culture screening systems and has reduced animal use by 80 to 90 percent, a decision based on scientific rather than animal welfare reasons.

Refinement refers to the modification of a technique to reduce the pain and distress experienced by research animals. For example, various jacket and tether systems have been developed to protect catheters inserted into research animals that allow an investigator to administer doses of test chemicals and take blood samples from an animal without having to restrain it.

Promoting Humane Laboratory Animal Care

Singer points out that most people may be unaware that scientists can be animal welfare advocates. The public may also be unaware of the difficulties of the research process. Furthermore, Singer asserts that the scientific community recognizes its professional obligation to safeguard and improve the welfare of laboratory animals.[39] The National Institutes of Health published the first federal laboratory animal guidelines in 1955. In 1966, the US Department of Agriculture developed the first federal regulations under the *Animal Welfare Act*. Congress amended the *Animal Welfare Act* as part of the *Food Security Act of 1985* (see chapter 12). Since then, standards for animals in research facilities have been established to ensure that pain and stress to the animals are minimized. Each research facility is required to permit inspection and to report annually that the rules are being followed.

However, implementation of the law may be limited by the staff to carry out inspections and enforcement. The US Office of Technology assessment report showed that on one list of 112 testing facilities, 39 percent were not even registered with the branch of the Department of Agriculture that inspects laboratories.[40] Rats, mice, and birds are still excluded. Although a lawsuit attempted to include these animals, an appeals court overruled the lower court order (see chapter 14).

The National Agricultural Library, officially a unit of USDA, was also required to establish an information service on employee training and animal experimentation to reduce animal pain and stress. To provide public accountability and assure humane care of laboratory animals, training and recognition programs have been established.

Formed in 1965, the American Association for Accreditation of Laboratory Animal Care (AAALAC) represents national professional scientific, medical, and educational organizations and promotes high standards for animal care, use, and well-being through the accreditation process. Any laboratory animal program that uses and cares for animals in research, teaching, or testing can qualify for the voluntary accreditation program. Members of the accreditation council visit laboratory sites to inspect the facilities and consult with the staff. The AAALAC has developed guidelines for proper laboratory animal care that are accepted by the biomedical community and complement AAALAC accreditation programs as well as government regulations.

The American Association for Laboratory Animal Science (AALAS) is a professional, nonprofit organization of persons and institutions concerned about the production, care, and study of laboratory animals. The organization provides a medium for the exchange of scientific information on all phases of laboratory animals care and use through its educational activities and certification programs. It has been certifying laboratory animal technicians for more than twenty years. The certification program has been accepted as a professional endorsement of an individual's general level of technical competence in animal care.

The Debate over Human and Animal Values

Research on humans is considered immoral since it causes pain and infringes on their freedom. If certain kinds of research on humans is considered to be immoral, then philosophers argue that such research is immoral when conducted on animals.[41]

Much of the debate over animals in research centers on the values of how people view animals, humans, and their relationships. The animal-oriented philosophers argue that there is no clear-cut line between humans and animals from a moral point of view and that animals have moral rights from their nature, even as humans do.

A fundamental distinction exists between the reformists who believe that animal research should continue, with various modifications or restrictions, and the abolitionists who believe that it should simply stop because, they believe, certain classes of animals have a moral status and should not be exploited. Others have expressed support for basic research but question certain types of animal testing.

In calculating the consequences of animal research, many scientists would ask the public to weigh the long-term benefits of the results achieved—to animals and to humans—and in that calculation, not have people assume the moral equality of all animal species.[42] In a sense, this is a utilitarian philosophy, in some ways similar to Peter Singer's philosophy, which suggests that all lives are not equal.

AVMA points out that most research can be conducted with minimal pain to the animals and that scientists accord animals the right to freedom from needless pain but not the right to self-determination. The rights of animals will expand as technology and understanding reduce reliance on them, the AVMA asserts. But most scientists do not believe they should apologize for the higher value they place on humans.[43]

In addition, the AVMA believes that animals play a central and essential role in research, testing, and education for continued improvement in the health and welfare of human beings and animals. The association also recognizes that humane care of animals used in research, testing, and education is an integral part of those activities. AVMA maintains that use of animals is a privilege carrying with it unique professional, scientific, and moral obligations. It encourages proper stewardship of animals but defends and promotes the use of animals in meaningful research, testing, and education programs.

AVMA also endorses use of "random-source" animals, if carefully controlled, since the association believes this practice contributes greatly to improving the health and welfare of both animals and human beings.[44] Random-source animals are those obtained from pounds and shelters, cost less, and can be used for practice surgery in veterinary colleges or for other uses that do not require uniform size, genetics, or known health background. However, AVMA encourages adequate funding for investigation and enforcement activities to prevent cruelty and enhance the welfare of animals.

Public sentiment for use of animals in research varies with the nature of the research and the expected benefits. One group, the Incurably Ill for Animal Research (IIFAR), gathered seventy thousand signatures on a petition to Congress in 1990 supporting responsible use of animals in medical research. The petition was presented at a Washington, D.C., press conference led by the IIFAR, the Association of American Medical Colleges (AAMC), and the Foundation for Biomedical Research (FBR).

Animal research has become more costly and difficult, in part because of self-regulation by scientists but also because of externally imposed regulation. Some animal researchers have left the field, and young researchers have chosen not to enter it.[45] The biomedical research community would like to see every possible measure taken to limit the number of animals used and to find new testing methods. However, most researchers strongly believe that replacement of animals entirely is impossible at present. Scientists most actively involved in the search for and development of nonanimal techniques concur that animal testing must continue. The unthinkable alternative is to risk human safety and human lives.[46]

An enlightened perspective for the biomedical community comes from Richard Vance who counsels, "We must respond in a forthright and honest way about what we do. We must continue to ensure that animal use in research is humane and appropriate."[47] John Krasney emphasizes that research scientists believe that the final judgment for animal research is the value of life, especially human life.[48]

Dr. Michael DeBakey, internationally recognized surgeon who developed many surgical advances and was consulted on the heart surgery for Russian president Boris Yeltsin asserts, "The fact is that the devastation, delay and outright intimidation that animal rights groups are imposing on the scientific community are greater today than at any time in the history of biomedical research. As a result, research to prevent, treat and cure many of mankind's greatest killers and cripplers is being slowed, halted or prevented. Animal research was absolutely essential to our victory over polio, our progress in treating diabetes, and what we learned to enable life-saving organ transplants."[49]

Lawrence Finsen and Susan Finsen, taking a historical approach to the animal rights movement, believe that it is very unlikely that the scientific validity of animal research can be successfully challenged by the animal rights movement. They believe that the "vivisection is fraud" campaign is unlikely to succeed. While research proposals may be challenged for concrete reasons, the rejection of vivisection on scientific grounds will only happen in response to crisis from within the halls of science.[50]

7

Intensive Animal Production: Efficient, Low-Cost Food or a Violation of Animals' Rights?

Confinement production of livestock and poultry has generated a major conflict between the meat, dairy, and poultry industries and reformist animal welfare and abolitionist animal rights groups. Animal activists identify this intensive production as factory farming. They claim animal crowding, suffering, and environmental degradation. Reformists have called for more space and alternative practices to make production more humane. Abolitionists call for an end to intensive production. In response, animal industry groups have supported research to measure stress and reduce it whenever possible.

The Setting

Animal products contribute about three-quarters of the protein and one-third of the food energy in the American diet. Consumers spent $244 billion on meat, poultry, eggs, and dairy products in 1993, or about half of the $491 billion they spent on all domestically produced foods.[1]

US farmers and ranchers received $88.1 billion in 1994 from the sale of animals and animal products, about half the value of all agricultural products marketed, according to the US Department of Agriculture.

Before World War II, most food animals and poultry were produced in relatively small-scale enterprises, often outside, except during extremely unfavorable weather. Intensive confinement methods, using more capital and less labor, have transformed meat, dairy, and poultry production into what animal activists call factory farming.

Food animal and poultry producers have adopted modern intensive production because they can produce more product with less labor and usually at lower cost. They believe that they are treating their animals humanely when the animals gain weight, appear healthy and free of disease, and are protected from rain, snow, and extreme cold and heat.

Critics see modern meat, dairy, and poultry production much differently. Their views are based on philosophical thinking, often with little exposure or understanding of the science or economics of food animal production.

Ruth Harrison led the criticism of intensive food animal production in Great Britain: "The factory farmer . . . uses new systems . . . developed primarily for his own convenience . . . which subject the animals to conditions to which they are not adapted . . . characterized by extreme restriction of freedom, enforced uniformity of experience, the submission of life processes to automatic controlling devices and inflexible time scheduling." [2]

Peter Singer, the philosopher, pointed out that the use and abuse of animals raised for food exceeds any other kind of mistreatment of living creatures, and he asserts that people are ignorant of the abuse behind the food they eat.[3]

Alex Hershaft, a former official at the Environmental Protection Agency and founder of the FARM, believes that farm animals experience abuse more often than other types of animals and suggests that the animal rights movement should focus on eliminating "farm animal abuse" and ultimately the need for animals for food consumption.[4]

Bernard Rollin, a philosopher-professor lecturing to animal scientists, asserts that "mechanistic animal agriculture must be rebuilt around satisfying the full range of needs flowing from the farm animals' natures—not only food, water, and shelter, but also exercise, alleviation of boredom, companionship, etcetera. Obviously, such modifications will take a major research effort." [5]

Critics of Food Animal Production Methods

Most animal activists and their organizations condemn and oppose "factory farming" because they view intensive production as inhumane, being carried out under unnatural conditions, and causing suffering for the animals and poultry. Their reasons listed here are not intended to advocate these positions or agree but to understand why they oppose intensive food animal production: [6]

• Factory farming is capital intensive, and success is not achieved by direct care for the animals, well-being of individual animals, or individual animal productivity.

• Animals are not machines—they feel pain, suffer frustration and boredom, and have lives of their own to lead. Do humans have the right to make animals live miserable lives just to satisfy their taste for a diet so rich in animal products that it is bad for their own health?

• Animals are raised under cruel and inhumane conditions in intensely confined quarters without freedom of movement.

• Intensive production systems use antibiotics and other drugs, and laws and regulations lack defined standards for raising food animals.

• Intensive animal agriculture has devastating impacts on consumer health and environmental quality.

• The life of a veal calf is one of deprivation, stress, and disease.

- The total-confinement pig farm is specially designed for maximum exploitation of the pig's reproductive and growth cycles.
- Chickens are ranging foraging animals by nature that need plenty of fresh air, sunshine, exercise, and fresh greens to stay healthy and feel good and will thrive best in small flocks with a rooster, several hens, and groups of young chicks playing about, so confinement broiler production, battery cage production, and associated management practices are opposed.
- In crowded battery cages, the hen's most basic instincts are cruelly violated and the life of a factory-farmed hen is one of intense suffering confined in a cage with barely room to stand or stretch her wings.
- Cattle are fed grain that should be used by humans. Beef is processed under unsanitary conditions and is a source of fat in the diet that can cause health problems. The land and the environment could be improved without vast acreage used for cattle production.
- Cattle production is destroying the earth's remaining tropical rain forests, depleting fresh water, causing organic pollution, exerting pressure on the carrying capacity of natural ecosystems, edging species of wildlife to the brink of extinction, causing global warming, and threatening the "chemical dynamics of the biosphere."
- The Bovine Growth Hormone (BGH) approved for use with dairy cows in 1994 is turning cows into high-tech milk machines and may be harmful to the cows and require greater use of antibiotics.
- Animal agriculture causes soil erosion, rain forest devastation, and pollution.
- Downed animals transported to auctions and stockyards suffer gross abuse and neglect.
- The right to life is the most fundamental right of all animals, and killing is unnecessary and detrimental to the welfare of humans.

Proposed Changes for Animal Agriculture

Jim Mason, an animal activist, and Peter Singer, a philosopher, recognize that individual dietary decisions will not be enough and suggest thirteen steps to bring about broader changes in agriculture and food policy:

1. Call for prohibition of antibiotics, growth stimulants, and feed additives in animal agriculture;
2. demand an end to government subsidies that "prop up factory farming";
3. end tax-supported research and technological development of confinement systems;
4. ask for local markets and food cooperatives where farmers and consumers can trade directly;
5. ask for meatless meals and "nonfactory" farm products from restaurants and other public food outlets;

6. have labeling laws that would mark all animals produced in confinement systems;

7. in supermarkets, separate foods produced by confinement from those produced by traditional methods;

8. tax meat and animal products to fund subsidized production of other crops;

9. stop "meat industry propaganda" in public schools and know how nutrition is being taught;

10. shift US Department of Agriculture policy to emphasize "good food and farm livelihood" first;

11. call for land reforms and zoning laws to restore small, diversified farms near populated areas;

12. have food products labeled to identify corporations owning the brand name; and

13. end animal product industry check-off programs for advertising that promote animal products.[7]

In their joint resolution, ASPCA, HSUS, and MSPCA called for enactment of legislation that requires meeting the "basic behavioral and physical needs of farm animals"; insists that food animals be protected from anticruelty statutes; and encourages state and federal legislation to study alternative systems of production.[8] This proposal is very similar to the plan adopted in England that has made livestock and poultry management a very bureaucratic process (see chapters 3 and 4).

ASPCA calls for humane slaughtering procedures to be constantly monitored to minimize any possible pain and suffering.

AHA calls for adequate air, water, and feed supply; safe housing and sufficient space to prevent injuries; appropriate "environmental complexity" to prevent harmful depravation and boredom; regular daily supervision and effective health care; and sensible handling in all stages to avoid unnecessary suffering.[9]

Henry Spira, ARI, has pushed for reforms on how veal calves are fed and shipped. He also believes that more use of electronic auctions would reduce the stress on animals, who must be shipped to live auctions.

HSUS has called for humane, sustainable agriculture. The term *sustainable agriculture* emerged in 1980s as a concept that finds support among many US farmers. However, its meaning may vary among different types of producers. Humane, sustainable agriculture as defined by HSUS adds an additional dimension.

Dr. Michael Fox, vice president of farm animals and bioethics at HSUS, suggests that supporting those farmers who carry out alternative, humane, and sustainable agricultural practices, rather than those who are allied with the conventional agricultural system, will hasten the day when products raised using humane, sustainable agriculture and husbandry will be readily available.[10]

HSUS asserts that its sustainable agriculture program produces adequate amounts of safe, wholesome food in a manner that is ecologically sound, economically viable, equitable, and humane. This system claims to meet "farm animals' basic physical and behavioral requirements for health and well-being through a system that respects all of nature—humans, soil, water, plants, and animals." [11]

Campaigns Against Intensive Food Animal Production

Campaigns against intensive food animal production paint a picture of animal suffering and abuse, may call for boycott of the product, and ask for money to further the campaigns. Despite these efforts, the overall effect on production or consumption seems to be very limited. Following are descriptions of some of these campaigns.

Eating with Conscience. A national effort of HSUS, bringing together three themes—promoting human health, saving the environment, and ending animal suffering, the program has promoted free-range eggs, a humane diet theme, and information in public forums.

Veal Ban Campaign. The purpose of this FARM campaign has been to persuade consumers and retailers to drop milk-fed veal from their menus. The actions have included advertising in the mass media, picketing veal restaurants, particularly on Valentine's Day and Mother's Day, a counterinaugural luncheon in January 1985, and legislative efforts to ban the veal crate and the anemic diet.

The Great American Meatout. This annual campaign, also sponsored by FARM, involves events featuring musical entertainment, speakers, exhibits and videos, sampling of meatless foods, and solicitation of the "Meatout Pledge," at least for one day or longer. The campaign has been headlined by Bob Barker, Doris Day, Casey Kasem, Ally Sheedy, River Phoenix, Chrissie Hynde, Kevin Nealon, and Elvira.

Compassion Campaign. Another FARM campaign, its purpose was to introduce the concept of animal rights in the 1988 presidential election debate. The campaign involved seeking a statement from presidential candidates, attending national party conventions, and conducting extensive media interviews.

Farm Ed. According to FARM, the program seeks to balance "the propaganda peddled to America's school children by the meat and dairy industries." [12] The Farm Ed program was funded by a grant from the Brach Foundation.

Campaign Against Factory Farming. HFA has placed full-page advertisements against veal production, bovine growth hormone, and the National Pork Producers Council "other white meat" campaign in national news magazines.

Animal Rights Awareness Week. Held in June, it was created by IDA to educate the public to the ways in which it can bring about a more just and compassionate world.

Targeting Perdue and poultry production. In 1989, Henry Spira and ARI launched a public awareness campaign to place farm animal welfare on the national agenda. A part of this program has been a major campaign against confinement poultry production, targeting Frank Perdue, a major broiler producer on the East Coast. Spira placed a full-page advertisement in the *New York Times*, challenging Perdue's claims that his chickens grow up in "chicken heaven." In addition, Spira called for a boycott of Perdue's chickens until their production methods are changed to reduce "pain and suffering." [13]

Coalition for Non-Violent Food. One of Henry Spira's projects has been to bring together animal activists under a single campaign.

"Adopt-A-McDonald's." Part of Jeremy Rifkin's Beyond Beef campaign, this effort was organized in April 1993. Volunteers were recruited to picket selected restaurants to persuade McDonald's to put a "veggie burger" on its menu. Only Fox Television carried the story and that included a rebuttal by an animal industry representative.

National Farm Animals Awareness Week. HSUS designated this week in September 1994. One report indicated that the event drew practically no attention from the media and apparently fizzled out. HSUS criticized confinement housing saying it is cruel and does not provide livestock and poultry with their most basic physical and behavioral needs. They called for consumers to "shop with compassion." [14]

Animal Well-Being: Science, Husbandry, and Economics

Animal producers along with many others in the food animal industry are concerned that misleading and false statements about food animal production by animal activists and their organizations could lead to misguided efforts by an uninformed public. According to Geoffrey Becker, the imposition of mandatory and unworkable regulations could be harmful not only to the industry but also to the animals themselves. [15]

To counter this disapproval of modern production methods, animal scientists have conducted and continue extensive research to measure farm animal well-being. They see a great need to study the animal's mental state—much more subjective and difficult to measure, analyze, and interpret. Janice Swanson points out that the science of animal welfare is still in its infancy and current investigations are revealing the complexities of well-being assessment. Researchers agree that a multidisciplinary approach is needed to assess and understand, alleviate, and prevent suffering. [16]

How do we know if animals suffer? Marian Dawkins emphasizes that "suffering" must be recognizable in some objective way, otherwise the laws that emerge are almost bound to be arbitrary and might even fail to improve the lot of the animals much, if at all. [17] Even with one measure of productivity, such as the amount of feed an animal needs to gain a certain amount of weight, there are still problems in establishing what this means for the welfare of the animal. The possibility of a split between the conditions that are commercially best for the farmer and those that favor the health of the individual animal becomes greater the more animals in the total unit. [18]

Does confinement cause suffering? Dawkins points out that an "unnatural" life, such as being raised in confinement, is not necessarily one of suffering, any more than a life in the wild is necessarily free from it. She advised not to confuse "romantic" notions about nature and freedom with scientific evidence on genetics, development, and what happens if animals are prevented from behaving in certain ways. [19]

Ian Duncan also calls for acceptable criteria for measuring animal welfare: "Scientific evidence on the welfare of farm livestock is urgently required so that rational decisions can be made on intensive production systems and practices." [20]

A major decision is what to do about animals, whether to pass laws and condemn conditions that cause suffering or to condone food animal production because it is believed necessary for some purpose. Dawkins emphasizes that the welfare of animals cannot be viewed in isolation. Changes in treatment of animals, particularly those backed up by law, could change what we eat, what we wear, the kinds of medicines available, and whether a treatment for a particular disease is available at all. [21]

Joy Mench and Ari van Tienhoven reported that modern farming methods may disrupt social structures in a number of ways. Overcrowding, which violates the personal spacing requirements of individual animals, is common. Animals may be deprived of normal social contacts by early weaning of piglets or artificial incubation and rearing of chicks. When population or density increases, such as on commercial poultry farms, the levels of aggression increase markedly. [22]

Yet devising a method to measure and interpret the emotional states of animals has become the central problem for animal ethologists investigating farm animal welfare. There is considerable controversy over whether emotional experiences like boredom, frustration, and apprehension of future suffering or pleasure exist in animals or are unique to human beings. [23]

In October 1992, scientists, food animal producers, food processors, food commodity association representatives, aquaculture specialists, and advocates from consumer, environmental, and animal well-being groups met in Kansas City to discuss future research needs for sustainable food animal production. [24]

A major goal identified at this conference was to enhance well-being throughout the life cycle of food-producing animals. The participants recognized that societal concerns about animal well-being have escalated in recent years without a corresponding increase in research funding to adequately define what constitutes a state of well-being.

Scientists believe that four types of indicators are needed to evaluate the overall well-being of an animal: (1) physiologic indicators, like leukocyte counts and hormone levels; (2) health indicators, like disease and death rates; (3) performance indicators, such as growth rates and reproduction; and (4) psychologic indicators.

The first three measures are related to the economic viability of the production unit and can be watched closely. But psychologic indicators are difficult to assess and little is known about the psychological well-being of farm animals. [25]

Poultry Production

Although poultry scientists observed differences in behavior between penned and caged laying hens, they did not find greater stress in the restricted cage environment as opposed to the pens. They also found that increasing the freedom of movement by using large indoor pens could result in increased social stress if larger numbers of birds are housed together.[26]

They concluded that the conditions under which a bird was reared, its past experience of confinement, and its relationship with its handler must all be taken into account when management practices are evaluated. No single technique of measuring welfare can be adequate by itself.[27]

Ian Duncan concluded that, generally speaking, caging as such does not lead to severe frustration. Displacement preening is seen in battery cages, which suggests that a state of mild frustration is fairly common under commercial conditions. However, it is also commonly seen under "natural conditions and seems to be the bird's way of responding to everyday problems."[28]

However, certain strains of hens pace back and forth and appear frustrated during the prelaying phase because they cannot find a suitable nest site. Since the main cause of reduced welfare seems to be frustrated nesting behavior, research in the United Kingdom is trying to incorporate a nesting site or sites into the battery cage.

Debeaking or beak trimming has been criticized as an inhumane practice. However, an outbreak of feather pecking or cannibalism in a group of chickens greatly reduces their welfare. The debeaking procedure uses a sharp, heated blade to remove about a third of the upper beak and a small part of the lower beak and effectively prevents cannibalism.

So it would seem that the birds gain some benefits. However, evidence suggests that beak trimming leads to acute and chronic pain and the behavior of beak-trimmed birds is radically altered for many weeks. So there is a welfare cost as well as a benefit.[29]

From a producer's perspective, housing the birds in cages protects them from the often fatal effects of mass panic and insures that each bird gets the correct amount of food. Caging increases hygiene, decreasing the need to give antibiotics, and therefore decreasing the amount of antibiotic residue. The eggs are cleaner, decreasing the rate of infections.

Producers view beak trimming, if properly done, as a good technique for preventing injury to other chickens. They trim the beaks of cage-layer chickens to prevent injury to other chickens. As chickens' natural behavior traits include feather picking and infighting, trimming of the sharp point of the beak—like trimming the sharp nails of a dog—is a good safety precaution for other chickens. Molting, which is a natural phenomenon, is induced scientifically so that all chickens are molting at the same time.[30]

Poultry scientists view performance as an important index of well-being. Healthy, productive animals are, by definition, not being abused, and the productive records provide the evidence. Until scientific evidence demonstrates the psychological indices of the animals, producers will judge animal welfare by the health, growth, and reproduction of the animals.[31]

The economic benefits of caged layers provides the strongest reasons for continuing the system, although modifications are possible. Although building and equipment costs per bird in the caged unit are slightly higher than the litter floor unit, operation costs and labor costs are almost four times higher in the floor unit. The most viable change seems to be reducing the number of hens per cage although costs per hen would rise somewhat. Shifting to a floor unit would require more space and greatly increase the costs of eggs to consumers.[32]

Pork Production

Pork producers are not at all sure how livestock feel or what they may need. So to learn more, the pork producers have allocated more than $200,000 in check-off funds to finance meaningful, scientific research into behavioral and psychological needs of livestock.[33]

Pork producers believe it is the animal's purpose to serve humanity and it is humanity's responsibility to properly care for the animals in their charge. Producers are constantly assessing and evaluating their long-established husbandry practices. They are doing it systematically because they do not want to do something in haste that would actually set back the welfare of their livestock.[34]

The pork industry has recently developed a voluntary set of guidelines for the proper care of livestock in confinement operations. Those guidelines are being widely distributed. Producers believe their operations will be more efficient and profitable if they manage them in a way consistent with good husbandry practices that have been well researched and recommended by animal husbandry scientists.[35]

Activists criticize sow gestation and farrowing stalls, since the sows cannot turn or walk around. Animal scientists and others counter that such systems permit the sow to stand and lie down; reduce death and injury to piglets due to crushing; control feed better; and reduce aggression. One company has produced a gestation stall with a swinging gate on one side that permits the sow to stand and turn around.

Animal protection groups view castration of boars and tail docking as painful and unnecessary, particularly if performed on older animals. Producers say such procedures are necessary to reduce animal aggressiveness; prevent physical danger to other animals in the herd and to handlers; enhance reproductive control; and satisfy consumer preferences regarding taste and odor of meat. These practices are usually performed on the animals at a young age so that the short-term discomfort leads to longer term benefit for the animals.[36]

Pork producers strongly prefer to work together as an association to improve care and environmental conditions for their animals rather than have mandatory government regulation.[37]

Veal Production

Veal calves may be raised in stalls, hutches, pens, or in small groups. The system used by a farmer varies by region and climate, type of calf, farmer preference, and size of farm.

Producers keep calves in individual stalls to provide individual attention, improve general health, separate aggressive young bulls from each other, minimize or eliminate injury to the animals, and aid in feeding efficiency and veterinary care.

In modern stall systems, calves can stand, lie down, see, touch, and react to other calves in well-lit, sanitary barns. The Animal Industry Foundation reports that it is not true that veal calves are kept in boxes or perpetual darkness.[38] A study of Western production shows that none of the facilities attempted to incorporate darkness as a deliberate component of the production system. Six of ten facilities had natural light sources and seven of ten used continuous low-level lights at night to observe calves without disturbing them.

Veal farmers demonstrate their concerns for the calf's welfare by providing individual housing and tethering and by monitoring the environment, diet and feeding, and health of the animals. Producers believe that current practices alleviate some of the problems that arise with raising groups of animals.[39]

The individual pens allow for individual treatment and avoid the difficulties arising from the "pecking order" that develops in groups of animals, such as getting the proper amount of the feed. Tethering keeps the eating and defecation in separate areas of the pen. Barns are rinsed daily. Group housing is viewed as inappropriate because it increases the likelihood of the spread of infectious diseases.[40]

The diet of milk replacer is a complete food ration that includes iron and enables the calf to gain efficiently. Iron is given when the calf arrives at the barn and after that, if needed. In the California study, iron was added to the milk replacer during the first sixteen weeks and limited during the last four weeks. At market weight, 25 percent were classed as marginally anemic and 10 percent clinically anemic.[41] In most barns, the animals have free choice water available daily. Antibiotics are given early as a preventive measure and after that, as needed. But they are not given continuously and are not in the finisher feed.

If any unacceptable residues are found, a joint assessment of the source and cause is to be made with the USDA's Food Safety Inspection Service, Food and Drug Administration, the producer, veterinarian, and feed company representative. However, overseeing an industry with so many producing units is a formidable task.

Veal producers claim to have changed and will continue to change their methods based on scientific facts. Through their trade association, producers are working together to improve their public image, which has been tarnished by animal rights campaigns against veal production methods. The American Veal Association has prepared *A Guide for Care and Production of Veal Calves* and has launched a quality assurance program. This program includes husbandry practices; keeping records of feed sources, water quality, feed medications, and individual treatments used according to a veterinarian's recommendations; periodic monitoring of carcasses; and extensive record keeping for individual animals.

Some evidence of veal producers' willingness to change includes a nationwide decrease in drug residue violations from 3.9 percent in 1988 to less than .24 percent in

1991. The average for all meat was .26 percent.[42] However, the veal industry received a setback in its public image when a federal grand jury indicted the Vitek Supply Corporation in December 1995, and convicted its president in 1996, for smuggling unapproved drugs into the United States and illegally adding the drugs to feed mixtures sold to veal producers.[43]

Consumers may also have some concern about veal-raising practices. A survey reported by the National Livestock and Meat Board Beef Industry Council showed that in 1989 5 percent of those responding never served veal at home because they objected to raising practices, and in 1991, 7 percent objected. However, expense, family dislike, taste, "not familiar with veal" were mentioned more frequently for not serving veal.[44]

Education and Responses

The scientific literature and conferences among animal scientists confirm that animal agriculture has an image problem. The general public is "ignorant of reality and today perceptions are what count." Regulations based on whims actually could decrease the well-being of animals.[45]

The Animal Industry Foundation (AIF) points out that farmers have always enjoyed broad public support for their efforts to provide abundant, nutritious food. But today they believe that groups that reject the raising of animals for food, and others, who because they do not have the facts or have bad information, are working to convince the public that farmers and ranchers no longer tend their animals as animals, but as "food machines."[46]

AIF believes that the consuming public today is generally unaware of farmers' relationship to their animals, and how meat, milk, and eggs are produced on modern farms. Industry leaders think that the average consumer may not make the connection between the attractively packaged meat, milk, and eggs in the supermarket and the process of getting these foods from the farm to the dinner table.[47]

On-farm experiences show that animals kept in housing are no more likely to get sick than animals kept in the open, and they are generally healthier because they are protected.[48] The animal industry and farm and livestock commodity organizations are conducting educational programs with producers to increase their knowledge of how to provide the best-known humane care for their animals.

Recent efforts by animal scientists working with 4-H and FFA animal projects reflect the public image concerns among farm animal owners. Leaders are called upon to instruct young people that they have an ethical obligation to care for their animals in humane ways that protect the animals' health and welfare. These responsibilities include providing food, water, and necessary care, well-kept facilities to allow safe, humane, and efficient movement, disease-preventing practices, and transportation and exhibition that avoid undue stress or improper handling.

A 1995 report commissioned by the American Farm Bureau Federation warned about European Union–style animal welfare directives and urged farmers to cut out nonessential production practices that might concern consumers, develop more animal-friendly systems, and communicate with the public.

Food animal industry leaders view Jeremy Rifkin and his "beyond beef" advocates as "naive and ignorant about the structure and operation of the nation's agricultural and livestock economy." [49] If Rifkin's campaign was successful in reducing US beef consumption, thousands of family cattle farms and ranches would be driven out of business, local economies and communities dependent on cattle and related business would be hurt or destroyed, and millions of consumers would go without beef.

The Food Facts Coalition cites the American Heart Association, American Cancer Society, and the National Academy of Science statements that lean beef can be an important part of a balanced diet and a good source of protein, vitamins, and minerals.

During the same week as the "Adopt-a-McDonald's" campaign, McDonald's launched their test market for their new "Megamac," a half-pound burger. The product promotion generated more news than the Rifkin boycott.[50]

Shortly after his appointment, John H. Gibbons, President Clinton's science adviser declared that he did not eat veal because of the way it was raised.[51] The American Feed Industry Association and the Farm Animal Welfare Coalition (US) called for its members to write Gibbons, pointing out that he was not informed on modern special-veal production; that calves are not kept in cages but in special stalls and may be tethered to prevent contamination of their feed; and that they are not force-fed. Members urged him to visit a barn and learn firsthand from those who raise veal.

When the Humane Farming Association launched their ad campaign against pork production in 1993, the National Pork Producers Council called the ad "a total fabrication designed only to raise money." They pointed out that America's hog farmers are committed to providing the best possible care for their livestock based on the latest scientific animal husbandry practices.[52]

Dr. Paul Dieterlen, past president of the Indiana Veterinary Medical Association and practitioner, stated that the *ASPCA Animal Rights Handbook* has "false and inaccurate statements on nearly every page."[53] The description of how chickens, eggs, pigs, milk, and veal are produced contains many inaccurate statements, yet those not informed about current production methods could accept these as true statements.

Animal Rights and Intensive Food Animal Production

Food animal producers have worked to improve the humane conditions under which their animals are raised. Most of the education and changes in production practices address welfare concerns. Those who take a reformist approach should see that producers take welfare concerns seriously. However, meeting the "abolitionist" demands of animal rights groups gets little if any serious attention.

The animal rights philosophy, if taken seriously, calls for the end of all food animal production. Consumers should shift to a vegetarian diet. Canvas and plastic should replace leather shoes and other leather products. Cotton and synthetic textiles should replace wool and silk in clothing manufacture.

When animal rights advocates cite the health problems associated with heavy consumption of animal products, animal producers have responded with efforts to reduce the fat content of meat and dairy products. They do not consider shifts from animal product to plant-based food production.

The economic disruptions for producers if meat, poultry, and dairy production was discontinued would devastate many farming communities and farm families. The firms that supply machinery, feed, and livestock supplies and others that process and market livestock, poultry, and dairy products would be forced out of business or into new product lines. And consumers would not have the protein and other nutrients available that they have traditionally received from animal-based food products.

However, a gradual decline in food animal production would cause less chaos than sudden changes. Dietary habits tend to change slowly, so the influence of those who choose not to consume animal products would probably evolve gradually over many years.

Can Animal Agriculture Survive?

Both in the United States and Europe, the efforts to thwart criticism of food animal production has concentrated on improving humane treatment. The food animal industry groups have usually taken a defensive position when confronted by animal rights groups, since their objectives appear so directly opposite. The nutritional benefits of meat, dairy, and poultry products offer strong incentives for many to continue consumption, though perhaps at a lower rate. Producers may also cite the valuable by-products for pharmaceuticals as an important reason for continued operation.

The lines of the animal rights debate for the future of farm animal production are quite clear. On one side are those who believe that animals have no place in the human diet and that other animal products such as fur, wool, leather, or silk should not be used.

Closer to the middle are groups who believe that animal protein in moderate amounts has a place in the human diet. They want to see food animals raised under the most humane conditions that producers can devise.

Animal behavior scientists are working to learn more about the psychological feelings of animals and how best they should be treated to reduce stress and pain during their life cycle.

Animal well-being is an important factor for moral acceptability of a given production system. However, moral acceptability advocates should not ignore the productivity of animals raised in such a system. Doing so would carry the danger that some alternative production systems may not generate enough income to be implemented by the producers or permit them to remain in business.[54]

Producers accept the concept of animal welfare and humane treatment since they believe that a healthy, productive, comfortable animal will also be the most profitable for their farming or ranching operation. However, food animal producers strongly oppose the philosophy that animals should not be produced for human food or other purposes. They see this issue as potentially the most disruptive threat to the future economic prosperity of their industry. Certainly, the food animal industries provide valuable food and fiber sources for millions of people. They also provide a livelihood for animal producers, processors, and distributors and for many related industries.

However, some food processors are taking steps to meet the demand for nonanimal products. Products made with vegetable proteins are becoming available as meat substitutes for those who wish to follow a vegetarian diet.

Taking an animal welfare orientation rather than animal rights doctrine, Bernard Rollin urges food animal producers and the animal industry "not to resist and combat the new ethic for animals—for they will not win—but rather to appropriate it into their production systems with the help of research that acknowledges and respects the patent truth that animals can both suffer and be happy." [55]

8

Expanding the Crusade
for Animal Rights

In actions to advance their movement, animal rights activists have created confrontations with hunters, compromised with filmmakers, criticized horse and dog racing, picketed aquariums, debated the value of zoos, objected to circuses, campaigned against carriage horses, and boycotted fur. The anti-fur campaigns have brought together reformists and abolitionist groups, who do not believe that fur in coats and other wearing apparel is necessary. Pets present a special dilemma for the most radical animal rights activists. Several groups work actively to place animal rights literature in the classroom.

The actions to enhance animal rights and animal welfare have expanded to include animals in sports, racing, trapping and hunting, entertainment, circuses, zoos, aquariums, and rodeos. Some groups focus their efforts on protecting wild animals, reducing overpopulation of pets, boycotting animal products in clothing and apparel, and reducing live animal use and dissection in education including elementary, secondary, college, and professional classes.

The Crusade Against Hunting

The crusade against hunting has provoked intense controversy. Animal rights groups and most animal welfare groups strongly oppose hunting because they believe:
- Hunting is cruel and inhumane;
- it is not necessary for gathering food;
- it may destroy threatened or endangered species; and
- it is not necessary to balance food supplies with deer population since deer, like any other mammals, are regulated by natural factors such as disease, extreme weather, predation, and availability of food. Deer, like other mammals, slow their reproduction rate in times of stress, producing fewer young when food is scarce.

Activists also oppose "canned" hunts. Private landowners and managers in rural areas of the South and West provide housing and the opportunity for hunters to pay a fee to shoot "wild game" enclosed inside the property boundaries. Texas, for example, had about 490 registered game ranches in 1991.

According to estimates, about one thousand commercial and more than two thousand private or semiprivate bird shooting preserves operated in the United States in 1991. The 1800 members of the North American Game Bird Association annually supply hunters with 44 million birds, about 80 percent of all those raised in the United States. Some of the animals involved are threatened or endangered species, and some hunters have been fined under the *Endangered Species Act*.

Major organizations that oppose hunting include these:

• ASPCA—opposes indiscriminate or cruel hunting and trapping of birds and other animals. This groups considers the steel-jaw leghold trap to be one of the cruelest and most indiscriminate of trapping devices.

• IDA—opposes sport hunting claimed to be "wildlife management" and works to depopularize hunting, which they view as a "blood sport."

• AHA—strongly opposes hunting in national wildlife refuges and the use of the steel-jaw leghold trap.

• HSUS—has strongly opposed the concept of sustainable use of wildlife because it places value on the hunting of wild animals for international trade.

• PETA—has moved to the forefront in promoting hunter harassment. It advises its members, "Help a few animals avoid becoming victims by organizing a hunt disruption. Join local hunters in the woods and follow them around, rustling leaves, chatting, perhaps playing a radio, to alert would-be prey to the presence of humans. Let local media know you'll be there and ask other activists to join in a demonstration at the entrance to the place hunters park their vehicles." [1]

In Defense of Hunting

Supporters of hunting cite a number of specific reasons for defending the sport.

• Hunting of some species helps balance the size of the wild herd and the available food so that species can survive. In recent years, deer populations have increased substantially. Hunters point to the undesirable increase in deer numbers to justify more deer hunting.

• Hunting helps the hungry. Hunters in several states donate venison from deer killed by hunters to shelters for the hungry. The Hunters for the Hungry program has served not only to help manage deer herds and feed the poor, but also to educate the public about the role of hunters and game in society. [2]

• Some Texas game ranches have become an important part of the endangered species survival strategy of the Association of Zoological Parks and Aquariums since the 1973 ratification of the Convention on International Trade in Endangered Species, which cut off legal imports of most of the rarest animals. [3]

• Well-regulated hunting is a beneficial use of renewable wildlife resources, which when left to nature are lost to predation, disease, starvation, or old age. As a population management tool, it is often the most humane way to keep big-game species in balance with shrinking habitat resources, thus avoiding further loss of habitat for nongame species as well, according to the National Rifle Association.[4]

• Proper hunting is in complete accord with the moral tenets of humans and the historical facts of their existence. The hunting heritage predates recorded history by many centuries.

• The hunter's interest in game is the principal factor in fostering the conservation of all wildlife and other natural resources. The privilege to hunt provides the incentive for the hunter's contribution to wildlife management, without which all else would be lost. The commitment of the hunter, along with licensing, regulation, and the contribution of voluntary taxes, assures the propagation of all wildlife.[5]

Hunting—a dying sport? Hunter numbers are down from 21 million in 1980 to 14 million in 1996.[6] Since the number of young hunters has declined, it seems likely that hunting activity will gradually phase out to small numbers of participants by the turn of the century.

Wayne Pacelle points out that the question of deer management is not one of the biological carrying capacity, but of cultural carrying capacity. How many deer will people tolerate in their environment?[7]

The growth of canned hunting could be the beginning of the end for all hunting. Canned hunts seem to expose the real reason for hunting—that hunting is strictly for killing, since it is not done for the chase, for meat, to protect domestic livestock, nor to cut alleged wildlife overpopulation.[8] Canned hunting may cause the sport to lose social acceptability and acquire public regulation or abolition.

Sport hunting has been targeted as especially cruel and inhumane. Hegins, Pennsylvania, has received notoriety among animal activists for its annual Labor Day pigeon shoot. For over fifty years, people in this small town of about a thousand people have marked the holiday by shooting live pigeons as they are released from holding boxes.

For several years members of PETA, Fund for Animals, and other animal rights groups have protested this activity in which participants kill an estimated five thousand pigeons. Many protesters have been arrested and received considerable media coverage. Eight protesters, refusing to pay fines for trying to impede the pigeon shoot, spent two weeks in Schuykill County, Pennsylvania, jail in 1991. Supporters held nightly vigils outside.[9]

The Crusade Against Animals in Entertainment and Public Display

Many animal activists oppose the use of animals in circuses, rodeos, zoos, and marine mammal shows. They believe the animals are exploited, subject to pain and suffering, and often injured or have their lives shortened.

Marine mammals. Animal rights groups argue that capturing wild dolphins for shows and entertainment may shorten their normal lives of forty years to less than twenty. Orca whales may live to be ninety in the ocean, but at Sea World, nineteen of twenty-five have died, lasting an average of only 6.5 years at the parks. Marine mammals in captivity commonly die of pneumonia, ulcers, and other stress-related illnesses.

Marine mammals breed very poorly in captivity, with high infant mortality rates. Because breeding programs have largely failed, marine parks and aquariums rely on the continual capture of wild dolphins, orcas, and whales. Wild dolphins swim 40 to 100 miles a day. Yet the required tank size for one dolphin is only 24 by 24 by 6 feet.[10]

Several animal groups strongly oppose killing or capture of whales. HSUS asked the National Marine Fisheries Service to deny a permit for the capture and display of the four beluga whales to be displayed at the Shedd Aquarium in Chicago in 1991. They charged that the permit was illegal and that the secretary of commerce had failed to meet the standards under US law for protecting marine mammals. But the court effort failed.[11]

Horse and dog racing. HSUS has long opposed horse racing in part because of the inherent problems of using horses or any other animals in competitive events for money and fame. In 1989, HSUS stated that

> ideally, horse racing could be humane if conducted properly. However, as long as horse racing is a business and not a "sport" money will take precedence over the welfare of the horse. Because of the large amounts of money waged at race tracks and the resulting potential for huge profits, it does not appear likely that pari-mutuel horse racing will ever become a humane sport. Gambling, quick profits, or tax shelters are the main incentives attracting participants to horse racing. Consequently the horse is viewed not as a living, feeling creature but merely as a tool for making money.[12]

HSUS opposes the use of drugs for horses and the slaughter of horses when their racing career is over. A large number of thoroughbreds end up as pet or human food.[13]

Animal protection groups have investigated the Iditarod sled dog race in Alaska. As a result of a critical report by an HSUS investigator, the trail committee implemented many suggested changes to improve the welfare of the dogs in the race.

Although a follow-up visit by the HSUS representative showed much improvement, some further specific changes to be made included attention and oversight for less-experienced mushers; prohibiting the leasing of teams and individual dogs; performing thorough prerace veterinary examinations of all participating dogs; changing the event into an elapsed time event to discourage overworking of the dogs; and setting mandatory twelve-hour rest periods for each third of the race.

Despite the improvements, HSUS still maintains reservations about some aspects of sled dog racing, such as the conditions of some dog yards and the culling and killing of surplus dogs.

Animal welfare and animal rights groups also oppose greyhound dog racing, a spectator sport that drew 29.4 million spectators wagering $3.5 billion at fifty-seven tracks in eighteen states in 1990. They oppose the use of live animals in training the dogs to race, the wholesale "culling" of thousands of greyhounds every year, and what they view as a substandard diet.

Industry spokesmen point out that most training is done with artificial lures and use of live lures is very low. However, an investigator for HSUS claims that 90 percent of all trainers use live lures and many live animals (frequently rabbits) are slaughtered every year.[14]

Most greyhounds not useful for racing are destroyed. An industry defender points out, "Killing surplus greyhounds is a necessity of the business. When a dog outlives its usefulness, it's got to be destroyed." [15]

The National Greyhound Adoption Program assists in placing dogs for adoption. When their racing careers are over, an estimated seven thousand per year may be adopted.[16]

Some may be used for research. But many more are euthanized. One source estimates as many as 30,000; another between 53,000 and 93,000 greyhounds are destroyed each year, depending on the number of puppies born.[17]

Animals in movies. AHA works with trainers, directors, and producers when animals are used in television programs and motion pictures to insure the animals' safety and well-being. AHA has developed four classifications for films on the basis of how animals were treated during the production: acceptable, "believed acceptable," questionable, and unacceptable.

Unacceptable films are so rated because outright animal cruelty occurred during the production. Questionable ratings are given when AHA was not on the set and was unable to obtain substantial or complete information on the film's animal action. Acceptable and "believed acceptable" ratings comply with the association standards for humane treatment. Of twenty-nine films rated in 1990, only two rated unacceptable and one rated questionable.[18]

PAWS maintains an animal sanctuary for animals that have appeared in movies or are surplus zoo animals. If they were not provided a sanctuary, they would probably have been killed or left to live under miserable conditions.[19]

PETA and a coalition of animal rights organizations urged Congress to hold oversight hearings into the US Department of Agriculture's implementation of the *Animal Welfare Act*. In the summer of 1992, a House agriculture subcommittee held a hearing specifically concerning animals used in entertainment.

Zoos and circuses. Zoos present a special dilemma for animal rights and animal welfare groups. At one time, zoos seemed to pose no special conflict. However, zoos as an institution for research, education, and preservation, beset by financial crises and targeted by animal rights activists, could become an endangered species.

Michael Hutchins, director of conservation and science for the American Association of Zoological Parks and Aquariums in 1991 called the activists "unrealistic and biologically naive, taking human moral precepts and trying to apply them to animals." He believes that the principles for conserving wildlife are different than those applying to domestic, farm, and laboratory animals.[20]

Hutchins makes a distinction between prestigious and carefully regulated zoos and the hundreds of roadside menageries, traveling shows, and petting zoos, many of which are substandard and ought to be closed.

Zoos claim that they are the key to the survival of endangered species. But animal activists claim the record of breeding in zoos and returning animals to the wild is probably more illusory than real. However, the San Diego Zoo, with over 150 species on the endangered list, has returned a dozen of them to the wild, including the rare California condor.[21]

Stephen Bostick declares that zoos can be defended from the charge of overriding animals' rights by showing that they are providing what the animals need, and that keeping animals is in the animals' interests.[22]

Animal rights groups have also targeted circuses for what they view as cruel and inhumane treatment of wild animals. Ringling Brothers Barnum and Bailey Circus defends its handling and treatment of animals over its 120 year history. They point out that they have worked with the US Department of Agriculture to set standards for animal care and maintenance. "We believe in the healthy interaction of animals and humans, not the 'separatism' as espoused by the cultists which would deny our children the opportunity to experience not only the beauty of animals firsthand, but to observe the harmony that can exist when humans and animals work and play together." [23]

Trade in wild and exotic birds is opposed by several organizations. A 1991 estimate reported that nearly 750,000 wild birds are legally imported into the United States each year and another 100,000 are smuggled into the country, principally across the Mexican border. Most of the trade is in parrots and macaws, and most of the birds are in danger of extinction.[24]

HSUS and others have supported legislation to make importation of wild birds as pets illegal. Birds imported for captive breeding purposes would still be permitted. Many of the birds die after capture before they leave the country of origin or in transit to this country. Some airlines have refused to transport wild birds.

Carriage horses present another cause for humane treatment of animals. In many cities with tourist attractions, horses pulling carriages provide rides for visitors. Animal rights groups have called for ending the use of carriage horses or for protective ordinances restricting the times and places that horses can be worked. They believe that horses' well-being is threatened by high heat and humidity, urban traffic, long hours, improper care, and untrained drivers. The carriage horse operators object to carriage bans and regulations as economic threats and interference with their private business.

In 1991, PETA members gathered 21,000 voter signatures in Washington, D.C., to outlaw carriage horses. The result was the first initiative vote in the nation's capital involving animals. PETA hoped for success since Paris, France, Santa Fe, New Mexico, and Reno and Las Vegas, Nevada, had previously banned carriage horses from their streets.[25]

However, animal industry groups, citizens, and Putting People First worked together to oppose this initiative. Sarah Davies, the only carriage operator in the city had only $1,500 to fight this move to put her out of business.

The amount spent by PETA in mailings and radio advertisements was estimated at $50,000 by one close observer and $100,000 by another. The opponents of the measure stumped the city, speaking to churches and civic associations, doing media interviews, and handing out literature as people approached the polls.[26]

By the day of the vote, Sarah Davies and her carriage horse business were endorsed by several newspapers, including the *Washington Post* and the *Washington Times*, and to some surprised people, the Washington Humane Society. Voters rejected by 62 to 38 percent the effort to ban carriage horses. The outcome may set back plans for similar referenda in other cities.

The Crusade Against Animals for Clothing and Apparel

The campaign against fur has been the most effective effort of all animal welfare/animal rights endeavors and the most harmful to a legitimate industry.

Mink production is the major part of commercial fur farming. The United States produces about 10 percent and Canada 3 percent of world fur pelt production. In 1990, US family fur farms produced 3.4 million mink and 50,000 fox pelts. There are about 1,400 mink and fox farms in the United States and 800 in Canada. Total value of production in 1990 was $110 million.[27]

Animal rights and some animal welfare groups target commercial mink production because they believe confinement production deprives the mink of its natural environment in the wild and because the animals are raised in close confinement and slaughtered by what the groups view as cruel and painful methods. They also view fur as an unnecessary product for clothing and apparel.

Trapping is also targeted. The steel-jaw leghold traps, illegal in sixty-five countries, brings slow death to wildlife. The trapped animals sometimes chew their legs off to escape, or they freeze. Many animals not wanted for fur, such as pets and other wild species, may also be caught in the traps.

As one anti-fur message stated, "Once a symbol of glamour and success, fur is now the symbol of vanity, insensitivity and greed. Out of style, less practical than alternatives and increasingly seen as offensive, a fur coat bought this year will be worthless a few years later. As people see the truth about fur, more and more furriers are going bankrupt."[28]

Fur sales have dropped and the number of fur stores have declined. Fur-Free Friday, a national effort originated by ARM! on the Friday after Thanksgiving, has given major emphasis to the animal activists' efforts to discourage wearing of fur. The Campaign for a Fur-Free America is an ongoing campaign. Its latest effort calls for a complete ban on all leghold traps, body-gripping kill traps, snares, and poisons, except in public health emergencies.[29]

One estimate showed that retail sales of fur dropped from $1.9 billion in 1989 to $1 billion in 1990.[30] In 1980, Upper Broadway in New York City had twenty-two fur stores, but ten years later, all had closed. In Denver, four major department stores dropped fur sales between 1990 and 1992.[31]

Besides picketing stores that sell furs, PETA has carried out persuasive efforts to convince fashion designers to drop their use of fur. But fur sales reportedly rose 9 percent in 1993, following a 10 percent increase the year before. Part of the fur debate has turned to advertising campaigns waged by the fur industry and the anti-fur activist organizations.[32]

An upswing in fur prices during the 1996–1997 winter marketing season indicated that the North American fur industry was showing signs of renewed life. Auction prices were higher, stimulated by demand from Russian importers. But the industry outlook remained uncertain as the European Union had threatened to ban fur from countries that permit use of leghold traps.[33]

Major organizations that have campaigned against fur and feathers in clothing and apparel are ASPCA, HSUS, PETA, IDA, ARM!, and the AHA. HSUS has also fought to save the elephant through successful retention of the ban on international trade in elephant ivory.

Companion Animals: The Dilemma for Animal Rights Advocates

Companion animals present one of the most serious predicaments faced by animal rights organizations. Some activists believe that having pets is in itself a form of "fascism." An *Animals' Agenda* survey in 1985 found that only half of the staff and leaders of animal rights groups approved of pet owning.[34]

John Kullberg, former president of the ASPCA, addressed the problem in 1991:

> Our biggest companion problem continues to be that inherent American attitude that treats animals like materialistic commodities. By what right do we incorporate the lives of companion animals into our own? . . . Some animal activists insist that having companion animals is ethically wrong, a remnant of slavery. For example, we masters own others, demand obedience, even shackle our commodities at times, and give rewards based on good behavior. Bad behavior often leads to beatings, dismissal, and even extermination. Ethical values indeed are not well-served unless stewardship, not ownership, is the norm for companion animal care.
>
> Shelters, spaying and neutering clinics, humane law enforcement and humane educational antidotes are still not adequately present to eradicate this societal thirst for pet-related products and pets. Radical initiatives (but always law abiding and rational) are needed.[35]

When *Harper's* senior editor, Jack Hitt, asked Ingrid Newkirk, cofounder of PETA, how she would envision a society that embraced animal rights and what would happen to pets, she revealed some of the conflicting philosophies. Newkirk replied that she did not use the word *pet* because she thinks it is speciesist language. She prefers the term "companion animal" and would like to prohibit breeding. In her thinking, people could not create different breeds, and there would be no pet shops.

If people did have companion animals in their homes, those animals would have to be refugees from the animal shelters and the streets. You would have a protective relationship with them just as you would with an orphaned child. "As the surplus of cats and dogs (artificially engineered by centuries of forced breeding) declined, eventually companion animals would be phased out."[36]

ARM! condemns the keeping of pets more boldly: "We believe that keeping of domestic animals is intrinsically exploitative. The degree of exploitation covers a wide range from the grossly abusive use of dogs for racing or fighting to the relatively benign paternalistic relationship which exists between a responsible pet 'owner' and his dog or cat."[37]

However, having created such dependent animals, ARM! believes that humans have the moral obligation to protect them and to provide for their needs, but pet populations should not continue to be proliferated. So ARM! strongly opposes the continued breeding of companion animals and their sale through pet stores.

Both John Kullberg and Ingrid Newkirk identify and recognize the problems, the suffering, and mistreatment of companion animals. Looking at the real world, the animal welfare and animal rights organizations have adopted similar policy positions:

Pet adoption. Several groups encourage people looking for pets to adopt one from their local animal shelter. They hope to get more pets coming out of shelters to balance the flow coming in.

Spay and neutering programs. Recognizing the overpopulation of pets, most organizations promote spaying and neutering to reduce the number of unwanted animals being born. Vigorous campaigns for spay/neutering provide some evidence that euthanization of homeless dogs and cats dropped roughly 40 percent from 1985 to 1990.[38]

The campaign against "puppy mills." This descriptive, derogatory term is used to target dog breeding farms that produce and supply puppies to pet stores. Some strategies against such enterprises include educational programs to encourage adoption of pets from animal shelters, working for legislation to regulate and license dog breeding enterprises, and requiring pet stores to give the source of the animals they offer for sale.

Some animal rights groups claim that the US Department of Agriculture has not enforced policies dealing with commercial dog breeding. They allege that some inspectors have not physically examined the animals in some commercial breeding facilities. They encourage people to write to the secretary of agriculture demanding closer inspections.

If a family or an individual wants to buy a pet, the animal rights groups recommend buying from small family enterprises where puppies are well-cared for and free from disease.

Seeing-eye dogs for the blind also present a difficulty for some animal protectors. For humane and sympathetic reasons, seeing-eye dogs are generally accepted as useful and necessary to help blind persons be more independent and self-sufficient than they could be otherwise. However, Kathy Guillermo of PETA, when asked on a radio talk show if PETA opposed use of seeing-eye dogs for the blind, admitted that she opposed the use of these.[39]

Regulation of animal shelters. Most local shelters are not directly affiliated with the national animal welfare groups, although their staff members may hold memberships in one or more of these groups. AHA has a major program through its Standards of Excellence program to help shelters upgrade their care of unwanted animals.

How should animal shelters dispose of surplus and unwanted dogs and cats? Animal rights groups have worked for legislation to prohibit animal shelters from selling or giving their surplus animals to research laboratories. So euthanasia is the most common disposal method when state laws or local policies prohibit sale for research purposes. For research laboratories, the cost of acquiring dogs and cats used in research has increased when they must go to buy them from commercial sources.

Wild horses present another issue for some animal rights groups. Descended from horses imported by the Spanish in the sixteenth century, thousands of wild horses roam over the public lands of the western United States. In 1972, the population was estimated at seventeen thousand, and their numbers have greatly increased in recent years. The Department of Interior through the Bureau of Land Management is responsible for their care.

Since the population has grown and feed supplies may be inadequate for their survival, the government has captured some of the horses and offered them for adoption to individuals who would give them humane care and promise not to send them to slaughter.

Animal rights groups have recommended that the Bureau of Land Management develop criteria for humane, fertility control methods, when such control is needed for managing wild-horse populations. HSUS wants to see wild horses stay free rather than see them captured and placed in private ownership.

Crusade in the Classroom

Recognizing that today's children will make tomorrow's decisions, some animal welfare and animal rights groups have developed programs for children. These materials present the philosophies and objectives of that organization.

HSUS publishes *KIND News.* The goal is to teach kindness to animals, people, and the environment. Interested persons may provide a subscription for a classroom for $18 a year.

The National Association for Humane and Environmental Education recognizes an outstanding teacher through its National Humane Education Teacher of the Year Award. The award highlights the accomplishments of an educator of kindergarten, elementary, or high school students.

ASPCA has published *For Kids Who Love Animals.* Although the first draft advocated vegetarianism, the revised published version included a chapter on how animals eat each other and suggests when families buy meat that they look for "organic or free-range" meat.[40]

ASPCA has also produced *The Other Side of the Fence*, a video aimed at school children that equates the emotional, physical, and environmental needs of an infant with those of a calf. Children are reminded that they can choose to eat meat or not, while a calf cannot make choices.

FARM developed a humane-farming curriculum for high schools. The program includes a *Healthy School Lunch Action Guide*, a new publication showing how to bring about healthier school lunches; "Choice USA," a packet for introducing meatless choices in school lunches; *How on Earth!*, a magazine on vegetarian living published by and for teenagers; *Otterwise*, a quarterly publication for children who are into saving animals and the environment; and "Living in Balance," a packet of educational materials based on *Diet for a New America*.[41]

PETA has developed materials for elementary-age school children to bring them the animal rights philosophies of that organization. Ingrid Newkirk's book, *Kids Can Save the Animals: 101 Easy Things to Do*, and a "PETA Kids Grab Bag," a "kit every PETA kid will love," are listed in the group's merchandise catalog.

PETA Kids, published especially to teach children the PETA philosophy, carries such features as "How to Start Your Own Animal Rights Club!"; "A Life Sentence", a condemnation of zoos; and "Taking Compassion to the Classroom," a report on one teacher who speaks on behalf of animals by teaching about animal rights.[42]

PETA has also formed PTN (PETA Teachers' Network) consisting of several hundred teachers committed to making education more humane. Members work to bring alternatives to dissection into science classes and to end the use of animals in the classroom. PETA has formed a staff writers group to write letters to the editor, operates print and video libraries to handle requests for information, and sponsors field trips for inner-city school children, student and teacher conferences, and one-day "Animal Rights 101" seminars across the country.[43]

AAVS, through their Animalearn program, has produced *Animals in Society: Facts and Perspectives on Our Treatment of Animals*, a secondary-school text to cover a range of animal issues, and *Saving Animals: A Student Guide*, a booklet providing general guidelines and specific ideas for young people.

AHA has developed Humane Education Aids. These include publications for elementary-grade children, including *The Animal Shelter: A Home Away From Home*, that introduces middle- and lower-grade students to the content of animal shelter facilities, services, and personnel; a publication on how to avoid dog bites; and a teacher's guide on pet owner responsibility.

Tom Regan, at the Culture and Animals Foundation in Raleigh, North Carolina, has written a booklet geared toward secondary-school students.

Some colleges and universities have also introduced the study of human and animal relationships. The Rutgers University Animal Rights Law Center teaches law students legal skills involving animal rights. The center sponsored its first conference, "A New Generation for Animal Rights," in 1993 to focus on the relationship of the animal rights movement to other social movements.

Opposition to Classroom Indoctrination

Not all schools accept materials from animal protection organizations without question. The Bloomsburg, Pennsylvania, public school system removed Newkirk's *Kids Can Save the Animals* because it did not support the ideas it contained.

PETA materials, given to school children in Bethesda, Maryland, infuriated Kathleen Marquardt and led to the founding of Putting People First, a citizen's anti–animal rights organization in 1989 (see chapter 11).

In Poland Township, Ohio, fifth-grade teacher Kathleen Markovich was placed on leave while the district investigated charges that she forced animal rights ideology on her students in the classroom. Parents complained, and after a school board meeting with sixty parents attending, Ms. Markovich agreed to avoid the subject of animal rights if she was permitted to return.[44]

Adrian Morrison expresses alarm by the animal rights efforts, which he sees as "the promotion of beliefs among the untutored by dishonest presentations of the ways animals are used by humans." He sees the animal rights tactics as discrediting biomedical research using animals and a prelude to the campaign against biology education. He concludes that "there is now a pernicious effort to lead children away from medical science by attacking the presence of animals in the classroom under the guise of a concern for animal welfare. He recognizes that a concern for animal welfare is appropriate but warns biology teachers that the animal rights movement is misrepresenting its own motive and the nature and necessity of medical research using animals.[45]

Success or Failure?

Have thousands of dollars, civil disobedience, and the efforts of hundreds of animal rights groups made a difference? The answer will depend upon the standard by which success is measured.

The efforts to stop hunting have resulted in hunter protection laws and special measures to stop harassment. Attempts to discourage use of fur have reduced the size of the fur production and retailing industry. But is animal rights activism the only cause of the decline? Efforts to reduce consumption of leather and wool seem insignificant, probably because people see leather and wool as more necessary commodities than fur.

Preventing destruction and capture of marine animals often requires international cooperation. There are instances of success and failure. Stopping international trade in ivory was aimed at saving elephants in the wild. Time will tell how successful this effort will be. Stopping international trade in wild birds and endangered animal species requires international cooperation and control of poachers. Pets, or "companion animals," the more preferred term among animal activists, remain an elusive dilemma among animal rights groups. Companion animals are near and dear to millions of people who often support the animal rights philosophies.

But the danger of alienating segments of the population, who support animal rights and welfare programs with their direct-mail contributions, requires treading lightly on the issue: Is keeping a pet morally acceptable to that animal rights organization? Pet owners who contribute to animal causes may demand an answer to this question.

Efforts to teach children about animal rights invokes intense conflict between animal rights groups and traditional animal industry and scientific groups. Both sides are competing for attention and time in the classroom to have their materials used and positions heard. The final outcome of these efforts will not be known until the classroom students of today become the thought leaders of tomorrow.

9

Vegetarianism and Animal Rights

People choose a vegetarian diet for health, ecological, and religious concerns; affection for animals; belief in nonviolence; and economic reasons. Compassion for animals attracts most animal activists to vegetarianism. Food animal producers resent the animal rights movement support for, and promotion of, vegetarian diets.

Vegetarianism is not a new idea. Plutarch, the Greek philosopher (A.D. 46–120), followed a vegetarian diet and based his vegetarianism upon a general duty of kindness to human and nonhuman alike. He argued that much of the world's cruelty arose from humankind's uncontrolled passion for meat.[1]

The arguments for a vegetarian diet among animal rights activists carry two basic themes: If animals are your friends, why eat them? If animal products cause health problems, wouldn't a vegetarian diet be more healthful? The answers to these questions are intertwined with social, economic, scientific, and moral values. On the other hand, food animal producers resent the support for and promotion of vegetarian diets by animal rights advocates.

Vegetarianism Explained

Vegetarian literature includes several definitions. Vegetarians do not eat meat, fish, or poultry. Traditional vegetarians who do not consume meat, but may consume dairy products, are termed lacto-vegetarians. Those who do not eat meat but eat dairy products and eggs are identified as lacto-ovo-vegetarians. Vegans, sometimes defined as ethical vegetarians, abstain from eating or using all animal products, including milk, cheese, other dairy items, eggs, honey, wool, silk, or leather. Some ethical vegetarians may reject any product or service, including medical procedures, tested on animals.

The number of vegetarians in the United States in 1992 was somewhere between 6 million and 14 million.[2] A 1990 survey by Opinion Dynamics revealed that 7 percent of Americans claim to be cutting meat out of their diet completely.[3] A survey conducted for

Time magazine and Cable News Network in 1992 concluded that 6.7 percent of all Americans consider themselves vegetarians, with another 5.6 percent reporting a commitment to vegetarianism in the past.[4] The study also reported that vegetarians eat many different foods, typically draw the line on red meat, and are more concerned about the environment than about animal welfare issues.[5]

A National Restaurant Association survey found that about 20 percent of American adults look for restaurants that serve vegetarian fare; 30 percent would order vegetarian meals when offered. Dr. Michael Klaper, animal activist and vegetarian, has commented that the meat industry is living in the last days of the Roman Empire.[6]

Why be a vegetarian? Vegetarians give several reasons for their dietary choices: health, ecological, and religious concerns; compassion for animals; belief in nonviolence; and economic reasons.

Animal rights activists practice vegetarianism because of their compassion for animals, as well as health and environmental concerns. Animal rights groups push vegan diets while the literature of the vegetarian industry recognizes that some will refrain from eating meat and continue to include dairy products and eggs in their diets.

Animal activists use the moral argument that meat eating causes unnecessary suffering and death to other "sentient" beings, and for this reason, it is wrong. If meat eating was necessary for survival, then the practices could be excused as a "necessary evil," vegetarians suggest. But the advocates claim that meat eating is not necessary for most people and that people in our society eat meat out of ignorance and habit, because they have developed a taste for it.

If animals have feelings but are killed for food, what about plants? Vegetarians acknowledge that plants react to various stimuli but that they do not have a nervous system like animals. The vegetarian recognizes the vitality of plants but points out that people must eat to survive.

Vegetarianism and Animal Rights Philosophy

Small vegetarian communities existed in the United States in the nineteenth century as utopian experiments. However, James Jasper and Dorothy Nelkin place the recent contemporary vegetarianism expansion in the 1960s, along with the growing interest in Eastern philosophy and alternative lifestyles. The growth of intensive food animal production produced a rallying point to encourage vegetarian diets among animal rights activist groups. For animal activists, eating meat is a form of cannibalism. A mass movement to vegetarianism would signify great success for the animal rights movement. But that probability seems a long time away, since a majority of Americans still eat meat.

The trends in meat consumption follow closely the trend of an increasingly affluent society. While beef and veal consumption per person has declined significantly, pork consumption has remained steady, and poultry and fish consumption have increased (see table 2).

Table 2. US Meat Consumption Per Capita, 1970–1996

	1970–72 (pounds)	1980–83 (pounds)	1996 (pounds)
Beef	78.9	72.9	67.2
Veal	1.8	1.3	0.9
Pork	49.5	48.6	50.8
Lamb/Mutton	2.1	1.1	1.2
Poultry	34.7	41.8	91.5
Fish[a]	11.9	12.7	14.7[b]

Sources: US Dept. of Agriculture, *Food Consumption, Prices and Expenditures, 1967–88*; *Food Review*, Sept.–Dec. 1993; *Agricultural Outlook*, July 1996.
[a] includes shell fish
[b] 1992 data

Vegetarians view the grain used to produce meat, milk, and eggs as the waste of resources. As John Robbins claims, "With a shift to a diet based on grains, vegetables, fruits, legumes, seeds and nuts, we would feed our entire population and have large amounts of grain left over for export. This could happen using less than one-third of the land we now use for meat production. Thus, vast tracts of farmland would be available for other purposes." [7]

Animal scientists and livestock producers quickly point out that cattle and sheep consume grass and other plant materials that are not suitable for human food. Some animals in certain production systems convert unusable plants into food for humans. However, pork and poultry production require large amounts of grain and plant protein meals in their rations. Although some grain could be used for human food if not fed to livestock, the undernourished and starving people in other countries do not have the money or goods to enter our markets to buy the current grain production. For many feed grain producers (growers of corn, sorghum, oats, and barley), food animals provide the best, and often the only, market for their products.

Vegetarian Promotion and Campaigns

PETA has actively promoted vegetarian diets. Its 1992 Vegetarian Campaign included members asking local restaurants to display "We Serve Vegetarian Meals" stickers if they served at least one vegetarian entree; providing morning radio rush-hour disc jockeys with free vegan "breakfasts in bed"; vegan campaign coordinator doing live interviews; organizing a vegetarianism demonstration in Moscow in front of McDonald's; holding "Meat Stinks" vigils at 4-H auctions at state and county fairs; distributing thousands of vegetarian cookbooks and bumper stickers, T-shirts, coffee mugs, and other items; holding exhibits, news conferences, and demonstrations at industry shows, including the

National Poultry Industries Federation, National Cattlemen's Association, American Meat Institute conventions, and the International Poultry Expo.

PETA also presents vegetarian endorsements from well known entertainers and includes vegetarian recipes in PETA News.[8] Although being a vegetarian is not required for employment on the PETA staff, most are vegetarians or may convert after seeing their literature.[9]

Other organizations that actively promote vegetarianism include Physicians Committee for Responsible Medicine, Farm Animal Reform Movement, Farm Sanctuary, Feminists for Animal Liberation (formerly Feminists for Animal Rights), Animal Rights Mobilization!, International Society for Animal Rights, EarthSave, National Anti-Vivisection Society, the North American Vegetarian Society, and the American Vegan Society.

What about the largest and oldest animal protection organizations? In the joint statement from the HSUS, ASPCA, and MSPCA, these groups express concern about food animal confinement systems, use of antibiotics, and lack of regulation for farm animals production. But no mention is made about vegetarian diets.[10]

ASPCA took a definite position on vegetarianism in 1991. In its *Animal Rights Handbook*, the chapter "Love Animals, Don't Eat Them" contains statements about food animal production that do not apply to most production systems but are intended to discourage meat, milk, and egg consumption. The handbook suggests not eating meat because of health concerns. "The easiest way to prevent needless animal suffering and the harmful environmental effects of meat-eating is to simply cut down on meat"—an oversimplified statement. The book also gives instruction on how to become a vegetarian and lists a number of vegetarian cookbooks.[11]

HSUS chief executive officer John Hoyt has declared, "We are not a vegetarian organization, and as a matter of policy do not consider the utilization of animals for food to be either immoral or inappropriate—a position that, as you might expect, earns us a great deal of criticism from various animal rights organizations." [12]

Animal Industry Perspective

AIF denies that a vegetarian diet is healthier than a diet that includes meat, milk, and eggs. The foundation cites the federal government and the American Heart Association statements that a diet containing meat, milk, and eggs is appropriate for both government and AHA dietary guidelines. They suggest that the approach to healthful eating should be common sense and a prudent diet that is low in fat, sodium, sugar, and alcohol.[13]

US Department of Agriculture Perspective

Early in 1991, the US Department of Agriculture was scheduled to publish *The Eating Right Pyramid: A Guide to Daily Food Choices*. The new graphic illustration was to replace the food wheel that displayed four food groups. Instead of the wheel that gave equal weight to the four groups, the pyramid was designed to place most emphasis on bread, cereal, rice, and pasta foods at the base; the fruit group and vegetable group on the next layer; and with fewer servings, the meat, poultry, fish, dried beans, eggs, nuts, milk, yogurt, and cheese layer. At the peak of the pyramid came fats, oils, and sweets, with advice to use sparingly.

After many months of review, the US Department of Agriculture Human Nutrition Information Service issued its *Food Guide Pyramid* in 1992. Also supported by the Department of Health and Human Services, the pyramid is based on USDA's research on what foods Americans eat, what nutrients are in these foods, and how people can make the best food choices.

The pyramid food guide focuses on fat because most Americans' diets are too high in fat. The goal is to keep the intake of total fat and saturated fat low, since a diet low in fat will reduce the chances of getting certain diseases and help a person maintain a healthy weight. The guide makes no mention of a vegetarian diet but emphasizes balanced eating and reduced fat intake.

The new food guide is based on the total diet rather than on a foundation or core diet. This focus was based on a response from two-thirds of nutritionists surveyed in 1983. The food group approach was used because the previous food guide used the group arrangement. The goal was to incorporate commonly used foods and allow consumers flexibility while meeting nutritional requirements.

Beginning at the bottom, the pyramid calls for daily consumption of six to eleven servings of bread, cereal, rice, and pasta; three to five servings of vegetables; two to four servings of fruit; two to three servings of milk, yogurt, and cheese; two to three servings of meat, poultry, fish, dried beans, eggs, and nuts; and the use of fats, oils, and sweets sparingly.[14]

Dietitians' Perspective

The American Dietetic Association stated its position on vegetarian diets in its March 1988 *Journal*: "It is the position of the American Dietetic Association that vegetarian diets are healthful and nutritionally adequate when appropriately planned." [15] The position paper pointed out that both vegetarian and nonvegetarian diets have the potential to be either beneficial or detrimental to health. In addition to possible health benefits, consideration may also be given to ecological, economical, and philosophical or ethical reasons for adopting such a diet.

The report cites studies of vegetarians indicating that this population generally has lower mortality rates from several chronic degenerative diseases than do nonvegetarians. It is likely that the effects are due not to diet alone but also to a healthy lifestyle, including desirable weight, regular physical activity, and abstinence from smoking, alcohol, and illicit drugs, with adequate health monitoring.

Even though the health benefits of a vegetarian diet make it attractive from a nutritional standpoint, this does not preclude the possibility of obtaining similar health benefits from a prudent nonvegetarian diet, if it can be planned in accordance with the "Dietary Guidelines for Americans." [16]

The American Dietetic Association issued a press release in response to a statement from the Physicians Committee for Responsible Medicine in which PCRM recommended dropping meat and dairy products from the diet. President Mary Abbott Hess commented:

> While the American Dietetic Association supports increased dietary emphasis on vegetables, fruits, grains and legumes, we can not advocate dropping meat and dairy products from the basic food groups.
>
> A diet with moderate quantities of lean meat, poultry, fish and low-fat dairy products is more likely to meet total nutrient needs than one without these foods.
>
> Although a vegetarian diet can be very healthy, it is difficult for the average person to plan one that provides all of the nutrients needed on a consistent, long term basis.
>
> Even now, many Americans don't meet recommended daily allowances for calcium, iron, zinc and critical B vitamins. Lean varieties of meat and dairy products remain the primary source of these nutrients, which are essential to maintaining healthy bones, blood and factors that promote immunity to disease.[17]

Suzanne Havala and Johanna Dwyer emphasize that the nutritional and health consequences of vegetarian diets are neither necessarily all good nor all bad.[18] Certain dietary inadequacies that may arise on vegetarian diets include deficiencies of iron, vitamin B-12, folic acid, calcium, vitamin D, zinc, and vitamin B-6. On the other hand, good evidence suggests that vegetarian diets and lifestyles have positive effects on weight, blood pressure, coronary artery disease, and laxation. But whether a vegetarian diet is conducive to good health or whether the effects are due to differences in specific nutrients or combinations consumed by vegetarians is not so clear.

Individuals at any age, especially older adults, if they suddenly adopt vegetarian diets should have careful monitoring since some may be avoiding treatment for some health problem and may unintentionally do themselves harm.[19] Recent work also suggests that similar advantages can accrue to nonvegetarian diets that are more in line with current dietary recommendations than people's usual eating patterns. With appropriate attention to nutrition, the health consequences of vegetarianism are neutral and, in some respects, may be positive. However, there is no magical, health-giving property that automatically adheres to vegetarian diets and, regardless of their composition, protects health.[20]

Judith Brown, School of Public Health, University of Minnesota, takes a practical view on vegetarianism. Although dietitians generally agree that it is possible to develop a balanced diet with plant foods, it is difficult to do and Brown does not recommend it for everyone.

Although calcium is available in other foods, it is hard to meet the calcium needs without dairy products. Vegetarianism is not the solution to health problems. A healthy diet contains a variety of foods. Brown recommends separating fact from fiction on diet issues.[21]

Dr. Dean Ornish points out that the rise of coronary heart disease in the United States has paralleled the increased consumption of animal fat and cholesterol. In a study of 24,000 vegetarian Seventh-Day Adventist men, after removing those who smoked, the risk of fatal coronary heart disease among meat-eating men (ages thirty-five to sixty-four) was three times greater than vegetarian men of comparable age, suggesting that the vegetarian diet may account for a large share of this low risk. Those who did not eat meat but consumed milk and egg products had a risk of fatal coronary heart disease about one-third less than the nonvegetarian men.

Studies in Framingham, Massachusetts, and seven countries showed a strong relation between the highest percentage of saturated animal fats in the diet and the highest cholesterol levels in the blood and the highest death rate from coronary heart disease.[22]

Vegetarian Diets for Pets

Many vegetarians who adopt a plant-based diet for themselves also want to provide vegetarian diets for their pets. Animal rights periodicals carry advertisements for vegetarian pet foods. But is this a wise choice for your dog or cat? Like vegetarian diets for humans, healthy vegetarian diets are possible if they contain the needed nutrients. Dr. James Corbin, a recognized authority on companion animal nutrition comments:

> Excellent vegetarian diets can be formulated and manufactured for dogs. These diets have been practical since 1950 and the development of microbiological production of vitamin B-12. Previously animal proteins with the vitamin B-12 source were necessary for dogs and most other nonruminant animals.
>
> Vitamin B-12 helps prevent anemia. Vegetarian diets have been proposed for dogs for many years, particularly by some groups which have a basis for the exclusion of animal blood from their own food and food fed to their animals. Vegetarian diets for dogs are feasible, practical, relatively inexpensive, and have been fed successfully.
>
> Cats also require vitamin B-12 plus taurine, a sulfonic acid derivative from methionine and cystine. Taurine is present in relatively large amounts in most mammalian tissues. When cat foods contain primarily animal protein sources, taurine is generally present in quantities to meet the cat's need and help prevent dilated cardiomyopathy, which is a condition resulting in impaired circulation and may cause death of cats. A similar problem can occur in humans eating a taurine-deficient diet. Both vitamin B-12 and taurine are available in pure and concentrated forms through chemical syntheses. That availability now permits the production of complete and balanced cat diets.
>
> Animal proteins contribute palatability to both dog and cat foods. Effective palatability enhancers of non-animal origin can now replace the flavor enhancement of animal proteins and provide nutritionally complete and balanced vegetarian diets readily acceptable to dogs and cats.[23]

So for vegetarians who also want to feed their dog or cat a healthy vegetarian diet, they must be sure that it contains the necessary ingredients. The diet must also be palatable—that means it must be appetizing so the animal will eat it. Although the vegetarian diet may contain all the necessary ingredients, if the dog or cat will not eat it, some animal-based components are most efficient in encouraging consumption needed for the benefit of the animal, even if this practice violates the ethical values of its owner. However, palatability enhancers from vegetable protein derivatives are almost as effective as those with animal-based protein enhancers.

Vegetarians in an Animal-Based Society

Just as followers of a particular religion may practice their beliefs in different ways, all vegetarians may not follow exactly the same practices in daily living.

Although strongly committed to a vegan diet, ARM! recognizes that under present conditions absolutely strict veganism is extremely difficult if not impossible to achieve. The group points out that excessive preoccupation with avoiding the consumption or use of minute amounts of an animal product can become an obsessive and egoistic concern with personal purity, rather than a genuine commitment to animal liberation. Such an obsession can actually retard efforts to free animals from pain and suffering by wasting valuable time and distorting one's focus.[24]

Vegetarians who want to avoid all animal products may find that it is virtually impossible to live that way. Many products, although primarily of plant origin, may have been processed or manufactured with the use of animal-based products. Not just food, but many other products, contain some animal-based product as part of their manufacturing process.

Some items that may use some form of animal product in their manufacture include rubber-soled canvas shoes, videotape, steel in automobiles, shampoo, cosmetics, paint, photographic film, glue, nonivory piano keys made from bones, household detergents, whole-grain bread, sugar made by filtering through charred animal bones, wax-coated fresh fruit, soy-based infant formula containing oleo acids, whey-based food products, tennis rackets and stringed musical instruments, building materials that may contain dried blood or animal tallow, food products that may contain albumin from eggs, wine or beer clarified with egg- or gelatin-based products, marshmallows made with gelatin, stuffed furniture with urea or animal blood used in the foam or textiles, and some pharmaceuticals with animal-based ingredients.

Vegetarians may console themselves by realizing that these by-products from the meat industry are just that—by-products. By eating less or no meat, the demand for meat declines, and fewer animals are slaughtered. As fewer animal by-products are available, nonanimal products will be developed.

Carol Wiley summed up the vegetarian's philosophy appropriately: "Being a vegetarian is the first step toward getting animal products out of our lives and the best way to make a positive impact for animals."[25]

Henry Spira takes a more realistic view of people's eating habits providing a more reformist perspective: "I don't see the whole world turning vegetarian tomorrow, but I can see the public that eats animals not wanting to be uncomfortable with what they are doing. . . . people are going to eat meat but they're going to be concerned about the quality of life of the animal." [26]

10

The Professions: Conflicts and Controversies

The major professions are caught in a dilemma over animal rights. Professionals and practitioners in medicine, law, veterinary medicine, psychology, natural resource management, and dietetics hold conflicting philosophical and scientific viewpoints that deal with animal and human relationships. Some animal rights–oriented groups have formed within these professions. How successful they will be in attracting a major part of their profession's members to their point of view remains to beeen.

The animal rights and animal welfare movements have influenced the professions of medicine, law, veterinary medicine, psychology, dietetics, and natural resource management. With their interests in animals and their products, practicing professionals have faced a choice on animal welfare and animal rights issues: to advocate, oppose, or straddle the fence. New advocacy organizations have emerged within these professions and have attracted advocates and sympathizers.

Physicians

The American Medical Association (AMA), established in 1847, is a voluntary service organization of physicians with nearly 300,000 members from every segment of medicine and representing 41 percent of all physicians in the United States. Its mission is to promote the science and art of medicine and the betterment of public health. Policies of the organization are decided through the American Medical Association House of Delegates. Physicians from every state, over eighty medical specialty societies, and federal service groups are represented. The controversies surrounding the use of animals in biomedical research have pulled physicians into the debate on animal and human relationships. The American Medical Association has consistently supported the humane use of animals for biomedical research, asserts that research involving animals is essential to improving the health and well-being of the American people, and actively opposes any legislation, regulation, or social action that inappropriately limits such research.

AMA believes that most Americans support the use of animals in research but want assurance that animals are treated humanely and used only when necessary. The association believes that animal rights activists have exploited the concern for animal welfare and have attempted to impede or stop the use of animals in biomedical research. AMA is concerned that animal rights organizations, in obtaining philosophic and financial support for legislative and regulatory changes, would compromise the future of biomedical research.

To clarify the issues, AMA published a white paper that clearly supports using animals in basic and applied research to assure continued medical progress. It supports regulator policies to protect animals from unnecessary pain or inappropriate use. However, in the association's view, human beings will experience pain and suffering if policies advocated by animal rights groups are adopted.

In a 1988 survey of active physicians, the AMA found that 99 percent agreed that animal experimentation had contributed to medical progress, 97 percent supported the use of animals in basic and clinical research, 96 percent supported the use of animals for drug testing, and 93 percent supported the use of animals for medical education. Compared to a similar survey in 1948, the survey showed that physicians' views on the use of animals in research were very similar to physicians' opinions forty years earlier.

In 1989, the AMA developed an Animal Research Action Plan, which suggested that AMA "promote the formation of a special investigative unit within government to examine animal rights activities." An animal activist editor labeled this a "cloak-and-scalpel" approach and standard operating procedure with the AMA.[1]

At its June 1990 annual meeting, the AMA passed two resolutions dealing with animal research. The first expressed strong support for the appropriate and humane use of animals in research and urged its members to inform their patients, community groups, and legislators. Use of nonanimal models in research is desirable when possible, the AMA emphasized, but continued use of animals is important for development of new and more effective medical treatments of diseases for both humans and animals.

AMA's second resolution condemned the Physicians Committee for Responsible Medicine (PCRM) for "implying that physicians who support the use of animals in biomedical research are irresponsible, for misrepresenting the critical role animals play in research and teaching, and for obscuring the overwhelming support for such research which exists among practicing physicians in the United States."[2]

Although PCRM openly "trades" on its medical credentials, its views do not represent the views of the medical and biomedical scientific community. In October 1990, AMA launched a campaign to stress the importance of animal research to human medicine and the need to continue animal research.[3]

PCRM has drawn together a group of physicians sympathetic to the animal rights philosophy. The committee president, Dr. Neal Barnard, has been criticized for pretended expertise in a wide range of areas when he is a psychiatrist—not a researcher, nutritionist, cancer specialist, internist, or general practitioner.[4]

Through newsletters, publications, public testimony, and nutrition, outreach, and public education programs, PCRM members champion the concept of alternatives to animal experimentation. They also have promoted the idea that effective alternative methods can and have been used to teach physicians and conduct research without inflicting pain and death on animals.[5]

In soliciting funds to carry on their programs, PCRM does not limit its membership or solicitation to physicians. Its solicitation letters list five major points of concern and support: (1) Opposition to the conditions under which laboratory animals are caged, transported and treated in laboratories; (2) support for the right of medical students to choose not to participate in laboratory experiments involving live animals; (3) support for effective alternative educational methods that do not use animals; (4) support for effective, humane research methods that reduce or replace use of animals in research, including epidemiological research, clinical studies, cellular research, and computer models; and (5) support for improved legal protection for all animals in laboratories.

PCRM has also targeted the use of animals for product testing. It opposes use of the Draize test for testing product toxicity on the eyes of rabbits. It petitioned U.S. Surgical Corporation to stop using live dogs to train sales personnel in use of their surgical staplers. They delivered signatures of over thirteen thousand doctors who opposed this practice.

The organization champions disease prevention rather than treatments developed through biomedical research with animals. Members want money to be spent on preventive medicine instead of animal research to find treatments for disease.

PCRM emphasizes diet as part of this disease prevention, strongly advocating less fat and more fiber. Rather than cutting down on meat and whole-milk dairy products because they are high in saturated fat, the PCRM recommends cutting them out altogether. The committee urges people to adopt the vegan diet of only plant products.[6]

With these recommendations, PCRM faces strong disagreement and objections from other physician groups, dietitians, and livestock, and dairy industry groups.

Veterinarians

The American Veterinary Medical Association (AVMA) represents fifty thousand veterinarians and includes about 70 percent of all veterinarians in the country. Its objective is to "advance the science and art of veterinary medicine, including its relationship to public health and agriculture." It provides a forum for discussion of issues of importance to the profession and for the development of official positions. Its positions on animal welfare clearly support humane care and treatment of animals but also recognizes that animals are used for human benefit.

AVMA sponsors an Animal Welfare Week annually. Since 1990, the association has held an annual Animal Welfare Forum in Chicago to enhance wellness in animals and people. AVMA takes a similar position to the Association for Biomedical Research on the value and importance of research to benefit both people and animals.

Guiding Principles

As professionals, veterinarians are encouraged to aid in developing a better understanding of all aspects of animal welfare and to aid in developing guidelines and standards to assure proper stewardship of animals.

The AVMA's official position deals primarily with scientific aspects of animal well-being. However, it recognizes veterinarians' rights to have ethical, philosophical, and moral values as they deal with animals.

AVMA sees animal welfare as a human responsibility that encompasses all aspects of animal well-being, including proper housing, management, nutrition, disease prevention and treatment, responsible care, humane handling, and, when necessary, humane euthanasia. It endorses and adopts animal welfare as official policy.

However, AVMA views animal rights as a philosophical and personal value characterized by statements of various animal rights organizations. Yet it emphatically does not endorse the philosophical views and personal values of animal rights advocates when they are incompatible with responsible use of animals for human purposes such as food, fiber, and research conducted for the benefit of both humans and animals. For AVMA, animal welfare and animal rights are not synonymous terms.[7]

AVMA Policies on Animal Welfare
Companion Animals, Horses, Wildlife

AVMA takes these positions regarding companion animals, horses, and wildlife. The organization

• opposes the use of dogs for dog fights and poultry for cock fights, encourages the humane use of animals by the entertainment media, and strongly opposes mistreatment or abuse;

• supports euthanasia of unwanted animals by properly trained personnel using acceptable, humane methods;

• supports deletion of cropped or trimmed ears from breed standards for dogs and prohibiting the showing of dogs with cropped or trimmed ears. It would also consider recommending elimination of docked tails for dogs from the breed standards if the American Kennel Club would follow the ear-trimming recommendation;

• supports declawing of cats when the cat cannot be trained to stop using its claws destructively;

• opposes use of drugs to alter normal horse-racing performance.

• recommends that animals be handled in a manner to minimize injury in spectator events, including rodeo, polo, horse racing, dog racing, dog sled racing, cutting and reining exhibitions, and field trials (its policy statement does not take a position on hunting); and

• recognizes the extensive injury caused by steel-jaw traps but also recognizes that they may be used legitimately in some aspects of wildlife management and predator control. It recommends discontinuance as soon as acceptable alternatives become available.

Animals in Research and Teaching

Concerning animals used in research and teaching, AVMA

• encourages adequate funding for investigation and enforcement activities to prevent cruelty and enhance welfare of animals used in research and teaching;

• endorses the latest principles and guidelines for use of animals in precollege education;

• supports carefully controlled use of animals from various sources for teaching and biomedical research, provided that all legal requirements and guidelines for acquisition, care, and use of animals are met; investigators have examined the need for such animals; safeguards are used to make sure that animals are unidentified and unowned; and only healthy animals are used; and

• encourages proper identification of pet animals, not only to guard against inappropriate use of pets in laboratories but also to assure that lost and stolen pets are not inadvertently destroyed in animal shelters. The veterinary medical profession claims that it works diligently to educate the public concerning responsible pet ownership and the need for animal birth control. However, AVMA reasons that given the existence of millions of unclaimed and unwanted dogs and cats, it does not appear to be either humane or practical not to use these animals, while raising additional purpose-bred animals, for research, safety testing, and teaching.

Animal Agriculture

AVMA holds these position on animal agriculture. The association

• affirms that animals raised for food, fur, or fiber should be treated and handled humanely and acknowledges that all animal owners and handlers must identify and take steps to abandon or correct practices that are cruel, abusive, neglectful, and contrary to the animal's well-being;

• recognizes that confinement livestock and poultry production is well established and should be humane; and

• encourages and actively promotes both applied and fundamental research on the welfare of livestock and poultry raised in confinement production systems.

As for transportation, sale, and slaughter of animals, AVMA

• recommends adequate protection from adverse environmental conditions during transport as well as time limits on railroads, excessive crowding, and deprivation of feed and water;

• recommends adequate and sufficient feed and water in sale yards, sorting and penning without abuse, safe and adequate vehicles for transport, and procedures to reduce occurrence and transmission of infectious diseases; and

• supports governmental regulations pertaining to humane slaughter of food animals and research on improved practices.

AMVA holds these positions on swine housing and the environment. It

• believes that tethers and stalls for sows are acceptable when monitored, maintained, and adjusted by responsible personnel;

• agrees with the standards for housing, flooring, environmental control, and stocking density as set forth by the North Central Extension agricultural engineers;

• accepts slotted floors and other open-floor designs that allow separation of the pigs from wastes and moisture; recommends properly designed and operated ventilation systems; and

• approves castration, ear notching, and tail docking of piglets as acceptable management practices when performed in a sanitary manner during the first week of a pig's life.

Regarding layer chickens, AMVA supports current use of cages to house layer chickens. Present knowledge is not sufficient to support a radical change or ban of this system, the association asserts.

The AMVA recommends the following for unwanted chicks, poults, and pipped eggs:

• killing unwanted chicks and poults by an acceptable humane method, such as carbon dioxide euthanasia, while condemning the smothering of unwanted checks or poultry in bags or containers; and

• killing pipped eggs prior to disposal, where the chick or poult has not been successful in escaping the eggshell during the hatching process.

AMVA recommends beak trimming to remove the sharp tip on young chickens and turkeys, thus preventing or reducing the natural traits of cannibalism, fighting, and feather picking. Beak trimming is considered a mild stress that often prevents serious future injury to other birds, even though this procedure has been criticized as cruel treatment. However, the association asserts that alternative methods for the control of cannibalism should be sought.

Induced molting of laying birds is designed to bring the entire flock in to a resting period at the same time. AMVA supports this practice when it is done under careful supervision, using reduced light and low sodium/calcium diets. The starvation/water deprivation methods of induced molting is not acceptable.

AMVA's positions on castration and dehorning of cattle include

• support of procedures that reduce or eliminate the pain, plus the recommendation that these procedures be completed at the earliest practical age; and

• endorsement of research in developing improved techniques for painless, humane castration and dehorning or alternatives to these practices.

The AMVA encourages veterinarians and producers to explore alternative housing systems for veal calf production. Guidelines, developed by the AVMA, should be followed so that the animals can stretch, stand, and lie down and to insure comfortable, clean, and safe growth and development of veal calves.

The Association of Veterinarians for Animal Rights (AVAR), started in 1981 by veterinarians Ned Buyukmihci and Neil C. Wolff, has these objectives: to inform and organize veterinarians to work for animal rights issues, provide expert testimony and advice to other humane groups, teach veterinary and other students about animal rights–related problems, and provide a sounding board for veterinarians and others in the animal rights field. Membership is open to both veterinarians and others as affiliate members. The estimated membership in 1990 was five hundred. The AVAR believes all animals have value and interests, independent of the value and interests of other animals, including people. As the physician protects the interests and needs of his or her patient, so should the veterinarian.

Veterinarians in AVAR support

• elimination of nonhuman animal testing in the creation or improvement of cosmetics, cleansers, and other household and industrial products;

• improved conditions under which food animals are reared so that so-called factory farming methods are eliminated, until there is a shift in dietary habits to vegetarianism;

• a ban on sport hunting, sport fishing, and trapping for furs, although AVAR does not condone hunting or fishing for food at all;

• education about inhumane and unnecessary cosmetic surgical operations such as tail docking, ear cropping, debeaking of chickens, tail docking of pigs, and declawing of cats;

• the ending of use of nonhuman animals in education where that use results in the harm or death of the animals;

• a solution to the companion animal overpopulation crisis through education and neutering; and

• prohibition of the patenting and genetic engineering of nonhuman animals used in agricultural, biomedical, and industrial experimentation. AVAR members view the creation of new species of animals by humans as unethical.

AVAR adamantly opposes the raising of calves singly in narrow stalls or crates. They believe this practice is inhumane and cruel. If calves are raised for slaughter, AVAR members assert that the only acceptable manner for raising the calves is in a loose housing system where the calves can exercise and socialize. But since the origin of veal cannot be determined from its packaging, the group urges its members and the public to refrain from buying veal altogether.

AVAR and AVMA have very different positions on animals in research. Although AVAR recognizes the desire for humans to better conditions for themselves, members believe that the ethical costs incurred, in terms of suffering and death of animals, have been astronomical. They seek an immediate end to dependence on use of animals in research that leads to the animals' harm—whether that harm be mental or physical suffering, loss of function, ill health, pain, inappropriate housing, isolation, or death.

Attorneys

The Animal Legal Defense Fund has brought together attorneys sympathetic with the legal rights of animals (see chapter 14). Although ALDF recognizes the injustice of treating other animals as property, this organization does not advocate stealing animals as a legal alternative for dealing with animal abuse. Their legal handbook states explicitly, "With few exceptions, our legal system does not recognize a difference between taking an animal from his (or her) owner, even for the animal's benefit, and taking a stereo. If you remove an animal from the possession of his owner without permission you are committing the criminal act of larceny." [8]

ALDF faces a dilemma in defending animal activists. The "necessity" defense is often used, saying that the action was taken because there was virtually no other way to prevent a greater harm to the animals. So far, this argument has been unsuccessful for defendants who have trespassed or blocked public access to bring attention to what they view as injustice to the animals.

Some activists think ALDF's sole function is the defense of criminal charges. Other supporters believe the group should not be involved in defending activists who violate the law.

Tischler points out that the underlying purpose is the pursuit of "major impact litigation"—litigation that allows them to question directly what they believe are abuses of animals. [9]

ALDF has observed other social reform movements to develop their strategies. One example is the civil rights movement, which saw the shift of the Supreme Court decisions from 1896 when separate but equal school facilities were acceptable to 1954 when the court declared that "separate but equal is inherently unequal." Tischler believes that animal rights litigation should be developed with a sense of this history.

In some lawsuits aimed at helping animals, the courts ruled that animal advocates had no "standing to sue" (see chapter 14). One of the group's major objectives is to come up with an innovative way to create standing so that they can go to court and protect animals against what they view as abuse.

ALDF prefers to be the plaintiff in litigation rather than a defendant. The group wants to spend its time and money on lawsuits that fight animal abuse, not on defending the organization. ALDF sees elevating the status of animals from property to person as a step-by-step process involving litigation, legislation, and public education. A long-range goal is to make fundamental changes in the legal system.

The Animal Rights Law Center directed by Gary Francione at Rutgers University School of Law in Newark, New Jersey, is the only center of its kind in the country.

Established in 1990 and funded with private contributions, the center serves four purposes: (1) to teach law students legal skills in the context of cases involving animal rights; (2) to litigate animal rights cases on a national basis; (3) to represent animal rights advocates; and (4) to educate the public on legal issues that involve animals. Gary L. Francione, professor of law, is director, and Anna E. Charlton, is codirector.

The teaching and litigation missions of the center are carried on by the Animal Rights Clinic, which provides real-life litigation experience to second- and third-year law students as part of the curriculum at Rutgers Law School. Students enrolled in the clinic earn six academic credits per semester and may earn up to twenty-eight credits while in law school.

Students work on cases that reflect the ways in which humans use animals including experimentation, agriculture, hunting, entertainment, and companionship. The clinic represents and advises animal advocates in a wide variety of cases and never charges for its professional services.

The center also works to educate the general public about species discrimination in the law and the relationship between animal rights and other progressive social movements. Center members, including law students enrolled in the clinic, provide public lectures and classes on animal law and prepare written materials for public distribution. The center also sponsors meetings and conferences on animal rights and the law.

Henry Mark Holzer, a professor of law at Brooklyn Law School, started the Institute for Animal Rights Law in 1991. It received varied annual support totaling $65,400 from 1991 through 1995 from the International Society of Animal Rights and its president, Helen Jones. The institute's objective is to make animal rights law a discrete field of law by creating materials that will allow teaching the subject in law schools; it also hopes to further its aims through publication of the *Journal of Animal Rights Law*.

Dietitians

Dietitians have been pulled into the animal rights debate because some animal rights organizations advocate vegan diets. The American Dietetic Association, whose 61,000 members comprise the world's largest group of food and nutrition professionals, supports the US Department of Agriculture's 1990 revision of the daily food guide (see chapter 9 for dietitians' views on vegetarian diets).

Psychologists

Psychologists for the Ethical Treatment of Animals (PsyETA), established in 1981, includes among its membership both clinical and research psychologists. In 1990, the group reported 450 members and an operating budget of around $40,000. Funding comes mainly from grants, along with membership dues and sale of publications.

The organization publishes a quarterly bulletin that includes articles, research reports, book reviews, and comments on animal welfare issues.

The most successful programs of the group include publication of *Humane Innovations and Alternatives in Animal Experimentation* and sponsorship of summer fellowships for graduate psychology students.

Differences between PsyETA and the American Psychological Association center on the use of animals in psychology-related research. PsyETA has held meetings at the annual convention of APA and has tried to influence APA positions on psychological treatment of animals. PsyETA was refused exhibit space at the 1990 APA convention when the group wanted to exhibit its publications on alternatives to animal experimentation.

Natural Resource Managers and Environmentalists

The philosophies and policies of those who manage our national parks and forests and other public wildlife habitats may be compatible or in conflict with animal protection groups, depending upon the policies that deal with wild animals.

A profound philosophical schism exists between the animal rights and environmental movements. One believes in the inherent value and equality of the individual, while the other believes in the superiority of the whole. Animal rights philosophers favor natural resource policy that protects the individual interests of animals, while most environmental philosophers favor policies that seek broad, systemwide goals.

Viewed in this context, the discrepancies and conflicts between animal rights activists and environmentalists become clear. Environmentalists see the whole; animal rightists see the parts. Thus, environmentalists support wildlife management, such as the managed hunt of deer herds and the eradication of mountain goats, policies that are based on holistic, ecological ideals. The animal rights advocates oppose these policies.

Conclusions

Physicians, veterinarians, attorneys, dietitians, psychologists, and natural resource managers face increasing debate over the philosophical and scientific views of animal rights and animal welfare groups. Animal rights–oriented organizations within some of these professions will continue efforts to recruit new members—both inside and outside. Although the organizations include the profession's name in their title, and many of their members are qualified in the profession, each group will accept contributions from outside sympathizers. Since these are generally respected professions, the general public may be more inclined to support these groups.

11

The Emerging Counterforce:
Animal Interest Groups,
Scientists, and Consumers
React

Food animal producers, research workers, scientists, and animal industries have reacted to the animal rights movement. Through educational efforts with their members and to the general public through the media, they are challenging and attempting to discredit the animal rights doctrines and beliefs.

T hose who produce, use, and enjoy animals have awakened to the potential consequences of a successful animal rights crusade. The opposition to animal rights activism has emerged in diverse and varied degrees of effectiveness. Most animal interest groups direct their anti–animal rights efforts toward their members and the general public. They often emphasize their strong support for humane treatment of animals, lending credibility to the animal welfare advocates, but, at the same time, make every effort to discredit the animal rights activists.

Albert Barber, chairman of the National Association for Biomedical Research, believes that scientists have been moved to act when alerted to the real dangers of what they see as an anti-intellectual force and its acceptance by the general public.

Farm Animal Welfare Coalition (FAWC)

The Farm Animal Welfare Coalition (FAWC), formed in 1981, is an ad hoc, informal group of forty-five major farm animal associations to solidify opposition to, and promote education against, animal rights activism (and should not be confused with the Farm Animal Welfare Council in the UK, which uses the same acronym). The coalition meets every three months to share information and decide on courses of action by individual organizations.

FAWC, alarmed by the premises of animal activists, the criticisms of modern confinement livestock and poultry production, and the promotion of vegetarianism, sees the animal rights movement as destructive to consumer choice and the farm economy.

The food animal industry faces a difficult task because "animal activists have aimed their appeals at a gullible public that, for the most part, knows little or nothing about current farming methods." [1]

The mission of the FAWC is to

- unite all farm organizations into a coalition committed to continued well-being and safe treatment of farm animals;
- study public opinion, attitudes, and knowledge about farm practices and modern farming technology; and
- educate the consumer, public officials, media, and other audiences about the farmers' essential concern for the well-being of their animals and the production of safe, low-cost food.

Organization members include the American Dairy Science Association, American Farm Bureau Federation, American Feed Manufacturers Association, American Meat Institute, American Society of Animal Science, American Veal Association, Animal Health Institute, Commission on Farm Animal Care, Farm and Industrial Equipment Institute, Holstein Association, Livestock Conservation Institute, Livestock Marketing Association, National Broiler Council, National Cattlemen's Beef Association, National Broiler Council, National Lamb Feeders Association, National Livestock and Meat Board, National Livestock Producers Association, National Milk Producers Federation, National Pork Producers Council, National Turkey Federation, National Wool Growers Association, Poultry Science Association, Provimi, and United Egg Producers. In addition to those industry groups, the US Department of Agriculture is also listed as a member.

Representatives of each organization review developments, decide on priority tasks, and contribute to policy development. By working together, the coalition aims to develop a common strategy, speak with one clear voice, and avoid efforts that are counterproductive in dealing with the animal rights movement.

FAWC works on ways to give positive answers to six basic issues covered by animal rights activism: vegetarianism; feed grain to farm animals versus hungry people overseas; animal rights and liberation; humane treatment of animals; use of antibiotics on animals; and health and diet issues. Its programs include

- continuing to monitor the direction of the animal rights movement, its attempts at coalition building, and themes used to alter public perceptions;
- establishing an effective system for monitoring state legislative and legal action;
- monitoring all studies on animal stress and advising members on implications for farming practices related to animal rights issues;
- developing positive themes to neutralize what coalition members see as irresponsible attacks on animal farming practices by animal rights groups;
- maintaining communications with other animal-rearing or user groups, particularly those concerned with laboratory animals;

- preparing their organizations to deal effectively with the challenge of the animal rights movement and implementing an ongoing communications program; and
- researching the attitudes and knowledge level about animal rights issues prevailing in the wider circle of agribusiness.

Animal Industry Foundation

AIF spun off from the FAWC in 1987. Its mission is to counter the work by animal welfare and animal rights groups. Its board of directors is comprised of producer groups, agribusiness associations, and agribusiness companies. Before 1993, these included the National Cattleman's Association, American Farm Bureau Federation, American Feed Industry Association, American Society of Animal Science, National Milk Producers Federation, National Pork Producers Council, and Southeastern Poultry and Egg Association. New trustees added in 1993 included the American Sheep Industry Association, National Broiler Council, United Egg Producers, Blue Seal Feeds, American Veal Association, National Turkey Federation, and Purina Mills. Membership includes corporate, national, and state agricultural businesses and organizations, trade associations, and individuals.

Steve Kopperud, legislative director for the American Feed Industry Association, also served as executive director of AIF from 1987 through 1992. AIF's budget is around $300,000 per year, and funding is provided by corporate and individual donations.

AIF works to educate consumers about how modern livestock and poultry producers operate and the importance of their service to the American public. It attempts to redefine animal agriculture in the context of top quality animal care, correcting misinformation and violence aimed at farmers, ranchers, researchers, processors, auction markets, and related businesses.[2]

The AIF mission is to create and disseminate professional communications for public education; serve as the umbrella organization through which livestock and poultry groups can develop and deliver coordinated, consistent messages to consumers; provide educational tools to farmers and ranchers to educate the public; and supply good, scientific information in the animal care debate.

To carry out its mission, the AIF
- produces and disseminates brochures that explain the role of animal agriculture and how animals are reared in a humane manner;
- conducts advertising programs where deemed necessary to respond to consumer concerns of public criticism of livestock and poultry producers;
- supports production and distribution of educational materials for schools;
- serves as a resource bank for research on animal welfare through creation of lists of materials and documents available;
- disseminates production and behavioral research data useful for livestock and poultry producers in improving their care and handling techniques; and
- provides speakers to appear in industry and public forums.

The American Feed Industry Association has many interests in common with the Animal Industry Foundation and its mission. Its location in Arlington, Virginia, across the Potomac River from Washington, D.C., provides a useful listening post for activities by Congress, animal welfare and rights groups, and federal government executive departments related to animal protection efforts.

American Farm Bureau Federation

AFBF is the largest general farm organization in the country with state organizations in forty-nine states and Puerto Rico and membership of more than 3.4 million farm operators, owners, and others associated with agriculture or rural communities. Its members include producers of all major crops, livestock, and poultry.

In 1982, as animal rights activism expanded, AFBF developed a steering committee and began to organize animal agriculture groups to deal with criticism of animal and poultry production. Dr. Hugh Johnson, head of the poultry division until his retirement in 1995, coordinated the animal welfare project and monitored activities of animal welfare and animal rights groups, state legislatures, and members of Congress and prepared newsletters and publications to keep state organizations informed of developments.

AFBF has actively supported or opposed legislation in Congress that would affect producers of livestock and poultry. They oppose bills that would prescribe specific management or production practices but support bills that aim to protect producers from abuse or damage. AFBF actively supported the Stenholm bill that, when enacted into law in 1992, made vandalism to animal research or production facilities a federal crime with stiff fines and penalties.

AFBF has also launched educational programs among its members to promote humane treatment and handling of livestock and poultry and among the nonfarm public and school children. In doing so, the federation hopes to foster favorable attitudes toward livestock and poultry production and those who produce these products.

The most significant AFBF effort to halt animal activists occurred in 1988. In Massachusetts, the Coalition to End Animal Suffering and Exploitation (CEASE) obtained enough signatures to place a referendum petition on the state's general election ballot, even though the state legislature rejected the proposition. The initiative would have eliminated the raising of milk-fed veal calves and would have required anesthetics for routine agricultural procedures. It would have established a scientific advisory board to set standards for animal production and marketing. The board was to be made up of four animal rights supporters and one representative from agriculture. Producers feared that the referendum would have imposed heavy regulation on livestock and poultry farming.

CEASE was founded on the principle that all animal exploitation is wrong. A successful effort in Massachusetts could have served as a model for other states. Massachusetts farmers feared that if the referendum were successful, the initiative would put most of the state's small farmers out of business.

The Massachusetts Farm Bureau members spearheaded an effort to defeat the initiative. With help from American Farm Bureau Federation, other state farm bureaus, and agricultural groups, they formed a political action committee, Massachusetts Committee to Save the Family Farm and hired Boston-based BMc Strategies, a public relations firm, to defeat the initiative. Their campaign succeeded. In November, the referendum initiative was defeated by a margin of 70 to 30 percent. A similar proposal could not be reintroduced in Massachusetts for at least six years.

The "I Care" program represents a positive farm bureau educational effort to foster humane treatment of animals among 4-H members and to demonstrate that young people do believe in good animal welfare. Established in Colorado in 1992, the program expanded across the country in 1992 and 1993. This program uses instructional materials, pledge cards, hats, clothing, and buttons. Young people receive instruction in proper handling, feeding, watering, bedding, and transporting of animals and in dealing with disruptive situations. The program gives them the chance to demonstrate that they believe in humane and responsible care of animals.

AFBF has encouraged each state farm bureau to designate someone to be the state animal welfare coordinator. To provide educational support and keep the membership informed, a handbook, *Meeting the Animal Rights Challenge*, was published and distributed in 1991. Another publication, *Handling the 20 Toughest Animal Rights Assertions*, was published in 1994.

National Pork Producers Council

Pork producers are sensitive to the criticisms pointed at them. Researchers have worked diligently to study the environmental conditions prevailing in modern confinement systems that animal activists label as "factory farming." Some progress has been made to improve buildings and equipment to accommodate humane concerns.

To counter what it considers as misleading information and to improve its image, the National Pork Producers Council prepared *The Pork Producer's Handbook on Animal Welfare/Animal Rights*. One section is devoted to the news media, when to talk to them and what to say at a meeting being picketed, and when and how to tell the producer's story.

To improve communication, the handbook suggests key points to make in interviews concerning animal welfare and animal rights. Members are advised to have a designated spokesperson and issue a statement along these lines:

> We recognize and respect the right of these people to express their views in a calm and non-disruptive way. We fully expect them to respect our rights to hold our meeting as well.
>
> We share with them their concern about the welfare of farm animals. We wish they were better informed about the way pork producers take care of their livestock.
>
> The American farmer has long been a leader in the best possible treatment and care of animals. . . . America's pork producers are dedicated to practicing the best animal

husbandry practices possible while at the same time offering American consumers a reasonably priced and nutritious product.[3]

The final chapter of the handbook lists security measures for the office and the farm. Members are advised:

> Today, actions against individuals are on the increase, and the violence is spreading. Radical environmentalists are uniting with animal rights activists and information-sharing between groups in different countries is increasingly evident. The animal rights movement is acquiring the earmarks of international terrorism.
>
> The animal rights movement constitutes a threat to the safety and the financial well-being of livestock farmers and those who represent them. . . . The goal is to establish a prudent balance between vigilance and confidence. Animal rights activists want the entire farm industry to live in a state of anxiety. Don't give them the satisfaction. On the other hand, don't be careless.[4]

National Cattlemen's Beef Association (NCBA)

Cattle producers have also faced strong criticism from the animal activists. In 1990, the National Cattlemen's Association (later renamed National Cattlemen's Beef Association) contracted with Hill and Knowlton, a Washington, D.C.–based public relations and research firm to prepare profiles on animal rights, consumers, nutrition/health, and environmental groups. The report was funded by the Beef Promotion and Research Board.

United Egg Producers

The United Egg Producers is a federated agricultural cooperative of five regional marketing cooperatives owned and operated by egg producer members. As part of its program, the cooperative has written animal welfare guidelines for the industry. Recommended guidelines encompass these basic requirements: suitable housing, adequate freedom of movement, rapid diagnosis and treatment of disease, access to feed and water, proper ventilation and environmental temperature, backup equipment for use in the event of electrical power failure, lighting for easy inspection of the flock, and properly designed equipment for the transportation of chicks, pullets, and replacement hens.

UEP emphasizes that the guidelines are representative of scientifically evaluated production practices and will change as new advances in science demonstrate alternatives and humane methods in producing eggs. In response to those who believe that confining egg-laying chickens in cages is undesirable, UEP states that this judgment is based on human perspective rather than the poultry perspective. They claim that chickens do much better in the safety of their cages than they did in either the barnyard or in outdated large-floor systems of housing. Chickens housed in large-floor systems may cause the weaker or submissive chickens to be deprived of food. Also, when chickens are housed en masse, they are subject to panic and mass hysteria from any sudden noise or other disturbance, and this could cause suffocation.

UEP also points out that trimming of the sharp point of the beak—like trimming the sharp nails of a dog—is a good safety precaution for other chickens. While UEP shares humanitarian concerns about animal welfare, the producers doubt that there can be any authoritative answer regarding the emotions of chickens. The only logical means of determining welfare is to measure productivity, which comes only with improvements in nutrition, health care, environmental care, housing, and protection from physical harm.

Fur Farm Animal Welfare Coalition

Fur producers have made some special efforts to defend their industry through the Fur Farm Animal Welfare Coalition. They accept a responsibility to assure "the continuation of both domesticated and wild animal species through responsible management"; call for survival of domesticated animals through a "symbiotic relationship of benefit to both man and various animal species"; and ensure the existence of species and the ecosystem by sustained and controlled harvest of fur-bearing animals in the wild to maintain essential environmental processes.

The coalition has developed guidelines for management, buildings and facilities, feeding and euthanasia, and humane care of mink.[5] The coalition's statement of environmental principles includes

- support for the CITES treaty, which prohibits traffic in the pelts of endangered species;
- pledge of adherence to industry standards for the humane care of fur-bearing animals on farms;
- endorsement of systems for harvest of animals in the wild that are appropriate, selective, efficient, and safe to use and that minimize injury and/or stress to the animal;
- endorsement of the internationally accepted principles set forth in 1990 by the Wildlife Society regarding proper natural resource conservation; and
- support for the use of renewable resources (natural fur), over nonrenewable resources (fake fur), wherever such alternatives exist.[6]

The retail fur industry appeals to individual freedom of choice to defend its position. Industry officials point out that garments from endangered species are not sold in the United States. They consider fur opponents animal extremists and call for the freedom of individuals to buy and wear fur.

Although fur has been the major target, the most dedicated animal rights advocates also eliminate other animal products from their personal use. They do not wear leather shoes, use leather purses, wallets, or belts. They do not wear silk or wool clothing, since these products are of animal origin. They also avoid purchasing any product made from feathers since they feel that use of any of these products supports what they see as exploitation of animals.

The biomedical research community expresses serious concern about animal rights campaigns: "The animal rights movement is not about reason. It is about eliminating the use of animals in research. . . . within the research world there is still no well-honed campaign to fight fire with fire."[7]

The National Association for Biomedical Research (NABR), formed in 1979 as the Research Animal Alliance, strives to give universities and industry a forum for responding to public policy issues affecting laboratory animals. As the alliance grew, its name was changed to the Association for Biomedical Research to convey clearly the reasons for its existence. In 1985, the National Society for Medical Research consolidated with ABR to become NABR.

Since its inception, NABR has faced intensified opposition to laboratory animal use and efforts by animal rights groups to abolish scientists' use of laboratory animals regardless of the consequences to human health. NABR carries out legislative efforts with members of Congress, state legislatures, government officials, and state groups. Representing science's interest in the responsible use of laboratory animals is the association's only mission.

From a budget of $100,000 in 1983 and less than 200 members, NABR had grown by 1993 to membership of more than 350 institutional members with $1.7 million in total assets and annual support and revenue of $967,100. Members include universities, medical and veterinary schools, teaching hospitals, voluntary health agencies, academic and professional societies, as well as pharmaceutical, laboratory animal breeder, and other research-intensive companies.

NABR supports the responsible use and humane care and treatment of laboratory animals in research, education, and product safety testing. The membership believes that only as many animals as necessary should be used, that any pain or distress animals may experience should be minimized, and that alternatives to the use of live animals should be developed and employed wherever feasible.

But the NABR believes that, now and in the foreseeable future, completely replacing animals is not possible and that the study of whole, living organisms is an indispensable element of biomedical research and testing that benefits all animals.

Closely affiliated, the Foundation for Biomedical Research (FBR) works with NABR to motivate and inspire the research community to become involved to influence public opinion supporting biomedical research. It is a nonprofit educational organization established to inform the public of the vital role played by humane animal research in the diagnosis and treatment of disorders that threaten human and animal health.

Scientists Center for Animal Welfare (SCAW)

The Scientists Center for Animal Welfare (SCAW), founded in 1979, is a nonprofit organization of scientists who promote the well-being of research animals. The committee supports responsible and humane treatment of animals used in research, testing, and education by encouraging exchange of information about animal well-being based on scientific data and observation. Through conferences and seminars, SCAW has fostered dialogue among professionals, researchers, and the animal protection community.

Livestock Conservation Institute (LCI)

For nearly eighty years, LCI has led animal industry efforts to reduce losses from disease and improper handling, advocate for improved animal health and handling programs, and, in recent years, respond to animal welfare and food safety concerns.

In 1995 and 1996, LCI coordinated the National Youth Livestock Program Ethics Symposia, prompted by public revelation of unethical and illegal activity associated with youth livestock programs across the United States. While the vast majority of exhibitors at youth and open livestock expositions are responsible stewards of livestock, the actions of a few unethical individuals are viewed as a threat to educational youth livestock programs.[8]

The symposia brought together animal educators, youth leaders, and teachers to focus on ethics, rules for livestock showing, and educational efforts to promote proper treatment of livestock shown at fairs and exhibitions.

The National Rifle Association

The National Rifle Association (NRA) was chartered in 1871 as an educational, recreational, and public service organization dedicated to the right of citizens to own and use firearms for recreation and defense. Since most animal rights and animal welfare groups oppose hunting and trapping, the NRA is concerned with these groups' campaigns. NRA official policies and objectives regarding hunting and wildlife conservation clearly define their position. The association also distributes educational materials and engages in political action when necessary to enhance its goals.[9]

National Animal Interest Alliance (NAIA)

NAIA is a coalition of diverse animal interest groups and concerned individuals working together to educate the public about the "critical difference between animal welfare and animal rights." [10] The alliance embraces the humane treatment and responsible use of animals and works to expose the value system and philosophy that seeks to end human use of animals. Its board of directors includes representatives of the livestock industry, animals in entertainment, education, medicine, biomedical research, outdoor sports, and the trapping, fishing, pet, and fur industries. Executive director Patti Strand is also coauthor of *The Hijacking of the Humane Movement: Animal Extremism*.

The coalition newsletter takes very strong anti–animal rights positions. The group has called the Humane Society of the United States a "closet animal rights group and mainstream legitimizer for the animal rights movement," partly because of the HSUS proposed a one-year moratorium on dog and cat breeding.[11]

Putting People First

Kathleen Marquardt, private businesswoman, homemaker, and mother, founded Putting People First (PPF) in September 1989 in Bethesda, Maryland, as a protest to what she considered animal rights propaganda. At that time, Marquardt owned "Elizabeth Quinn," described as "an upscale Washington silk, clothing company." [12] The organization used a Washington, D.C., post office box for a mailing address, even though Marquardt used her husband's Bethesda, Maryland, law office as the office for PPF until the summer of 1993. At that time, Marquardt moved PPF to Helena, Montana, her native state. Interestingly, Marquardt's husband, attorney William Wewer, had previously provided legal counsel for the Doris Day Animal League.

When Marquardt suspected that her children were being "brainwashed" in their classes by the materials supplied to schools by People for the Ethical Treatment of Animals, she decided to act.[13]

With membership at $15 per year, PPF enlisted twenty thousand members in its first year. The promotion literature described Putting People First as "a group of concerned citizens from all walks of life who object to being intimidated by so called 'animal rights' activists. Our organization opposes the terrorists who proclaim that physical harassment, arson, property destruction, burglary, and theft are 'acceptable crimes' when used as civil protest to promote the interests of animals over people." [14]

PPF defined its major objectives: to enlighten middle America about the work of animal rights groups, to provide balanced education about animals and their use with school-age children, and to protect human health through disease control and support for biomedical research.

Marquardt served as chairman and prepared a tabloid newspaper, *The People's Agenda*, to inform and encourage members to support the organizations objectives and programs. Each issue reported activities of animal activist groups, the successful efforts of members to counter the animal rights activities, and defends the uses of animals for food, clothing, research, and pleasure. As a consumer-oriented voice, PPF defended people's rights to use animals for hunting, trapping, fur production, carriage horses, zoos, and other leisure activities.

In 1990, PPF spearheaded a campaign against a referendum that would have banned use of carriage horses in Washington, D.C. With other animal support groups joining the opposition, PPF defeated the referendum. PPF also worked to ease restrictions on use of carriage horses in New York City.

In addition, PPF investigated the positions of leading presidential candidates on animal rights issues. Through its publications and mailings to solicit membership dues, PPF took a more confrontational approach than most other animal industry and research groups. *People's Agenda* targeted, condemned, or severely criticized

• presidential candidate Paul Tsongas (1992), for working as a paid lobbyist for animal rights causes such as banning hunting on federal lands, crippling medical research using animals, and attempting to shut down the Canadian fur and trapping industry; PPF claimed that although Tsongas at one time had been a critic of animal research, he changed his position, pointing out that his successful fight against cancer was possible with the help of experimental treatments developed through animal research;[15]

• Ingrid Newkirk, cofounder of PETA, for pushing her animal rights philosophies through *PETA Kids*, a publication for children; "because she does not educate children, merely indoctrinates them to become fund raisers for PETA's coercive agenda and encouraging children to demand that their schools serve only vegetarian meals, despite warnings from the American Medical Association and American Dietetic Association that such diets are nutritionally dangerous for children;"[16]

• Alex Pacheco, president of PETA, for suggesting that arson, property destruction, burglary, and theft are acceptable crimes when used to promote the interests of animals over people;

• Kathy Guillermo of PETA for her public denunciation of the use of seeing-eye dogs;

• Paul Harvey, radio commentator, for his support of animal rights philosophies and criticism of trappers and hunters;

• Michael Fox, HSUS, veterinarian, for his article in the *Encyclopedia Britannica*, which PPF viewed as slanted toward animal rights philosophy;

• Paramount studios, for hiring Chris DeRose, known to support animal rights causes, to produce a television show, *Hard Copy*;

• Greenpeace, an environmental group, for producing a documentary film, *Survival in the High North*, which showed a seal being beaten, not by a seal hunter but by a hired actor;

• PETA activist Jennifer Woods, dressed as a giant chicken, for hitting broiler producer Frank Perdue in the face with a pie on February 29, 1992, while attending a University of Maryland Board of Regents meeting;

• Representative Frank Pallone, Jr., a Democrat from New Jersey, for proposing a House Joint Resolution to designate Animal Rights Awareness Week (later withdrawn after letters of criticism arrived);

• Combined Federal Campaign, for including PETA as a charity for which federal employees could designate their contributions;

• the Sierra Club, for its efforts to stop two scientific research groups in central Texas from conducting biomedical research;

• Representative Barbara Boxer, a Democrat from California and later a US Senator, for introducing HR 3918, the *Consumer Products Safe Testing Act*, because the legislation assumed that valid nonanimal models are available;

• Columnist Jack Anderson, for blaming the decline in certain shorebird populations on duck hunters, instead of upon the loss of habitat, people taking over more land for houses and other uses, and the overpopulation of furbearers, especially a species called nutria, since these animals destroy fragile wetlands and eat the eggs and young of nesting birds;

- Robin Walker, PETA, and Elliot Katz, IDA, for attacking PPF's "Hunters for the Hungry" project for donating venison to the needy at church shelters;

- FOA, for demanding that New Yorkers turn their furs over—not to charities— but to FOA, whose members receive coats at "fur amnesty rallies," put them into storage, and use them for demonstration and propaganda purposes;

- HSUS, for proposing a bill that would impose a licensing fee of $500 for pet breeders and getting it introduced in the Ohio Senate by State Senator Barry Levey; and

- *60 Minutes*, for its presentation on fur production that used videotape that did not represent true conditions on fur farms and that gave no opportunities for veterinarians or wildlife biologists to present their perspectives on commercial fur production.

Despite its nationwide efforts to rally citizen support against the animal rights movement, Putting People First has struggled financially. Its 1991 financial statement showed total revenue of $159,000 and expenses of $321,000, leaving a deficit of $162,000. Wewer and Marquardt have evidently used personal funds to keep the organization in operation.[17]

Marquardt, with two coauthors, wrote *Animal Scam: The Beastly Abuse of Human Rights*, to expose the "fraud and reveal the tactics of animal rights activists and their organizations." [18] The book attacks the animal rights agenda and its effects on science, health, the economy, food, and other aspects of American life.

In 1996, PPF associated with the American Policy Center. Marquardt continued to speak at various meetings and write for the APC newsletter.

Legislative Cooperation

Probably the most successful coordinated anti–animal rights effort by the opposition organizations culminated in 1992 when Congress passed the *Animal Enterprise Protection Act*. Representatives for biomedical research, patient groups, agriculture, and other animal interests formed an effective working coalition to obtain passage of the law. What the full benefits will be, if any, remain to be seen (see chapter 12).

12

Animal Protection in Congress

Congress and the executive branch set national policy for humane treatment of animals. Policies to regulate acquisition, care, and treatment of laboratory animals and to protect wild animals have been established. Attempts to mandate management practices for food animal production have not succeeded. The Congressional Friends of Animals was formed to keep abreast with animal welfare issues. The Animal Welfare Coalition was organized to counter animal welfare and animal rights influence among members of Congress. The Congressional Sportsmen's Caucus was viewed by animal activists as antienvironmental and unfriendly to protection of endangered species and marine mammals.

State laws and local ordinances to prevent cruelty to animals and provide animal shelters date back to the nineteenth century. However, national policy to enhance humane treatment of animals has occurred since World War II.

Protection Measures into Law

The successful legislative efforts fall into several categories: (1) humane treatment of animals in slaughter plants, in research facilities, and in transit; (2) protection of endangered animal and bird species; (3) protection of marine mammals, fish, and wildlife; (4) establishment of standards for conducting research with laboratory and other animal species; (5) protection and humane treatment of pets; and (6) antiterrorism control.

Members of Congress have introduced many bills on various aspects of animal protection. While some bills become law or are incorporated into legislation as amendments, others get only scheduled hearings or receive no attention (see appendix 5 for a detailed list of successful federal animal welfare legislation).

Federal Efforts to Stop Animal Terrorism

The death threat against Dr. John Orem at Texas Tech University prompted Congressman Charles Stenholm (Democrat, Texas) to introduce his bill making damage to animal research and production facilities a federal crime.

Senator Howell Heflin (Democrat, Alabama) and Stenholm led the successful legislative efforts, along with other members of the House and Senate, to protect research and animal production facilities from illegal acts. The biomedical research and food animal production interests applauded the legislation, saying it was vital for researchers and animal producers so that they and their work are protected.

The *Animal Enterprise Protection Act of 1992* was passed after the illegal actions and threats to life and property aroused animal owners and users, who then sufficiently convinced their representatives in Congress to take action. Because interested members of Congress introduced bills that approached the problems in different ways, several years were required to bring final action. Most animal welfare and rights groups did not believe the legislation was necessary, however, because state laws already made vandalism and theft illegal. Yet they were not able to stop this bill, which made vandalism to animal research and production facilities a violation of federal law.

Humane Intentions But No Action

Many bills dealing with animal protection that are introduced in Congress are never enacted. Some authors may not expect their bills to pass, but they may think they have represented their constituents by introducing them. The major efforts are categorized here even though they have not been successful.

Animal Welfare Act Amendments

Bills have attempted to permit any person to commence a civil action to compel any responsible official to enforce the *Animal Welfare Act*; to broaden the scope of the *Animal Welfare Act* by adding the phrase "mouse, rat, bird," after "rabbit"; to give the secretary of agriculture authority to issue a restraining order or injunction if there were reason to believe that any dealer, carrier, exhibitor, or handler was endangering the health of any animals or was dealing in stolen animals; and to provide for the humane treatment of animals used for exhibition purposes.

Farm Animals

Bills have attempted to identify humane animal husbandry practices for livestock and poultry; to establish a farm animal husbandry committee to investigate all aspects of intensive farm animal husbandry; to establish the Commission on Modern Farm Animal Practices to determine if intensive farm animal husbandry has any adverse effect on human health; and to examine the economic, scientific, and ethical considerations with respect to the use of intensive farm animal husbandry.

The effort to legislate farm animal husbandry and management practices has most frequently targeted veal calves. Bills have been introduced to mandate facilities to enable a calf raised for veal to turn around, lie with legs outstretched, and groom itself; and to require a daily diet containing sufficient iron and digestible fiber.

Bills have also aimed to regulate and insure humane poultry slaughter and humane handling of downed animals; and to regulate or prohibit the use of bovine growth hormone for dairy cattle. Bills to study food animal husbandry and management practices, especially veal production, have been introduced without success.

Although several animal welfare and animal rights groups have strongly criticized intensive food animal confinement production, the bills to study or regulate intensive production practices have been strongly opposed by the food animal industry. Food animal producers dislike what they see as unnecessary government regulation. Their organization leaders have close ties with members of the Senate and House Agriculture Committees who are sympathetic to farmers' problems. Consequently, until the makeup of the House and Senate Agriculture Committees include more animal welfare and non-farmer interests, legislation to regulate food animal production practices will not succeed in Congress.

Use of Animals in Research and Testing

Use of animals in biomedical and product testing research has created serious confrontations and debates. Bills have attempted to establish a National Center for Medical Rehabilitation Research and a Senior Biomedical Scientific Service, with a staff to conduct and support biomedical research and training; to disseminate health information; to conduct programs relating to medical rehabilitation; and to establish wherever possible nonanimal acute toxicity testing as an acceptable standard for government regulations without compromising human safety.

Related bills have also proposed to promote the dissemination of biomedical information through modern methods of science and technology, to prevent the duplication of experiments on live animals, and to modernize testing of consumer products that contain hazardous or toxic substances.

Animal Patenting and Genetic Engineering

Bills in this area have attempted to place a five-year moratorium on granting of patents on invertebrate or vertebrate animals, including those that have been genetically engineered; to establish a Biotechnology Science Coordinating Committee to regulate the use of genetically engineered animals in agricultural activities and amend the federal law relating to animal patents; and to require the secretary of agriculture to reduce the price received by producers for milk from cows injected with bovine growth hormone.

Companion Animals

Bills involving companion animals have attempted to prohibit greyhound racing and greyhound race training unless artificial or mechanical lures are used; to make the

Animal Welfare Act applicable to facilities that are used for dog racing or dog training; to establish pilot programs using dogs and monkeys to aid quadriplegic veterans; and to provide signal dogs to hearing-impaired veterans.

Hunting and Trapping

Since most animal activists oppose hunting and trapping, bills have attempted to stop recreational hunting and trapping on wildlife refuges; prohibit airborne hunting of the Alaska gray wolf; establish specific criteria and solutions dealing with wildlife management problems; and end the use of the steel-jaw leghold trap by prohibiting the shipment in interstate or foreign commerce of such traps and articles made of fur from animals trapped by that means.

Because some hunters have been harassed by animal activists, bills have been introduced to protect persons engaged in a lawful hunt within a national forest; to establish a penalty for persons who intentionally obstruct, impede, or interfere with the conduct of a lawful hunt; and to reaffirm recreational hunting on national wildlife refugees.

Protecting Marine Mammals

Bills have aimed to protect dolphins that might get caught by tuna fishermen; to prohibit commercial hunting of whales; to ban the use of large-scale drift nets by fisherman from the European Community; and to ensure that incidental taking of marine mammals will not reduce the optimum sustainable population and monitor the level of incidental take in commercial fishing.

Protecting Wildlife

Bills to protect wildlife have attempted to prohibit the importation of Australian kangaroos and kangaroo products into the United States; monitor and conduct research on migratory nongame birds in the Western Hemisphere; and prohibit the killing of wildlife for sport, recreation, or commercial purposes on national wildlife refuges and sanctuaries.

Endangered Species and Animal Protection Amendments

Bills have attempted to amend the original legislation or make new laws to establish an ecologically significant old-growth forest reserve system; ensure the conservation of the northern spotted owl and the protection of other species associated with old-growth forests; secure a predictable supply of timber to afford stability to timber dependent communities; and provide economic adjustment assistance to communities and employees dependent on the forest industry. Other bills would maintain fish and wildlife populations, including the California condor in the Los Padres National Forest and the habitats to support such populations; make grants for projects for propagation of species listed as endangered or threatened; ban importation of all ivory products into the United States; revoke Most Favored Nation treatment of the products of elephant-producing countries that do not have or enforce appropriate protection for the animals; list the African elephant as an endangered species; make the Florida panther an endangered species; ban exportation of American black bear viscera; prevent the issuing of permits for the taking of any marine mammal from protected state waters for public display if inconsistent with state law; enhance the conservation of exotic birds in the wild by reducing and ultimately ending the import of such birds for the pet trade; reform the avian import process to decrease mortality and facilitate captive breeding of such birds; determine whether a species is endangered on the basis of the best scientific and commercial data available; to assure balanced consideration of scientific, economic, and social factors in the implementation of the act; and provide private property protection.

Member Coalitions

Animal rights and animal welfare concerns gained further public attention in the national policy arena when two coalitions formed among members of Congress in the early 1990s.

Congressional Friends of Animals

In March 1990, Congressman Tom Lantos (Democrat, California) and Robert C. Smith (Republican, New Hampshire) invited their colleagues to join the Congressional Friends of Animals. They pointed out a growing interest in animal issues beyond the traditional concerns of welfare and conservation of species. As members of Congress who want to act responsibly, they called on their colleagues to join Congressional Friends of Animals.

The organization provided its members and staffs information about animal welfare issues and legislation. The group sponsored a number of educational seminars and meetings, including a briefing by world-renowned primatologist Dr. Jane Goodall and a staff tour of the National Institutes of Health Animal Research Facility in Poolesville, Maryland.

Lantos and Smith stated that the Congressional Friends of Animals would provide a forum for discussion of a broad range of issues and expression on a variety of views. The agenda was to be open, shaped by those who joined. The coalition was to serve as a clearinghouse for information on animal issues and sponsor activities, such as debates and panel discussions, staff briefings, and field trips to places of interest to its members.

By the end of the year, twenty-four members of Congress were listed as members of the coalition, and twenty-eight were identified as interested. Among members of the 101st Congress (1991–1993) who were reported as members were Tom Lantos (Democrat, California), chairman; Bob Smith (Republican, New Hampshire), co-chair; Charles

Bennett (Democrat, Florida); William Broomfield (Republican, Michigan); Tom Campbell (Republican, California); Ron Dellums (Democrat, California); Bob Dornan (Republican, California); Walter Fauntroy (Democrat, Delegate, District of Columbia); Peter Kostmayer (Democrat, Pennsylvania); Jerry Lewis (Republican, California); John Lewis (Democrat, Georgia); Ed Markey (Democrat, Massachusetts); Bob Mrazek (Democrat, New York); Major Owens (Democrat, New York); Frank Pallone (Democrat, New Jersey); Matthew Rinaldo (Republican, New Jersey); Robert Roe (Democrat, New Jersey); Ileana Ros-Lehtinen (Republican, Florida); Steve Schiff (Republican, New Mexico); Larry Smith (Democrat, Florida); Harley Staggers (Democrat, West Virginia); Robert Torricelli (Democrat, New Jersey); and Edolphus Towns (Democrat, New York). In the 102nd Congress (1993–1994), Lantos continued to chair the Congressional Friends of Animals.

In March 1993, the group sponsored a briefing on marine mammal protection, in view of the coming reauthorization of the *Marine Mammal Protection Act*. Speakers included representatives from the API, NEAVS, the Campaign Against US Exportation of Dolphins, and the National Marine Fisheries Service.

In May 1993, Lantos invited members to a briefing on the proposed poultry slaughter legislation. The briefing featured Christine Stevens, AWI; Karen Davis, UPC; and Alex Hershaft, FARM. Only a few congressional staff members attended.

The caucus also helped keep the Washington, D.C., animal shelter open. At the time, it was threatened with closure due to lack of funds.

Turnover of membership in Congress has affected the continuity of the Congressional Friends of Animals. Among the twenty-four members listed in 1993, only twelve were still in Congress in 1995. After the change of leadership in Congress in 1995, funding for congressional caucuses was eliminated, and the strong effort to balance the budget hampered efforts to build strong support for animal welfare issues.

The Animal Welfare Caucus

By October 1990, some other members of Congress led by Representative Vin Weber (Republican, Minnesota) had formed the Animal Welfare Caucus, partly to counter perceived influence of the pro-animal welfare and pro-animal rights positions of the Congressional Friends of Animals. Some animal rights groups were critical of the name chosen by this group, which supported the use of animals for human benefit as well as humane treatment. The announced purpose was "to battle animal rights groups that threaten to undermine the livestock industry and block medical research that could cure Alzheimer's disease or cancer."[1]

The name Animal Welfare Caucus was chosen intentionally to distinguish it from groups that claim animals have rights similar to humans. Weber believed that animal rights groups were small but growing in number and influence. He cautioned that "if their agenda gains support our region's economy and quality of life could be seriously damaged."[2]

Weber's objective was to "bring common sense voice to the debate and to raise the concerns of medical researchers, farmers, sportsmen, and consumers about animal rights activities."[3] The group agreed that animals should not be mistreated. But group members also stressed that animals should not be elevated to the same status as human beings. They view animal research as vital to public health, the livestock industry as a vital part of the rural economy, and meat as an important part of a balanced diet. They believe that these are all legitimate uses of animals that must be protected.

The core members of the coalition were Byron Dorgan (Democrat, North Dakota), Joe Skeen (Republican, New Mexico), Joe Early (Democrat, Massachusetts), and Charles Stenholm (Democrat, Texas). At the time, Stenholm served as chairman of the House Agriculture Subcommittee on Livestock and Dairy.

This group's aim was to serve "as a clearinghouse for animal welfare information and raise public awareness of animal rights groups' activities."[4] The first priority of this group was to pass the Stenholm bill to make vandalizing farm animal facilities or research laboratories a federal crime. The coalition viewed the violent acts by animal rights groups as economic sabotage, causing millions of dollars in damage to animal research and production facilities.

In their call to attract members to the Animal Welfare Caucus, Weber claimed that no one had welcomed the concern for humane care of animals more than the people who work with animals. In the call for membership, he based his concern on the premise that in the last few years legislation had been introduced that would negatively affect "farmers, ranchers, food processors, biomedical researchers, and other responsible animal users."[5] The stated purpose of the caucus was to ensure that any responsible legislation dealing with animal care be based on fact and driven by a need to correct real problems—not create new ones. The goal of the caucus was to protect farmers, ranchers, sportsmen, and researchers from unreasonable laws. The organizers felt that the time had come for a commonsense approach to the animal rights issue.

When Weber did not return to Congress, Representatives Charles Stenholm (Democrat, Texas) and John Boehner (Republican, Ohio) took over leadership of the Animal Welfare Caucus. Their main focus in 1993 and 1994 was to watch for emerging issues where coalition effort would be required; but no issues emerged that required attention. All but one core member remained in Congress in 1995. However, without major animal welfare issues on the legislative agenda, no activity from this group took place during 1995 and 1996.

Congressional Sportsmen's Congress

The Congressional Sportsmen's Caucus (CSC) includes 215 senators and representatives and is the largest bipartisan caucus. As viewed by the Human Society of the United States, CSC "stands for recreational destruction of wildlife and industry-driven spoliation of the environment." Its members, who are viewed as antienvironmentalists, have led efforts to open the Arctic National Wildlife Refuges to oil exploration, to destroy wetlands protection, and to pervert both the *Endangered Species Act* and the *Marine Mammal Protection Act*.[6]

On the other hand the fur, firearms, tobacco, chemical, and coal industries have raised funds to form the Congressional Sportsmen's Caucus Foundation to support a balance between development and environmental concerns.

Perspectives on Past and Future Legislative Efforts

Legislative efforts by animal protection organizations fall into two categories: (1) the bills that get enacted into law and (2) those bills that die in committee or are voted out along the legislative trail. The successful legislation brought together those groups that had concern for animals from a humane, environmental, or economic perspective and rallied support from a significant segment of the concerned public. The opposition was not strong enough to prevent a final compromise and passage of the animal protection acts.

Since the *Animal Welfare Act* and *Endangered Species Act* have been passed, a number of amendments have been introduced. But few have been passed. Evidently, the original legislation was considered adequate and further action did not seem a high priority. Bills to further protect wildlife, marine mammals, and regulate animal research, product testing, and exhibitions have not gained enough support to become law. Revisions of the *Endangered Species Act* were considered under new leadership in the 104th Congress.

Lobbying and legislative efforts to enhance humane treatment of animals will continue despite limited success on some issues. Although animal protection is a top priority issue for the animal protection organization leaders, it has limited appeal to many citizens who place other issues much higher on their agendas. Members of Congress will be guided by the people they represent. The shift in leadership in the 104th Congress during 1995 and 1996 placed animal protection and environmental groups in a defensive position on endangered species, environmental issues, and property rights issues. The future leadership in Congress and in the White House will determine future success on animal protection legislation.

13

Freedom of Expression
Out of Control

Direct actions by extremists, both legal and illegal, have undermined the credibility and acceptance of the animal rights movement. Illegal and destructive actions against animal research and production facilities occurred in England in the 1970s and spread to the United States in the 1980s. While property damage has been substantial, no person has been injured despite threats and intimidation.

Since 1977, the federal government has documented 313 individual actions, varying widely in nature and scope, against enterprises or individuals using or marketing animals or animal-derived products.[1] The media reports, sought by the perpetrators of these acts, fulfill one of their goals—attention and publicity for the animal rights movement. Richard Ryder, a philosopher sympathetic to animal causes, suggests, "The chronic deafness of governments to the animal rights message has certainly added fuel to the flames of protest."[2]

Animal activists' activities have been delineated between those that are legal and those that are not. The first group involves protests or demonstrations at institutions using animals or selling products that fall short of being illegal.[3] The most controversial actions involve deliberate breaking of the law. Such activities include

- nonviolent acts of civil disobedience, such as sit-ins and breaking into laboratories to gather information and release animals;
- break-ins and destruction of buildings and equipment; and
- threats to human life and safety, such as adulteration of products, fire bombs in stores, and car bombs directed at individual scientists.

In the early 1980s, the Animal Liberation Front (ALF) began to claim credit for incidents in the United States involving vandalism and the theft or release of animals. Although the exact circumstances surrounding the ALF appearance remain a matter of speculation, the emergence of ALF activity apparently coincided directly with the popularization of the modern animal rights movement and the formation of its advocacy organizations.[4]

Although not legally recognized as an organization, the Animal Liberation Front is responsible for many of the illegal actions taken to "liberate" animals that they believe are being abused and exploited. The ALF claimed credit for approximately 60 percent of the total incidents documented in the US Department of Justice report.[5]

Animal Extremism in England

The Animal Liberation Front, better known as ALF, traces its origins back to the Band of Mercy, a nineteenth-century antivivisection group originating in England. In 1972, Ronald Lee and Clifford Goodman started a group known as the Band of Mercy, which began direct attacks on hunters in England. The new name, Animal Liberation Front, emerged in 1976 with the first attack on the Charles River Laboratories where vehicles were damaged.[6]

In recent years, ALF raids in England have targeted institutions connected with animals—furriers, research laboratories, and confinement farming operations. Scotland Yard has identified ALF as an international underground terrorist organization active in the United Kingdom, France, Canada, and the United States. In the United Kingdom, ALF claims about 2,500 activists, although police estimate the hard-core number is around 2150 and only about 50 are prepared to use explosives and incendiaries.[7] Most of the protesters at public demonstrations are young; women appear to outnumber men. About half of the ALF activists are working class and half, middle class, with a strong presence of lawyers, teachers, and civil servants. The majority have secure jobs.[8]

Despite the apparent absence of tangible connections, animal rights extremism in the United Kingdom is believed to exert considerable influence in the United States. Not only has animal rights extremism in the United Kingdom set the ideological stage for adherents in the United States and other countries, but it also has established the example for violence and destruction.[9] The frequency of extremist animal rights activity and the more severe destruction to animal enterprises in the United Kingdom has far exceeded that in the United States. ALF and other groups have demonstrated an increasing willingness to use timed or electrical incendiary devices and to cause harm to an individual or his or her personal property. Threats and claims of product tampering or contamination have also been more common.

David Hardy identifies four characteristics of ALF as it has operated in the United Kingdom. These characteristics explain their success and resistance to law enforcement authorities.

1. ALF is organized in small, independent "cells," with no clearly defined command structures. The compromise of one cell by undercover work or capture has minimal risk of compromising other cells.

2. It has formed links with aboveground groups that can raise funds, register for charitable exemption, mail newsletters, and lobby. These linked groups can also distribute press releases for the underground group, stage press conferences, and deplore the

excesses of their illicit counterpart, even as they take advantage of ALF's products—videotapes, photographs, and lab notes.

3. ALF and its sympathizers in the United Kingdom attempt to take over established animal welfare organizations. These older organizations have useful identification and an image of reasonableness, funds built up by decades of contributions and endowments, and often a relatively small number of members who could easily be voted down by a concerted drive.

In the United Kingdom, takeover efforts have succeeded with these organizations: the British Union for the Abolition of Vivisection (BUAV) and the National Anti-Vivisection Society (NAVS). One of the new leaders of BUAV pointed out that with the newly controlled funds, the new leadership was able to provide not only public relations but defense funds for those arrested. When asked if the organization supported illegal groups, the official replied, "Our policy is to support the activists in their direct action tactics morally, but not in a physical or financial way. We give them space in our newspaper because we think they have a very important role to play."[10] This strategy has been repeated in the United States.

4. ALF operations involve a rapidly expanding use of violence against research facilities and medical researchers. In 1989 alone, fourteen attempted bombings were attributed to British animal rights groups, together with over four hundred other criminal acts. There are ALF groups all over the world—in the United States, Canada, Netherlands, Germany, New Zealand, Australia, South Africa, and France. Despite the fundamental differences between extremist activities in the United Kingdom and the United States, the general momentum of animal rights extremism in the United States has and continues to follow closely the example established in the United Kingdom.[11]

Parallel Patterns from Great Britain to the United States

Small independent cells. It is widely believed that ALF is a loose configuration of small, autonomous cells with no centralized common structure and with no formal membership requirements beyond the willingness to inflict damage upon an animal enterprise. In each country where it operates, ALF is believed to be composed of one hundred or fewer "hard-core" members and more numerous activists or sympathizers who are willing to engage in less-destructive activities.[12] Consequently, it has been difficult for law enforcement authorities to track down the persons responsible for the acts of vandalism and theft that have occurred.

Links with aboveground groups. In the United States, People for the Ethical Treatment of Animals has publicized ALF activities soon after their occurrence. Though never publicly condoning ALF's illegal activities, PETA representatives almost always voiced support for the motive or principle underlying any given incident.[13]

Takeover of established animal welfare organizations. Kim Stallwood, who had been active in animal rights activity in the United Kingdom, emigrated to the United States and became PETA'S executive director, where he served from 1981 to 1992. In 1987,

PETA brought their members and supporters to the New England Anti-Vivisection Society meeting, at which they elected PETA's director candidates to the NEAVS board (see chapter 4).[14]

Animal Terrorism in the United States

The Animal Liberation Front's goals are as follows:

1. to liberate animals from places of abuse and place them in good homes where they can live out their natural lives free from suffering;

2. to inflict economic damage upon those who profit from the misery and exploitation of animals; and

3. to reveal the horrors and atrocities committed against animals behind locked doors.[15]

Their operation style includes always striking under cover of night, activists concealing their identities with ski masks, and victimizing major targets with evident forethought and precision.[16] It is widely believed that ALF activists conduct careful surveillance of a selected target before victimizing it; and they are also suspected of infiltrating selected targets by gaining employment in the enterprise or by cultivating close contacts with employees having ready access to the facility.[17] ALF raids usually appear to be very well organized, which may account for their relative infrequency. Also, it is commonly asserted that ALF raiders are able to reduce their chances of being caught by not having individuals go on successive raids. The ALF seems to be a loose collection of individuals who keep no membership lists or telephone numbers. No one has ever publicly admitted being a member.[18]

One set of ALF documents lists its "Ten Rules for Direct Action":

1. Make sure the operation will be effective. Never waste time with an operation which you feel will be ineffective.

2. Hit the enemy where they least expect it and where it will hurt them the most.

3. Almost all sabotage should be carried out at night.

4. Timing must be perfect, as the longer the operation takes the greater the chances of something going wrong.

5. Work only with people you trust, undercover cops who infiltrate activist groups are extremely dangerous. Work in small groups or cells, consisting of no more than four to six people.

6. All operations should be simple and fast, and several means of escape should be planned.

7. All equipment should be concealed. Volatile substances should be handled with extreme caution.

8. All groups should have a leader. He or she should be picked for their leadership qualities and will make all decisions.

9. The need for secrecy is obvious. Security and secrecy must be maintained without reservation. If it is not, you deserve to be caught.

10. Any member who breaks the code of the group must be cast out immediately and permanently.[19]

ALF activists are believed to use alternating names and group titles as a tactic for evading detection. Altogether, twenty-three different entities (listed in appendix 4) were documented as having claimed responsibility for violent or disruptive acts against animal enterprises since 1977. ALF claimed about 60 percent of the documented incidents. No information has been found to link these groups, whether they operate independently, in competition, or in conflict with the ALF.[20]

From 1977 through June 1993, a total of twenty-eight different types of animal enterprises were victimized by animal rights extremists. They most frequently targeted university animal research facilities, fur retailers, individuals, meat retailers, food production, private research, department stores, and federal research units. The biomedical, food industry, and retail fur industry represent about 82 percent of all animal enterprises harmed. Extremists targeted biomedical research scientists using animals or their personal property on forty-three occasions or about 14 percent of all documented incidents.[21]

ALF claimed its initial act in the United States in 1982. ALF and other animal liberation groups have committed more than 300 incidents, about half classed as minor vandalism, such as spray-painting graffiti, breaking windows, gluing locks, and defacing property. Theft or release of animals ranked next as the most frequent action. The high incidence of minor vandalism suggests that most extremist animal rights–related acts continue to be small scale and fairly haphazard. However, 26 of the 313 documented incidents involved major structural damage and property loss and significant disruption of commercial or research operations, resulting in the FBI labeling this destructive and costly form of "economic sabotage" as "domestic terrorism." [22]

The illegal acts also included break-ins and destruction of laboratory equipment; damage to vehicles owned by research institutions; trespassing and blocking of entrances to research facilities; bomb threats; theft or destruction of research data and audio- and videotapes; taking employment in research facilities to spy on the operations and taking illegal photos of the operations; and vandalism and attempted arson to offices and animal and poultry production facilities (see appendix 6 for a list of known direct actions by ALF and other animal rights groups).

The most destructive act in which animal activists were suspected occurred on April 16, 1987, when intruders set fire to the animal diagnostic laboratory under construction at the University of California at Davis and caused an estimated $4.5 million damage.

Among the documented incidents in twenty-nine states from 1977 through June 1993, California reported 143 incidents, or 46 percent of the total. The next highest numbers occurred in Maryland, Pennsylvania, Florida, New York, North Carolina, and Washington State. The numbers reached a peak in 1987 with 53 incidents and 1988 with 52 incidents. Only 11 incidents were reported in 1992 and 13 in the first half of 1993.[23] Incidents continue to be documented (see appendix 6).

The rapid expansion of ALF in the United States was possible because the organizational experience had been tested in England, and there were aboveground groups that could become ALF's parallel organizations.[24]

In 1986, Farm Sanctuary of Rockland, Delaware (later located in Watkins Glen, New York), issued a press release announcing that the Farm Freedom Fighters had "liberated" twenty-five laying hens from a Mid-Atlantic cage-laying operation. The group claimed this was the first direct farm animal "liberation" conducted in the United States.[25] Although such incidents have caused substantial damage, none of the activities documented in the report to Congress is known to have resulted in injury or death of another individual.[26]

Official Actions

Although many of the break-ins and destructive acts of vandalism occur with no arrests, some of the participants have been apprehended and convicted. One of the first American ALF raiders to get caught was Roger Troen, who was convicted of theft, burglary, and conspiracy. PETA paid the ALF member's $27,000 legal tab and, in January 1989, informed its members that it had. The $34,900 restitution assessment against Troen was reported to have been paid by PETA, but PETA claimed that it had not.[27] Troen was released early because of good behavior and began working and living at a shelter for animals.

In 1992, Virginia Bollinger was fired from her position as an assistant at Laboratory Animal Resources at Wright State University in Ohio for violating facility policies. A coworker saw her entering the laboratory at unauthorized times, making videotapes, and removing documents from their proper place.

When a warrant was issued to search her locker on the premises, police found a video camera, a 35-millimeter camera, and audio recording equipment. She was arrested and charged with disorderly conduct and obstructing official business after she refused to allow police to inventory her locker.

Bollinger was identified as an undercover investigator for PETA. A PETA spokesman claimed that Bollinger had provided "shocking evidence" that would enrage the public when the information was released. PETA sent a representative to hold a press conference for the group, but she did not provide any of the photos or documents that were alluded to.[28]

The FBI identified a person who distributed the ALF statement claiming responsibility for the August 1991 break-in at Washington State University. Rodney Coronado, a member of the Coalition Against Fur Farms said he faxed the release to the Associated Press but denied involvement in the break-in.

On July 16, 1993, a federal grand jury in Grand Rapids, Michigan, returned a five-count indictment against Rodney Coronado, a suspected ALF member, in connection with the February 1992 break-in and arson at an animal research facility at Michigan State University. Coronado was also wanted in Canada on charges relating to vandalism of fur retailers. After a year on the run, Coronado was arrested on a reservation outside

Tucson, Arizona. On March 3, 1995, Coronado pleaded guilty to two felony charges, one of them for the 1992 arson. On August 11, a federal judge sentenced Coronado to fifty-seven months in prison for the arson and for stealing a cavalry man's journal from a museum in Montana. In addition, he had to pay more than $2.5 million in restitution and spend three years on supervised release. Coronado is only the second person to be convicted of participation in an incident attributed to the Animal Liberation Front.[29]

Threats Against Research Scientists and Others

Although ALF has mainly targeted its efforts to property damage and animals thefts, individuals have been threatened. Following a break-in at the Texas Tech Health Science Research Center, Dr. John Orem, who had been conducting research on Sudden Infant Death Syndrome, received death threats and an allegedly AIDS-contaminated condom.[30]

Stanford University researchers also were reported to have received death threats. Two University of California at Los Angeles faculty members had their homes attacked. A Columbia University researcher received a telephone threat followed by red paint thrown in front of his house and the burning of his guest house. Death threats have also been directed to research scientists at Johns Hopkins, Duke, Harvard, National Institutes of Health, and Cornell University.[31]

Animal rights activist Fran Stephanie Trutt placed a radio-controlled pipe bomb at the parking space of Leon Hirsch, president of U.S. Surgical Corporation in Norwalk, Connecticut.[32] Had the bomb exploded, it probably would have killed everyone within 30 feet. The grounds were evacuated, and the bomb was successfully disarmed. As a lover of dogs, Trutt was enraged by the use of as many as ten thousand live dogs each year, in demonstrating the use of surgical staples.

On November 11, 1988, Trutt was arrested. She pleaded no contest to charges of attempted murder, possession of explosives, and bomb manufacturing.[33] Friends of Animals, located in the same city, provided legal and moral support for Trutt, following the disclosure that her two accomplices were in contact with the police and were employed by a surveillance organization hired by U.S. Surgical.

Although no arrests were made, an illegal pie-throwing incident at the World Pork Expo in Des Moines, Iowa, in May 1991 sparked some disagreement between two animal rights activists. A PETA staff member dressed in a pig costume threw a nondairy cream pie at the teenage Iowa Pork Queen.

Vickie Eide, representing the Iowa Alliance for Animals, reprimanded the PETA staff members involved—"from a humane perspective it was a mean and hateful deed"—and reminded the staffers that it was a legally actionable case of assault. As an animal rights supporter, Eide regretted that PETA, a leading national animal rights organization, had launched an incident of sensationalism like this hit-and-run publicity stunt.[34]

PETA Lifestyles Campaign Director, Kathy Snow Guillermo, defended the incident, pointing out that the opportunity to discuss the issue of pork industry abuses would not have presented itself if the pie-throwing incident had not occurred. She pointed out that, as a result, media interviews about vegetarianism took place in sixty markets, and pork industry representatives had to answer questions about their treatment of animals.

Chris DeRose, president, Last Chance for Animals, and Aaron Leider, director, began serving a ninety-day prison sentence in the Los Angeles County Jail in October 1992 for refusing to leave a research facility and taking pictures at the UCLA cat vivarium in 1988 where research was taking place.[35]

In March 1997, Syracuse, New York, police arrested Jeffrey Watkins and Nicole Rogers of the Syracuse Animal Defense League. Watkins was sentenced to seven months for splashing red paint on a passerby's fur coat and jumping on a police car at separate protests. Rogers drew sixty days for chaining herself to a fur store security gate.[36]

The Strategies and Procedures of Illegal Animal Activists

Ingrid Newkirk describes some inside details of the most noted attacks on animal research facilities. Although she gives the individuals involved assumed names, she identifies the places where attacks actually took place. A *People* magazine interview with "Valerie" confirms the Newkirk report.[37] How much of the account is fictionalized is difficult to say.

The Internet became a part of activists' activities in 1997. The Animal Liberation Frontline News Service quoted *Fur World* concerning a posting of names, addresses, and phone numbers of firms engaged in the fur business. The list, "The Final Nail: Destroying the Fur Industry," to be used by anti-fur forces, included instructions and diagrams to construct incendiary devices. Because the Internet is a worldwide computer-based network, messages can be posted from anywhere, and it is not clear if the originator is subject to the laws of the United States or Canada.

The Extremists' Justification

Those who take personal risks of injury, arrest by participation in demonstrations, or illegal actions undoubtedly do so with a dedication that many find hard to understand. Although only a few participate in demonstrations and illegal activities, they are strongly motivated to save animals that they believe are abused and mistreated. They see animals in research as the most abused and often in the most need of rescue. They question the value of many research projects that involve many years' work before favorable results can be identified. Cleveland Amory, president of the Fund for Animals and the New England Anti-Vivisection Society, describes the activists as "the people who, often at risk of life and limb as well as of jail, break into laboratories and rescue animals from experimenters and vivisectionists."[38]

Tim Dailey defends ALF tactics, including the use of letter bombs and planting of bombs on researchers' automobiles. "In a war you have to take up arms and people will get killed, and I can support that kind of action by petrol bombing and bombs under cars, and probably at a later stage, the shooting of vivisectors on their doorsteps. It's a war, and there's no other way you can stop vivisectors." [39]

Following an editorial in *Animal People* that condemned the planting of fire-bombs in the fur sections of Chicago department stores, Gary Francione of Rutgers Animal Rights Law Clinic asserted that he would not advise any person to break the law. But he suggested that there is a significant moral difference between planting a firebomb and removing animals from a laboratory. In removing animals from a laboratory, this illegal act threatens only the property rights that people claim over animals. It is a fundamental premise of the animal rights movement that it is morally wrong to treat animals as property.[40]

Direct Actions and Their Consequences

Illegal acts, vandalism, and threats against animal research workers have marked the animal welfare and animal rights movements, even though the extremists comprise a small part of those sympathetic to humane treatment of animals in legal and legitimate ways.

Violence in pursuit of animal liberation is universally condemned in public by all mainstream animal rights groups. Many groups stay away from direct action to further their goals. However, breaking into laboratories and undercover work of activists disguised as employees has provided materials used in antivivisection campaigns. The public does not have access to laboratories since research scientists may feel that information about their work may overestimate animal suffering and underestimate the public benefit of their work.[41] Ryder claims that no one has been seriously injured by actions of animal activists. However, in England, activists have been severely injured during demonstrations against hunting, circuses, and hare coursing. Claudia Ross, an American reporter for the *Bangkok Post* who wrote about international trade in animals, Dian Fossey, a protector of gorillas in Africa, and Chico Mendes, a Brazilian conservationist, were murdered.[42]

Activists in the United States have also suffered injuries. A demonstrator at the Hegins, Pennsylvania, pigeon shoot in 1991 received a broken collar bone and another, a broken arm. During a demonstration against the baboon liver transplant operation in Pittsburgh in February 1993, a demonstrator was injured when knocked down by a hunter carrying a gun. During an anti-fur demonstration in New York, a photographer was hit by a fur dealer.[43]

The Effects of Animal Extremism

The consensus among practitioners in industry, government, academia, and law enforcement alike is that animal rights extremism in the United States has significantly affected the enterprises and industries it has victimized. These effects include the direct costs of physical destruction or stolen property; the collateral costs of enhanced security, higher insurance rates, and lost clientele; and the indirect costs of disrupted, delayed, or canceled research. These compounded effects on targeted animal enterprises has not been reliably quantified.[44]

Actions by animal activist groups have intimidated the animal production industries and biomedical research communities and have led to defensive measures to protect their property and facilities. The result is greatly increased costs to conduct research and reduced funds for research output.

In some instances, public farm tours to visit livestock and poultry facilities have been suspended because of possible vandalism. State fairs and 4-H livestock shows have been placed on alert to deal with any demonstrations or harassment by animal activists.

The consequences of militant actions by dedicated animal rights advocates are summed up by Michael Fox who condemned "militant animal liberation fundamentalists" for going too far in burning research laboratories, vandalizing production facilities, and stealing animals. He concludes, "Progress in animal protection will be seriously compromised so long as there is violence in the name of animal liberation, and that violence is linked in the public's mind and by the media with any proposition of animal protection." [45]

Lawrence Finsen and Susan Finsen conclude that the direct-action, illegal tactics of ALF are the most controversial of any in the animal rights movement. Some see ALF as a dangerous terrorist organization with the potential for destroying the movement by discrediting it as violent. However, some who are sympathetic to animal causes see ALF as the most dedicated and important arm of the movement, providing information through no other means and liberating animals where all other efforts have failed.[46]

Many dedicated animal activists would probably agree that an *Animal People* editorial, an independent voice within the animal rights movement, expresses their feelings about animal extremism:

> Most of the animal protection community has privately regarded the ALF with exasperated embarrassment, while a more militant minority has extolled the ALF as heroes and heroines. . . . The ALF and imitators are practically singlehandedly responsible for rationalizing the organized backlash against the animal rights movement, are the major reason why animal protection representatives still have virtually no place on institutional care and use committees; and have managed to equate the term "animal rights activist" with "terrorist" in the minds of many people in law enforcement and media, even those otherwise sympathetic to the cause of animals.[47]

Animal Rights Violence in Canada

In the United States, actions by the ALF have involved vandalism and theft of animals. In 1996, a radical entity, the "Justice Department," which had been active for three years in England, began to take credit for violent actions in Canada. It has been described as an

ALF splinter group. But one observer in England sees the Justice Department as a style of activity rather than a distinct set of people.

While ALF has not targeted people, the Justice Department actions in England have involved sending letter bombs and blowing up milk trucks. The first Canadian strike involved sending out sixty-five envelopes containing razor blades coated with rat poison to guide outfitters who led hunting trips across British Columbia and Alberta.[48]

14

Seeking Legal Rights
for Animals

The key issues involved in litigation for animals are standing to sue and forcing a government agency to follow the intent of legislative bodies; other key issues in litigation concern animal sacrifice and religious rituals, protection of wild animals, and animal damage control programs to protect domestic livestock owned by farmers and ranchers.

Although state and federal laws insure humane treatment of animals, the existence of the law itself will not guarantee that animals will be cared for humanely. Individuals and organizations concerned about animal welfare and protection are taking legal action to force government agencies to implement more protectionist interpretations of the law.

The Animal Legal Defense Fund has pioneered efforts through the courts to compel humane treatment of animals. ALDF encourages attorneys to use the laws to demand appropriate action by those responsible for animals' care and protection. Fund members believe that all animals deserve to be defended against human exploitation.

The Key Issues

The key issues involved in litigation for animals include (1) standing to sue, (2) forcing a government agency to follow the intent of legislative bodies, (3) determining legal status for animal sacrifice and religious rituals, (4) protecting wild animals, and (5) deciding on the use of animal damage control programs to protect domestic livestock owned by farmers and ranchers.

Standing to sue. In some lawsuits aimed at helping animals, the question is whether the courts will permit animal advocates the standing to sue. Standing to sue is a legal doctrine that determines the plaintiff's eligibility to bring suit and is usually decided by the presiding judge. To qualify for standing, the plaintiff must show that the conduct of the defendant will "invade a private substantive legally protected interest of the plaintiff citizen." [1]

However, owners of animals have an economic interest and direct relationship, so courts may question whether animal activists have the right, or standing, to sue the farmer or laboratory on behalf of the activist, their organization, or the animals.

ALDF points out that without an attorney's participation, limited legal protections granted animals will have little impact behind the doors of the slaughterhouse, the laboratory, the pound, the airport, and many other facilities in which people interact with nonhuman animals. So one of ALDF's major goals is to come up with innovative ways to create standing so that attorneys can get into court.

Enforcing the law. Animal activists have used the courts when a federal, state, or municipal agency disregards a legislative directive that the agency is supposed to implement.

Freedom for religious practices. Religious practices that involve kosher slaughtering practices or religious rituals that involve animal sacrifice generate strong opposition from animal activists.

Protecting wild animals. The cases for wild animals involve protecting them in their natural environment and stopping what activists see as abuse in zoos, aquariums, entertainment, and sporting activities.

Killing predators or saving endangered species. Long-standing government policy has favored extermination of wild animals that are viewed as predators to domestic livestock and poultry. Litigation issues involve protection of endangered or threatened species; determination of risks to birds, other wildlife, and people with the use of poison baits; and, in the view of some animal activists, the contention of "an effort to limit the government's systematic, century-old extermination of countless wildlife as a favor to farmers and rancher." [2]

Taking the Animals' Cases to Court

State and local court cases against individuals to enforce the anticruelty laws go back many years. But actions to protect the animals' rights through litigation in state and federal courts have emerged most frequently since 1981.

Animals in Research and the Silver Spring Monkeys

The case involving the Silver Spring monkeys was among the first to challenge the use of animals in research and established animal rights as a growing movement. In 1981, Alex Pacheco, an undergraduate student at George Washington University and a cofounder of People for the Ethical Treatment of Animals, worked as a lab volunteer for Dr. Edward Taub, a medical researcher at the Institute for Behavioral Research (IBR) in Silver Spring, Maryland.

Taub was using primates that had been captured in the forests of the Philippines to study the ability of monkeys to use a limb after nerves were severed. He surgically severed all nerves in the limbs of a number of monkeys and then forced the monkeys to use the deadened limbs. The stated purpose of this research was to help humans who had suffered a stroke.

While working at IBR, Pacheco found that the lab did not provide the research primates with what he believed was sufficient food and water, a sanitary environment, or adequate veterinary care.

Pacheco brought in animal research authorities at night to inspect the situation and then notified local police, who raided the lab and rescued the monkeys. Dr. Taub was arrested and tried for cruelty to animals. He was convicted of not providing proper veterinary care on one count but later, through appeal, was found not guilty. The rest of the litigation centered on what to do with the monkeys and how to stop further research on them. The animal rights groups were unsuccessful in their efforts (see appendix 4 for the history and chronology of the Silver Spring monkeys and the litigation that followed).

Lessons from the Silver Spring Monkeys

Why were animal rights supporters unsuccessful? The judge declared that to sue in federal court, the plaintiffs had to show that they personally suffered from actual or threatened injury as a result of the conduct of the defendant.

The court concluded that the *Animal Welfare Act* did not authorize private individuals and organizations to be named guardians of research animals seized from a medical research institute whose chief was convicted of state animal cruelty law violations.[3]

The court had previously declared that "a mere interest in a problem, no matter how long that interest and no matter how qualified the organization to evaluate the problem is not sufficient by itself to create a standing" to bring suit. So even though commitment and strength in membership may enhance legislative access, it does not necessarily provide entry to a federal court.[4]

Even though the plaintiffs asserted that their tax payments entitled them to ensure that the *Animal Welfare Act* was respected by the National Institutes of Health (NIH), the Supreme Court had previously rejected this reasoning—that payment of taxes does not purchase authority to enforce regulatory restrictions. Although the plaintiffs claimed that they had contributed to the maintenance of the monkeys after Sergeant Swain seized them and before NIH took possession, this expenditure was a voluntary offer to help Maryland authorities and did not give them any ownership interest in the monkeys.

However, despite its setbacks in court, the animal rights movement gained significant attention from the Silver Spring incident.[5] Katie McCabe reported that Pacheco's pictures cast the first shadow of suspicion over the research community's treatment of animals and gave the animal rights movement a rallying cry. The case also stimulated activists' efforts to gain legal standing in behalf of animals.

Yet Pacheco and People for the Ethical Treatment of Animals challenged McCabe's reporting as libelous and inaccurate. To settle a lawsuit, the *Washingtonian* published corrections and clarification that acknowledged that some of the statements reported by McCabe came from unreliable sources.

The statements of correction were as follows: (1) Pacheco did not stage the photo of the monkey Domitian but took the picture during the day and had not told a different story about the photo to the Maryland court. (2) Pacheco was not responsible for cleaning the laboratory, so the pictures he took depicting unsanitary conditions did not support an inference that they were not representative. (3) Statements by former employees, who had been fired by PETA, were questionable. PETA continues to be audited each year, and these audits have not shown any financial irregularities. (4) PETA funds were not used in the election for the board of NEAVS, but the funds were raised separately by Mr. Pacheco through a special action campaign fund. (5) When Roger Troen was convicted, PETA did not pay any of the $34,900 restitution fund but did pay legal fees of $27,000.

Forcing Government to Implement the Law

Environmental impact statements. In 1990, People for the Ethical Treatment of Animals brought action against the secretary of health and human services, charging that federal agencies were failing to prepare environmental impact statements before awarding research grants to institutions conducting animal research, thus violating the *National Environmental Policy Act.*

On October 22, the US Court of Appeals ruled in favor of the government agencies. The court held that PETA and other animal activists failed to establish injury sufficient to give them standing to challenge the granting of funds to research institutions.[6]

The *Animal Welfare Act* and its 1985 amendment mandated basic humane standards of care for animals in laboratories. The act charged the secretary of agriculture to prescribe regulations and standards for the proper treatment of animals.

Although the amendment was passed in 1985, the first draft of regulations to implement the law were issued in March 1989. Researchers complained about the high cost of implementing the regulations, so a second set were issued in August 1990.[7] ALDF thought that advocates of the research industry went to work to undermine and delay enforcement by the USDA.

In 1988, ALDF sued the USDA for failing to enforce the *Animal Welfare Act.* Under court order, the USDA proposed comprehensive regulation for use of anesthesia and painkillers, for daily exercise, adequate cage size, and safeguards for psychological well-being of primates.

On March 15, 1989, the secretary responded to public comments by saying that USDA was not changing its definition of *animal* to cover birds, rats, and mice. He admitted that the department had the authority to regulate, but except for wild rats and mice, it had never covered them in its regulations. But in response to comments, he said USDA was considering regulations.

On November 15, 1989, ALDF petitioned the secretary of agriculture to conduct rule-making proceedings to include birds, rats, and mice in the definition of *animal* and set up standards for their care.

On June 8, 1990, the Department of Agriculture, after a review of the ALDF petition, concluded that initiating rule-making to regulate handling of birds, rats and mice was not appropriate. The department based its decision on manpower, funds, and resources available to effectively administer the animal welfare program.

On April 1, 1991, Animal Legal Defense Fund brought suit in the US District Court of the District of Columbia. The group alleged that the secretary of agriculture violated the federal *Laboratory Animal Welfare Act* by promulgating regulations that failed to include birds, rats, and mice as *animals* within the meaning of the act.

The Department of Agriculture tried to dismiss the suit. But the judge denied the request for dismissal and ruled that the plaintiffs were "aggrieved by agency action" within the meaning of the act and had standing to seek judicial review. The judge also ruled that the secretary was not necessarily acting within discretionary authority delegated by Congress when he determined that birds, mice, and rats were not covered by the act.

The court ruling stated that under the *Administrative Law and Procedure Act*, animal welfare organizations satisfied the injury-in-fact standing requirement to challenge regulation of the Department of Agriculture. ALDF alleged that lack of data on condition of mice, rats, and birds caused by failure to consider such fauna as animals injured the ability of organizations to disseminate to their members information about treatment and conditions of such fauna.[8]

On January 8, 1992, ALDF again brought suit challenging the Department of Agriculture's failure to include birds, rats, and mice as animals within the federal *Laboratory Animal Welfare Act*. Judge Charles Richey ruled that the department's failure to include birds, rats, and mice was "arbitrary and capricious" and not in accord with the law. The court also declared that the secretary did not have complete discretion in defining for which animals the department will prescribe treatment standards.[9]

On February 25, 1993, ALDF and others brought suit again in the District of Columbia federal district court alleging that USDA and the former secretary of agriculture had violated the *Improved Standards for Laboratory Animals Act*. ALDF claimed that the final regulations issued by USDA were arbitrary and capricious and contrary to law under the *Administrative Law and Procedure Act*. Judge Charles Richey concluded that the plaintiffs had successfully demonstrated that the USDA had violated the *Administrative Law and Procedure Act* by enacting regulations that did not comply with the mandate of Congress in the *Animal Welfare Act* as amended. He ordered the USDA to issue new regulations without unnecessary delay.

The plaintiffs specifically cited these concerns: the lack of minimum requirements in regulations regarding dog exercise and nonhuman primate psychological well-being; the delay permitted until February 1994 in complying with new cage requirements; special cage designs that permitted entities to evade existing minimum cage size requirements; and regulations that permitted regulated entities to store their plans for dog exercise and nonhuman primate enrichment on-site where such plans would not be subject to *Freedom of Information Act* requests.

The USDA claimed that it had a broad mandate from Congress and that the regulations were properly within that mandate. The department contended that the call for minimum requirements did not require absolute numerical criteria.[10]

On May 20, 1994, the US Court of Appeals for the District of Columbia ruled in favor of the US Department of Agriculture stating than none of the plaintiffs, the Animal Legal Defense Fund, the Humane Society of the United States, or two individuals, could demonstrate both constitutional standing to sue and a statutory right to judicial review under the *Administrative Law and Procedure Act*. So the lower district court judgment was overturned, and the suit against the Department of Agriculture was dismissed.

The Animal Welfare Act under Review

Review of the *Animal Welfare Act* underscores two points in view of court decisions: (1) a commitment of administrative supervision of animal welfare and (2) subordination of such supervision to the continued independence of research scientists.[11] Recent amendments to the *Animal Welfare Act* reaffirm the congressional finding that "the use of animals is instrumental in certain research and education or for advancing knowledge of cures and treatments for diseases and injuries which afflict both humans and animals.[12]

Humane Treatment and Food Safety

On June 25, 1985, Animal Legal Defense Fund of Boston sued Provimi Veal Corporation under the Massachusetts consumer protection statute in the Massachusetts state court. Provimi removed the case to the US District Court of Massachusetts in August 1985. ALDF argued that (1) their members ate veal and wanted to be assured that animals were raised in a healthy manner, free from cruelty and (2) veal calves were fed subtherapeutic doses of antibiotics and other chemical additives that ALDF claimed were bad for the individuals who ate the calves' meat.

After considerable argument, the court acknowledged that ALDF raised very important issues but did not agree that ALDF had standing to raise them. The court saw the suit as an attempt to indirectly enforce anticruelty laws, something only the state had the right to do. It also pointed out that comprehensive federal regulations for labeling, packaging, and marketing of meat and use of medicated animal feeds were designed for consumer protection.[13]

Protecting Wildlife and Endangered Species

Congress passed the *Endangered Species Act* in 1973 in response to a concern that various species had been rendered extinct as a result of economic growth and development and a lack of conservation. One of the greatest strengths of the act is that the courts have taken Congress at their word in interpreting the act.

Efforts to protect endangered species have produced conflicts and litigation in recent years. When the endangered species has been classed as a predator, the conflicts become more difficult to resolve.

The Timber Wolf: Endangered Species or Predator?

On April 11, 1977, the State of Alaska brought action against the secretary of the interior, Defenders of Wildlife, and others seeking the right to maintain a wolf-hunting program to protect the Western Arctic caribou herd. The judge ruled that the secretary of the interior had power to halt the wolf-hunt program on federally controlled lands.[14]

Six months after passage of the *Endangered Species Act*, the Minnesota Department of Natural Resources (DNR) issued an administrative order that allowed the taking of endangered timber wolves under certain circumstances. When this state agency attempted to continue wolf trapping under its Directed Predator Control Program, the federal Fish and Wildlife Service (FWS) notified the agency that the program violated the federal law and ordered the DNR to revoke this state authorization to take timber wolves. But the Minnesota DNR petitioned FWS to exclude Minnesota from the endangered wolf's range.

In February 1977, Julius Brzoznowski, a northern Minnesota farmer sued the secretary of the interior based upon alleged loss of cattle to predator wolves. In May 1978, an agreement was reached that the department would begin to trap wolves on Brzoznowski's farm. The trapped wolves were to be impounded for relocation. On June 9, a court order dissolved the May agreement.

On June 6, 1978, Fund for Animals and a group of nonprofit conservation-oriented organizations brought suit against US government officials including the secretary of the interior, the secretary of agriculture and the director of the US Fish and Wildlife Service. FFA wanted to stop the defendants from trapping and killing wolves.

On June 22, 1978, the Fish and Wildlife Service issued rules that allowed the taking of the gray wolf in Minnesota because there had been unusually large numbers of human/wolf conflicts; large numbers of wolves would cause these conflicts to continue; and the taking would not have adverse consequences on the wolf population. The court judgment recommended: (1) that the defendants be directed to stop trapping and killing Eastern timber wolves in four zones in Minnesota, except when the action is necessary and the defendants remove a gray wolf or wolves when the animals have committed a significant depredation upon livestock lawfully present in the area; and (2) no trapping of Eastern timber wolves on public lands in these four zones of Minnesota would be permitted except for the public lands immediately bordering privately owned land upon which significant depredation has occurred.[15]

The court decision left many unanswered questions: How close to privately owned lands could trapping occur on public lands? How would the trapper know if the presence of a wolf would actually justify trapping it because of the possibility that it would attack livestock? And how would "significant depredation" be identified?

The court report admitted that the determination left the government agencies and the farmers in a difficult situation. But it also stated that the remedy for this problem must come from law makers and not be "judicially legislated."

In 1981, the Minnesota DNR stated that the wolf was not endangered or threatened and that as a state agency, it should manage the resources in its state. So the DNR requested control of the program in Minnesota to maintain optimum wolf density, regulate harvest, provide enforcement and public information, and provide for population monitoring and research.

The Minnesota DNR developed timber wolf management plans in 1980 and 1981, but both were rejected by the US Fish and Wildlife Service.[16] On August 15, 1983, the government moved to reopen the case of *Fund for Animals v. Andrus* and asked for the court to either clarify or dissolve its order so as to not conflict with new regulations. Although the plaintiffs objected, the court ordered that the case be reopened. In this case, both sides were interpreting the *Endangered Species Act* to support their positions.

On January 5, 1984, the Sierra Club and Defenders of Wildlife asked for a judgment against the secretary of the interior and officers of US Fish and Wildlife Service. They wanted to stop the implementation of new government regulations allowing a sport-hunting season on the Minnesota gray wolf. In addition, the court blocked the implementation of new federal regulations published August 10, 1983, expanding the current livestock depredation control program.[17]

On February 19, 1985, the US Court of Appeals affirmed the decision on the illegality of the sport season but sent back to the district court to reconsider regulation involving depredation control.[18]

On May 2, 1985, the court ordered the secretary of interior and the Fish and Wildlife Service to amend the regulations to prohibit (1) trapping and killing Minnesota gray wolves except when such action is necessary and is directed to the removal from a farm or other privately owned land of a specific wolf when reasonable evidence exists that the wolf or wolves have committed a significant depredation upon domestic animals; (2) trapping and killing Minnesota gray wolves on public lands in Minnesota except that portion of the public lands that immediately border upon privately owned lands for a distance not to exceed one-half mile and upon which significant depredation has occurred; and (3) the sale or export of Minnesota gray wolves in interstate or international commerce.[19]

Protecting the Bison in Yellowstone Park

On January 15, 1991, the FFA brought suit against the secretary of the interior; the secretary of agriculture; the director of the Montana Department of Fish, Wildlife, and Parks; the director of the Montana Department of Livestock; and the Montana attorney general. The fund requested an injunction to stop the shooting of bison outside the boundaries of Yellowstone National Park, to prevent migration of bison out of that park, and stop any action that would reduce the bison population, pending completion of an environmental impact statement.

The court ruled that the FFA (1) failed to show likelihood of success of their request, irreparable harm, or public interest favoring it; (2) did not have standing to sue based on psychological injury its members would suffer knowing that bison would be shot if they wandered outside the park; and (3) failed to make claims against the State of Montana for which relief could be granted. So the request for an injunction was denied.[20]

On February 24, 1993, FFA took action against the secretary of agriculture, challenging a February 18 decision to fund, approve, and implement a research program that involved the capture of ten to sixty pregnant wild bison. The bison were to be taken from just outside the boundary of Yellowstone National Park, transported to Texas where they were to be infected with brucellosis, corralled with cattle, and, after a few months, slaughtered.

FFA, as a group committed to preservation of animal species in their natural habitats, claimed that the secretary of agriculture failed to comply with the *National Environmental Protection Act*, deprived FFA members of crucial information and input regarding the project, and reduced opportunities for members to observe, photograph, and enjoy bison in their natural habitat. The plaintiffs also claimed that the capture of the bison and their handling and destruction would be "less than humane." [21]

The defendants reported that the State of Montana would continue to eliminate the potential spread of brucellosis from Yellowstone National Park bison to Montana by capturing and sending to slaughter all bison that wander into Montana from the park. If the research were delayed beyond February, it would have to be postponed for at least a year with no guarantee that funding would be available later.

The court decided to support a preliminary injunction against the research project because of the apparent violation of the environmental law by a public agency, the questionable value of the research project, and the possibility for study of brucellosis in bison at a location closer to Yellowstone Park.

Hunting Grizzly Bear in Montana

On September 20, 1991, the Fund for Animals requested an injunction to stop officials in the Department of Interior who had authorized a sport hunt of the grizzly bear in parts of northwestern Montana. The plaintiffs contended that the regulation violated the *Endangered Species Act*. On September 27, the court granted a preliminary injunction as requested.[22]

Deer Hunting in Florida

On November 10, 1982, the Fund for Animals, Herbert Hoover Environmental Defense Fund, the Ad Hoc Committee to Save the Deer, and others sued the Florida Game and Fresh Water Fish Commission. They sought to prevent a deer hunt planned to take place in the South Florida Everglades.

The hunt had been proposed by the Florida authorities to eliminate what they perceived as serious overcrowding, which they predicted would result in starvation of the entire deer population and other problems. Since the proposed hunt was to be conducted by state officials on state-owned land, there was no federal involvement.

The court held that the defendant action did not violate the *National Environmental Policy Act*, the *Administrative Law and Procedure Act*, the *Endangered Species Act*, the *Migratory Bird Conservation Act*, the *Fish and Wildlife Coordination Act*, or the *Bald and Golden Eagle Protection Act*. So the plaintiffs were not entitled to an injunction to prevent the deer hunt.[23]

Killing Ravens to Save Desert Tortoises

In 1990, HSUS brought action against the secretary of the interior to stop the poisoning of Mojave Desert ravens as a method of protecting desert tortoises. The plaintiff secured a temporary restraining order, but before the hearing on the preliminary injunction, the parties settled the matter. The Department of the Interior decided to discontinue the poisoning program at the time but to continue it when needed under controlled conditions.

Under the *Equal Access to Justice Act*, HSUS asked for reimbursement of its attorneys' fees, costs, and expenses. The government claimed that irreparable harm to the desert tortoises would occur if poisoning were halted during rainy periods, when the tortoises surfaced. The tortoise population had been declining, and the government wanted to prevent every tortoise death that it could.

The court ruled that the government's position in the litigation was substantially justified and that there was no evidence of bad faith. So there would be no award of attorneys' fees. But the court did rule that the HSUS was justified in raising concerns about other desert wildlife and so was awarded its costs in the amount of $120 for its filing fee.[24]

Adopting Wild Horses

On July 8, 1987, the Animal Protection Institute of America and the Fund for Animals brought suit against the secretary of the interior and officials of the Bureau of Land Management. They wanted to stop the government from allowing adoption of wild horses and burros for commercial slaughter or other exploitation.

The government officials claimed that they had issued regulations permitting adoptions of such animals and that as long as the animals were humanely cared for for one year, the secretary had no authority or obligation in connection with the animals. The Bureau of Land Management policy had included inquiry into a prospective adopter's ability to provide humane care of otherwise unadoptable wild horses for one year before giving title.

The district court in Nevada held that where the secretary knew in advance of transfer of title of wild, free-roaming horses and burros and that the potential adopter intended to slaughter or exploit the animals, that such persons must be rejected and title transfer refused under the *Wild Free-Roaming Horses and Burros Act.*[25]

Importing Whales for Exhibition

Several animal protection organizations have worked to prevent importation of whales for aquariums and zoological parks. Two recent cases support the keeping of whales for public exhibition.

On April 28, 1989 the secretary of the interior issued a permit to the Shedd Aquarium for importation from Japan of six false killer whales for public display in Chicago. On July 31, 1992, the Animal Protection Institute of America, the International Wildlife Coalition, Midwest USA, Whale Protection Federation, Humane Society of the United States, Greenpeace USA, Cetacean Society International, Sea Shepherd Conservation Society, and the American Humane Association sought to stop the importing of false killer whales from Japan.

On November 29, 1991, the secretary authorized importation by Shedd Aquarium of four, yet-to-be-captured beluga whales from Canada also for display in Chicago. In this second case, the International Wildlife Coalition was joined by Animal Protection Institute of America, Greenpeace, American Humane Association, Humane Society of the United States, Fund for Animals, Sea Shepherd Conservation Society, and Whale and Dolphin Conservation Society in objecting to the Canadian importation.

In each case, the plaintiffs argued that the secretary of the interior had violated the *Marine Mammal Protection Act of 1972* in authorizing the importations. On June 12, 1992, the Supreme Court issued its decision in *Lujan v. Defenders of Wildlife*, holding that environmental groups did not have standing to challenge a rule promulgated by the secretary of the interior interpreting the *Endangered Species Act of 1973*. After determining that the whales to be imported were not a threatened or endangered species and that they would be moved in a humane manner, the court denied the petitions of the animal protection organizations and permitted the import of the whales from Japan and Canada to Shedd Aquarium in Chicago.[26]

Protecting Animals in Entertainment

Animal activists groups have attempted to stop what they see as animal abuse in the entertainment industry. Such suits can be costly and may do little to change the way that animals are treated.

On August 2, 1989, Bobby Berosini, a Las Vegas night club entertainer with an orangutans act, filed suit against two groups and several individuals for defamation; misappropriation of name, likeness, and character (in other words, fund-raising using Bobby Berosini's name); and invasion of privacy. The suit, filed at the Clark County,

Nevada, district court, named PETA, PAWS, and other individuals. Berosini claimed that PETA and others falsely accused him of abusing his orangutans and distributed an altered videotape, which supposedly proved the abuse. This case involved years of litigation and a heavy judgment against PETA, which was appealed to the Nevada Supreme Court and reversed (see appendix 7 for details).[27]

On March 11, 1994, the American Humane Association accepted $315,000 to end a libel suit filed in 1989 against game show host Bob Barker, Nancy Burnett of United Activists for Animal Rights, the City of Los Angeles, and former Los Angeles animal control director Robert Rush. Barker alleged that AHA Hollywood office director Betty Denny Smith ignored cruelty on the sets of two films, *The Tender* and *Project X*. Barker, Burnett, and Rush tried to remove the AHA from the oversight authority over the use of animals in films. AHA had held this authority since 1939 through a contract with the Screen Actors Guild. After Barker lost a motion for summary judgment against the AHA in 1993 and lost appeals at both the appellate and state supreme court, his insurer moved to settle, and the other parties agreed to the terms.[28]

Humane and Ritual Slaughter

In 1974, Helen E. Jones, designated as "next friend and guardian of all livestock animals now and hereafter awaiting slaughter in the United States," brought action against the secretary of agriculture. She challenged provisions of the *Humane Slaughter Act*, relating to ritual slaughter under the free-exercise and establishment clauses of the First Amendment. A three-judge district court agreed that the plaintiffs had standing to bring such action, but they ruled that ritual slaughter was not in violation of the free exercise clause and the plaintiff's motion was denied.[29]

In 1991 and 1992, kosher slaughter practices again came up for debate in court. A New Jersey kosher food company brought action, challenging New Jersey's kosher food regulations. Following dismissal in the superior court, the food company appealed. The appellate court ruled that the state regulations did not violate the establishment clause of the First Amendment. However, on further appeal, the New Jersey Supreme Court ruled that the regulations violated establishment clauses of the federal and state constitutions by imposing "substantive religious standards" for the kosher products industry and authorizing civil enforcement of those standards with the assistance of clergy. The supreme court majority determined that the kosher regulations fostered excessive entanglement because they "impose substantive religious standards" and authorized the State to monitor the adherence to those standards."[30]

Religious Rituals

The practice of animal sacrifice in the name of religion was involved in a suit by the City of Hialeah against the Church of the Lukumi Babalu Aye, brought to the federal district court in Florida. The court ruled that the City of Hialeah could prohibit the practice, the circuit court of appeals agreed. On June 11, 1993, the US Supreme Court reversed the appeals court decision. At stake was whether animal protective legislation could be nullified by supposedly religious practices abhorrent to a civilized society. This case involved the scope of free exercise of religion guaranteed in the First Amendment of the Constitution.

Justice Kennedy, in delivering the opinion of the Supreme Court, concluded that the laws in question were enacted contrary to free exercise principles. The Court viewed the city ordinance as specifically targeted against Santeria church members. Justice Blackmun noted the large number of animal rights organizations that filed amicus briefs in support of the City of Hialeah and stated that their interest demonstrated a concern that should not be treated lightly. Legal authorities on animal rights emphasized that the Supreme Court did not approve of animal sacrifice but held that these practices could not be prohibited by legislation that was specifically intended to target religious practices alone.[31]

These organizations in support of the City of Hialeah included the Washington Humane Society, PETA, New Jersey Animal Rights Alliance, Foundation for Animal Rights Advocacy, HSUS, AHA, ASPCA, ALDF, MSPCA, ISAR, Citizens for Animals, FARM, IDA, PAWS, Student Action Corps for Animals, Institute for Animal Rights Law, American Fund for Alternatives in Animal Research, Farm Sanctuary, Jews for Animal Rights, United Animal Nations, and United Poultry Concerns.[32]

Patents on Animals

From 1989 to 1991, animal rights and animal welfare groups joined with some farm groups to challenge the commissioner of the US Patent and Trademark Office and the secretary of commerce. They disagreed with the patent office rule to allow patenting of "nonnaturally occurring, nonhuman multicellular organisms including animals."[33] The suit was filed by ALDF, ASPCA, the Marin Humane Society, Wisconsin Family Farm Defense Fund, HFA, AVAR, PETA, and other individuals.

On March 29, 1989, the federal district court ruled that the Patent Office had made an "interpretative rule" that was exempt from public notice and comment requirements of the *Administrative Law and Procedure Act* and that the patent office did not exceed its authority to make that rule.

On March 15, 1990, the same group of organizations submitted arguments before the US Court of Appeals, seeking to invalidate the rule issued by the commissioner of the US Patent and Trademark Office. The appeals court judge ruled that the case arose under patent law and that the federal circuit court had exclusive jurisdiction over any appeal. So the case was transferred.[34]

On April 30, 1991, the federal circuit court judge ruled that (1) the rule was an "interpretative rule" exempt from the notice and comment requirements of the

Administrative Law and Procedure Act; and (2) the farmers, husbandry groups, and organizations did not have standing to seek a declaration that animals are not patentable subject matter nor to seek an injunction against the issuance of animal patents.[35]

Although the court has supported the patent office on this issue, many still question its authority to enact a rule with such complex and far-reaching consequences. The decision to allow patents for the products of biotechnology is fraught with unfathomable complexities.[36] Thus, as the consequences of new biotechnical research become more evident, this issue can be expected to show up in future court cases.

Can Animal Advocates Win in Court?

The cases reported here are only part of the litigation that animal activist groups have undertaken on behalf of animals. Some key legal issues will determine if animal advocates can succeed in their litigation efforts.

Getting standing to bring suit is the first step necessary. If the judge grants standing, then the case can be heard. Many times the animal activist groups as plaintiffs were not given standing, and their cases were dismissed or rulings were made in favor of the defendants.

One of the problems in gaining standing is to justify or prove that the members represented by an animal plaintiff group have suffered some injury or loss personally. This obstacle is often difficult to overcome since the animals are usually owned by private individuals or institutions. Where certain government actions interfered with the activities or programs of an organization, the court would recognize that the organization had standing to undertake legal action.

Conflicts have developed between state and federal government agencies involving animal treatment. The conflict arises between federal laws dealing with endangered species and state laws authorizing state agencies to control animal predators or maintain wild animal populations to match the available food supplies through selective hunting policies.

Although federal law provides for review committees to monitor humane treatment of animals used in research, questions often remain as to what is useful research and what is cruel and inhumane treatment of animals. The Berosini orangutans case in the Nevada courts indicates that dedicated efforts and sufficient funding can give animals used in entertainment a hearing in the courts.

Changing human values toward animals and the continuing public support of animal protection groups could bring about change in laws and court decisions in the future. David Favre and Murray Loring suggest that the animal rights movement has a substantial task to establish that animals, as living beings, have a right to access the judicial system. The arguments to support such a goal are based upon a mixture of moral and ethical beliefs, as well as scientific information.[37]

15

Financing Animal Rights
and Animal Welfare Activities

Animal protection has become an industry financed by donations and bequests from a generous society. Incomes and assets of animal rights and animal welfare organizations vary widely, and financial security is not guaranteed. Some groups thrive while others struggle as they lose support. Emotional appeals for contributions to help stop mistreatment of animals flood the mails continuously. Scattered reports suggest that some funds may be used for purposes that the donors did not suspect.

W hether identified as animal welfare, animal rights, animal liberation, or animal protection, activism to improve the conditions by which animals are raised, cared for, used by humans, or protected in the wild has evolved into a substantial charitable industry. In 1989, the budgets of major national and regional organizations totaled an estimated $107 million and asset holdings, $232 million. When including all state and local animal and habitat protection groups, the estimate for public contributions totaled $3.12 billion for 1992.[1]

Organization Leadership

The accomplishments and success of an animal protection organization depends upon the dedication and capability of its leaders as well as its financial strength. Animal welfare and animal rights leaders fall into one or more of these categories:

1. Those who have independent wealth or other sources of income and choose to devote part of their time to promote animal protection and humane treatment without additional salary. Some leaders that fit this group include Cleveland Amory, president, FFA; Shirley McGreal, president, International Primate Protection League; and Christine Stevens, president, AWI. Ingrid Newkirk, vice president and cofounder of PETA draws no salary, but the extent of her wealth or other sources of income are uncertain. She should also be classified in the third group.

2. Those professionals employed to manage and direct the organization and the policies established by a board of directors and who receive substantial salaries

comparable to other organization executives. Leaders that best portray this category include John Stevenson, president of the North Shore Animal League; John Hoyt, chief executive officer, and Paul Irwin, president, HSUS; Brian Davies, International Fund for Animal Welfare; and Gus Thornton, president, MSPCA. The reported individual salaries of these professionals each exceeded $150,000 in 1994.[2]

3. Those dedicated persons who probably have little if any personal wealth but have strong feelings and desire to help animals, work hard at modest salaries to further their beliefs in animal causes, attract support from others, live modestly, and attract volunteers to help carry out part of their programs. Persons in this group would include Kim Bartlett, publisher, and Merritt Clifton, editor, of *Animal People*; Robin Duxbury, president of ARM!; Lori Bauston, president, and Gene Bauston, vice president, of Farm Sanctuary; Alex Pacheco, president of PETA; Jeanne Roush, former executive director, PETA; Kim Stallwood, editor, *Animals' Agenda*; Bradley Miller, president and codirector, and Bonnie Miller, codirector, HFA; and Henry Spira, president, ARI.

Legal Status

The organizations discussed in this chapter operate under Section 501 (c)(3) of the *Internal Revenue Code*, which gives them tax-exempt status. Most contributions are tax exempt and the organization does not have to pay federal income taxes on net income. They must file an annual IRS Form 990 for tax-exempt organizations.

DDAL devotes a major part of its program to lobbying for specific legislation to help animals. The league specifically points out to contributors that contributions are not tax deductible.

Since each charitable organization must file an annual report with the Internal Revenue Service, and with some state agencies overseeing charitable fund solicitation, the income and expenditures of these organizations are usually available for public inspection. The financial statements show the income and expenses in various categories. But in the day-to-day operations, alarming reports suggest that some organization leaders have spent money in ways that are not entirely within the scope for which the money was donated.

Fund-Raising and Financial Management

The major sources of funds are program services, dues, public contributions, bequests, grants from foundations or government agencies, investment income, sales of merchandise, gifts and loans from other animal protection groups, and rental of mailing lists.

Program Services

Earnings from direct services characterize thousands of local humane societies, which operate animal shelters, arrange adoptions of companion animals, conduct spay and neuter clinics, and provide visible help for animals in distress. However, most national animal rights and animal welfare organizations are not affiliated with these local humane societies, and only a few operate animal shelters or serve animals directly.

In 1995, ASPCA reported $2.6 million from animal hospitals and adoption program fees, about 15 percent of its total support and revenue. However, how much of this income from animal programs will be reduced after 1994 is uncertain as the ASPCA phases out its animal control contract with New York City.

MSPCA received $16.5 million in 1995 for health and hospital services and for farm and cemetery income. The American Humane Association received over $1,070,222 for program services in fiscal year 1995 in addition to its public contributions from membership and other donations. Friends of Animals reported payments from pet owners for spay/alter services of $2.3 million, about half of its total 1995 fiscal year income.

In its early years, the Food Animal Concerns Trust, a much smaller organization, received about half of its income from its egg and veal education programs, until it set up Nest Eggs in 1989 as a wholly owned subsidiary. Its major source of funding now comes from donations.

Membership Dues and Donations

Membership dues and contributions are a very significant source of income for most animal activist organizations. Although membership dues may be solicited annually, many organizations also make special appeals during the year to bring in additional contributions. For some organizations, all contributors are considered as members. Membership dues, donations, and contributions are often reported together. Total revenues, fund balances, and assets of selected national organizations are shown in table 3. The significance of contributions as a part of an organization's total revenue is illustrated in table 4.

The Humane Society of the United States leads all organizations in its contributions and dues received, with $24.7 million in 1995, comprising 65 percent of its total revenue. The organizations receiving the next highest income from contributions and dues were ASPCA, PETA, and MSPCA. However, because of its large animal program services, MSPCA received only 30 percent of its total revenue and support from dues and contributions.

Bequests, Grants, Special Gifts

The animal protection industry has built up substantial assets by securing bequests from supporting and sympathetic donors. Bequests, grants, and special gifts can make the big difference for an organization's program and financial stability. These are illustrated for selected organizations in table 5.

In 1995, HSUS reported $9.4 million in bequests, 25 percent of its total revenues.

Table 3. Revenues, Fund Balances, and Assets of Major Animal Rights/Welfare Organizations

Organization (Year)	Total Support & Revenues $(000)	Fund Balance $(000)	Total Assets $(000)
HSUS (1995)	38,102	11,823[a]	47,616
MSPCA (1995)	21,390	36,092	74,681
ASPCA (1995)	13,370	36,371	38,714
PETA (1995)	10,742	906	7,691
Intl. Fund Animal Welfare (1995)	7,657	2,009	2,919
NHES (1995)	7,240	779	1,722
AHA (1995)	6,190	2,499	3,586
FFA (1995)	5,154	12,016[b]	13,152
FOA (1995)	4,667	2,436	3,063
NAVS (1995)	2,092	4,350	356
ALDF (1995)	1,819	656	677
DDAL (1994)	1,814	459	542
IDA (1995)	1,443	374	440
PCRM (1995)	1,377	20	188
AAVS (1995)	1,308	8,017	8,055
HFA (1995)	1,111	1,270	1,452
NEAVS (1995)	1,198[c]	5,004	5,559
Farm Sanctuary (1995)	931	227	1,173
AWI (1995)	639	566	566
FACT (1995)	491	1,511	1,516
United Animal Nations (1995)	428	44	58
Intl. Primate Protection (1995)	396	468	471
ISAR (1994)	375	434	486
FARM (1995)	200	75	83
Veterinarians for Animal Rights (1994)	110	115	117
PsyETA (1995)	62	3	3
UPC (1995)	44	44	?
ARM! (1995)	29	6	6
Vegan Outreach (1995)	24	8	?

Sources: Foundation for Biomedical Research, *Directory of Animal Rights/Welfare Organizations, 1994*; US House of Representatives, Committee on Agriculture, Subcommittee on Department Operations, Research, and Foreign Agriculture, *Review of U.S. Department of Agriculture's Enforcement of the* Animal Welfare Act, *Specifically of Animals Used in Exhibitions, July 8, 1992; Animal People,* December 1996; author's mail survey of individual organizations; and annual financial reports of individual organizations.

Note: Total revenues include amounts received from contributions, grants, bequests, program services, and interest on investments. Fund balance is the amount of cash, cash equivalents, and liquid assets after fixed assets, liabilities, and expenses are deducted and will usually be less than total assets. Assets usually take into account the amount of the organization's liabilities and may also include property held in trust.

[a] Includes general and designated funds but does not include $24 million held in investments.

[b] Includes $9.9 million in marketable securities, $1.8 million in cash or equivalents.

[c] Amount budgeted. Actual revenues not reported.

Table 4. Public Support Received by Selected Organizations in Relation to Total Revenues

Organization (Year)	Dues & Contributions (including bequests) $ (000)	% of Total Revenues
HSUS (1995)	24,710	65
ASPCA (1995)	12,907	74
PETA (1995)	10,825	92
MSPCA/AHES (1995)	6,348	30
Intl. Fund for Animal Welfare (1995)	4,859	63
FFA (1995)	3,646	71
NHES (1995)	3,369	47
AHA (1995)	2,367	58
FOA (1995)	2,138	46
DDAL (1994)	1,743	90
ALDF (1995)	1,726	94
NAVS (1994)	1,542	73
IDA (1995)	1,341	89
Animal Protection Inst. (1995)	1,315	97
PCRM (1994)	1,165	97
HFA (1993)	1,070	95
NEAVS (1993)	1,032	77
Farm Sanctuary (1995)	811	97
AWI (1995)	578	95
AAVS (1995)	547	42
United Animal Nations (1995)	377	90
FACT (1994)	417	85
ISAR (1994)	293	78
Animal Rights Network (1994)	241	80
Intl. Primate Protection League (1995)	396	75
FARM (1995)	198	100
United Action for Animals (1993)	193	99
AVAR (1994)	110	93
ARM! (1994)	29	100
UPC (1995)	83	99
SUPPRESS (1995)	77	64
Vegan Outreach (1995)[a]	10	40

Sources: Organization annual reports; New York State Department of State, Charitable Division; Illinois Attorney General, Division of Charitable Trusts; *Animal People*, IRS Form 990 as filed by that organization.
[a] July 1, 1995 – May 28, 1996

Table 5. Bequests of Selected Animal Organizations

Organization (Year)	Bequests $ (000)
HSUS (1995)	9,377
MSPCA (1994)	5,538[a]
ASPCA (1994)	2,666
FFA (1995)	1,789
PETA (1995)	1,636
FOA (1995)	1,378
NAVS (1995)	1,220
NEAVS (1993)	940
AHA (1995)	922
API (1995)	536
Intl. Fund for Animal Welfare (1995)	518
AAVS (1995)	476
NHES (1995)	237
ALDF (1995)	223
ISAR (1994)	190
FACT (1995)	129
DDAL (1994)	106
Farm Sanctuary (1995)	60
PCRM (1995)	40
AWI (1995)	33
United Animal Nations (1995)	6

Sources: Organization financial statements supplied by the organization; the New York Department of State, Department of Charitable Trusts; and State of Illinois Attorney General's Office, Charitable Trust Division.
[a] Includes MSPCA and AHES.

If bequests exceed $50,000, HSUS places part into the general fund and the remainder in its designated fund for use over five years. Fund for Animals received $1.79 million in bequests, comprising 35 percent of its total public support. PETA received $1.6 million from bequests, 14 percent of its revenues.

Investment Income

Those organizations with the most assets will usually have the largest investment incomes. Investment income is a substantial part of annual revenue for some organizations and a very small part for others. HSUS, MSPCA, and ASPCA earned more than $1 million per year in 1994 or 1995, contributing significantly to their other revenues (see table 6).

Table 6. Investment Income of Selected Animal Rights and Welfare Organizations

Organization (Year)	$ Amount (000)
HSUS (1995)	3,275
MSPCA (1994)	2,121
ASPCA (1994)	1,100
FFA (1995)	605
PETA (1995)	278
FOA (1995)	137
United Animal Nations (1995)	383
AHA (1995)	122
NHES (1995)	117
NAVS (1995)	63[a]
AWI (1995)	41
ISAR (1994)	15
IDA (1995)	11
Farm Sanctuary (1995)	8
ALDF (1995)	6
Intl. Primate Protection League (1994)	4
Intl. Fund for Animal Welfare (1995)	3

Sources: Data from annual financial reports of individual organizations.
[a] NAVS also reported $454,888 gain from sale of securities.

Merchandise Sales

Many animal protection organizations sell merchandise—calendars, T-shirts, mugs, bumper stickers, photos, posters, banners, and many other items. These items provide additional net revenue as well as advertising and promotion for animal protection groups.

PETA's merchandise far outsells other organizations. Cruelty-free merchandise sales totaled $600,774 in 1993, $851,000 in 1994, and $510,374 in 1995. After deducting catalog expenses, HSUS reported literature and other materials sales of $606,824 in 1993, $1.037 million in 1994, and $740,000 in 1995.

Smaller organizations also get income from merchandise and literature sales. However, in most cases they total less than $15,000 a year.

Mailing list rentals are also a source of income. In 1995, PETA collected $85,000 and PCRM, $14,000 from mailing-list rentals. Animal Legal Defense Fund received $45,671 for sale of its mailing list in 1994 and $67,293 in 1995. In 1994, Doris Day Animal League collected $38,000 from its mailing-list rentals.

An organization may also receive financial support from other animal protection groups. Assistance is also given through networking support—speaking on programs, serving on boards of directors, giving recommendations, working together on jointly sponsored projects.

In August 1990, PETA faced a $1.5 million judgment in a district court in Las Vegas, Nevada, alleging defamation of a man accused of striking animals in a Las Vegas casino. The organization filed an appeal of the verdict in the Nevada Supreme Court and restricted a portion of its net assets for this contingency. In October, the district court ordered the judgment be stayed on condition that PETA post a bond of $800,000, which it did. In 1993, PETA had outstanding a $300,000 note payable to a related animal rights organization and also executed a contingent note payable for $500,000. The contingent note payable was to take effect if the letter of credit was called. The related organization filed a security interest for $800,000 against the assets of PETA.

In January 1994, the Nevada Supreme Court reversed the judgment against PETA in its entirety. In May 1995, the Nevada Supreme Court entered its final order upholding the reversal and dismissing the plaintiff's case.[3]

HSUS reported $199,855 in 1995 and 247,785 in 1994 for "gifts and grants to other humane organizations." FFA allocated $139,960 for "gifts and services to allied organizations" in 1995.[4]

Expenditures: Program, Overhead, and Fund-Raising

The boards and management of animal protection groups must allocate their available funds to provide program support, pay their staffs and officers, and allocate enough for fund-raising to keep a viable organization.

Direct-mail campaigns are the most frequently used method to raise money. The costs of fund-raising are usually identified in the organization reports. But accounting methods will vary. Some include mailing costs along with other overhead costs. Some allocate part of the mailing of fund-raising literature as part of their educational program since the campaign letters also deal with animal rights and animal welfare concerns.

The National Charities Information Bureau (NCIB) requires approved charities spend at least 60 percent of their budgets on programs, not including direct mail associated with fund-raising. This standard is stricter and more indicative an organization's priorities than the IRS rules, which allow charities to write off some direct-mail costs as program service under the heading of public education. So the figures that organizations declare and the figures as amended in accordance with NCIB rules guidelines are often very different.[5]

According to *Animal People*'s six years of monitoring, DDAL has spent not less than 68 percent, and some years up to 98 percent, of its annual budget for direct-mail fund-raising and executive salaries.[6] On December 3, 1991, the bureau listed FOA, NAVS, and PETA because they failed to meet one or more standards set by NCIB, including spending at least 60 percent of annual expenses for program activities; accurate disclosure; no high pressure tactics; and proper use of funds.[7]

The FOA and PETA were cited because Priscilla Feral of FOA and Alex Pacheco of PETA are salaried employees and also chair their boards of directors. NAVS was listed because it paid honoraria to board members for attendance at board meetings. The total reported for the 1991–1992 fiscal year was $16,290.[8] *Animals' Agenda*, after private investigations among present and former staff members, reported that NAVS was functioning mainly "as a private charity for family and friends of executive director Mary Margaret Cunniff."[9] The 1995 audited report showed that PETA spent $1.98 million for membership development, 15 percent of total expenditures.[10]

Andrew Rowan, a close observer of animal protection groups, does not fully agree with accounting practices used. He called attributing a portion of direct-mail pieces to public education "outrageous." He refers to the content of the direct-mail pieces as "pabulum and self-congratulatory copy" and does not believe they can be described as education. He feels that organizations could do a better job using their direct mail to educate rather than to raise funds and should report how the funds raised have been used.[11]

Overhead costs will vary with the nature of an organization's program and activities. Some organizations with shelters and sanctuaries have high overhead costs because of their labor-intensive programs. They may also rely on volunteer labor and donated supplies that do not show up in cash accounting.[12]

The major program expenses will vary with the organization's program emphasis. In 1995, PETA reported $2.7 million for research and investigations and $3.6 million for public outreach and education and 4.1 million for "international grassroots campaigns."[13]

In 1995, ASPCA spent $3.9 million operating animal hospitals and spay/neuter clinics and $1.5 million for animal placement. Law enforcement work took $1.2 million and national humane education and publications, $4.8 million.

In 1995, HSUS spent $9.99 million for public education, membership information, and publications. They spent $2.5 million for cruelty investigations and regional office operation. Wildlife animal habitat and sheltering required $2.6 million from their budget.

Legislation, Litigation, and Legal Fees

In 1995, HSUS reported $1.3 million spent for legal assistance, legislation, and government relations. PETA reported $1.1 million for professional services and consultants. ASPCA spent $737,000 for legislation and humane advocacy and $1.2 million for humane law enforcement and litigation in 1995.

The Doris Day Animal League 1994 report showed program services of $1 million, of which $333,000 was spent for public advocacy (usually referred to as lobbying) and

$665,000 for public education, some of which was probably spent for direct mailings that included requests for contributions.[14] DDAL actually reported $404,000 for fund-raising.

Animal Legal Defense Fund spent $571,698 for legal services in 1995 for lawsuits to protect animals and to provide legal information, advice, and assistance to members and the public.[15] In contrast, Fund for Animals reported $58,000 for legislative activities in 1995 but spent $1.7 million for animal rescue and protection and $799,000 for humane education.[16]

Staff Salaries

Personnel can be a major part of the costs of many organizations. The salaries paid to top executives vary with the size of the organization, its ability to pay, and internal policies. Compared with private-sector corporate executives, many animal protection group employees' salaries are relatively low. The average 1993 salary of all paid US charity chief executives was $111,000 with budgets of $10 to $25 million and $93,800 for those with budgets of $1 to 10 million, compared to $52,000 for animal shelter executive directors.[17]

Opposition Salaries

In all fairness, the salaries of the highest paid animal protection executives appeared to be in the same range as those paid chief executives of organizations that often oppose animal rights policies and activities. However, many animal activist staff members receive far less than the salaries of the highest paid executives. A 1991 survey of twenty-two farm commodity checkoff boards and farm, commodity, and agribusiness organizations showed the average salary of top executives was $93,094 with salaries in the middle 50 percent from $62,500 to $105,000.[18]

Fund-Raising Strategies

Most national animal activist organizations use direct-mail solicitations to raise money. A person who has joined or contributed to one of these organizations will probably receive several letters each year asking for contributions. Also, donors may be included on a mailing list of charity contributors or animal sympathizers and receive solicitation letters from several organizations.

The letters frequently include one or more of these emotional themes: animals mistreated and suffering from laboratory research or product testing; inhumane factory farming methods, especially veal production; animals crowded into trucks being injured, disabled, and abandoned; the horrors of puppy mills; abandoned pets that must be euthanized; unnecessary cruelty of commercial fur production; the need to boycott companies that use animal testing; or the opportunity to save wild animals and exotic birds. Names of prominent entertainers may be listed to endorse the appeals. Surveys, free address labels, calendars, bumper stickers, or other merchandise are often included to encourage responses.

One of the newest appeals for funds links violence toward animals with violence toward human beings. Following a major feature in the March/April 1994 issue of *Animals' Agenda*, PETA sent out a fund-raising appeal to support its educational program "to give educators the tools they need to teach respect for animals—and putting children on the road to developing into responsible, caring, compassionate adults." [19] Some letters appeal to diet-conscious persons and the opportunities to improve health by use of a vegetarian lifestyle.

Most appeals for funds focus on animal rights, animal welfare, and related issues. As Ann Charlton points out, "Most of the large (and rich) national groups quite intentionally avoid speaking about other social issues lest they offend their conservative donors." [20]

Instability and Risks of Public Support

Depending upon public donations to operate any organization can carry risk and uncertainty. What happens when mail campaign appeals do not bring in the needed funds? In the 1990s, DDAL, ARM!, AAVS, FARM, FOA, HFA, ISAR, NEAVS, and NAVS experienced sharp fluctuations in year-to-year contributions.

Yet some organizations continued to draw increased public support. Although smaller than some groups, Farm Sanctuary attracted 94 percent more support in 1991 than in the previous year and, in 1992, 14 percent more than in 1991. HSUS, AHA, PCRM, IDA, and ASPCA drew increased contributions and bequests during the early 1990s.

Why do some organizations lose public support while others gain it? The recession and general economic conditions might suggest that discretionary money that came to some groups in earlier years has disappeared. But why did some groups gain while others lost? Have the same mailing lists been "milked" by the same organizations too often? Do the successful appeals of past years no longer apply?

While there may be no definite answers to these questions, one conclusion seems certain: Public support for all animal protection organizations is no sure pot of gold.

Making a Donation?

"What You Should Know Before You Give," an article that appeared in the December 1995 issue of *Animal People*, made the following recommendations for giving to animal welfare organizations: People wishing to contribute to an animal protection organization outside their local communities should first find out something about the programs and financial structure of that group. Although animal protection is one of the smallest and least-lucrative branches of charity, probably raising less than 1.1 percent of all charitable contributions, one report estimates that more than ten thousand organizations, ranging from multinational advocacy groups with corporate-sized budgets to local cat-rescue societies, are seeking donations.[21] Whether to contribute to an animal protection organization is a personal decision that each individual must make. National Charities Information Bureau exists to help people make informed decisions about contributing to charitable causes.

A *Wall Street Journal* report points out that even though charities are required to make financial statements available, people who go to the trouble of requesting them do not always get the whole truth. According to the *Journal*, that is because under accepted accounting procedures, charities can call a substantial part of their direct-mail costs "public education," because their pleas for money are wrapped in statements to raise public awareness of a problem.[22]

So those considering a donation will want to ask what their money is used for. How much goes into program? How much is spent for fund-raising? How much salary do the executives receive? Are the programs and activities those that the individual wants to support? Donations to most animal protection groups are usually tax-deductible, and the solicitation letters will usually say so.

How the Money Is Used

The money contributed to the regional and national animal rights and welfare groups is used for much different purposes than a local humane society. In most cases, a local humane society that cares for homeless dogs, cats, and other companion animals is not connected with the national groups. Only a few of the national groups that advertise about animal mistreatment spend any donations for direct animal care.

The animal protection organizations operate with money raised mainly by direct-mail solicitation and bequests, special gifts, interest and investment income, merchandise sales, and fees paid for services rendered. Their revenue is spent for investigations of animal abuse; legal fees; publicity of what they perceive as abuses of animals by individuals, research laboratories, animal owners engaged in recreational and leisure-time activities, and food animal producers. Revenue is also spent to generate mailings to raise more funds. Organization leaders travel widely to lecture, participate in conferences, network with other animal activists, and further their organization objectives.

Although most leaders in these groups are dedicated and honestly pursue their organizations' missions, some abuses have been reported, just as individuals in private and business may stray from honest and ethical conduct.[23] Editors of *Animal People* have monitored fund-raising and spending patterns of the major national animal protection groups for several years. They believe that some contributions for animal advocacy are wasted, and they suggest that those who donate should investigate how their money is used.

16

Resolving Conflict: Hopes or Dreams?

How animals are treated and used in the future will depend on public attitudes and changing ethical and social values. If the European experience provides any guide, owners and users of animals can expect that step by step, changing values will influence animal production, marketing, processing, research, and entertainment practices.

Assessment for the Future

L ooking at the entire scope of human-animal relationships, one may wonder if there is any way to resolve the conflicts of philosophies, values, traditions, and economic interests between animal rights activists and animal owners, scientists, and practitioners. Bernard Rollin suggests that more public dialogue must be sought between animal activists and those who use animals. He believes such open dialogue could lead to the discovery of common ground where none was suspected. For example, he believes that there is plenty of room between keeping the status quo and abolishing research altogether.[1]

Public Attitudes Support Human Rights

The general public has mixed reactions to animal rights. A *Parents Magazine* survey published in 1989 revealed that a surprising 80 percent of its mainstream, middle-class readership believes that animals have rights—though 85 percent also believed that it was morally permissible to use animals for human benefit. Similar results were obtained when veterinary students were surveyed. Therefore, at a minimum, 70 percent of those polled agree that animals have rights but that it is still okay for humans to kill and eat animals.[2]

A 1990 survey conducted by Opinion Dynamics showed that 76 percent believed that farmers treat their animals humanely and only 9 percent believed they did not. A majority (58 percent) believed that farm practices such as trimming the beaks of chickens, the horns of cattle, and the tails of pigs did not hurt the animals and that such procedures are done for the animals' safety. About 20 percent believed these practices are cruel and done just to make money for farmers.

A substantial majority (84 percent) agreed that consumers have a right to choose what they eat and that a small minority of activists should not dictate consumer choices. Celebrities influence public attitudes only marginally on both sides of the farm animal and meat issues.[3]

The Animal Rights Ideology

The philosophical writings that have formed the ideologies of the modern animal rights movement do not completely agree or form a single doctrine for animal rights activists. However, some major principles identify areas of controversy that will make compromise or reaching common ground most difficult:

- Animals are sentient beings that have feelings of pain, fear, enjoyment, and boredom, and animals can suffer from mistreatment.
- Animals have a moral right not to be killed or used for any purpose by humans.
- If humans really respect animals, they will not eat them but instead will follow a vegetarian diet.
- Animals should not be raised and slaughtered for their fur.
- Wild animals should not be captured and impounded in zoos or aquariums or nor should they be taken to wildlife parks where they will be hunted.
- Animals should not be used in experiments for testing products.
- Intensive production of livestock and poultry, labeled factory farming by activists, is cruel, causes great suffering, and is the most widespread abuse of animals in America in the 1990s.
- Students should have the right to refuse dissection as part of their biology courses, if they choose to do so.

From Ethical and Social Values to Changing Policies

Animal welfare activists have worked to change public policies and practices that they believe cause pain and suffering for animals produced for food or used for research, entertainment, or leisure activities. As reformists, they have achieved some successes.

Animal rights activists face important decisions as to whether they will work exclusively to put an end to the institutions that they believe exploit animals or whether they will focus their energy to reform the existing structures involved with the use of animals. Tom Regan and Gary Francione believe that the reformist approach only perpetuates what they see as conditions of exploitation. Others, working to improve how animals are treated, see the possibility or the necessity of achieving their ultimate goals by working for improvements in the conditions of laboratory animals, more humane slaughter methods, and humane transport laws. FARM, for instance, works for both abolition and reform.[4]

Although animal rights organizations can cite accomplishments, they face some crucial challenges: How can they measure genuine progress toward their goals of animal rights? What form of activism on behalf of animals should they take? Which forms of animal "exploitation" should be emphasized by activists trying to achieve change?[5]

The welfarists, working for humane reform, may resent the so-called fundamentalism of animal rights groups, who are viewed as sacrificing attainable welfare goals for the sake of hypothetical abolitionist goals later.[6] But the animal rights activists see reformist efforts as measures that will exploit some animals today for the possibility of saving some from being exploited in the future.

Animal rights leaders point out some of the reasons why the movement may not be doing so well: There is lack of understanding of ideology; some activists are committed to other social justice movements; some reject speciesism and refuse to recognize that biological differences do not justify moral differences.[7]

Protecting and Defending Animal Industries

Animal activism has influenced animal industry leaders, scientists, and educators to encourage animal owners and users to care for and handle animals more humanely and under more stress-free conditions than in the past. However, animal owners and users are resisting encroachment of activism that would restrict or destroy the industries and institutions that thrive on the traditional uses of animals. These defensive countermeasures include educational programs; advertisements; educational materials for schools and civic and community organizations; tours; orientation of producers and users of animals on how to deal with public demonstrators; and promotion of the accomplishments of scientific research and product testing.

Animal industry's strong public support from customers, close ties through trade associations and government agencies, and continuous rapport with legislators and members of Congress provide major advantages over new, and often tagged "radical," organizations with philosophies that would allegedly disrupt the economic base and living standards of many communities across the country.

Power clusters within the food animal and agriculture industries and the biomedical research and medical communities, along with sportsmen, hunters, trappers, and other animal users all provide established public support and facilitate legislative action to maintain and protect the use of animals for food, research, sport, and entertainment.

Consequently, how animals are treated and used in the future will depend on public attitudes and changing ethical and social values. If a majority of citizens accept these changing attitudes and values, they can influence change in public policies and government regulation. The crucial question is, will owners and users of animals sense greater personal responsibilities for humane care and treatment that move their actions closer to the positions of the reformist animal welfare philosophies? Or will the abolitionist philosophies of the animal rights groups gain control and achieve legislation that mandates strict controls?

The ethical dimension of animal care and use has become established in some European countries. If the European experience provides any guide to the future in the United States, then owners and users of animals can expect that step by step, ethical values will influence change in animal production, marketing, processing, research, and entertainment practices.

As more Americans want assurance that animals are raised and handled under humane conditions and in a stress-free environment, the pressure for more regulation and public policies will persist. Animal activists will continue surveillance of and publicize farm production practices, treatment of animals in research laboratories, handling of animals in entertainment and leisure pursuits, and conservation and preservation of wild animals.

Those who want to change public policies through federal legislation face some major obstacles. In the 1990s, the overriding public issues drawing policymakers' attentions have been reducing annual deficits and moving toward a balanced budget, achieving national health care, fighting the drug traffic, and reorienting foreign policy with the revolutionary political changes in the former Soviet Union, in China, in Eastern Europe, and in the Middle East. The time and efforts of the federal executive and legislative branches will be so occupied with these issues that moving animal rights issues to the forefront for new legislative action will be a formidable task.

Success for Animal Activists

Animal rights leaders can cite their successes. The *Humane Slaughter Act of 1958*, the *Animal Welfare Acts* (1966, 1970, and 1976), the *Health Research Extension Act*, the 1985 *Improved Standards for Laboratory Animals Act*, and the *Endangered Species Act* all aimed to insure more humane treatment of animals and initiate reforms rather than abolish any current uses of animals. However, bills to regulate veal production and establish standards for farm animal management practices have been introduced in Congress, but no action had been taken by 1997.

In 1976, activist Henry Spira rallied public support against the American Museum of Natural History in New York because of its cat experiments.[8] In response, the National Institutes of Health cut off funding for the research. His campaign for alternatives to use of animals in testing cosmetics led to changes in policies at Revlon. Since then, Revlon and Avon have funded research projects to find alternatives to animal testing. Another activists' success came when a sit-in at the National Institutes of Health led to the cut off of funding for the University of Pennsylvania Head Injury Laboratory.[9]

Animal activists' exposure of downed animals arriving at the St. Paul stockyards in 1991 led to legislative proposals, rules, and regulations to prohibit acceptance of injured animals at some public stockyards. However, Humane Farming Association and some other animal activists were not pleased with the California law that permits slaughter of disabled animals.

On other fronts, the campaign against use of animals in crash tests forced General Motors to change their policy in 1993. In addition, fur sales have declined, perhaps partly because of fashion choices or cost, and partly because of changing ethical values and animal activists campaigns against fur. Some fur stores have closed.

In February 1994, McDonald's, the world's biggest beef buyer, pledged to issue a statement of humane principles to all the meat and poultry suppliers for its restaurants in the United States. The agreement to ratify and distribute the statement came in exchange for the withdrawal of a stronger and more specific statement advanced as a shareholder resolution by Henry Spira of Animal Rights International.[10]

So the question is, not if, but when further efforts will be made to regulate, restrict or force voluntary changes in animal care and use. Finding a common ground on all issues that will satisfy animal rights and animal welfare organizations and be acceptable to animal owners and users will probably not be possible.

Animal Rights Groups Take Strong Stand

The positions of many animal rights organizations leave little room for compromise with the community of animal owners and users. The viewpoint that animals are not to be used for any human purpose is a call for eventual elimination of animal production and use for food and clothing, research, and entertainment or leisure purposes.

However, Andrew Rowan believes that some in the animal liberation movement are willing to compromise and to indulge in horse trading, while others hold on to their positions with almost religious fervor and refuse vehemently to consider the possibilities of compromise.[11]

When Peter Singer suggested "an ethical, not an exploitative, relationship with other species" as a long-term goal, he also recommended being practical and flexible. The first step to progress is to reduce the "suffering the animals are now undergoing."[12]

Singer's view of flexibility is to divide the movement into short-term goals to stop "some of the suffering now" and long-term goal of "animal liberation."[13] His statement reveals that he is not an ardent animal rights advocate, rather a more moderate reformist concerned with animal suffering, who is willing to suggest reformist actions that reduce present animal discomfort. He suggests that by reducing animal discomfort now that animal use might be phased out in the future. But animal rights advocates do not believe this will happen and do not want a compromise that may maintain animal suffering.

Henry Spira, a pragmatic, yet willing arbitrator of animal rights issues, believes that problems are not resolved without dialogue and patience. By showing his willingness to work with large-animal owners, Spira moves out of the abolitionist animal rights camp and into the reformist group. Other animal rights advocates do not approve of his compromising strategies and tactics.

James Jasper and Dorothy Nelkin observe that animal rights fundamentalists share a reluctance to moderate their demands or actions because they are convinced that they are morally correct and it appears immoral to accept partial solutions.[14] This observation is confirmed by Tom Regan's declaration, "We will not be satisfied until every animal who suffers at the hands of human exploiters is set free!" [15] But those advocates who take a realistic view are willing to accept incremental changes that are abolitionist in nature, such as when some practice is stopped. Larry Horton describes the strategy: "Most sophisticated activists are quite satisfied to take one step at a time while keeping their ultimate objective firmly in mind." [16]

Regan and Francione point out that it is perfectly consistent with the philosophy of animal rights to take a gradual approach to end animal exploitation as long as the steps that need to be taken are abolitionist in nature. They view such steps as ending the Draize, LD-50, and other toxicity and irritancy tests, the use of animals in product testing, and the use of maternal deprivation, military, and drug addiction experiments as abolitionist steps in the animal rights movement. They also view bans on commercial whaling and trade in fur, along with an end to the killing of elephants, rhinos, and other big wild game as abolitionist steps.

For food animals, the abolitionist approach is to use education and "seize the vegan initiative that contemporary society, for a variety of reasons, presents to them." [17]

Reform or Abolition?

Organizations that are more oriented to animal welfare and humane treatment offer more opportunity for dialogue and compromise, though not on every issue. The chief executive officer of HSUS once declared, "We are not a vegetarian organization, and as a matter of policy do not consider the utilization of animals for food to be either immoral or inappropriate." [18]

However, HSUS is also committed to pursuing reforms within agriculture and other animal-related industries. [19] HSUS and other animal welfare–oriented groups have taken strong stands against fur animal production, hunting, trapping, certain aspects of horse and dog racing, circuses, aquariums, rodeos, dog breeding, and product testing with animals. Some opportunities for reform that might be pursued in the laboratory animal research area include refinement of research techniques, reduction in numbers of animals used, and replacement of some animal methods with other procedures.

The companion animal industry presents a special challenge. Rather than oppose the keeping of pets, some animal welfare organizations have launched massive educational campaigns to encourage pet owners to spay and neuter their animals to prevent further reproduction, obtain their pets from animal shelters, and avoid purchases from breeding farms, sometimes termed "puppy mills," and pet stores.

Efforts to stop all breeding of dogs and cats in local areas for a year have been suggested but have been unsuccessful. Proposals to require a license for anyone who wants to dispose of puppies or kittens have usually been unsuccessful. These efforts had a special motive to reduce new births of puppies and kittens, but enforcement could be difficult.

Strategies for Animal Industries

Recognizing the campaigns against their traditional uses of animals, animal owners and users have organized and developed strategies to protect their interests.

Food animals. Since defense of the status quo will not usually succeed, research programs are underway to find scientific evidence of animal behavior and humane treatment. In addition, educational programs among producers aim to encourage the highest standard of humane treatment obtainable.

If humane animal treatment carries a favorable ethical and social value, can this desirable trait be translated to economic value? Does the comfort and well-being of food animals when growing to maturity make them more desirable and in demand after they are transformed into meat, milk, eggs, wool and leather?

Such differentiation of product is occurring. Meat processors in England are contracting with producers to follow a "humane" production system that differentiates their product and encourages its purchase. Retail stores feature "free-range" and "barn-raised" eggs along with those produced in battery cages. To translate this concept into US production will require a self-disciplined core of cooperative producers who would follow the guidelines and carry out their contract obligations honestly and on schedule. Producing and marketing a "humanely produced" product might succeed if marketing is beamed toward consumers who strongly believe in humane care and treatment of animals and are willing to pay the higher cost.

Spira would like to adapt the "three R's"—replacement, reduction, and refinement—to the food animal industry. Recognizing that people's eating habits tend to change slowly, he sees a realistic program that would focus on ethical reasons for a meatless diet (replacement); eating fewer animal products on ethical and health grounds (reduction); and pressuring industry and government to develop, promote, and implement systems that reduce farm animal "pain and suffering," as long as people continue to eat animal products (refinement).[20]

Animal producers and processors would almost certainly reject parts of Spira's plan. They would like to expand the market for their product, not replace it with vegetables and cereals. Reduction could also reduce the demand and the market potential for meat and other animal products. Refinement offers more opportunity for cooperation and compromise. Research has been underway to produce leaner products with lower fat content. The pork products of the 1990s are much leaner and contain less fat than a few years ago. Beef grades have been changed, and leaner beef is available to the diet-conscious consumer. Turkey and broiler producers, with the help of research and breeding, now market a bird with a higher proportion of lean meat and less fat than a few years ago.

On refinement, food animal producers and researchers are working to make facilities more "animal friendly." A turn-around gestation stall developed by researchers at the University of Illinois has been produced by a farm equipment manufacturer. Veal producers have developed standards permitting the individual calves to move about more freely. The calves' diets are formulated to meet recommended nutritional needs.

The Indiana Commission on Farm Animal Care was created in 1981 to promote sound husbandry practices, inform the public on how modern production practices are beneficial to farm animals, and provide information to interested groups. In 1988, the Consortium for Developing a Guide for the Care and Use of Agricultural Animals in Agricultural Research and Teaching published a guidebook authored by experienced animal, dairy, and poultry scientists, along with agricultural engineers and veterinarians. Animal educators have staged conferences and conducted programs for 4-H and FFA members to encourage humane treatment and social responsibility in caring for their animals.

In April 1993, the USDA and Purdue University sponsored a conference on food animal well-being, which recognized the social and ethical dimensions of animal care. The conference participants called for unified, animal agriculture well-being guidelines based on scientific research and an educational program for the public and animal producers.

Animals in research. Scientists engaged in animal research are very sensitive to the criticisms and destruction by animal activists and the need to maintain a favorable public image to support their research. Major educational efforts have been launched to explain biomedical research and the benefits that scientists see in continuing this work.

Animals in entertainment, exhibitions, and leisure activities. There is little room to find common ground when activist groups want to abolish entire industries or institutions. However, reasoning and changing public attitudes will bring about change. Some areas for resolving conflicts are underway.

Groups concerned with how animals are treated in movie production have worked with the producers so that animals are handled to avoid injury. Zoos and aquariums have established standards for animal care and have carried out educational programs showing their role in maintaining endangered species and rescuing and caring for sick and imperiled animals. Additionally, complaints about the carriage horse trade has led to rules and regulations for humane care and treatment of these horses.

Hunters have attempted to improve their public image by donating venison and other game for food at shelters for the homeless. Conscious of the campaigns against sport hunting, sportsmen's groups have launched public relations programs to promote their views of the benefits of hunting in controlling overpopulation of wild animals.

Ethics and Standards for Animal Activists and Owners

In the mid-1990s, critics have targeted animal owners for improper treatment of their animals. They have cited animal activists and their organizations for improper use of donated funds.

A veal feed supplier has been cited for use of illegal drugs in feed supplied to producers. A few incidents of improper drug use to improve the muscular appearance of show cattle have tarnished the image of young people and their parents who show animals at fairs. Crowding animals into transport trucks has resulted in a few animals arriving at the stockyards crippled and unable to walk. As a result of these incidents, the door has been opened for animal activist protests, fund-raising appeals, and legislative efforts.

Unfortunately, a few reports have placed a cloud of suspicion over the fund-raising efforts, management practices, and uses of donated funds by individual animal activist leaders.

Animal People has identified five standards for financial integrity that every animal welfare and animal rights organization should follow to be worthy of public financial support:

- evidence from sources outside the organization that it is carrying out successful activities;
- detailed record keeping and trustworthy financial statements—and willingness to release them;
- salaries, if any are paid, that do not exceed the regionally adjusted median and/or the median for the job;
- organizational strategy—a defined focus, not just reacting to current events or trying to climb aboard bandwagons; and
- organizations not using outdated information or making erroneous claims.[21]

The practices that *Animal People* target as unethical conduct include spending large percentages of organization funds for fund-raising; having a board of directors dominated by the family of the executive director; owning stocks of companies that use animals in research and testing; paying high salaries to chief executives; and conducting no ongoing feeding, sheltering, or rescue programs that really help animals in distress. Some scattered "bad apple" incidents involving both animal owners and animal activist leaders tarnish the image of many more dedicated, ethical, and honest individuals and organizations.

Values in Conflict

The different views about animal and human relationships held by groups and individuals derive from the values instilled by family, education, home community influences, ethnic origins, and the social and cultural environment. Very few who own and handle animals deliberately inflict pain or injury.

Raising animals for food and clothing, conducting research on animals, or using them in exhibitions and leisure activities are judged to serve a useful purpose, especially for the benefit of society. The major conflicts of values surrounding animal rights are social, economic, and cultural.

As a social movement, animal rights doctrine confronts established systems and practices that many accept without question. For example, most people accept intensive and large-scale production of livestock and poultry. They accept the eating of meat and other animal products; hunting, fishing, and trapping; the use of animals for classroom dissection and laboratory research; exhibition of animals in zoos and aquariums; and the use of animals in circuses and in horse and dog racing. Many of these customs came about as part of the culture brought to this country by immigrants. Some customs were adopted from Native Americans.

The animal rights philosophy and its related recommended actions threaten markets, income, jobs, and livelihood for those who produce animals and animal products, who use animals in research, or depend on animals as part of leisure and entertainment pursuits.

The income and employment associated with producing, handling, processing, and marketing animals and animal products is substantial but difficult to measure completely. For example, the cash receipts from farm marketings of livestock and livestock products totaled $86.3 billion in 1992. This 1987 Census of Agriculture reported the production of cattle and calves, dairy products, hogs, sheep, broilers, turkey, and eggs came from 1.9 million farms that provided employment to the operator and additional hired labor. There were also 415,000 farms that had horses or ponies.

The 1987 Census of Manufacturers reported value added by manufacturing of dairy products totaled $11.8 billion and employment of 159,000. In the meat and poultry processing industries, the value added totaled $11.3 billion with employment of 340,000. The pet food industry produced 7 million tons of dog and cat food in 1991 with a sales of $7.6 billion.[22] Besides buying food for companion animals, their owners spent millions for accessories, equipment, and veterinary services.

Employment and related expenditures for equipment and supplies are substantial in the area of animal research and in entertainment events such as circuses, rodeos, horse and dog racing, as well as in institutions such as zoos and aquariums. These industries also provide income for managers, owners, and employees.

Citing these data is not intended to defend these activities and oppose reform in how the animals are treated. However, eliminating all these industries and related activities, even over time, could create severe financial losses and adjustment to new employment and means of livelihood for millions of people. On the other side, eliminating all of these animal industries would require a shift in consumption habits for the millions of people who now buy or use animals and animals products in their daily lives. But in a market system, these industries would gradually decline and go out of business if no one wanted to buy their products or services.

Contradictions and Conflicts

The conflicts of values that lie at the root of the animal rights debates will never be completely reconciled. Within the animal rights and animal welfare groups and the animal industry and scientific communities, contradictions will remain. Animal activists criticize castration, tail clipping, and debeaking in food animals. Animal industry groups view these practices as appropriate and beneficial to the animal.

However, most animal activist organizations advocate spaying and neutering for controlling dog and cat populations. Most animal rights groups oppose injuring or killing of animals in research and testing programs, yet some recommend euthanasia for disposing of unwanted animals in shelters and disabled livestock at public stockyards.

While some animal activists advocate letting all animals roam freely outside in their "natural state," many animals that have been sheltered and protected by human husbandry would suffer from exposure and might not survive.

Other animal activists oppose intensive confinement production of livestock and poultry. However, they realize that companion animals, specifically dogs and cats, are often confined in their owners' homes from morning to night while their owners are at work. Seldom can they run free outside as their ancestors once did. So animal activists recognize that dogs and cats have long been domesticated, and many would not survive if left to run free.

Tolerance and Compromise Needed

Unless different individuals and groups accept and tolerate the values held by others, conflicts will continue. Yet there are some signs of acceptance and tolerance.

For example, while animal owners and handlers still maintain their economic and social interests in animals, they have begun to recognize the rising tide of ethical concerns about how animals are used and cared for.

On the other hand, animal rights and animal welfare groups face a greater challenge. They must appeal to and persuade the gift-giving public that their positions on animal issues are right, to maintain and enlarge the flow of charitable dollars flowing from almost continuous mail solicitations. For the more activist animal rights organizations, the flow of dollars to their treasuries may depend upon their continued campaigns in "exposing" alleged animal atrocities and suffering at the hands of owners, handlers, and research workers.

Animal activist groups must also convince local, state, and national policymakers that laws and regulations are needed to validate their value system into public policy. As in most public decisions, the future public policies established for animal-human relationships will depend on compromises with the side with the most votes—the votes won through the debate for change in public feelings and attitudes toward animals.

How and when to protect animals illustrates the conflict of philosophical, scientific, economic, and social values. Animal rights proponents follow the philosophical views of Singer, Regan, and others, that humans should treat animals humanely because they are sentient beings and should not be treated differently because they are of another species.

Animal industry proponents support scientific research and its findings for humane treatment of animals. They also believe that humans have the right to use animals to meet their needs for food, wearing apparel, biomedical research, product safety testing, and entertainment. These uses of animals serve the best interests of people, they assert.

From an animal welfare perspective, Dr. David O. Weibers quite appropriately expresses the hope that "as more humans awaken to the deeper identity of other sentient beings, the seeds of evolution are created—seeds that will ultimately foster not only harmony between humans and other animals, but also between humans and other humans." [23]

Appendixes
Notes
Bibliography
Index

Who's Who in Animal Rights and Animal Welfare in the United States

Individuals listed here are or have been active in national or regional efforts. Many dedicated people working in state or local efforts could not be listed for lack of space. Since people actively involved in animal protection may change employment or leave the movement, the information presented here is believed to be accurate at the time of publication.

Adams, Carol. Author, *The Sexual Politics of Meat: A Feminist Vegetarian Critical Theory*.

Albright, Jack L. Professor of animal sciences and animal management and behavior, Purdue University, School of Agriculture and Veterinary Medicine; member of Indiana's Commission of Farm Animal Care.

Altiere, Susan. President, International Society for Animal Rights, after removal of longtime president Helen Jones in 1996; former secretary-treasurer.

Amory, Cleveland. Author; president and founder, Fund for Animals; former president, New England Anti-Vivisection Society; adviser, Farm Animal Reform Movement; vice president, Beauty Without Cruelty; steering committee member, Coalition to Abolish the LD-50 and Draize Tests; advisory board member, Concern for Helping Animals in Israel; advisory committee member, Food Animal Concerns Trust; former board member and cofounder, Humane Society of the United States.

Anthony, Donald H. President, American Humane Association; general manager, Humane Society of Missouri.

Armstrong, Martha. Vice president, companion animals, Humane Society of the United States; former director, humane education, Massachusetts SPCA.

Bahouth, Peter. Executive director, Greenpeace USA.

Barber, Albert A. Past chairman of the board, National Association for Biomedical Research.

Barker, Bob. Television personality and vocal animal rights activist.

Barnard, Neal. President, Physicians Committee for Responsible Medicine; board member, New England Anti-Vivisection Society; former advisory board member, Animal Rights Network.

Barnes, Donald J. Director of education, National Anti-Vivisection Society; former board member, Animal Rights Network.

Bartlett, Kim. Publisher and cofounder, *Animal People*; former editor, *Animals' Agenda* magazine; adviser, Farm Animal Reform Movement.

Bauston, Gene. Cofounder, Farm Sanctuary, an animal rights organization and animal shelter operation in Watkins Glen, New York; board member, Animal Rights Network.

Bauston, Lorri. Cofounder, Farm Sanctuary.

Bello, Michael J. Former executive director, Chicago-based International Foundation for Ethical Research.

Bemelmans, Madeleine. President, Society for Animal Protective Legislation; board member, Animal Welfare Institute.

Berger, Alan H. Executive director, Animal Protection Institute.

Bernstein, Emmanuel. President, Psychologists for the Ethical Treatment of Animals.

Bernstein, Madeline. Regional vice president, Los Angeles, American Society for the Prevention of Cruelty to Animals.

Berosini, Bobby. Entertainer who used orangutans in his act at the Stardust Hotel in Las Vegas, Nevada. He was secretly videotaped before his act to show alleged abuse of the animals.

Biondi, Vicki. Director, Iowa Alliance for Animals; board member, Animal Rights Network.

Boehner, John. Member of Congress from Ohio; co-chair of Animal Welfare Caucus.

Briggs, Anna C. Founder and president, National Humane Education Society.

Brown, Larry C. Former executive director, American Humane Association.

Brown, Robert A. President, Food Animal Concerns Trust; former president, Chicago Anti-Cruelty Society; advisory board member, Humane Farming Association and Animal Protection Institute.

Bullington, Allan. Director, Animal Rights Information Services, a New York–based producer and distributor of video programs on animal rights.

Buyukmihci, Nedim C. Veterinarian; president, Association of Veterinarians for Animal Rights; honorary board member, California Political Action Committee for Animals; advisory board member, Humane Farming Association and Animal Protection Institute; advisory committee member, Food Animal Concerns Trust.

Capaldo, Theo. President, New England Anti-Vivisection Society, following retirement of Cleveland Amory in 1995.

Caras, Roger A. President, American Society for the Prevention of Cruelty to Animals, since 1991; former television wildlife commentator.

Cave, Eleanor. Vice president, Beauty Without Cruelty.

Cave, George P. Former president, Animal Rights Mobilization! (formerly Trans-Species Unlimited).

Cave, William. President, American Anti-Vivisection Society, until his death in February 1990.

Clark, James A. Former executive vice president, American Anti-Vivisection Society.

Clifton, Merritt. Animal activist writer; editor, *Animal People*; former news editor, *Animal's Agenda*.

Close, Doreene. President, Coalition to End Animal Suffering and Exploitation, a Massachusetts-based animal rights organization.

Cohen, Murry J. Chairman, New York–based Medical Research Modernization Committee.

Coronado, Rodney. Animal rights activist; founder, Coalition Against Fur Farms. Coronado was indicted by a Michigan federal grand jury and convicted in connection with 1992 break-in at Michigan State University.

Cunniff, Kenneth L. Adjunct professor of law, John Marshall University; attorney, National Anti-Vivisection Society.

Cunniff, Mary Margaret. President and executive director, National Anti-Vivisection Society; vice president, International Foundation for Ethical Research.

Curtis, Stanley L. Professor of animal science, Pennsylvania State University; former professor of animal science, University of Illinois; recognized authority on environmental conditions for swine.

Davis, Karen. Founder, United Poultry Concerns.

Day, Doris. Actress; president, Doris Day Animal League; chair, People Protecting Primates; national co-chair, Farm Animal Reform Movement.

DeBakey, Michael E. Chancellor, Baylor University College of Medicine; chairman, Foundation for Biomedical Research, 1993.

Dell'Amico, Louise. Director, Citizens to End Animal Suffering and Exploitation.

Derby, Pat. President, California-based Performing Animal Welfare Society.

Dinshah, H. Jay. President, American Vegan Society.

Douglass, Adele. Director, Washington office, American Humane Association.

Duxbury, Robin. Director, Animal Rights Mobilization! headquartered in Denver; former staff member, Rocky Mountain Humane Society.

Eide, Vickie. Board member, Animal Rights Network; founder and director, Iowa Alliance for Animals.

Eldon, Margaret. Former president, American Anti-Vivisection Society.

Feral, Priscilla. President, Friends of Animals; executive director, Committee for Humane Legislation.

Fields, Ann. Founder, Love and Care for God's Stray Animals, labeled as one of the most lucrative no-kill animal scams ever. She died from a drug overdose, believed to be suicide, at age 49 in 1995. During her lifetime, she was involved in several lawsuits alleging fraud, deceit, and deceptive trade practices.

Finch, Patty A. Vice president, youth education, Humane Society of the United States.

Fischer, David U. Executive director, Animal Protection Institute.

Forkan, Patricia. Executive vice president, domestic operations, Humane Society of the United States.

Fox, Michael. Veterinarian; author; vice president, farm animals and bioethics, Humane Society of the United States; adviser, Farm Animal Reform Movement; head, Center for Respect for Life; director, Humane Farming Association. Fox is an international authority on animal behavior and animal welfare science.

Francione, Gary. Law professor; director, Rutgers University Animal Rights Law Clinic, active in animal rights activities; chair, Animal Protection Committee of the American Bar Association Young Lawyers Division; legal counsel, People for the Ethical Treatment of Animals; founder, Animal Rights America in 1995, which split due to disagreement among the founders on how to deal with the 1996 March for the Animals in Washington, D.C.

Fraser, David. Animal scientist, Center for Food and Animal Research, Agriculture Canada; organizer, Canada's Expert Committee on Farm Animal Welfare and Behavior.

Galvin, Roger W. Vice president, Animal Legal Defense Fund; secretary, Physicians Committee for Responsible Medicine; former Maryland state's attorney.

Gennarelli, Thomas. Research scientist, University of Pennsylvania, targeted by animal rights groups for his work on head injuries. His laboratory was closed down as a result of protests at the National Institutes of Health.

Gerard (formerly Linck), Peter. Executive director, National Alliance for Animals; sponsor, 1990 and 1996 March for Animals; sponsor, Animal Rights Symposiums; president of the board, Animal Rights Network; publisher, Animals Agenda.

Goldberg, Alan M. Director, Johns Hopkins Center for Alternatives to Animal Testing, Baltimore, Maryland.

Goodwin, J. P. Founder and executive director of the Dallas-based Coalition to Abolish the Fur Trade. In 1993, he was convicted of vandalizing three Memphis fur stores by gluing their locks and spray-painting slogans on their walls. He has been quoted frequently in the Animal Liberation Frontline Information Service and was hired in 1997 as campaign coordinator for In Defense of Animals.

Grandin, Temple. Animal scientist, Colorado State University; leading livestock handling consultant specializing in reducing stress; designer of handling systems for the livestock industry.

Grandy, John W. Staff vice president for wildlife and habitat protection, Humane Society of the United States.

Granoski, Charles M., Jr. President, American Humane Association.

Greanville, David Patrice. Animal and environmental activist; president, National Anti-Road Kill Project and Voice of Nature Network; former advertising director and acting publisher, *Animals' Agenda*; former board member, Animal Rights Network.

Guerrero, Kenneth E. Chairman of the board, Animal Protection Institute of America, a California-based organization seeking to promote "unity-with-diversity" in the humane movement.

Guillermo, Kathy Snow. Lifestyles campaign director, People for the Ethical Treatment of Animals; author, *Monkey Business*.

Hardy, David T. Washington, D.C., attorney experienced in wildlife and environmental law; author, *America's New Extremists: What You Need to Know About the Animal Rights Movement*.

Hart, Robert F. X. Executive director, American Humane Association since 1993.

Hazard, Holly. Attorney, Galvin, Stanley and Hazard, Washington, D.C.; executive director, Doris Day Animal League.

Hershaft, Alex. President, Farm Animal Reform Movement; advisory board member, Humane Education Committee.

Hindi, Steve. Founder of the Chicago Animal Rights Coalition; leader of anti-hunting protests.

Holzer, Henry Mark. Professor of law, Brooklyn Law School; president, Institute for Animal Rights Law; board member and counsel, International Society for Animal Rights.

Hoyt, John. Chairman, Humane Society of the United States; board member, Animal Rights International; director, National Association for the Advancement of Humane and Environmental Education, animal welfare–oriented but opposes fur and confinement livestock production.

Irwin, Paul G. President, treasurer, and past executive vice president, Humane Society of the United States.

Jamieson, Dale. Philosophy professor, University of Colorado; advisory committee member, Food Animal Concerns Trust.

Jones, Helen. Founder and former president, International Society for Animal Rights; vice president, Beauty Without Cruelty; advisory committee member, Animal Liberation Network. Jones was removed from her president's post by the ISAR board in January 1996 and accused of converting organization funds for personal use and other alleged misconduct.

Jones, John F. President and board member, American Humane Association.

Juliano, Sharon. Associate professor of anatomy, Uniformed Services University of the Health Sciences, Bethesda, Maryland. Her research, under a National Institutes of Health grant on how the brain reorganizes its nerve signals after a trauma, made her the target of extensive protests by animal rights activists.

Katz, Elliot. President, In Defense of Animals.

Kheel, Marti. Cofounder and West Coast coordinator, Feminists for Animal Liberation.

Kimber, Evelyn. Vice president, New England Anti-Vivisection Society; board member, Animal Rights Network.

Kindler, Roger A. Vice president and general counsel, Humane Society of the United States.

Klaper, Michael. Author; physician; activist for animal rights and vegetarian diets.

Knapp, Richard M. Chairman of the board, National Association for Biomedical Research.

Kopperud, Steven. Lobbyist, American Feed Industry Association; former executive director, Animal Industry Foundation and Farm Animal Welfare Coalition.

Kullberg, John F. Director of companion animals and investigations, HSUS; former president, American Society for the Prevention of Cruelty to Animals; advisory committee member, Animal Rights International; advisory committee member, Food Animal Concerns Trust; former president, Guiding Eyes for the Blind (1992–1994).

Lantos, Tom. Member of Congress from California; strong supporter of animal welfare and animal rights; advisory board member, Concern for Helping Animals in Israel.

La Valette, Mary de. President and treasurer, GAIA Institute; supporter of the animal rights movement.

Leary, Sue. President, American Anti-Vivisection Society.

Lockwood, Randall. Vice president, field services, Humane Society of the United States.

Lyman, Howard. Executive director, Eating with a Conscience campaign, Humane Society of the United States; former executive director, Beyond Beef, a coalition of environmental and other groups supporting Jeremy Rifkin philosophies; former Montana rancher; former lobbyist, National Farmers Union.

Mackie, Murial. President, Texas-based Primarily Primates.

Maggitti, Phil. Author; copy editor, *Animals' Agenda*.

Marquardt, Kathleen. Founder, Putting People First; vice president, American Policy Center.

Mason, Jim. Author, *Animal Factories*; lecturer, animal rights issues; advisory board member, Animal Rights Network.

McArdle, John. Scientific adviser, American Anti-Vivisection Society.

McCabe, Katie. Writer, *Washingtonian* magazine. Her stories on the animal rights movement led to a lawsuit against her by PETA, later settled out of court.

McCartney, Paul. Entertainer and longtime animal rights supporter.

McGreal, Shirley. Chairwoman, International Primate Protection League; advisory board member, Animal Protection Institute.

McMillan, Marjorie. Former head of radiology, Massachusetts Society for the Prevention of Cruelty to Animals. McMillan sued the president for gender-based salary discrimination and was awarded $787,621.

Medlock, Aaron. Executive director, New England Anti-Vivisection Society.

Mench, Joy. Poultry scientist, University of California–Davis; formerly at University of Maryland; board member, Scientists Center for Animal Welfare.

Michaels, Gil. President, Compassion for Animals, a California-based animal rights organization with an educational orientation; publisher, *Animals' Voice*.

Miller, Bonnie. Secretary, treasurer, and board member, Humane Farming Association.

Miller, Bradley. Executive director, Humane Farming Association; former advisory board member, Animal Rights Network; president, Buddhists Concerned for Animals; board member, California Political Action Committee for Animals; advisory committee member, Food Animal Concerns Trust.

Millsaps, Reed. Former attorney, National Anti-Vivisection Society.

Montavalli, Jim. Writer; former editor, *Animals' Agenda*; former board member, Animal Rights Network.

Morgan, Richard. Chair, Political Action Committee for Animal Welfare and Protection.

Morrison, Adrian R. Director, Program for Animal Research Issues, National Institute of Mental Health; professor of anatomy, School of Veterinary Medicine, University of Pennsylvania; member, board of directors, National Animal Interest Alliance.

Mouras, Belton. Development director, Performing Animal Welfare Society; former secretary general, United Animal Nations–USA; advisory board member, *Animals' Agenda*.

Natelson, Nina. President and director, Concern For Helping Animals in Israel.

Nelson, Tina. Executive director, American Anti-Vivisection Society.

Newkirk, Ingrid. Cofounder, People for the Ethical Treatment of Animals; director, New England Anti-Vivisection Society.

O'Barry, Richard. Authority on preparing marine mammals to return to natural habitats, Dolphin Project.

Orem, John M. Professor of physiology, Texas Tech University in Lubbock. Orem lost ten years of work on sudden infant death syndrome after the Animal Liberation Front raided his lab, confiscated his research cats, and destroyed data and equipment.

Pacelle, Wayne. Vice president for legislation, Humane Society of the United States; former national director, Fund for Animals; former board member, Animal Rights Network.

Pacheco, Alex. Animal activist; cofounder, People for the Ethical Treatment of Animals; board member, executive committee, New England Anti-Vivisection Society; officer, People Protecting Primates; adviser, Farm Animal Reform Movement; board member, Humane Farming Association.

Paulhus, Marc S. Vice president for companion animals, Humane Society of the United States.

Prescott, Heidi. National outreach director, Fund for Animals. Prescott has been called a "hunt saboteur" by *Animals' Agenda*. She has been arrested at least six times for violating hunter harassment laws and has spent thirteen days in a Maryland jail rather than pay a $500 fine.

Reeve, Christopher. Actor, famous for his role as Superman; animal rights activist. In speaking to the Animal Rights March audience in Washington on June 10, 1990, he urged moderation and "one step at a time" approach to animal rights, but he was shouted down and strongly criticized by other activists.

Regan, Susan. Executive director, Association of Veterinarians for Animal Rights.

Regan, Tom. Author; philosopher; animal rights activist; president and founder, Culture and Animals Foundation, North Carolina State University; national co-chair for the March for the Animals, which took place in Washington, D.C., on June 10, 1990; board member, Marian Rosenthal Koch Fund; cofounder, Animal Rights America in 1995.

Reines, Brandon. Veterinarian; founder and president, Center for Health Science Policy.

Rifkin, Jeremy. Environmental activist, Foundation for Economic Trends; board member, Farm Animal Reform Movement; author, *Beyond Beef*.

Robbins, John. Author, *Diet for a Small Planet*; board member, Farm Animal Reform Movement; founder, EarthSave.

Roberti, David. Founder, California-based Respect Our Animals' Rights.

Rollin, Bernard. Professor of philosophy, professor of physiology and biophysics, and Director of Bioethical Planning, Colorado State University; author and lecturer on animal ethics.

Rose, Chris de. Founder and president, California-based Last Chance for Animals.

Rose, Naomi. Member, Humane Society of the United States; authority on marine mammals.

Roush, Jeanne. Former executive director, People for the Ethical Treatment of Animals; former Director of Research and Investigations.

Rowan, Andrew N. Senior vice president, Humane Society of the United States; founder and former director, Center for Animals and Public Policy, Tufts School of Veterinary Medicine; science adviser, Animal Rights International; vice-president, Scientists Center for Animal Welfare; advisory panel member, American Humane Association.

Ryder, Richard. British psychologist; author; originator of the term *speciesism*; representative, British Political Animal Lobby.

Scholz, Tom. Member, "Boston" rock group; board member, Farm Animal Reform Movement.

Seiling, Eleanor. Founder, United Action for Animals.

Shapiro, Kenneth. Executive director, Psychologists for the Ethical Treatment of Animals; former president of the board, Animal Rights Network.

Singer, Peter. Philosopher; author *Animal Liberation*, often regarded as the bible for the animal rights movement; consultant, Animal Rights International; adviser, Culture and Animals Foundation; adviser, Farm Animal Reform Movement.

Spira, Henry. Coordinator, Animal Rights International; honorary board member, California Political Action Committee for Animals; coordinator, Coalition to Abolish the LD-50 and Draize Tests; coordinator, Coalition to Abolish Classroom Dissection; adviser, Farm Animal Reform Movement; advisory board member, Animal Protection Institute; member, Coalition for Nonviolent Food

Stallwood, Kim. Editor in chief, *Animals' Agenda*, 1993; executive director, People for the Ethical Treatment of Animals, 1987–1992; former advisory board member, Animal Rights Network. Before coming to the United States, he was acting general secretary to the British Union for Abolition of Vivisection.

Stanley, Valerie. Attorney, Washington, D.C., law firm of Galvin, Stanley and Hazard; attorney, Animal Legal Defense Fund suits against the secretary of agriculture from 1991 to 1993; board member, Animal Legal Defense Fund.

Stenholm, Charles. Member of Congress from Texas, serves on House Agriculture Committee; co-chair of Animal Welfare Caucus.

Stephens, Martin L. Vice president, laboratory animals, Humane Society of the United States.

Stevens, Christine. President and director, Animal Welfare Institute.

Stevens, Roger. Treasurer, Animal Welfare Institute.

Strand, Rod, and Patti Strand. Coauthors, *The Hijacking of the Humane Movement*. Patti is executive director, National Animal Interest Alliance.

Tannenbaum, Margo. Contact person, California-based Animal Liberal Front Support Group; president, Action for Animals; secretary, Last Chance for Animals.

Taub, Edward. Researcher, Institute for Behavioral Research at Silver Spring, Maryland, in 1981. His research with monkeys and the poor housekeeping and care of monkeys at the laboratory developed into the Silver Spring monkeys cases.

Thalberg, Katharine. Cofounder, Aspen Society for Animal Rights. Her campaign to ban fur sales in the city of Aspen failed. The campaign was supported by her husband, the mayor of Aspen.

Thornton, Gus. President, Massachusetts Society for the Prevention of Cruelty to Animals; advisory committee member, Animal Rights International.

Thurston, Ethel. Chair, Beauty Without Cruelty, a New York–based group working to inform the public about suffering of animals imposed by the fashion, cosmetics, and household product industries; trustee, American Fund for Alternatives to Animal Research; advisory board member, Animal Rights Network.

Tischler, Joyce. Attorney, executive director, Animal Legal Defense Fund; national advisory board member, Animal Protection Institute; board member, California Political Action Committee for Animals; advisory board member, Humane Farming Association.

Todd, Betsy. Registered nurse, associated with Feminists for Animal Rights; cofounder, National Association of Nurses Against Vivisection.

Trapp, George J. Former president, Chicago-based National Anti-Vivisection Society.

Trull, Frankie L. President, National Association for Biomedical Research, an organization representing member institutions in national policy making concerning the use of animals in research; president, Foundation for Biomedical Research.

Weibers, David O., M.D. Chairman, Scientific Advisory Council; director, Humane Society of the United States.

Wessels, Marc A. Executive director, International Network for Religion and Animals.

Wewer, William. Attorney, Putting People First; one-time attorney, Doris Day Animal League.

White, Dennis J. Field representative, HSUS; former director, Animal Protection Division, American Humane Association.

White, MacDonald. President, United Action for Animals.

Wills, David K. Former vice president for investigations, Humane Society of the United States; past president, Michigan-based National Society for Animal Protection. Wills was sued by the Humane Society of the United States for allegedly embezzling funds. He countersued HSUS, the HSUS president, and three staff members.

Wise, Steven. Attorney and former president, Animal Legal Defense Fund; president, Center for Expansion of Fundamental Rights, dedicated to obtaining rights for chimpanzees and bonobos.

Woods, Jennifer. Executive director, National Association of Nurses Against Vivisection.

Wyler, Gretchen. Actress; adviser, Farm Animal Reform Movement; board member, Fund For Animals; advisory committee member, Food Animal Concerns Trust; founder and president, the Ark Trust, a nonprofit animal protection organization.

Zawistowski, Stephen. Senior vice president for humane education and science adviser, American Society for Prevention of Cruelty to Animals.

Animal Bill of Rights

(A Petition to the 102nd United States Congress)

I, the undersigned American citizen, believe that animals, like all sentient beings, are entitled to basic legal rights in our society. Deprived of legal protection, animals are defenseless against exploitation and abuse by humans. As no such rights now exist, I urge you to pass legislation in support of the following basic rights for animals:

The right of animals to be free from exploitation, cruelty, neglect and abuse.

The right of laboratory animals not to be used in cruel or unnecessary experiments.

The right of farm animals to an environment that satisfies their basic physical and psychological needs.

The right of companion animals to a healthy diet, protective shelter, and adequate medical care.

The right of wildlife to a natural habitat, ecologically sufficient to a normal existence and a self-sustaining species population.

The right of animals to have their interest represented in court and safeguarded by the law of the land.[1]

Chronology of Animal Welfare in Europe, 1964–1995

1964   In England, Ruth Harrison wrote *Animal Machines*, which stimulated concerns and led to development of animal welfare policies and regulations in several western European countries. This book initiated much of the public concern for the welfare of farm animals under modern production methods.

1965   The report of the Technical Committee, commonly referred to as the Brambell Report, defined certain principles of animal welfare and recommended certain mandatory standards in the care and production of food animals in the United Kingdom. The Brambell Report set the stage for animal welfare policy and regulations. This report identified the "five freedoms" that established the basis for animal welfare controls: (1) freedom from thirst, hunger, and malnutrition; (2) appropriate comfort and shelter; (3) the prevention or rapid diagnosis and treatment of injury, disease, or infestation; (4) freedom from fear; (5) freedom to display most normal patterns of behavior.

1967   The United Kingdom Ministry of Agriculture, Fisheries and Food set up the Farm Animal Welfare Advisory Committee, later renamed and enlarged as the Farm Animal Welfare Council, as a response to the Brambell Report.

1968   Parliament passed the *Agriculture (Miscellaneous Provisions) Act*, which recommended codes of practices for the housing and management for intensively kept livestock.

1969   The Council of Europe issued the *European Convention for the Protection of Animals during International Transport*.

1971   The United Kingdom Ministry of Agriculture issued its first *Codes of Recommendations for the Welfare of Livestock*, which at that time were advisory, not mandatory.
        The Swedish parliament passed a law that required that new housing for animals must be approved by the County Agricultural Board; the board would consider animal protection before government credit could be obtained. In 1973, the law was extended to include all remodeling and construction whether government credit was involved or not.

1972	The West German Parliament passed the *Animal Protection Act* to "protect the life and well-being of the animal."
1975	The Netherlands National Council for Agricultural Research issued its report on animal husbandry and welfare.
1976	The Council of Europe issued the *European Convention for the Protection of Animals Kept for Farming Purposes*. In 1978, the European Economic Community Council adopted it.
1978	The Swiss Federal Assembly passed the *Federal Act on Animal Welfare*. In a public referendum, 80 percent approved it.
	The Danish National Committee for Poultry and Eggs held the first seminar on poultry welfare and egg production in cages.
1979	The Council of Europe issued the *European Convention for the Protection of Animals for Slaughter*. The European Community Commission was invited to report on keeping laying hens in cages, propose minimum standards for their protection, and consider economic factors. The first European Animal Welfare Conference was held in Amsterdam.
	The High Court in Frankfurt, Germany, as a result of alleged infringements of the German *Animal Protection Act of 1972*, ruled that the battery cage system for keeping hens was cruel because the "hens are permanently deprived of exercising such behavior patterns as scratching, stretching, wing flapping, preening, flight behavior, resting, undisturbed laying and unhindered movement." The West German Agriculture Minister was required to take action.
	In the United Kingdom, the Ministry of Agriculture, Fisheries and Food created the Farm Animal Welfare Council, an independent advisory body, giving it the responsibility of reviewing the welfare of farm animals on agricultural land, at markets, in transit, and at the place of slaughter.
1980	The European Community Council recognized that battery cages were widely used and profitable but also pointed out that they could lead to "unnecessary and excessive suffering" and a common minimum standard should be set.
	The European Community Eurogroup for Animal Welfare was established at Brussels, composed of representatives of the most influential animal welfare organization from each of the member countries.
	In the United Kingdom, the House of Commons Agriculture Committee held hearings and issued its report, *Animal Welfare in Poultry, Pig, and Veal Calf Production*.
1981	The European Community Commission proposed that the council approve setting minimum standards for protecting laying hens in battery cages.
	In Denmark, the World Poultry Science Association held the First European Symposium on Poultry Welfare.
	In Switzerland, regulations for the Swiss *Federal Act on Animal Welfare* became effective.
	In the United Kingdom, the Ministry of Agriculture responded to the report on

animal welfare in poultry, pig, and veal calf production, concluding that much work remained in research, development, and other fields.

The Universities Federation for Animal Welfare held a two-day symposium, Intensive Husbandry Systems.

1982 The second European Conference on Protection of Farm Animals was held in France.

In Sweden, regulations were rewritten for the animal welfare code as applied to farm animals.

The European Commission held a workshop on housing and welfare in Scotland and on the welfare of confined sows in France.

1986 The European Community Council issued a directive to insure that where animals are used for experimental or other scientific purposes, the provisions laid down by law, regulation, or administrative provisions are followed.

The United Kingdom passed *The Animals (Scientific Procedures) Act* with new provisions to protect animals used for experimental or other scientific purposes.

1987 The United Kingdom Ministry of Agriculture announced an eventual ban on veal crates and issued a *Code of Practice for the Transport by Air of Cattle, Sheep, Pigs, Goats and Horses.*

1988 The Swedish Parliament passed the *Animal Protection Act*, specifying management practices for livestock and poultry and consolidating previous animal welfare legislation into one act.

1989 The United Kingdom Ministry of Agriculture issued *Guidelines for the Transport of Farmed Deer* and *Code of Practice for the Welfare of Horses, Ponies, and Donkeys at Markets, Sales, and Fairs.*

1990 The United Kingdom Ministry of Agriculture published a *Code of Practice on the Welfare of Animals in Livestock Markets.*

Sweden passed an animal welfare law to ban tethering of sows, to ban gestation crates, to limit sows in farrowing crates to one week after farrowing, and to allow only partly slatted floors.

In April, the European Parliament voted for a ban on sow stalls and tethering with a phaseout in five years.

A seminar held in Brussels in November looked at alternatives to replace stalls and tethers. The EU Council of Ministers was to make the final decision.

1991 The United Kingdom Ministry of Agriculture issued (1) *Codes of Recommendations for Welfare of Livestock: Pigs, Cattle*; (2) *Operations on Farm Animals*, listing the provisions of legislation relating to procedures carried out on animals, the operations permitted, age, need for anesthetic, and qualifications of the person performing it; and (3) *Guidance Notes for Exporters of Horses and Ponies from Great Britain.*

Most regulations implementing recommendations of the Farm Animal Welfare Council's Interim Report went into operation. Others were scheduled to begin January 1, 1992.

Lufthansa (German airline) announced a bird embargo and would not transport tropical birds caught in the wild. It had already banned transportation of animals threatened with extinction, hunting trophies, and products made from endangered species.

1992   Commission of the European Community issued the report of the Scientific Veterinary Committee, working group on Transport of Farm Animals and Pets.

Commission of the European Communities, Directorate-General for Agriculture, issued a report of the Scientific Veterinary Committee on the welfare of laying hens kept in different production systems.

1993   Commission of the European Communities issued a communication to the council and European Parliament on the protection of animals.

Commission of the European Communities issued a proposal to amend the directive on protection of animals during transport.

1995   In the United Kingdom, protesters demonstrated against the transporting of live animal across the English Channel to the European mainland.

Chronology of the Silver Spring Monkeys

Week of August 27, 1981. Alex Pacheco brought other researchers to the Institute of Behavioral Research (IBR) at night to inspect the monkeys and the lab facilities. They corroborated the abuses. Pacheco also shot videotape showing unsanitary lab conditions and monkeys apparently in need of veterinary care. It was that videotape, along with other evidence gathered by Pacheco, that led to a police raid.

September 11, 1981. Under a search warrant, Sgt. Richard W. Swain, Jr., seized seventeen monkeys from the IBR used by Dr. Edward Taub.

October 9, 1981. The Circuit Court of Montgomery County instructed Sergeant Swain and Dr. James Stunkard, a veterinarian, to transfer the monkeys to an NIH facility in Poolesville, Maryland, considered the best place for temporary care and custody.

November 1981. The Taub trial centered on Taub's handling of complex problems associated with deafferentation—the severing of nerves—in this case, to deprive limbs of sensation to simulate human stroke and spinal cord injury. Experts on the two sides of this issue disagreed as to whether the monkeys' limbs should have been bandaged.

December 2, 1981. Taub was found guilty of six of seventeen counts for cruelty to animals under Maryland law. The Montgomery County Maryland Court of Appeals found Taub guilty of one count of cruelty to animals. Although Taub was prosecuted, the bulk of the litigation focused on the fate of the monkeys. Sometime between September and December, two of the seventeen monkeys died.

December 3, 1981. When Taub was acquitted on eleven of seventeen counts, People for the Ethical Treatment of Animals, along with other groups and individuals, feared that the monkeys would be returned to the lab. So they filed a bill of complaint in the Maryland Circuit Court. They also felt a civil inquiry would show violations of the federal *Animal Welfare Act*. The case was removed to the US district court.

December 17, 1981. NIH requested removal of the case to the US district court in Maryland. Within two days, IBR asked for dismissal on the grounds that the plaintiffs lacked standing to sue. Within two weeks, NIH moved to dismiss the action for improper venue or to transfer the case to the US district court in Washington, D.C., to consolidate with two other cases. The case, *Humane Society of the United States (along with PETA) v. Block*, was a civil suit to force the secretary of agriculture to enforce the *Animal Welfare Act* against Taub and

IBR. The other case, *Fund for Animals v. Malone*, was to control the research treatment of animals and to prevent the return of the seized monkeys to Taub and IBR.

April 1982. The Washington, D.C., district court dismissed *HSUS v. Block* and *Fund for Animals v. Malone*, stating that the enforcement authority of NIH and the Department of Agriculture was "wholly discretionary"; and with no laws that required enforcement action for standards of care, they have no duties to meet the concerns of the plaintiff organizations.

August 1983. The Maryland Court of Appeals reversed the conviction of Dr. Taub on the grounds that the Maryland statute did not apply to medical research conducted with federal funding. The Maryland law was later amended to cover abuses conducted by medical researchers who work under a federal program.

January 1985. A federal magistrate in the Maryland district recommended that the district court dismiss for lack of standing the suit against IBR, NIH, and Swain. (The case against Stunkard has been dismissed earlier.) Three months later, the district court adopted the magistrate's report and recommendation.

November 1985. Maryland district court refused to set aside the January judgment. The plaintiffs appealed.

May 8, 1986. Arguments were given before the US Court of Appeals for the Fourth Circuit in the case of *International Primate Protection League, Animal Law Enforcement Association, People for Ethical Treatment of Animals, Alex Hershaft, Pamela Chapman, Jo Shoesmith, Virginia Bourquardez, Peter W. Solem, Bertha K. Solem, and Sherryl R. Thomas v. Institute for Behavioral Research, Inc., Richard W. Swain, Jr., National Institutes of Health, Animal Laboratory and James V. Stunkard*. The plaintiffs wanted to be named guardians of the Silver Spring monkeys.

September 4, 1986. Judge John R. Hargrove dismissed the action, declaring that individuals and organizations lacked standing to bring the action and that the *Animal Welfare Act* did not confer private cause of action. The individuals and organizations appealed.

October 7, 1986. A rehearing took place, but the appeal for the animal rights organizations and individuals was again denied.

July 1988. NIH transferred the monkeys to the Delta Regional Primate Center, a component of Tulane University. NIH proposed an experimental research procedure, or protocol, that led to further litigation. The protocol involved the participation of four researchers in the use of electrodes to take brain measurements in the monkeys during a four-hour period before each monkey was to be euthanized. The procedure also contemplated a postmortem examination of the monkey's brain tissues and spinal cords. Through these experiments, NIH hoped to obtain information that could benefit the rehabilitation of stroke and accident victims.

December 1989. Louisiana district court issued a temporary restraining order, sought by the same animal rights groups involved in previous Silver Spring monkey case, barring Tulane University and NIH from euthanizing certain of the Silver Spring monkeys and conducting autopsy research. NIH removed the case to the US district court. The federal district judge issued an injunction prohibiting disposal of the animals. Appeal was taken.

January 11, 1990. Physicians Committee for Responsible Medicine, (PCRM) et al. as plaintiffs filed action against Louis D. Sullivan, in his official capacity as secretary of health and human services, seeking to prevent experiments on one of seven surviving Silver Spring monkeys. They claimed that the NIH research plan was defective and constituted misconduct in science. They also asked NIH to investigate allegations of scientific misconduct. In addition, they urged NIH to terminate all actions directed at implementing the research and sought release of the monkeys to an appropriate primate sanctuary.

January 12, 1990. A temporary restraining order was issued.

January 14, 1990. The temporary restraining order was vacated by agreement of the parties because of the deterioration of the monkey's condition. The research and euthanasia of the monkey proceeded that evening.

January 25, 1990. The Office of Scientific Integrity Review, to which the January 11 petition had been referred, dismissed all of the allegations, declining to pursue any inquiry or investigation into the matter.

January 30, 1990. The court dismissed the actions of January 12 and 14 on the grounds that issues presented appeared to have been resolved with the death of the monkey.

March 8, 1990. The United States Court of Appeals for the Fifth Circuit (Louisiana) heard the case of *International Primate Protection League et al., v. Administrators of the Tulane Education Fund, and the National Institutes of Health*. The court of appeals held that animal rights groups lacked standing and that dismissal was required rather than remand to state court and NIH had sufficient interest in the monkeys to support removal of the case to federal court.[1]

April 13, 1990. Rehearing of the case was denied.

June 25, 1990. PCRM and others came before the US district court in Washington, D.C., arguing that the issues presented had not been resolved and asked for an injunction to prevent further experiments on the surviving monkeys. They claimed that a newspaper article on March 14, 1990, stated that three additional monkeys were targeted for experimentation. The defendants pointed out that plaintiffs assumption of the challenged experiments without public notice was erroneous. They claimed that plaintiffs would have at least forty-eight hours' notice of any plans to implement the research in question and could call for a temporary restraining order if they desired. The defendants did not deny that the challenged experimentation would take place on the remaining monkeys. They merely refuted the lack of notice argument. Judge John Garret Penn ruled that plaintiffs motion to vacate the dismissal was granted, that the plaintiffs could file an amended complaint and a motion for a preliminary injunction, and the motion for preliminary injunction was accepted.[2]

June 28, 1990. PCRM et al. as plaintiffs, in the US district court in the District of Columbia, sought an order restraining the implementation of the experimental procedure on the remaining Silver Spring monkeys. Judge Penn denied the motion for a temporary restraining order. So NIH and the researchers at the Delta Regional Primate Center could proceed with their research.[3]

March 20, 1991. The Supreme Court heard arguments in the case of *International Primate Protection League et al. v. Administrators of Tulane Education Fund et. al.*

May 20, 1991. The Supreme Court and Justice Marshall held that (1) the statute authorizing removal of state suits by federal officers does not permit removal by federal agencies (the National Institutes of Health was the agency in this case); (2) that animal rights groups had standing to challenge removal of the case from state to federal court; and (3) that the case be returned to the state court.[4] NIH did not see the Supreme Court decision as having much effect since it could designate one of its officers as the party in a case, if it were returned to state court.

Successful National Legislation for Animal Welfare

Humane Slaughter Act of 1958, Public Law 85-765. Defines methods of humane slaughter: "No method of slaughter or handling in connection with slaughtering shall be deemed to comply with public policy of the United States unless it is humane."

Animal Welfare Act of 1966, Public Law 89-544. Regulates the transportation, sale, and handling of dogs, cats, and certain other animals to be used for research or experimentation.

Animal Welfare Act, Amendments of 1976. Public Law 94-279. Increases the protection for animals in transit and assures treatment of certain animals. Animal fighting ventures prohibited.

Endangered Species Act of 1973, Amendments of 1979. Requires the secretary of interior to examine the status of a species before declaring it endangered or threatened, designates critical habitats, provides guidelines for establishment of endangered species, and develops programs for conservation.

Marine Mammal Protection Act of 1972 and 1976. Prohibits the killing, capturing, or harassing of any marine mammal without a permit.

Lacey Act, Amendments of 1981. Public Law 97-79. Makes it unlawful for any person to sell, import, export, or receive any illegally taken fish or wildlife or to transport fish and wildlife in any container that has not been properly stamped or marked.

Health Research Extension Act of 1985. Public Law 99-158. Establishes animal research standards that include formation of animal care committees and development of research plans to reduce animal use, provide alternatives to animal use, and reduce pain and discomfort to research animals.

The Food Security Act of 1985. Public Law 99-198. Requires the secretary of agriculture to set standards governing the humane care, treatment, and transportation of animals by dealers, research facilities, and exhibitors. Each research facility must establish at least one committee to assess animal care and practices.

Emergency Wetlands Resources Act of 1985. Public Law 99-645. Provides funding for the maintenance of wildlife refuges and the acquisition of wetlands and provides for inventory and status information on wetland habitats.

Wildlife Sanctuary for Humpback Whales 1986. House Joint Resolution 67. Public Law 99-630. Directs the president and the International Whaling Commission to seek a treaty or international agreement that would establish a sanctuary for humpback whales in the West Indies.

Mice for Biomedical Research 1989. H.J. Res. 3091. Public Law 101-190. Provides for the construction of biomedical facilities to ensure a continued supply of specialized strains of mice essential to biomedical research.

Department of Defense Appropriation 1989. Public Law 101-165. Prohibits the use of funds to purchase dogs or cats for training students in surgical or medical treatment of wounds caused by any type of weapon.

Food, Agriculture, Conservation and Trade Act of 1990 ("Pet Theft Act of 1990"). Public Law 101-624. Provides that a dealer may not obtain any live dog or cat from a source other than a city, county, or state pound, a private entity under contract with a local agency, a registered research facility, or an individual who bred and raised the animals.

Be Kind to Animals and National Pet Week. H.J.Res. 458, S.J.Res. 236. Public Law 101-282. Designates May 6–12, 1990, as "Be Kind to Animals and National Pet Week," to celebrate the firm commitment of Americans to responsible pet ownership and humane education.

National Prevent-a-Litter Month. S.J.Res. 229. Public Law 101-261. Designates March 1990 as "National Prevent-A-Litter Month."

To Establish the Red Rock Canyon National Conservation Area 1990. Public Law 101-621. Establishes this area to be managed following existing land policy and management of wild free-roaming horses and burros. Hunting restriction may be implemented.

International Dolphin Conservation Act of 1992. Provides for an international agreement that should end the intentional slaughter of dolphins.

Wild Bird Conservation Act of 1992. Establishes a moratorium on importation of the most threatened bird species and a ban on importation of other bird species, if there is evidence that continued trade is imperiling bird populations.

Driftnet Moratorium Enforcement Act of 1992. Calls for a global moratorium on use of large-scale driftnets on the high seas. Nations continuing to use drift nets will be denied access to US ports and face an embargo of their fish products and possibly other products.

Animal Facilities Protection Act of 1992. Public Law 102-346. Provides a broad range of protection to animal facilities classed as research or farm production. The law maintains a minimum amount of damage ($10,000) that must be inflicted to make it a federal crime and is aimed at halting attacks by radical animal rights groups on farms and research laboratories.

California Desert Protection Act of 1993. Preserves the desert wilderness and its wildlife and creates the Mojave National Park, where hunting would be prohibited.

Direct Actions by US Animal Rights Activists

December 9, 1980, Ringling Brothers & Barnum & Bailey Circus, Venice, Florida. Slogans were spray-painted on trailers.

September 1, 1981, Institute for Behavioral Research, Silver Spring, Maryland. Alex Pacheco volunteered to work in the lab, collected data, and took photos implying inhumane treatment and unsanitary conditions. He supplied materials to county police who then confiscated the seventeen research monkeys.

April 2, 1982, University of Maryland, Animal Science Department, College Park. Forty-two rabbits were stolen.

Fall 1982, Chicago, Illinois. An animal laboratory veterinarian received a bomb threat.

December 25, 1982, Howard University, Medical Science Building, Washington, D.C. Nerve transmission studies were interrupted when cats valued at nearly $3,000 were stolen. The ALF was allegedly involved.

December 25, 1982, University of Florida, School of Medicine, Miami. ALF allegedly stole two rats.

December 27, 1982, US Naval Research Laboratory, Bethesda, Maryland. ALF allegedly stole one dog.

December 28, 1982, University of California, Berkeley. "Urban Gorillas" stole one cat and two kittens.

January 14, 1983, Naval Medical Research Institute, Bethesda, Maryland. ALF allegedly stole three dogs.

March 20, 1983. A bomb was placed outside the home of a researcher. It was found by a family member.

June 26, 1983, Toronto Western Hospital, Toronto, Ontario. ALF allegedly stole five cats.

August 15, 1983, dog pounds in Ohio. ALF allegedly spray-painted trucks and slashed tires, causing damage estimated at $6,000.

October 1983, University of Maryland, College Park. ALF allegedly broke in and stole a number of rabbits.

December 23, 1983, fur shops, Miami, Florida. ALF vandalized the shops.

December 25, 1983, Harbor-UCLA Medical Center, Los Angeles, California. ALF claimed credit for stealing twelve dogs involved in heart research, including five with experimental pacemakers, along with six rats being used in Alzheimer's disease studies.

December 25, 1983, Johns Hopkins University, Baltimore, Maryland. ALF allegedly stole six rats being used in Alzheimer's disease studies.

April 22, 1984, VA Medical Center, Minneapolis, Minnesota. The ALF allegedly stole a dog recuperating from experimental gall bladder surgery.

April 24, 1984, California Primate Research Center, Davis. After a twenty-four-hour vigil, fifteen people were arrested for blocking entrance to the center.

May 1984, California Primate Research Center, Davis. The director and associate director found ticking packages outside their homes. The associate director's car was spray-painted with animal rights slogans. The bomb squads found each package contained a clock and a copy of Peter Singer's book *Animal Liberation*. ALF was allegedly responsible.

May 16, 1984, California State University, Psychology Department, Sacramento. The ALF allegedly stole twenty-three rats with an estimated value of $1,900.

May 31, 1984, University of Pennsylvania, Head Injury Laboratory, Philadelphia. The ALF allegedly stole six years of research data, including audio- and videotapes, and damaged computer and other equipment.

June 30, 1984, Folsom Rodeo, Sacramento, California. Slogans were spray-painted on facility gates, walls, and seats.

July 28, 1984, University of Pennsylvania, Veterinary School, Philadelphia. ALF, claiming dissatisfaction with results of previous break-in, allegedly stole dogs being used in arthritis research, cats used in research of sudden infant death syndrome, and pigeons used in wing repair research.

August 27, 1984, University of California, Berkeley. The Animal Rights Direct Action Coalition members demonstrated causing arrests of twenty-six demonstrators.

October 1984, Vernon, California. Murals defaced on outside of pork slaughterhouse.

November 12, 1984, Knudson facility, Stockton, California. Windows were broken and paint thrown on facility.

November 15, 1984, Ohio State University, Dentistry Laboratory, Columbus. An activist was arrested for illegally trespassing and demonstrating.

November 28, 1984, National Cancer Institute, Bethesda, Maryland. The ALF staged a bomb threat.

December 1984. Individual researchers in the United States and Great Britain received threatening letters; some included bomb threats.

December 9, 1984, City of Hope Research Institute and Medical Center, Duarte, California. ALF allegedly broke in and stole 36 dogs involved in cancer research, 11 cats being used in emphysema studies, 12 rabbits, 28 mice, and 13 rats. Authorities placed the total damage at $500,000.

December 12, 1984, Fur Outlet, Inc., Tampa, Florida. Building was spray-painted with slogans.

December 22, 1984, University of California, San Diego. The southern California unit of the ALF threatened three researchers. Local police provided protection.

January 1985, San Diego, California. Simulated bomb left in fur department store restroom.

January 14, 1985, University of California, School of Medicine, San Diego. Death threat to dog laboratory professor caused cancellation of seminar.

February 13, 1985, University of California, Laboratory for Energy Related Research, Davis. ALF claimed to take two dogs, but no animals were found missing from the facility.

February 17, 1985, Napa County Animal Shelter, Napa Valley, California. ALF allegedly stole ten rabbits that had been recovered from the City of Hope break-in on December 9.

March 10, 1985, Los Angeles County Department of Animal Control and Care, Los Angeles, California. ALF splattered paint and left a threatening note at the residence of the director.

March 13, 1985, House of Furs, Sacramento, California. A plate-glass window was broken, and slogans were spray-painted on the front of the building and on the garage door.

April 11, 1985, University of California, Veterinary Medical Teaching Hospital, Davis. Vehicles were spray-painted with slogans.

April 20, 1985, University of California, Riverside. In a break-in and theft, ALF allegedly stole approximately 460 rats, mice, pigeons, monkeys, cats, rabbits, opossum, and gerbils having an estimated cost of $600,000.

April 23, 1985, University of California, Davis. The Animal Rights Direct Action Coalition participated in demonstrations and trespassing.

May 23, 1985, University of California, School of Veterinary Medicine, Davis. PETA activists accompanied by local press disrupted the dog surgery laboratory.

July 15, 1985, National Institutes of Health, Bethesda, Maryland. PETA activists occupied the office of the director of the National Institute for Neurological and Communicative Disorders and Stroke to protest the University of Pennsylvania Head Injury Laboratory.

August 10, 1985, Leather #1 (store), Bethesda, Maryland. The building was spray-painted with slogans on walls, awnings, and windows.

September 9, 1985, New York City. Demonstrators gathered outside the home of a researcher for the New York State Psychiatric Institute to protest. They later hurled an ax into his front door and left a threatening letter.

February 27, 1986. University presidents (at least forty across the United States) received threats from IDA.

April 21–22, 1986, University of California, Riverside. Attempted break-ins occurred during World Week for Laboratory Animals.

May 1, 1986, Simonsen Laboratories, Gilroy, California. An estimated twelve thousand pathogen-free rodents were exposed to contaminants, and equipment valued at $165,000 was damaged.

June 4, 1986, Sydel's Egg Farm, Hartly, Delaware. Farm Freedom Fighters broke into the facility, stole twenty-five chickens, and spray-painted buildings.

July 1986, Gillette Company, Rockville, Maryland. With the support of animal activist organizations, individuals intentionally obtained employment at the facility, collected data, took unauthorized photos, and supplied the materials to the media at press conferences.

July 21, 1986, Cedars-Sinai Medical Center, Halper Research Lab, Los Angeles, California. SUPPRESS and Last Chance for Animals protesters formed a picket line preventing employees from entering the building. Ninety-six protesters were arrested for trespassing.

August 5, 1986, Dept. of Health and Human Services, Washington, D.C. PETA activists were arrested as they demonstrated for the Silver Spring monkeys.

October 26, 1986, University of Oregon, Eugene. ALF broke in and stole 150 animals including cats, rabbits, rats, and hamsters, with total property damage exceeding $50,000.

November 10, 1986, Stanford University, Palo Alto, California. IDA activists demonstrated and were arrested outside the president's office.

November 24, 1986, Omega and HMS Turkey Ranches, Sacramento, California. ALF cut gas lines, put sugar in gas tanks, put glue in engines, spray-painted extensively, and stole turkeys. Damage was estimated at $12,000.

December 7, 1986, SEMA, Inc., Rockville, Maryland. True Friends stole four chimpanzees, valued at $50,000, that were slated for AIDS and hepatitis research.

January 1987, Tarlow's Furs, San Jose, California. At the store, locks were glued, slogans painted, paint bombs thrown.

February 1987, Kentucky Fried Chicken, Beaumont, California. The store's billboard was cut down, and slogans were spray-painted.

March 19, 1987, Tarlow's Furs, San Jose, California. Windows were broken, gasket sealer was put in key slots, and slogans were spray-painted.

April 16, 1987, University of California, Davis. The ALF allegedly painted and damaged seventeen to twenty state-owned vehicles.

April 16, 1987, University of California, Davis. The ALF allegedly set fire to a diagnostic laboratory under construction, causing $4.5 million damage.

April 16, 1987, Wolfe Poultry Farms, Milan, Pennsylvania. The Farm Freedom Fighters stole forty chickens.

April 17, 1987, Universal Animal Care, Bloomington, California. One hundred fifteen rabbits were stolen.

April 18, 1987, rabbit breeding farm, San Bernardino County, California. ALF allegedly stole one hundred rabbits.

April 1987, Lake Havassu City, Arizona. At Burger King and Kentucky Fried Chicken stores, a butcher shop, and a hunting and fishing shop, slogans were spray-painted.

April 1987, Fresno, California. Tarlow's Furs, slogans painted.

April 1987, Harris Ranch, Collings, California. Spikes were placed under truck tires, slogans were painted, and property vandalized.

May 24, 1987, Bureau of Land Management, Litchfield, California. The Western Wildlife unit broke in and stole six horses.

June 2, 1987, Hallmark Furs, St. Louis, Missouri. Store was firebombed. A device was hurled through a window, causing more than $1 million damage.

June 13, 1987, University of California, Davis. The ALF broke in and released five turkey vultures being used in a study to increase survival rates of birds in the wild. Researchers feared that the birds were not capable of surviving in the wild.

August 12, 1987, University of Nevada, Las Vegas. The ALF broke in and stole three goats from goat farm.

August 23, 1987, Animal Parasitology Institute, US Dept. of Agriculture, Beltsville, Maryland. The Band of Mercy allegedly stole seven miniature pigs and twenty-seven cats. The cats were infected with a potentially harmful bacteria. A nationwide alert for recovery of the animals was sent out.

September 1, 1987, San Jose Valley Veal, Inc., Santa Clara, California. Damage was done to a paper products warehouse. Damage was estimated at between $7,500 and $10,000.

October 1987, Birds Landing Pheasant Hunting Club, Fairfield, California. A replacement billboard was paint-bombed.

October 1987, Roberts' Furs, Fresno, California. The facility was paint-bombed and locks were glued.

October 1987, Olivers Egg Farm, California. Trucks and battery units were spray-painted.

October 1987, taxidermist's shop, Fresno, California. The shop was paint-bombed and spray-painted.

November 9, 1987, National Institutes of Mental Health, Bethesda, Maryland. IDA, PETA, and other activists were arrested as they protested against psychological research.

November 9, 1987, Marysville rodeo, Marysville, California. A billboard was cut down and slogans were painted.

November 14, 1987, Faith Home Poultry, Ceres, California. Thirty-eight hens were stolen, equipment was sabotaged, and slogans painted.

November 17, 1987, Birds Landing Pheasant Hunting Club, Fairfield, California. A billboard was cut down and slogans spray-painted.

November 19, 1987, Davis Egg Ranch, Gilroy, California. A truck was spray-painted with slogans.

November 26, 1987, Ferrara Meat Company, San Jose, California. A suspicious fire broke out in a grain building.

November 28, 1987, V. Melani Poultry, Santa Clara, California. Arson and vandalism caused an estimated $230,000 damage.

January 29, 1988, University of California, Irvine. The ALF allegedly broke in and stole thirteen beagles used in lung research.

February 14, 1988, Cal-Cruz Hatcheries, Santa Cruz, California. The company was picketed, and protesters were arrested when they climbed on the building roof to place a banner.

March 6, 1988, Sun Valley Meat Company, San Jose, California. Trucks were stripped of their paint.

March 21, 1988, US Dept. of Health and Human Services, Washington, D.C. Various groups demonstrated, and eight activists were arrested as they protested against psychological research.

March 21, 1988, San Jose Valley Meat Company, San Jose, California. Windows were etched with fluid, trucks were spray-painted with slogans.

March 27, 1988, Nitabell Rabbitry, Hayward, California. ALF stole twenty-three rabbits.

April 4, 1988, Davis Poultry Company and Egg Ranch, Gilroy, California. ALF allegedly stole twenty-four rabbits and sixty-three chickens.

April 5, 1988, Race Street Fish and Poultry, San Jose, California. Slogans were spray-painted.

April 21, 1988, University of California, Los Angeles. Last Chance for Animals activists videotaped animals in the lab and then released the tapes to local media. In October 1992, Chris DeRose and Aaron Leider began serving a ninety-day sentence in Los Angeles County jail for their part in the incident.

April 27, 1988, Harris Ranch, Collings, California. A water tank and signs were spray-painted.

May 10, 1988, Harris Ranch, Collings, California. Near the ranch, slogans were spray-painted on a freeway overpass.

June 5, 1988, Sun Valley Meat Packing Company, San Jose, California. Arson and vandalism caused an estimated $300,000 damage.

June 14, 1988, Beaver Farm, Stevensville, Montana. PETA activists allegedly stole two hundred beavers.

June 23, 1988, Santa Rosa Veal Farm, Santa Rosa, California. Two baby veal calves were stolen.

August 1988, Biosearch, Inc., Philadelphia, Pennsylvania. With the support of animal activist organizations, including PETA, individuals intentionally obtained employment at the facility, collected data, took unauthorized photos, and supplied the materials to the media at press conferences.

August 15, 1988, Loma Linda University, Loma Linda, California. ALF allegedly stole seven dogs, took records of earlier transplant research, spray-painted ALF slogans on the walls, and caused an estimated damage of $10,000.

September 24, 1988, University of California, Santa Cruz. Although an organization was not identified, police interrupted a raid and arrested seven people. Vandals spray-painted animal rights slogans on campus buildings and walkways.

September 25, 1988, University of Massachusetts, Amherst. The apiary was broken into.

October 1, 1988, wild game and taxidermist shops, San Francisco, California. Slogans were painted and windows etched.

October 14, 1988, San Diego, California. Homes of three San Diego Wild Animal Park elephant keepers were vandalized. ALF, which claimed responsibility, doused cars with paint stripper and red paint and painted sidewalks with the slogans, "Dundas's revenge" and "No excuse for animal abuse."

November 1988, Del Conte's Furrier, Santa Rosa, California. The facility caught on fire, causing $100,000 damage. A caller to the Associated Press said the ALF was responsible.

November 11, 1988, U.S. Surgical Corporation, Norwalk, Connecticut. Fran Stephanie Trutt placed a homemade, radio-controlled pipe bomb on the premises.

November 12, 1988, turkey ranch, Manteca, California. Thirty-three turkeys were injured, and slogans were painted.

December 23, 1988, Stanford University, Stanford, California. The ALF addressed a threatening letter and a fake bomb to the director of the Lab Animal Facility.

January 6, 1989, Veterans Administration Medical Center, Tucson, Arizona. The ALF allegedly stole seven dogs and returned three. None were part of research projects at the time they were stolen.

January 29, 1989, Dixon Livestock Company, Sacramento, California. Earth First protested against the livestock industry by setting a fire that caused damaged estimated at $250,000.

January 29, 1989, California Cattlemen's Association, California Wool Growers Association, California Council on Agriculture office building, Sacramento. Earth First! caused vandalism, including graffiti etched with acid.

February 21, 1989, University of California, Berkeley. In an attempt to halt construction on the Northwest Animal Facility, six people climbed a crane and hung banners from the top.

February 26, 1989, Duke University, research farm, Durham, North Carolina. A chain-link fence was cut to gain access to the farm. Documents were stolen, along with keys to the facility and vehicles.

March 26, 1989, Northwestern University, Evanston, Illinois. Several buildings spray-painted with slogans and death threats were made against a Northwestern researcher.

April 2, 1989, University of Arizona, Tucson. ALF took responsibility for theft of over one thousand animals. Four buildings were broken into, and two were set on fire. Estimated damage from arson was set at $100,000. There was a potential public health threat from mice infected with cryptosporidium.

April 24, 1989, National Institutes of Health, Bethesda, Maryland. Approximately two hundred IDA and PETA activists protested, and fifty-eight were arrested after blocking traffic on a main thoroughfare. Ingrid Newkirk, Tom Regan, and Alex Pacheco spoke at the demonstration. Three activists were charged with assault of a National Institute of Health police officer. The protest was in observance of World Laboratory Animal Liberation Week.

April 24, 1989, University of California, Los Angeles. Last Chance for Animals activists staged a sit-in in the hallway leading to the chancellor's office. Security police arrested twenty of about seventy-five activists who refused to leave when asked. The sit-in was held in observance of World Laboratory Animal Liberation Week.

April 25, 1989, Cedars-Sinai Medical Center, Los Angeles. Last Chance for Animals activists protested outside of the medical center. One arrest was made from among fifty protesters observing World laboratory Animal Liberation Week.

April 27, 1989, University of California, Los Angeles. Last Chance for Animals activists returned to continue protests. Jack Carone, a spokesperson for LCA, was arrested and charged with felony theft. Police said Carone stole an officer's handcuffs during the demonstration on April 24. The protest was held in observance of World Laboratory Animal Liberation Week.

April 28, 1989, Luce-Carmel Meat Company, Monterey, California. ALF was linked to incendiary devices found by an arson squad. Vandals spray-painted vans and trucks with graffiti.

April 29, 1989, Emory University, Atlanta, Georgia. ALF allegedly staged a break-in, left incendiary devices found by an arson squad, and spray-painted vans and trucks with graffiti.

May 22, 1989, partridge rearing facility, Elko, Nevada. ALF allegedly destroyed 1,400 ready-to-hatch eggs, released 600 to 700 chukars, and extensively damaged rearing pens and office facilities.

May 26, 1989, California Cattlemen's Association, Sacramento. Bricks and an unlit molotov cocktail were thrown through an office window.

June 1, 1989, Nevada Youth Training Center, Elko, Nevada. ALF claimed responsibility for releasing more than 600 chukar birds owned by a hunters group and cared for by boys at the youth center. The sheriff's department reported that many of the birds were killed by passing cars after running onto a nearby interstate highway. Another 1,400 chukar eggs in incubators and hatchers were feared lost because of vandalism. Estimated damage was $2,500.

June 5, 1989, Avon Company, Atlanta, Georgia. Two bomb threats occurred, but no bomb was found.

July 4, 1989, Texas Tech University, Health Science Center, Lubbock. ALF broke into the lab and office of a researcher, stole five cats and research data, and vandalized equipment and personal records. The estimated damage was $50,000 to $70,000.

July 15–16, 1989, Florida Cattlemen's Association Animal Disease Diagnostic Lab, Saddle Rack Store, Kissimmee. Buildings were vandalized and a truck spray-painted with animal rights slogans.

1989, Elko County, Nevada. Vandalism reported by ranchers included oil drained from tractors, fence and water pipelines cut, troughs and watertanks overturned, windmills decommissioned, and steel dropped into well casings.

January 14–15, 1990, University of Pennsylvania, Philadelphia. The ALF allegedly launched an intimidation campaign against an outspoken researcher, broke into his office, stole computer disks, personal files, videotapes, and a manuscript.

January 22, 1990 University of Pennsylvania, Philadelphia. Mike Winikoff, a PETA member, worked undercover as a lab assistant, then stole two rats from the university's psychology department laboratory.

April 24, 1990, National Institutes of Health, Bethesda, Maryland. Various activists trespassed after being warned not to cross police lines. Police charged twenty-seven with trespassing and fined first fifteen offenders, then scheduled ten others for trial on charges ranging from resisting arrest to assault and battery of a police officer.

April 25, 1990, University of California, Berkeley. At a demonstration by various activists, twenty-eight were arrested for trespassing.

May 2, 1990, Dawson Research Laboratory, Orlando, Florida. The ALF allegedly broke into the laboratory by forcing the door, stole eight rabbits, spray-painted walls, and issued press release through PETA in Washington.

July 1990, Simonsen Laboratories, Gilroy, California. ALF activists broke in by cutting through the roof, stole one hundred guinea pigs valued at $2,500, and spray-painted the walls.

July 1990, Lincoln, Illinois. Farmer Wayne Conrady was harassed by an animal activist on the highway as he was hauling hogs to market.

October 2, 1990, US Dept. of Agriculture, Washington, D.C. FARM activists forced their way into the building. Police arrested five activists and charged three with trespassing.

October 5, 1990, American Medical Association, Chicago, Illinois. The AMA office received bomb threats causing two evacuations.

October 27, 1990, State University of New York, animal facility, Buffalo. Twelve research projects were interrupted when 750 laboratory animals, including 89 rats, 620 mice, 35 hamsters, 1 quail, and 5 chickens were released.

November 9, 1990, Chicago, Illinois. A researcher received a bomb threat.

January 1, 1991, Cook County Hospital, Chicago, Illinois. ALF allegedly stole twenty-one rabbits and guinea pigs, fed fruit to caged baboons, and removed tops from rat and mice cages.

April 14, 1991, Seattle, Washington. The car of the director of the Regional Primate Center Director and a neighbor's home were spray-painted with animal rights slogans.

May 25, 1991, Seattle, Washington. The homes and cars of two Seattle scientists were spray-painted.

May 31, 1991, Des Moines, Iowa. An anonymous PETA member pushed a nondairy cream pie into Iowa Pork Queen Dainna Jellings's face at the World Pork Expo.

June 1, 1991, Des Moines, Iowa. Pork supporter Sandra O'Neill hit PETA protester Denise Berner with a pie.

June 10, 1991, Corvallis, Oregon. ALF destroys a laboratory farm where minks were kept.

June 15, 1991, Northwest Farms Food Cooperative, Edmunds, Washington. ALF allegedly burned down empty building that supplies feed to mink producers and research animals at Oregon State University.

June 17, 1991, Bowman Gray School of Medicine, Winston-Salem, North Carolina. ALF allegedly phoned in bomb threat to the school.

June 20, 1991, Mellowville, California. Naturalists United for Terrorism (NUT) blew up the sewage treatment plant at Stinkwater Junction, sending millions of gallons of raw sewage into the Rio Des Muertes "to stop genocide of billions and billions of bacteria by health department fascists."

August 13, 1991, Washington State University and USDA facility, Pullman. Vandals destroyed research materials and computers and turned animals loose.

February 29, 1992, Michigan State University, East Lansing. Vandals broke into the offices of a mink researcher, removed identification tags from 350 mink, burned offices, and destroyed records covering thirty-two years. Damage was estimated at $125,000.

February 29, 1992, University of Maryland, College Park. PETA activist Jennifer Woods, dressed as a giant chicken, hit Frank Perdue, major chicken producer and member of the Maryland Board of Regents, in the face with a pie. Woods was arrested for assault and disorderly conduct.

October 24, 1992, US Dept. of Agriculture Predator Research Laboratory, Logan, Utah. ALF allegedly firebombed the office and injured coyotes.

October 28, 1992, Wright State University, Dayton, Ohio. PETA undercover investigator Virginia Bollinger was arrested on charges that she entered the laboratory at unauthorized times, made videotapes, and removed documents from their proper places.

November 8, 1992, Swanson Meats, Minneapolis, Minnesota. Vandals set fire to trucks and placed glue in locks, causing $100,000 loss. Some trucks were spray-painted with the slogan "Meat is murder."

1992, Minneapolis, Minnesota. Simek's Meats and Seafood, Johnson's Meats, and Summit Meats were vandalized. In Bloomington, Minnesota, at the Alaskan Fur Company, vandals damaged trucks and store facilities.

January 3, 1993, National Cattlemen's Convention, Phoenix, Arizona. PETA special projects director Dan Matthews in a bloody "butcher's" costume, a woman dressed as a cow, and four others left their designated picketing site and attempted to gain entrance to the convention site and were arrested for trespassing and disturbing the peace.

January 10, 1993, National Turkey Federation annual convention, Newport Beach, California. Animal activists entered the reception room, pulled out signs, and marched around the room chanting "Meat stinks." Hotel security escorted the group from the room.

April 28, 1993, Montgomery County and Greenbelt, Maryland. Cars and homes of four researchers and the president of an animal services facility were vandalized by animal rights activists identified as Animal Avengers. Car windshields were broken and garage doors, vehicles, and driveways were spray-painted.

May 30, 1993, Johns Hopkins School of Public Health, Baltimore, Maryland. Students Against In Vivo Experiments and Dissection (SAVED) stole four dogs and three cats from the animal housing facility. The dogs were involved in a study concerning the effects of ordinary levels of a common air pollutant. The testing in which they were involved was identical to allergy testing performed on human subjects elsewhere at Johns Hopkins.

June 1, 1993. Animal Liberation Action Foundation mailed letters in the United States threatening a campaign of destruction and bloodletting upon individuals and facilities.

November 27, 1993, Chicago, Illinois. In four department stores, ALF claimed to have planted incendiary devices protesting the sale of fur. The eight devices ignited fires in three of the stores, causing minimal damage and no injuries.

January 27, 1994, San Diego Meat Company, San Diego, California. The Farm Animal Revenge Militia ignited two meat company refrigerated trucks with flammable liquid and spray-painted "Meat is Murder" on the company's building.

January 30, 1994, San Diego Meat Company, San Diego, California. Farm Animal Revenge Militia splashed flammable liquid that started fire in two rooms of the meat company. The fire caused $60,000 damage to the building and $15,000 to the contents.

May 19, 1994, Honolulu, Hawaii. Alex Pacheco and three other PETA activists attempted to protest the Nature Conservancy's use of snares to control pigs in Hawaiian forests. They were arrested on criminal trespass charges.

July 27, 1994, Philadelphia, Pennsylvania. Three PETA members attempted to throw urine at the headquarters building at Wyeth-Ayerst Laboratories but hit police instead. They were arrested.

September 29, 1994, American Meat Institute, San Francisco, California. Two PETA members were arrested after animal rights activists dumped a large pile of manure outside a meeting of the institute.

October 18, 1994, Gillette Company, Annapolis, Maryland. Seven protesters were arrested for disorderly conduct and trespassing during a meeting of company representatives.

February 3, 1995 Boston, Massachusetts. Three PETA members dressed in bunny suits climbed flagpoles and hung a large banner at Gillette corporate headquarters. The activists were arrested after spending two hours dangling eighty feet above the street.

April 5, 1995, Ringling Brothers Circus, Washington, D.C. Eighteen members of PETA, wearing prison garb and elephant masks, protested a special performance of the Ringling Brothers Circus and were arrested for unlawful entry and obstructing passage on the Capitol grounds.

April 30, 1995, Dairygold Distribution Center, Olympia, Washington. Vandals damaged trucks and spray-painted animal rights slogans on walls. Damage was estimated at $15,000.

June 1995, Majestic Meats plant, Salt Lake City, Utah. The plant was firebombed.

November 24, 1995, Valley River Center Mall, Eugene, Oregon. An estimated $75,000 worth of furs were spray-painted on Fur Free Friday.

January 1996, Sheboygan, Wisconsin. From 200 to 400 mink were released from a fur farm owned by Robert Zimbal.

May 3, 1996, Oregon Regional Primate Center, Beaverton. Activists blocked entrance to the facility and locked themselves to the blockade.

May 18, 1996, Central Meat Packing Plant, Chesapeake, Virginia. Intruders cut refrigeration equipment freon lines, electrical lines, and two natural gas lines. Slogans painted on the building read, "Meat is murder," "Killers," and "ALF".

June 21, 1996, fur farm, Riverton, Utah. Mink were released from cages.

July 4, 1996, Latzig Mink Farm, Howard Lake, Minnesota. Activists released one thousand mink from pens. About nine hundred were recovered.

July 17, 1996, Holt Mink Ranch, South Jordan, Utah. Vandals attempted to release three thousand mink; and they committed extensive property damage to the farm.

August 10, 1996, mink farm, Hinsdale, Massachusetts. Vandals released one thousand mink and caused $10,000 damage to the mink farm.

August 12, 1996, Justice Jorney's mink ranch, Alliance, Ohio. Two thousand five hundred mink were released.

August 13, 1996, Boys Town National Research Hospital, Omaha, Nebraska. Unidentified person obtained employment and collected data, including unauthorized videotapes alleging inhumane treatment. Videotapes were released to the media, and complaints were filed by PETA with the USDA and NIH.

August 17, 1996, Boston, Massachusetts. The home of a semi-retired furrier was splashed with red paint.

August 31, 1996, Rus Dun Egg Farm, Fayette County, Tennessee. A truck was firebombed and burned.

September 2, 1996, Hegins, Pennsylvania. Animal rights activists protested at a Labor Day Pigeon Shoot. Fifteen people were arrested.

October 2, 1996, Rancho Slaughterhouse, Petaluma, California. Four activists were arrested for blocking the entrance to the facility during a protest.

October 3, 1996, home of Georgio Politis, Onondaga, New York. Vandals splattered the furrier's home with red paint and painted "You can't hide" on a door.

October 7, 1996, U.S. Surgical, ACS Medical Convention, San Francisco, California. Sixteen activists were arrested during a protest.

October 8, 1996, University of California, Los Angeles. Six activists protested inside the office of a researcher and were arrested. Videotapes and paperwork were stolen.

October 13, 1996, Ringling Brothers & Barnum & Bailey Circus, Denver, Colorado. Thirty activists protested at the circus. Four were arrested for trespassing, after locking themselves to the main doors of the arena where the circus was appearing.

October 25, 1996, mink farm, Morgan County, Utah. Two thousand mink and two hundred foxes were released.

October 30, 1996, National Aeronautics and Space Administration, Washington, D.C. PETA activists protesting a mission occupied the office of the administrator, Daniel Goldin. They chained themselves together, using bicycle locks, and were arrested for trespassing.

November 12, 1996, Alaska Fur Company, Bloomington, Minnesota. An incendiary device was thrown through the window of the fur company, causing damage estimated at $2 million.

November 18, 1996, National Air and Space Museum, Washington, D.C. Activists chained themselves together at the base of the *Apollo 11* command module for two hours, protesting NASA's BIOW mission.

November 28, 1996, Carmel Mink Ranch, Hinsdale, Massachusetts. One thousand mink were released. All but fifty were recovered.

December 11, 1996, office of *Vogue* editor Anna Wintour, New York City. Activists were arrested while protesting comments Wintour made regarding wearing fur and eating meat.

December 19, 1996, Lewis Morris Park, Morris Township, New Jersey. Activists blockaded the entrance to the park, trying to prevent hunters from shooting deer for population control.

December 25, 1996, Jack Brower Fur Farm, Bath, Michigan. Activists released an estimated one hundred fifty mink and sprayed green paint on the premises.

December 26, 1996, Haertel Company, Eden Prairie, Minnesota. Incendiary devices were left on a company truck. The company produces a pelt cleaner used on fur farms. An estimated $18,000 damage was claimed.

January 3, 1997, Georgio's Furs, Syracuse, New York. Eight activists were arrested, including one charged with assaulting a police officer, while protesting in front of the store.

January 1, 1997, Cornell University, Poultry Virus Isolation Facility, Ithaca, New York. Activists cut a padlock on the back door, took pictures, walked through a virus isolation area without protection, and contaminated their shoes with the infection. The Band of Mercy claimed responsibility.

January 25, 1997, Macy's Harold Square, New York City. Five anti-fur activists, covered in fake blood and with steel-jawed traps attached to their legs, were arrested during a protest.

January 27, 1997, Producers Livestock Marketing Association, Salt Lake City, Utah. Windows were broken, and the building was vandalized; damages of $3,000 to $5,000 were estimated.

January 29, 1997, Producers Livestock Marketing Association, Salt Lake City, Utah. Windows were broken, and firebombs were hurled into the building. Extensive damage was estimated at $75,000 to $100,000.

February 19, 1997, Rancho Slaughterhouse, Petaluma, California. Activists firebombed the slaughterhouse with two molotov cocktail–type bomb.

March 4, 1997, Outdoorsman, hunting and trapping store, Indianapolis, Indiana. Windows were broken, the building spray-painted, and the back of the building burned.

March 6, 1997, Jack-in-the-Box restaurant, Perris, California. The construction site was burned.

March 6, 1997, Douglas Burgers restaurant construction site, Lake Elsinore, California. An incendiary device failed to go off at the site.

March 7, 1997, Lloyd's Furs, West Hartford, Connecticut. The building was painted with red letters, "ALF."

March 11, 1997, Utah Fur Breeders Agricultural Cooperative, Sandy, Utah. Activists set fire to the business, destroying an office and four trucks, causing $1 million in damage.

March 14, 1997, New York Meat Products, South Windsor, New York. ALF slogans were painted on the building.

March 14, 1997, New York Meat Company, Hartford, Connecticut. Windows and delivery vans were smashed, locks damaged, and red paint used to write the slogan "Meat is murder."

March 18, 1997, Montgomery Fur Company, Ogden, Utah. Activists doused the company's building with gasoline, but the incident was foiled by a security guard.

March 18, 1997, University of California, Center for Comparative Medicine, Davis. Activists claimed responsibility for setting fire to a construction site to mark the tenth anniversary of the campus diagnostic laboratory. Damage was minor.

March 18, 1997, Exclusive Furs by Ramon, West Hartford, Connecticut. Slogans, including "Ramon = Death," were scrawled in red on the side of the building.

March 23, 1997, Acme chicken slaughterhouse, Seattle, Washington. Machinery was damaged and offices vandalized with acid and paint. Three chickens were stolen.

March 23, 1997, Flemmington Fur Company, Flemmington, New Jersey. A rock was thrown through a front window, followed by an incendiary device. Fire caused only a small amount of smoke and fire damage because the store's sprinkler system doused the fire. An undetermined amount of damage was caused.

April 4, 1997, L. W. Bennett and Sons, fur farm, East Bloomfield, New York. An estimated three thousand mink were released.

April 9, 1997, home of John Marcopolis, owner of Elan Furs, Indianapolis, Indiana. Vehicles were covered with paint stripper. The house was doused with red paint, and slogans were painted on a door.

April 9, 1997, Don Kelly Chinchilla Farm, Deberry, Texas. Ten chinchilla were released.

May 30, 1997, fur ranch, Mt. Angel, Oregon. Vandals released an estimated eight to nine thousand mink from their cages on a fur ranch, and many of the animals died of exposure; this incident is probably the largest attack on the US mink industry.[1]

The Bobby Berosini Orangutans Case

On August 2, 1989, Bobby Berosini, a Las Vegas night club entertainer with an orangutan act, filed suit at the Clark County, Nevada, District Court for defamation, misappropriation of name, likeness, and character (for fund-raising using his name), and invasion of privacy against PETA, PAWS, and other individuals. In the lawsuit Berosini claimed:

- PETA had contact with entertainers in the production show in which Berosini's orangutans appeared;
- PETA identified Berosini as a principal target in their fund-raising campaign based on stopping the use of animals in entertainment;
- an entertainer working with PETA secretly filmed Berosini trying to get the animals under control;
- PETA edited and altered the tapes and then distributed the doctored tapes;
- PETA waged a massive misinformation media campaign, falsely accusing Berosini of criminal animal abuse;
- PETA falsely called him a child abuser;
- PETA falsely accused him of beating the orangutans with a steel pipe;
- PETA falsely stated that the striking of the orangutans was routine and unprovoked;
- US Department of Agriculture conducted an investigation and found no signs of abuse; and
- the producer of the tape admitted he altered the sound and the visual portion of the tape in order to sensationalize the tape.

PETA filed a counterclaim against Berosini, requesting confiscation of the orangutans due to Berosini's alleged abuse. The court dismissed the counterclaim "with prejudice."

On August 11, 1990, the jury ruled in favor of Berosini and against PETA, PAWS, Jeanne Roush, Pat Derby, and Ottavio Gesmundo as follows:

- Invasion of privacy, unreasonable intrusion upon seclusion of another:
  Ottavio Gesmundo, $250,000
- Invasion of privacy, appropriation of another's name or likeness:
  PETA, general and special damages, $500,000
  Jeanne Roush, general and special damages, $250,000

- Invasion of privacy and publicity that unreasonably places the other in a false light before the public:

    PETA, general and special damages, $500,000

    Jeanne Roush, general and special damages, $250,000

    Ottavio Gesmundo, $250,000

    PAWS, $50,000

    Pat Derby, $50,000

- Defamation:

    PETA, general and special damages, $1,000,000

    Jeanne Roush, general and special damages, $1,000,000

    Ottavio Gesmundo, $500,000

    PAWS, $50,000

    Pat Derby, $50,000

After determining the verdicts of the jury, the court determined that the plaintiff did prevail on his claim of invasion of privacy and publicity that unreasonably places the other in a false light before the public and that such remedy is an alternative or additional remedy to the claim for defamation. So the court ruled that Berosini could not recover damages on both, and damages were to be awarded on the defamation claim only.[1]

PETA appealed the verdict to the Nevada Supreme Court. Before the court made its ruling, PETA set up a contingency fund to pay the awarded damages if they were required to do so (see chapter 15). On January 27, 1994, the Nevada Supreme Court reversed the decision against PETA, ruling that the videotape reflected clear and unequivocal depiction of how Berosini treated the orangutans. PETA claimed that the judge in the trial was a former college roommate of Berosini's employer and had received a sizable campaign contribution from him. They further claimed that the previous judge had refused to allow many of the defendant witnesses to testify. After the Nevada Supreme Court decision, PETA submitted a petition to the district court of Las Vegas asking that Berosini be required to pay court costs of close to a quarter of a million dollars.[2]

Although Berosini sought reconsideration of the supreme court decision, on May 22, 1995, the Nevada Supreme Court entered its final order upholding the reversal and dismissing the plaintiff's case.[3]

In 1996, PETA reported that a Las Vegas judge ordered Berosini to pay PETA $387,000 in costs and legal fees as a result of the failed lawsuit he filed against PETA.[4]

Notes

Preface

1. Rollin, "Animal Welfare," 3456.

1. The Evolution of Animal Welfare and Animal Rights

1. Thomas, 92–142.
2. Thomas, 180.
3. Thomas, 182.
4. Thomas, 184.
5. Thomas, 185.
6. French, 26–27.
7. Guither and Curtis, 2.
8. Harrison, *Animal Machines*, 1.
9. Ruth Harrison, interview by author, May 1982.
10. Brambell.
11. AHA is the parent organization for the American Association for Protecting Children.
12. US Dept. of Justice, 3.
13. Holden, "Animal Regulations," 882.
14. Hill and Knowlton, 8.
15. Kenneth J. Shapiro, Address before the 7th International Animal Rights Symposium, Washington, D.C., July 9, 1994.
16. Richard D. Ryder, Address before the 7th International Animal Rights Symposium, Washington, D.C., July 9, 1994.
17. Jasper and Nelkin, 51.
18. Ogden, 6.
19. Regan, Francione, and Newkirk, 40–42.
20. This is a frequently used slogan, probably originated by Ingrid Newkirk, founder of PETA.
21. Rowan, "Animal Well-Being."
22. Rowan, "Animal Rights," 5.
23. "A New Fundamentalism?" *Animals' Agenda* 11.9 (Nov. 1991): 2.
24. Guither, 4.
25. Francione, "Animal Rights and Welfare," 28–29.
26. *Animal People*, Mar. 1997, 2, 13.

27. *Animal People*, Aug.–Sept. 1996, 2.
28. Charrow quoted in Hardy, iii.
29. Rollin, *Animal Rights*, 12.

2. A Changing Philosophy for Human and Animal Relationships

1. Garner, 6.
2. Garner, chapter 1.
3. *Webster's New World Dictionary of the American Language*, college ed., s.v. "philosophy."
4. Singer, *Animal Liberation*, 1st ed., 7.
5. Bentham, *Introduction to the Principles of Morals and Legislation*, quoted in Singer, *Animal Liberation*, 1st ed., 8.
6. Leahy, "Animals and the Ethics of Slaughter."
7. Singer, *Animal Liberation*, 1st ed., 9.
8. Regan, *Case for Animal Rights*, 235.
9. Regan, *Case for Animal Rights*, 142–43.
10. Singer, *Animal Liberation*, 1st ed., 82.
11. Singer, *Animal Liberation*, 1st ed., 172.
12. Garner, 243.
13. Regan, *Case for Animal Rights*, 261.
14. Leahy, *Against Liberation*, 10.
15. Singer, ed., *In Defence of Animals*, 1.
16. Frey, 29.
17. Frey, 100.
18. Clark, 14.
19. Clark, 27.
20. Clark, 28.
21. Clark, 182.
22. Regan, *Case for Animal Rights*, xii.
23. Regan, *Struggle for Animal Rights*, 122.
24. Regan, *Struggle for Animal Rights*, 45.
25. Regan, *Struggle for Animal Rights*, ix.
26. Ryder, *Victims of Science*, 1–2.
27. Ryder, *Victims of Science*, 5
28. Ryder, *Victims of Science*, 10.
29. Sapontzis, xii.
30. Sapontzis, xiv; Finsen and Finsen, 206–7.
31. Midgley, "Persons and Nonpersons," 60; Finsen and Finsen, 228–29.
32. Rollin, *Unheeded Cry*, 270.
33. Jamieson, 109.
34. Leahy, *Against Liberation*, 176.
35. Leahy, *Against Liberation*, 251.
36. Vance, 1715, 1717.
37. Tester, 5.
38. Singer, *Animal Liberation*, 1st ed., 259.
39. Singer, *Animal Liberation*, 1st ed., 97.

40. There are some who would avoid use of wool products, but Singer believes that wool is not a major issue since the sheep are not killed to obtain their fleece.

41. Regan, *Philosophy*, 2.

42. Regan, in Singer, ed., *In Defence of Animals*, 13.

43. Singer, "A Conversation," 26–27.

44. Singer, ed., *In Defence of Animals*, 8.

45. Leahy, *Against Liberation*, 169.

46. Linzey, *Christianity*, 28–29.

47. Linzey, *Christianity*, 30.

48. Linzey, *Christianity*, 33.

49. Linzey, *Christianity*, 49.

50. Linzey, *Christianity*, 44.

51. Warren, 201.

52. Warren, 206.

53. Garner, 243.

54. Rowan, letter to the editor, 1114.

55. Vance, 1718.

56. Tweeten.

57. Halverson, 37.

58. Finsen and Finsen, 233.

59. Gary Francione, interview in Hitt, et al., 44.

3. Animal Welfare in Europe

1. Rollin, "Animal Welfare," 3456.

2. Commission of the European Communities, "Council Directive of 24 November 1986," 1.

3. Commission of the European Communities, "Council Directive of 24 November 1986," 1–6.

4. Birbeck, 1378.

5. MAFF (UK), *Summary of the Law*, 1.

6. MAFF (UK), *Codes of Recommendations*.

7. NFU (UK), *Animal Welfare*.

8. MAFF (UK), *Animal Health 1990*, 28.

9. Dun, 28.

10. Dun, 30.

11. Swedish Ministry of Agriculture, *The Animal Protection Act*.

12. Roland Printzskold, Swedish livestock producer, interview by author, July 15, 1993.

13. Hill and Sainsbury, 19.

14. Guither and Hollis, 24.

15. Birbeck, 1379.

16. Windhorst, 31.

17. Guither and Curtis, 49.

18. For more information on the RSPCA's work, see *Animal Life* 9 (Aug. 1992), 29; 10 (winter 1992), 29.

19. Free, 12.

20. Hill and Sainsbury, 35.

21. PETA, *Annual Review*, 2.

22. Rollin, "Animal Welfare."

4. Reformists and Abolitionists: Organizations and Their Leaders

1. In this chapter, every effort was made to bring together the latest available information on the groups listed. However, officers, addresses, and other developments are subject to frequent change. Financial data were the latest that could be obtained at the time of publication.

2. *Animals' Agenda*, Mar. 1991, 33.

3. *International Society of Animal Rights Newsletter*, spring 1994.

4. Greene, 45.

5. Hill and Knowlton, 19; ASPCA, *Animal Rights Handbook*.

6. MSPCA, *Toward the Future: 1994 Annual Report*, 8–9.

7. FBR, *Directory*, 1994, 6.

8. Kelley, 1

9. Kelley, 1.

10. Kelley, 1.

11. Statement by Cleveland Amory and Frank Cullen in "Declaration of the Rights of Animals."

12. Martin, 9.

13. "Correction and Clarification," *Washingtonian* 27.3 (Dec. 1991): 36.

14. FBR, *Directory*, 1994; "Layoffs at NEAVS," *Animal People*, Sept. 1993, 9.

15. "The Watchdog," *Animal People*, July 1996, 13; Philip G. Peabody Coalition, South Lynnfield, Mass., letter to Cleveland Amory, Sept. 1995; correspondence with Cleveland Amory, Alex Pacheco, and members of the board, NEAVS, Sept. 27, 1995–May 15, 1996.

16. "Organizations," *Animal People*, Jan.–Feb. 1997, 12.

17. Hill and Knowlton, 54.

18. *Animal People*, July–Aug. 1994, 2.

19. *Animal People*, Mar. 1993, 11; June 1996, 13.

20. *Animal People*, July–Aug. 1993, 11.

21. Hoyt, "Report," 7.

22. Hoyt, "Tilling a Common Ground."

23. Fox, "Animal Agriculture," 26–27.

24. Oliver, 27.

25. Paul Irwin, president, HSUS, letter of Apr. 2, 1993, soliciting funds for new program dealing with "animal suffering, human health and the environment."

26. Hill and Knowlton, 49.

27. Irwin, "Eating with Conscience."

28. *Foundation for Biomedical Research News*, 13.1 (Jan.–Feb. 1996): 1.

29. *Animal People*, June 1996, 13.

30. Hill and Knowlton, 43.

31. Statement by Kenneth E. Guerrero, chairman, and Duf Fischer, executive director, Animal Protection Institute, in "Declaration of the Rights of Animals."

32. Hill and Knowlton, 43.

33. Statement from ARI in "Declaration of the Rights of Animals."

34. Hill and Knowlton, 27.

35. *Animals' Agenda*, Dec. 1991, 52; Nov.–Dec. 1994, 41. Editor Kim Stallwood stated in a national seminar in July 1994 that 20,000 copies were printed; 12,000 were mailed to subscribers, and 4,500 were sent out for newsstand sales.

36. Kim Stallwood, letter to author, May 1, 1993.

37. Newkirk, *Save the Animals*, xiv.

38. *Foundation for Biomedical Research News* 13.1 (Jan.–Feb. 1996), 8.

39. Newkirk, *Save the Animals*, xiv.

40. AFBF, *Meeting the Animal Rights Challenge*, 14.

41. *Foundation for Biomedical Research News*, 13.1 (Jan.–Feb. 1996): 5.

42. "Revulsion and PETA," *Des Moines Register*, Aug. 9, 1991, 12A.

43. The ad appeared in the *Des Moines Register*, under the heading "Milwaukee . . . July 1991," 14T. Steve Kopperud, head of the FAWC (US), made the comment during a personal conversation following publication of the ad.

44. AFBF, *Meeting the Animal Rights Challenge*, 14.

45. *Animal People*, July–Aug. 1994, 2.

46. ARM! "Comprehensive Policy Statement," 1–2.

47. Statement from FARM in "Declaration of the Rights of Animals."

48. Mail survey and information to author.

49. Katz.

50. *Animal People*, Jan.–Feb. 1994, 11–12.

51. Hill and Knowlton, 45.

52. Organization statement in "Declaration of the Rights of Animals."

53. Albright, 10.

54. *Wall Street Journal*, Oct. 29, 1990, 1.

55. US Dept. of Justice, 7.

56. American Animal Protection Organizations, "Joint Resolutions."

57. "Animal Welfare," Monitor Bulletin 88.24, *International Business Issues Monitor* (New York), May 31, 1988, 9.

58. Strand and Strand, 51.

59. *Animal People*, Sept. 1993, 11; Nov. 1993, 3.

60. *Animal People*, May 1997, 13.

5. A Profile of Animal Rights Activists

1. Almond, 138–39.

2. Lunch, *Nationalization of American Politics*.

3. Jamison and Lunch.

4. Richards and Krannich.

5. "The Emerging Face of the Movement," *Animals' Agenda* 5.2 (Mar.–Apr. 1985): 10.

6. Sperling. For a more complete idea of Sperling's profile of the animal rights movement, see her chapters 2, 3, 4, 5, and 8.

7. US Dept. of Commerce, 51.

8. US Dept. of Commerce, 14.

9. US Dept. of Commerce, 47.

10. Jasper and Nelkin, 20, 38, 39.

11. Ranney, 6–9.

12. US Dept. of Commerce, 58.

13. L. White, 1206.

14. Regan, ed., *Animal Sacrifices,* x; Linzey, in Regan, ed., *Animal Sacrifices,* 115–48; Linzey, *Christianity*; Singer, *Animal Liberation*, 2d ed.

15. Newkirk quoted in McCabe, "Who Will Live, Who Will Die?" 21.

16. Wilson; Lichter and Rothman.

17. Barke, 127.

18. Jamison and Lunch.

19. Nie, Verba, and Petrocik.

6. The Debate over Animals in Research, Testing, and Teaching

1. Beck et al., 50.

2. Rowan, Loew, and Weer, 14–15; *Animal People*, Apr. 1994, 17.

3. Rollin, *Animal Rights*, 136–37.

4. Rowan, *Of Mice, Models, and Men*, 63.

5. The Silver Spring monkeys case began in the summer of 1981 after Alex Pacheco, later co-founder of People for the Ethical Treatment of Animals, began working as a volunteer for Dr. Edward Taub at the Institute for Behavioral Research in Silver Spring, Maryland. See chapter 14 and appendix 4.

6. Rowan, *Of Mice, Models, and Men*, 58.

7. Reines, 7.

8. McKeown, 157

9. McKeown, 198.

10. Joel Brinkley, "Many Say Lab-Animal Tests Fail to Measure Human Risk," *New York Times*, Mar. 23, 1993, A1, A16.

11. Cunniff, 2.

12. Tiger, "Is There Really a Conflict?" 11.

13. Roberts, 26–27.

14. Tiger, "Is There Really a Conflict?" 11.

15. Tiger, "Is There Really a Conflict?" 11.

16. DeBakey, "For the Sake of Your Patients," 17.

17. NAS, *Science, Medicine, and Animals*, 12.

18. AMA, "Use of Animals in Biomedical Research," 2.

19. Leader and Stark, 476.

20. Krasney, 7.

21. *NABR Issue Update*, 1992.

22. The Delaney Amendment was viewed by many as out of date with today's technologies for detecting substances in extremely minute amounts. It was replaced with new legislation in 1996 that changed the rules for defining food safety. However, the need for animals in research was not changed by this law..

23. William Lijinsky, "Animal Tests Are the Only Way to Discover Toxic Substances," *Washington Post*, Oct. 9, 1990, health sec.

24. "The Use of Animals in Product Safety Testing," *NABR Issue Update*, Washington, D.C., 1997, 4.

25. FBR, "Scientists and Patient Advocates Denounce Animal Rights Movement," press release, Washington, D.C., June 17, 1996.

26. Dr. Don Simmons, AVMA, conversation with author, June 17, 1997.

27. AVMA, *Animal Welfare Positions*, 9.

28. Shapiro, "Psychology of Dissection," 20.

29. Rowan, *Of Mice, Models, and Men*, 101.

30. "NABT Moves Toward Stronger Support For Classroom Dissection," *Animal People*, Apr. 1994, 18.

31. FBR, *FBR Facts*, 2.5 (n.d.): 1.
32. Rowan, "The Alternatives Concept," 1.
33. "Use of Animals in Product Safety Testing," 5.
34. FBR, *Animal Research*, 1.
35. Weibers, "Vision of a New Era," 10.
36. Cohen, 869.
37. NAS, *Science, Medicine, and Animals*, 15–16.
38. *SCAW Newsletter* 12.4 (winter 1990–91): 5–6.
39. Singer, *Animal Liberation*, 2d ed.
40. Cohen, 869.
41. Rollin, *Animal Rights*, 137.
42. Masta, letter to the editor.
43. AVMA, *Animal Welfare Positions*, 7.
44. AVMA, *Animal Welfare Positions*, 9.
45. Beck et al., 50–59. "Of Pain and Progress" appeared in the Dec. 26, 1988, issue of *Newsweek*. It reports on the campaign by Trans-Species Unlimited (now ARM!) against Michiko Okamoto and the drug experiments with cats that led to the decision by Cornell University to forfeit a $530,000 three-year research grant from the National Institute on Drug Abuse (NIDA).
46. FBR, *Use of Animals*, 8.
47. Vance, 1718.
48. Krasney, 13.
49. DeBakey, "Health and Hypocrisy."
50. Finsen and Finsen, 280.

7. Intensive Animal Production: Efficient, Low-Cost Food or a Violation of Animals' Rights?

1. William R. Stricklin, quoted in Becker, 1; data from Economic Research Service, US Dept. of Agriculture.
2. Harrison, "Welfare Requirements," 11.
3. Singer, *Animal Liberation*, 2d ed., 95.
4. Alex Hershaft, statement at Decade of the Animals Conference, Bethesda, Md., Nov. 8–11, 1991.
5. Rollin, "Animal Production," 12.
6. Although specific organizations and individuals have made this criticism, other organizations or individual activists also hold similar views.
7. Mason and Singer, 192.
8. American Animal Protection Organizations, "Joint Resolutions."
9. AHA, *Policy Statement*.
10. Fox, "Humane Sustainable Agriculture," 26.
11. Fox, "Humane Sustainable Agriculture," 26.
12. FARM, Fund solicitation letter, 1994, to launch its education campaign.
13. *New York Times*, Oct. 20, 1989, A17; Feder, 34.
14. Paul Irwin, inside front cover, *HSUS News*, spring 1994.
15. Becker, 8.
16. Swanson, "Welfare Concerns," 3.
17. Dawkins, 2.
18. Dawkins, 31.

19. Dawkins, 38.

20. Duncan, 4.

21. Dawkins, 128–29.

22. Mench and Tienhoven, 598.

23. Mench and Tienhoven, 00.

24. This symposium was sponsored by the Federation of American Societies of Food Animal Sciences and the Forum for Animal Agriculture.

25. *Farm Animal Welfare in Indiana*, 14.

26. Mench and Tienhoven, 602.

27. Mench and Tienhoven, 602.

28. Duncan, 5.

29. Duncan, 5.

30. UEP, "Recommended Guidelines," 4–5.

31. Ash, 7–8.

32. Southeastern Poultry and Egg Association, "An Economic Impact Analysis."

33. NPPC, *Pork Producer's Handbook*, 36.

34. NPPC, *Pork Producer's Handbook*, 36.

35. NPPC, *Pork Producer's Handbook*, 36.

36. Becker, 10.

37. Hardin, 5.

38. AIF, *Animal Agriculture*, 11.

39. Stull and McMartin, 7–8.

40. Becker, 10.

41. Stull and McMartin, 15.

42. Kenneth Cheatum, American Veal Association, phone conversation with author, May 3, 1993; Kopkey, 7.

43. "Federal Grand Jury Indicts Top Veal Feeder," *Animal People* Jan.–Feb. 1996, 1; "Dead Meat," *Animal People*, June 1997, 10.

44. National Livestock and Meat Board, *Building Stable Market Growth*, 9.

45. Curtis, 3.

46. AIF, *Animal Agriculture*, 5.

47. AIF, *Animal Agriculture*, 3.

48. AIF, *Animal Agriculture*, 18.

49. Lambert, 1.

50. *AIF Newsletter*, May 1993.

51. Associated Press, *Washington Post*, Mar. 9, 1993.

52. Statement prepared by NPPC in response to inquiries.

53. Paul Dieterlen, *Farm Animal Welfare in Indiana*, 19.

54. Hurnik, 1831.

55. Rollin, "Animal Production," 13.

8. Expanding the Crusade for Animal Rights

1. Chambers, 27.

2. Marquardt, Levine, and LaRochelle, 34; "Hunters for the Hungry Feed Poor, Irks Fringe," *People's Agenda*, Feb. 1991, 2.

3. Clifton, "Killing the Captives", 23–24.

4. NRA, *NRA and Hunting*.

5. NRA, *NRA and Hunting*.

6. Merrit Clifton, editor of *Animal People*, phone conversation with author, June 25, 1997. Two surveys report numbers of hunters. The US Fish and Wildlife Service, noted here, bases its figures on numbers of hunting licenses issued. The National Shooting Sports Federation bases its numbers on surveys that probably include some hunters who do not buy licenses. Both show a decline in the number of hunters in recent years.

7. Pacelle, 18.

8. Clifton, "Killing the Captives," 25.

9. "Grassroots Campaign, Stopping the Shoot," *PETA News* 8.1 (winter 1992): 25.

10. IDA, *Performers or Prisoners?*

11. "Whales Die at Shedd Aquarium," *HSUS News* 37.3 (summer 1992): 5.

12. " 'Doing the Derby' in Kentucky: Racing's Problems Overshadow Its Big Day," *HSUS News* 37.3 (summer 1992): 3.

13. " 'Doing the Derby,' " 3.

14. Maggitti, "See How They Run," 12.

15. Marshall Gifford, lawyer for a greyhound trainer, US House of Representatives, Committee on Agriculture, Subcommittee on Livestock and Subcommittee on Department Operations, Joint Hearing, 891.

16. Letter from David G. Wolf, director, National Greyhound Adoption Program, to Representative Charles Rose, US House of Representatives, Committee on Agriculture, Subcommittee on Livestock and Subcommittee on Department Operations, Joint Hearing, 887–88.

17. Data from National Greyhound Adoption Program, quoted in US House of Representatives, Committee on Agriculture, Subcommittee on Livestock and Subcommittee on Department Operations, Joint Hearing, 918, 965.

18. "1990s Movie Ratings as of May 30," *Advocate* (AHA) 8.2 (spring 1990): 17.

19. Carbone, 9.

20. Birnbaum, 60.

21. Birnbaum, 60.

22. Bostick, 46.

23. "Genuine Animal Welfare," statement from Ringling Brothers Barnum and Bailey Circus, n.d.

24. *HSUS News*, fall 1991, 16.

25. "Carriage Horse Ban Makes Ballot," *PETA News* 6.4 (fall 1991): 11.

26. "D.C. Voters Display Horse Sense: 'Whoa' to Carriage Ban, 'Neigh' to PETA," *People's Agenda*, Jan. 1992, 1; interviews by author.

27. Fur Farm Animal Welfare Coalition, *Fur Farming*.

28. IDA, *Fur*.

29. Robin Duxbury, *Animal Rights Mobilization! Newsletter*, spring 1995, 2.

30. *PETA News* 7.4 (fall 1992): 9.

31. Duxbury, "Fur Free Friday," 11.

32. Advertisement, *Washington Post*, Apr. 1, 1994, D1–2. While the fur industry ads in 1993–1994 were showing "charmed life-style situations" to promote fur, PETA placed advertisements and demonstrated with live models the slogan, "I'd rather go naked than wear fur." This ad campaign that gained much media coverage also backfired against PETA with complaints that the ads were insulting to women. At a national animal rights conference in July 1994, Ingrid Newkirk, cofounder of PETA, apologized to the audience for any humiliation this campaign may have caused to feminist and women's groups.

33. *Wall Street Journal*, Dec. 24, 1996, B5.

34. Jasper and Nelkin, 52.

35. Kullberg.

36. Hitt et al., 50.

37. ARM! "Comprehensive Policy Statement," 4.

38. Clifton, "Network," 8.

39. LaRochelle, "Will Fund for Animals Ban Pets?" 4.

40. John Kullberg in *Animals' Agenda*, Sept. 1991, 40.

41. "Youth Education Programs," *Farm Report* (FARM), spring–summer 1994, 6.

42. See *PETA Kids*, no. 4 (summer 1990).

43. *PETA News* 8.1 (winter 1992): 14.

44. Associated Press story quoted in *People's Agenda*, May 1992, 9.

45. Quotes here and in following paragraphs are from Morrison, 204, 208.

9. Vegetarianism and Animal Rights

1. Ryder, *Animal Revolution*, 23.

2. Jasper and Nelkin, 148.

3. Unpublished report by Opinion Dynamics, Cambridge, Mass., "American Attitudes Toward Farmers and Farm Animal Issues," based on a random survey of six hundred American adults in Oct. 1990.

4. See Skelly Yankelovich and White/Clancy, Shulman, Inc., "The American Vegetarian: Coming of Age in the 90's," a study of the vegetarian marketplace conducted for the *Vegetarian Times* in 1992.

5. Yankelovich et al.

6. Comment made by Dr. Michael Klaper, animal activist and vegetarian at the Decade of the Animals Conference, Bethesda, Md., Nov. 8–11, 1991.

7. Robbins, "A Vegetarian Direction," 3.

8. McCartney and McCartney, 6–7.

9. Jenny Woods, PETA staff member, phone conversation with author, Nov. 29, 1990.

10. American Animal Protection Organizations, "Joint Resolutions."

11. ASPCA, *Animal Rights Handbook*, 40–41.

12. Hoyt, "Tilling a Common Ground."

13. AIF, *Animal Agriculture*, 15.

14. US Dept. of Agriculture, *Food Guide Pyramid*.

15. Havala and Dwyer, 351.

16. Havala and Dwyer, 352.

17. American Dietetic Association, "Diet Without Meat and Dairy Products Is Not Best for Most Americans, Dietitians Say," press release, Chicago, Apr. 8, 1991.

18. Havala and Dwyer, 352.

19. Havala and Dwyer, 352.

20. Havala and Dwyer, 354.

21. Brown made these comments at the conference, "The Ethics of Humans Using Animals for Food and Fiber," Univ. of Minnesota, Apr. 18–19, 1991.

22. Ornish, 145–47.

23. Statement by Dr. James Corbin, professor of animal science, emeritus, Univ. of Illinois at Urbana-Champaign. Before joining the university faculty, Corbin worked for a major pet food manufacturer for twenty-five years developing balanced pet foods using a variety of plant and animal ingredients.

24. ARM!, "Comprehensive Policy Statement," 5–6.

25. Wiley, 89.

26. Henry Spira, quoted in Houghton, 23.

10. The Professions: Conflicts and Controversies

1. Maggitti, "AMA Makes Us Sick," 42.

2. Horton, "Physicians," 218.

3. "AMA to Fight Back in Animal Rights War," *Chicago Tribune*, Oct. 5, 1990, sec. 1, 4.

4. Marquardt, Levine, and LaRochelle, 48–49.

5. PCRM, financials statement, July 31, 1994; organization statement, "Declaration of the Rights of Animals."

6. Burros.

7. AMVA, *Animal Welfare Positions*.

8. ALDF, *Animals' Advocate*, 7.

9. Bring, 40–41.

11. The Emerging Counterforce: Animal Interest Groups, Scientists, and Consumers React

1. Stanley Curtis, former head of the Dept. of Animal Sciences, Pennsylvania State Univ., quoted in Quaife, 19.

2. Hill and Knowlton, 20.

3. NPPC, *Pork Producer's Handbook*, 31.

4. NPPC, *Pork Producer's Handbook*, 43.

5. Fur Farm Animal Welfare Coalition, *Standard Guidelines*.

6. Fur Farm Animal Welfare Coalition, *Statement of Environmental Principles*.

7. Culton, 517.

8. Announcement of the National Youth Livestock Program Ethics Symposium, sponsored by LCI, Dec. 6–8, 1996.

9. Richard J. Dunn, NRA Hunter Information Services, correspondence with author, Apr. 17, 1991.

10. NAIA, *Alliance Alert*, 1.

11. NAIA, *Alliance Alert*, 3.

12. Smith, 5.

13. Kathleen Marquardt, interview by author, Apr. 1991.

14. PPF, information letter, Feb. 1991.

15. "Tsongas, Brown Linked to Animal 'Rights,'" *People's Agenda*, Mar.–Apr. 1992, 1.

16. "PETA Files Out of School Library," *People's Agenda*, May 1992, 2; LaRochelle, "Brainwashing," 6.

17. The 1991 financial statement, IRS Form 990, showed loans of $178,000 from the William Wewer Keogh Plan and IPSO Profit Sharing.

18. Marquardt, Levine, and LaRochelle, book jacket.

12. Animal Protection in Congress

1. Congressman Vin Weber, "Weber Forms Animal Welfare Caucus," press release, Nov. 17, 1989.

2. Weber, press release, Nov. 17, 1989.

3. Weber, press release, June 7, 1990.

4. Weber, "There Is an Alternative to the Animal Rights Movement: Join the Animal Welfare Caucus," letter inviting members of Congress to join the caucus.

5. Weber, letter.

6. "Caucus No Friend of Animals," *HSUS News* 39.3 (summer 1994): 5.

13. Freedom of Expression Out of Control

1. US Dept. of Justice, 8.

2. Ryder, *Animal Revolution*, 279.

3. Garner, 216–17

4. US Dept. of Justice, 5.

5. US Dept. of Justice, 8.

6. Ryder, *Animal Revolution*, 274.

7. Garner, 220.

8. Ryder, *Animal Revolution*, 278.

9. US Dept. of Justice, 25.

10. Hardy, 22.

11. US Dept. of Justice, 7.

12. US Dept. of Justice, 6.

13. US Dept. of Justice, 7.

14. Hardy, 29; McCabe, "Beyond Cruelty," 36.

15. US Dept. of Justice, 5–6.

16. US Dept. of Justice, 6.

17. For further insights into operations of the Animal Liberation Front, see Newkirk, *Free the Animals!*

18. Reed and Carswell, 39.

19. "Animal Liberation Front," *People's Agenda*, July 1992, 9.

20. US Dept. of Justice, 7.

21. US Dept. of Justice, 9.

22. US Dept. of Justice, 14.

23. US Dept. of Justice, 20.

24. Hardy, 25.

25. Farm Sanctuary, press release, Rockland, Del., June 4, 1986.

26. In February 1990, Dr. Hyram Kitchen, Dean of the Veterinary School of the University of Tennessee, was shot and killed at his home. One month before the incident, a local police department issued an alert through the FBI's National Crime Information Center that various sources, including mail received by the University of Tennessee, indicated that animal rights extremists had threatened to assassinate a veterinarian dean within the following twelve months. No one was ever arrested for the act and there was no claim of responsibility. Some suspect that ALF or another extremist animal rights group or individual was responsible. It must be emphasized, however, that this suspicion has never been substantiated (US Dept. of Justice, 11).

27. Hardy, 32; "Correction and Clarification," *Washingtonian* 27.3 (Dec. 1991): 36.

28. "Putting People First," *People's Agenda*, Nov.–Dec. 1992, 1.

29. *Foundation for Biomedical Research News*, 12.3 (May–June 1995): 1; *FBR Facts* 2.2.

30. Hardy, 33.

31. Hardy, 33.

32. Kirk Johnson, "Arrest Points Up Split."

33. "Fran Trutt Freed from Prison," *NAVS Bulletin*, spring 1991, 28.

34. Vickie Eide, letter to the editor, *Animals' Agenda*, Nov. 1991, 4.

35. PETA phone hot line message, Oct. 12, 1992.

36. *Animal People*, Apr. 1997, 20.

37. Reed and Carswell, 35.

38. Newkirk, *Free the Animals!* xi.

39. Dailey quoted in Hardy, 15.

40. Francione, "In Defense," 5.

41. Garner, 221–22.

42. Ryder, *Animal Revolution*, 281–83.

43. PETA staff member, phone conversation with author, Oct. 21, 1993.

44. US Dept.of Justice, 23.

45. Fox, "Putting Animal Rights in Perspective."

46. Finsen and Finsen, 99–100. Speaking before the 1994 Animal Rights Symposium, Ingrid Newkirk, cofounder of PETA, commented that "a few laboratories have been creatively recycled into the ground." The comment brought laughter and applause from the audience. However, she followed up saying, "Radical thoughts are ok, radical actions are not."

47. *Animal People*, Jan.–Feb. 1994, 2.

48. "Animal Rights Violence," *Foundation for Biomedical Research News* 13.1 (Jan.–Feb. 1996): 1.

14. Seeking Legal Rights for Animals

1. *Black's Law Dictionary*, 4th rev. ed., s.v. "standing to sue."

2. *International Animal Rights Reporter*, fall 1992, 5.

3. *International Primate Protection League et al. v. Institute for Behavioral Research, Inc. et al.*, 799 F.2d 934; 7 U.S.C.A. 2143, 2146, 2146(a), 2149(b).

4. *Sierra Club v. Morton*, 405 U.S. 727, 735 n.8; 92 S.Ct.1361, 1366 n.8; 31 L.Ed.2d 636 (1972).

5. McCabe, "Who Will Live" 116.

6. *People for the Ethical Treatment of Animals et al. v. Department of Health & Human Services*, 917 F.2d 15 (1990).

7. "Round Three for AWA Dog, Cat and Primate Standards," *Animals' Agenda* 11.4 (May 1991): 32.

8. *Animal Legal Defense Fund et al. v. Yeutter et al.*, 760 F.Supp. 923 (1991).

9. *Animal Legal Defense Fund, et al. v. Madigan et al.* 781 F.Supp. 797 (1992).

10. *Animal Legal Defense Fund et al. v. Secretary of Agriculture et al.* 1993 WL 50719 (D.D.C. 1993).

11. *International Primate Protection League et al. v. Institute for Behavioral Research, Inc. et al.*, 799 F.2d 934 (4th Cir 1986).

12. US House of Representatives, House Conference Report No. 99-447.

13. *Animal Legal Defense Fund v. Provimi Veal Corporation*, 626 F.Supp. 278, (1986).

14. *State of Alaska v. Andrus et al.*, 429 F.Supp. 958 (1977).

15. *Fund for Animals v. Andrus*, 11 ERC 297 (1978).

16. *Sierra Club et al. v. Clark*, 577 F.Supp. 783, 784, 786.

17. *Sierra Club et al. v. Clark*, 577 F.Supp. 783 (D.Minn. 1984).

18. *Sierra Club et al. v. Clark*, 755 F.2d 608 (8th Cir. 1985).

19. *Sierra Club et al. v. Clark*, 607 F.Supp. 737 (1985).

20. *Fund For Animals, Inc. v. Lujan*, 794 F.Supp. 1015 (1991).

21. *Animal Legal Defense Fund et al. v. The Secretary of Agriculture*, 1993 WL 49936 (D.D.C. 1993).

22. *Fund for Animals, Inc. et al. v. John H. Turner et al.*, 1991 WL 206232 (D.D.C. 1991).

23. *Fund for Animals, Inc. et al. v. Florida Fish and Fresh Water Fish Commission*, 550 F.Supp. 1206 (1993).

24. *Humane Society of the United States v. Lujan et al.*, 1990 WL 134832 (D.D.C. 1990).

25. *Animal Protection Institute of America, Inc. et al. v. Hodel et al.,* 671 F.Supp. 695 (1987).

26. *Animal Protection Institute of America, et al. v. Mosbacher et al.*, 799 F.Supp. 173 (1992).

27. US House of Representatives, Subcommittee on Department Operations, *Review*, 671–93.

28. "Civil Suits," *Animal People*, Apr. 1994, 16.

29. *Jones v. Butz*, 374 F.Supp. 1284 (1974).

30. *Ran-Dav's County Kosher, Inc. v. State of New Jersey*, 129 N.J. 141; 608 A.2d. 1353 (1992).

31. Charlton, Coe, and Francione, 29–34.

32. "Animals Have Advocates in Three Major Cases," *International Society of Animal Rights Report*, summer 1992, 4.

33. *Animal Legal Defense Fund et al. v. Quigg*, 710 F.Supp. 728; 27 U.S.L.W. 2467; 9 U.S.P.Q.2d 1816 (1989).

34. *Animal Legal Defense Fund et al. v. Quigg*, 900 F.2d 195; 14 U.S.P.W.2d 1485 (1990).

35. *Animal Legal Defense Fund et al. v. Quigg* 932 F.2d 920; 18 U.S.P.Q.2d 1677 (1991).

36. Mark, 4.

37. Favre and Loring, 2.

15. Financing Animal Rights and Animal Welfare Activities

1. Information from the American Association of Fund Raising Counsel's Trust for Philanthropy, in *Animal People*, Jan.–Feb., 12.

2. "Who Gets the Money?" *Animal People*, Dec. 1995, 12–13.

3. PETA, financial statements for 1992, 1993, and 1995.

4. HSUS, "Combined Financial Statements, 1995"; FFA, financial statement, 1995, 6.

5. "Who Gets the Money?" *Animal People*, Dec. 1995, 12.

6. "Help the Ones Who Really Help Animals," *Animal People*, Dec. 1995, 2.

7. "Nepotism at NAVS?" *Animals' Agenda* 12.2 (Mar. 1992): 29.

8. NAVS, 1992 fiscal year annual report, prepared by Selden, Fox and Associates, Certified Public Accountants, Aug. 12, 1992.

9. "Nepotism at NAVS?" 29

10. PETA, "Financial Statements and Supplementary Information, July 31, 1995," 13.

11. Rowan, letter to the editor, *Animals' Agenda*.

12. "Who Gets the Money?" *Animal People*, Dec. 1996, 12.

13. PETA, "Financial Statements," 1995, 12–13.

14. DDAL, "Report for Year Ending December 31, 1994, from Charitable Organization Supplement," Attorney General Jim Ryan, State of Illinois.

15. ALDF, financial statement, Dec. 31, 1995.

16. FFA, financial statement, 1995, 6.

17. "Who Gets the Money?" *Animal People*, Dec. 1995, 2, 13–14.

18. Wyant, 15.

19. PETA, fund-raising letter, 1994.

20. Charlton, Coe, and Francione, 33.

21. "What You Should Know Before You Give," *Animal People*, Dec. 1995, 1.

22. Crossen, 1.

23. "What You Should Know," 2.

16. Resolving Conflict: Hopes or Dreams?

1. Rollin, *Animal Rights*, 234, 235.

2. Rollin, "Animal Production," 3; Rowan, "Animal Well-Being," 23.

3. "American Attitudes Toward Farmers and Farm Animal Issues," a report based on a survey by Opinion Dynamics Corp. of Cambridge, Mass., taken with six hundred telephone interviews among adult Americans from Oct. 10–14, 1990.

4. Finsen and Finsen, 258–59.

5. Finsen and Finsen, 258.

6. Finsen and Finsen, 261.

7. Tom Regan, speaking at the 1994 National Animal Rights symposium, Washington, D.C., July 9, 1994.

8. Jasper and Nelkin, 26–29.

9. Jasper and Nelkin, 126–27.

10. *Animal People*, Apr. 1994, 1, 7.

11. Rowan, "Animal Rights," 5.

12. Singer, statement at the March for Animals, Washington, D.C., June 10, 1990.

13. Singer, statement.

14. Jasper and Nelkin, 51.

15. Regan, statement at the March for Animals, Washington, D.C., June 10, 1990.

16. Horton, "Enduring Animal Issue," 743.

17. Regan, Francione, and Newkirk, 40.

18. Hoyt, "Tilling a Common Ground."

19. Paul Irwin, HSUS letter of Apr. 2, 1993, to solicit funds for a new program dealing with food animal production, healthy diets, and the environment.

20. Spira, 15.

21. "Help the Ones Who Really Help the Animals," *Animal People*, Dec. 1995, 2.

22. *Feedstuffs*, Feed Industry Reference Issue 64.29, Minneapolis, Minn., July 16, 1992, 82–83.

23. Weibers, "Healing Society's Relationship."

Appendix 2: Animal Bill of Rights

1. From a mailing by ALDF that accompanied a request for support through a tax-deductible membership contribution of $15–$100 or more.

Appendix 4: Chronology of the Silver Spring Monkeys

1. *International Primate Protection League et al. v. Administrators of the Tulane Educational Fund et al.,* 895 F.2d 1056 (1990).
2. *Physicians Committee for Responsible Medicine v. Sullivan et al.,* 1990 WL 95423 (D.D.C. 1990).
3. *Physicians Committee for Responsible Medicine v. Sullivan,* 1990 WL 95430 (D.D.C. 1990).
4. *International Primate Protection League et al. v. Administrators of Tulane Education Fund et al.,* 111 S.Ct. 1700, 1991. For an extensive legal analysis of the cases cited, see Klauber.

Appendix 6: Direct Actions by US Animal Rights Activists

1. Data compiled from NABR; AFBF; PETA hotline; ALF Information Service; US Dept. of Justice; Hardy; *Animal People,* Mar. 1996; *Newsweek,* Dec. 26, 1988, 52; *Chicago Tribune,* Nov. 30, 1996, and June 2, 1997; and other newspaper reports.

Appendix 7: The Bobby Berosini Orangutans Case

1. US House of Representatives, Subcommittee on Department Operations, *Review,* 673–88.
2. "Nevada Supreme Court Rules for PETA," *PETA News* 9.2 (spring 1994): 12–13.
3. PETA, "Financial Statements and Supplementary Information, July 31, 1995."
4. Pacheco.

Bibliography

Addcox, Nancy G. "The AALAS Certification Program." *Animal Welfare Information Center Newsletter* (National Agricultural Library) 2.3/4 (July–Dec. 1991).

Albright, J. L. "Animal Well-Being/Animal Rights Issues and Food Animal Agriculture." Paper presented at the winter meeting of the Virginia Veterinary Medical Association, Tysons Corner, Va., Feb. 15, 1992.

Almond, Gabriel A. *The American People and Foreign Policy*. New York: Harcourt, Brace, 1950.

American Animal Protection Organizations. "Joint Resolutions for the 1990s." *New York Times*, Jan. 29, 1992, D22.

American Farm Bureau Federation. *Handling the Twenty Toughest Animal Rights Assertions*. Park Ridge, Ill.: AFBF, 1994.

———. *I Care About My Animals: A Discussion Guide for Dealing with Animal Rights Activities at Youth Fairs and Exhibits*. Park Ridge, Ill.: AFBF, 1991.

———. *Meeting the Animal Rights Challenge, A Handbook for State Farm Bureau Animal Welfare Coordinators*. Park Ridge, Ill.: AFBF, 1991.

American Humane Association. *Policy Statement: Farm Animal Welfare*. Denver, 1993.

American Medical Association. "Use of Animals in Biomedical Research: The Challenge and Response." AMA White Paper. Chicago, Mar. 1988.

American Society for the Prevention of Cruelty to Animals. *The Animal Rights Handbook*. Los Angeles: Living Planet Press, 1990.

———. *Origin, Purpose, Principles and Beliefs*. New York: ASPCA, n.d.

American Veal Association. *Guide for the Care and Production of Veal Calves*. 3d ed. Naperville, Ill., 1990.

American Veterinary Medical Association. *Animal Welfare Positions, Recommendations and Background Information*. Rev. ed. Schaumburg, Ill., 1991.

Amundson, Sara. "Congressional Friends of Animals." *Animals' Agenda* 15.3 (n.d.): 33.

Animal Industry Foundation. *Animal Agriculture, Myths and Facts*. Rev. ed. Arlington, Va., 1989.

Animal Legal Defense Fund. *The Animals' Advocate: Investigating Animal Abuse*. Rockville, Md., 1987.

"Animal Research, A Hazard to Health." In *Health and Humane Research*, 9–11. Jenkinstown, Penn.: AAVS, n.d.

Animal Rights Mobilization! "Comprehensive Policy Statement on Animal Rights as Adopted by the Board of Directors." Denver, n.d.

Animal Rights Network Board of Directors. "Page Two." *Animals' Agenda* 13.7 (Sept.–Oct. 1992): 2.

Anunsen, C. "Saving the Goats: A Showdown in Washington State." *Animals' Agenda* 13.1 (Jan.–Feb. 1993): 24–27, 42.

Ash, Marianne. "A Poultry Producer's View." In *Farm Animal Welfare in Indiana*, 9–10.

Association of Veterinarians for Animal Rights. *Position Statement*. Vacaville, Calif., n.d.

Barke, R. *Science, Technology, and Public Policy*. Washington, D.C.: Congressional Quarterly Press, 1986.

Beck, Melinda, Karen Brailsford, Lynda Wright, and Jacob Weisberg. "Of Pain and Progress." *Newsweek*, Dec. 26, 1988, 50–59.

Becker, Geoffrey S. *Humane Treatment of Farm Animals: Overview and Selected Issues*. Washington, D.C.: Congressional Research Service, Library of Congress, 1992.

Bell, Robert. *Impure Science*. New York: Wiley, 1992.

Bentham, Jeremy. *An Introduction to the Principles of Morals and Legislation*. 1823. Reprint, Oxford: Clarendon Press, 1907.

Bernstein, Mark H., Tom Regan, Andrew Rowan, Peter Singer, and Richard Vance. "Is Justification of Animal Research Necessary?" *Journal of the American Medical Association* 269.9 (1993): 1113–15.

Berschauer, David P. "Is the 'Endangered Species Act' Endangered?" *Southwestern Univ. Law Review* 21.3 (1992): 991–1018.

Birbeck, Anthony L. "A European Perspective on Farm Animal Welfare." *Journal of the American Veterinary Medical Association* 198.8 (1991): 1377–80.

Birnbaum, Jesse. "Just Too Beastly for Words." *Time*, June 24, 1991, 60.

Boehlje, Michael. "Animal Agriculture in Search of a Policy." *Purdue University Agricultural Report*, Dec. 1992, 13–16.

Bostick, Stephen St. C. *Zoos and Animal Rights: The Ethics of Keeping Animals*. London: Routledge, 1993.

Brambell, F. W. Rogers. *Report of the Technical Committee to Enquire into the Welfare of Animals Kept under Intensive Livestock Husbandry Systems*. 1965. Reprint, London: Her Majesty's Stationery Office, 1974.

Bring, Ellen. "Joyce Tischler: Legal Activist." *Animals' Agenda* 11.6 (July–Aug. 1991): 40–43.

Broad, William, and Nicholas Wade. *Betrayers of the Truth*. New York: Simon and Schuster, 1982.

Burd, Stephen. "President Signs Bill Imposing Federal Penalties for Vandalizing Facilities Used in Animal Research." *Chronicle of Higher Education*, Sept. 2, 1992, 30.

Burros, Marian. "Rethink Four Food Groups, Doctors Tell U.S." *New York Times*, Apr. 10, 1991, C1.

Carbone, Susan. "Pat Derby and PAWS: A Home for 'Retired' Animal Actors." *Animals' Agenda* 12.2 (Mar. 1992): 9.

"Challenging Animal Labs and Winning: Respect for Compassion in Medical School." *PCRM Update*, Nov.–Dec. 1990, 1–2, 6–10.

Chambers, Cindy. "Deer-Hunters: America's Unsung Heroes?" *PETA News* 7.4 (fall 1992): 27.

Charlton, Ann E., Sue Coe, and Gary Francione. "The American Left Should Support Animal Rights: A Manifesto." *Animals' Agenda* 13.1 (Jan.–Feb. 1993): 29–34.

"Chronology of Grand Jury Events Relating to the Animal Liberation Front." *FBR Facts*. Washington, D.C., n.d.

Clark, Stephen R. L. *The Moral Status of Animals*. Oxford: Clarendon Press, 1977.

Clifton, Merritt. "Fur Farms: Where the Sun Doesn't Shine." *Animals' Agenda* 11.9 (Nov. 1991): 12–15.

———. "Killing the Captives." *Animals' Agenda* 11.7 (Sept. 1991): 20–25.

———. "Network." *Animals' Agenda* 11.8 (Oct. 1991): 8.

———. "Who's in Charge at the National Humane Education Society." *Animal People*, July–Aug. 1993, 11.

Clingerman, Karen. *Animal Welfare Legislation: Bills and Public Laws, 1990.* AWIC Series, no. 4. Washington, D.C.: US Dept. of Agriculture, National Agricultural Library, 1991.

———. *Animal Welfare Legislation: Bills Submitted to the 102nd Congress, January 1991–March 1991.* AWIC Series, no. 9; Preliminary Report, no. 1. Washington, D.C.: US Dept. of Agriculture, National Agricultural Library, 1991.

———. *Animal Welfare Legislation: Bills Submitted to the 102nd Congress, April 1991– June 1991.* AWIC Series, no. 9; Preliminary Report, no. 2. Washington, D.C.: US Dept. of Agriculture, National Agricultural Library, 1991.

Clingerman, Karen, Sean Gleason, and Janice Swanson. *Animal Welfare Legislation: Bills and Public Laws, 1980–1988.* AWIC Series, no. 8. Washington, D.C.: US Dept. of Agriculture, National Agricultural Library, 1991.

———. *Animal Welfare Legislation: Bills and Public Laws, 1989.* AWIC Series, no. 2. Washington, D.C.: US Dept. of Agriculture, National Agricultural Library, 1990.

Cohen, Carl. "The Case for the Use of Animals in Biomedical Research." *New England Journal of Medicine* 315.14 (Oct. 2, 1986): 865–70.

Commission of the European Communities. "Council Directive of 19 November 1991 on the Protection of Animals During Transport." *Official Journal of the European Communities* (Brussels) L340/17, Dec. 11, 1991.

———. "Council Directive of 24 November 1986." *Official Journal of the European Communities* (Brussels) JL358, Dec. 18, 1986, 1–6.

———. *Proposal for a Council Directive Amending Directive 91/628/EEC on the Protection of Animals During Transport,* COM (93) 330, adopted July 13, 1993. Brussels, 1993.

Commission of the European Communities, Directorate General for Agriculture. *Communication to the Council and the European Parliament on the Protection of Animals,* COM (93) 384, adopted July 23, 1993. Brussels, 1993.

———. *Report of the Scientific Veterinary Committee (Animal Welfare Section) on the Transport of Farm Animals.* Brussels, 1992.

———. *Report of the Scientific Veterinary Committee (Animal Welfare Section) on the Welfare of Laying Hens Kept in Different Production Systems.* Brussels, 1992.

Consortium for Developing a Guide for the Care and Use of Agricultural Animals in Agricultural Research and Teaching. *Guide for the Care and Use of Agricultural Animals in Agricultural Research and Teaching.* Champaign, Ill.: Editorial and Production Services, 1988.

Council of Europe. *European Convention for the Protection of Animals Kept For Farming Purposes.* T-AP (91)4. Strasbourg, 1991.

———. *European Convention for the Protection of Animals Kept for Farming Purposes, Recommendation Concerning Cattle.* T-AP (91)4 Addendum 1. Strasbourg, 1991.

Crossen, Cynthia. "Organized Charities Pass Off Mailing Costs as Public Education." *Wall Street Journal,* Oct. 29, 1990, 1.

Culton, Barbara J. "Can Reason Defeat Unreason." *Nature* 351.6327 (June 13, 1991): 517.

Cunniff, Mary Margaret. "The Truth Will Set Them Free." *NAVS Bulletin* (spring 1991): 2.

Curtis, Stanley. "Keynote Speech." In *Farm Animal Welfare in Indiana,* 3–4.

Dawkins, Marian Stamp. *Animal Suffering: The Science of Animal Welfare.* London: Chapman and Hall, 1980.

DeBakey, Michael E. "For the Sake of Your Patients, You Must Defend Animal Research." *Physician's Management* (June 1989): 17–19.

———. "Health and Hypocrisy on Animal Rights." *Wall Street Journal,* Dec. 12, 1996.

"Declaration of the Rights of Animals." Statement adopted and proclaimed at the March for Animals, Washington, D.C., June 10, 1990, organized by NAVS.

"Development of Non-Animal Product Safety Test." *SCAW Newsletter* 12.4 (winter 1990–91): 16.

Dieterlen, Paul. "A Veterinarian's View." In *Farm Animal Welfare in Indiana*, 11–13.

Dun, P. "Cages Are at Present Still the Best System for Egg Producers." *Misset-World Poultry* 8.8 (1992): 28–32.

Duncan, Ian J. H. "The Science of Animal Well-Being." *Animal Welfare Information Center Newsletter* (National Agricultural Library) 4.1 (Jan.–Mar. 1993): 4–5.

Dutch Society for the Protection of Animals. *Farm Animals Kept in Intensive Systems, Evaluation of Existing Systems and Future Prospects*. Report of the Study Committee on Intensive Farming (translation), Dec. 1990.

Duxbury, Robin. "Fur Free Friday '92." *Animals' Agenda* 12.7 (Sept.–Oct. 1992): 11.

Dwyer, Johanna T. "Nutritional Consequences of Vegetarianism." *Annual Review of Nutrition* 11 (1991): 61–91.

EarthSave Foundation. *Our Food, Our World: The Realities of an Animal-Based Diet*. Santa Cruz, Calif., 1992.

Eide, Vickie. Letter to the editor. *Animals' Agenda*, Nov. 1991, 4.

Farm Animal Reform Movement. *A Decade of Progress for Farm Animals*. Bethesda, Md., n.d.

Farm Animal Welfare Council (UK). *Report on the European Commission Proposals on the Transport of Animals*. Tolworth, Surbiton, Surrey, Sept. 1991.

———. *Report on the Welfare of Broiler Chickens*. Tolworth, Surbiton, Surrey, April 1992.

———. *Report on the Welfare of Laying Hens in Colony Systems*. Tolworth, Surbiton, Surrey, Dec. 1991.

Farm Animal Welfare in Indiana: A Special Program on Animal Welfare Issues. Conference proceedings. West Lafayette, Ind.: Purdue Univ. School of Veterinary Medicine, 1990.

Favre, David S., and Murray Loring. *Animal Law*. Westport, Conn.: Quorum Books, 1983.

Feder, Barnaby J. "Pressuring Perdue." *New York Times Magazine*, Nov. 26, 1989, 32–34, 60, 72.

Feedstuffs. Feed Industry Reference Issue 64.29. Minneapolis, Minn., July 16, 1992, 82–83.

Finsen, Lawrence, and Susan Finsen. *The Animal Rights Movement in America*. New York: Twayne, 1994.

"Food Graphic Shows USDA Conflict of Interest." *Animals' Agenda* 11.6 (July–Aug. 1991): 33.

Foundation for Animal Rights Advocacy. *Rutgers Animal Rights Law Center*. Newark, N.J.: Rutgers Univ. Animal Rights Law Center, n.d.

Foundation for Biomedical Research. *Animal Research and Human Health*. Washington, D.C.: FBR, 1992.

———. *Directory of Animal Rights/Welfare Organizations*. Washington D.C.: FBR, 1990.

———. *Directory of Animal Rights/Welfare Organizations*. Washington, D.C.: FBR, 1994.

———. *The Use of Animals in Biomedical Research and Testing*. Washington, D.C.: FBR, 1988.

Fox, Michael W. "Animal Agriculture: Human and Animal Well-Being." *HSUS News* 36.3 (summer 1991): 26–27.

———. "Humane Sustainable Agriculture: A Simple Way to Help the Animal Kingdom and the Good Farmer." *HSUS News* 37.1 (winter 1992): 26.

———. "Putting Animal Rights in Perspective," *Des Moines Register*, Aug. 11, 1991, 1C.

Francione, Gary L. "Animal Rights and Welfare: Five Frequently Asked Questions." *Animals' Agenda* 14.3 (1994): 28–29.

———. "In Defense of the Animal Liberation Front." *Animal People*, Mar. 1994, 5.

Free, Ann Cottrell. "Eastern Europe's Animals: Help Needed." *Animal Welfare Institute Quarterly* 44.1 (winter 1992): 12.

French, Richard D. *Anti-Vivisection and Medical Science in Victorian Society*. Princeton, N.J.: Princeton Univ. Press, 1975.

Frey, R. G. *Rights, Killing and Suffering: Moral Vegetarianism and Applied Ethics*. Oxford, Eng.: Basil Blackwell, 1983.

Fur Farm Animal Welfare Coalition. *Fur Farming in North America*. St. Paul, Minn., n.d.

——. *Standard Guidelines for Operation of Mink Farms in the United States*. St. Paul, Minn., n.d.

——. *A Statement of Environmental Principles*. St. Paul, Minn., n.d.

Garner, Robert. *Animals, Politics and Morality*. Manchester, Eng.: Manchester Univ. Press, 1993.

Glaser, Lewrene K. *Provisions of the Food Security Act of 1985. Agricultural Information Bulletin no. 498. Washington, D.C.: Economic Research Service, US Dept. of Agriculture, 1986.*

Grandy, John W. "Zoos: A Critical Reevaluation." HSUS News *37.3 (summer 1992): 12–14.*

Greanville, Patrice, and Doug Moss. "The Emerging Face of the Movement." *Animals' Agenda* 5.2 (Mar.–Apr. 1985):10–11.

Greene, Stephen G. "Animal Charity in the Doghouse." *Chronicle of Philanthropy*, Mar. 8, 1994, 45.

Guillermo, Kathy Snow. *Monkey Business*. Washington, D.C.: National Press Books, 1993.

Guither, Harold. *The Food Lobbyists*. Lexington, Mass.: Lexington Books, 1982.

Guither, Harold D., and Stanley E. Curtis. *Animal Welfare: Developments in Europe: A Perspective for the United States*. No. AE4536, AS 675. Urbana: Univ. of Illinois Agricultural Experiment Station, 1983.

Guither, Harold D., and Gilbert R. Hollis. *The Economics and Policy Dimension of Animals Rights and Animal Welfare for the U.S. Swine Industry*. No. AE4696. Urbana: Univ. of Illinois Agricultural Experiment Station, 1992.

Guither, Harold D., and Michelle Van Buer. *The Evolution, Ethics, and Politics of Animal Protection*. No. AE4675. Urbana: Univ. of Illinois Agricultural Experiment Station, 1991.

Halverson, Marlene. "Farm Animal Welfare: Crisis or Opportunity for Agriculture?" Staff Paper P91-1. Dept. of Agricultural and Applied Economics, Univ. of Minnesota, Jan. 1991.

Hardin, John. "The Pork Industry View." In *Farm Animal Welfare in Indiana*, 5–6.

Hardy, David T. *America's New Extremists: What You Need to Know About the Animal Rights Movement*. Washington, D.C.: Washington Legal Foundation, 1990.

Hargrove, Eugene C., ed. *The Animal Rights Environmental Ethics Debate*. Albany: State Univ. of New York Press, 1992.

Harrison, Ruth. *Animal Machines*. London: Vincent Stuart, 1964.

——. "The Welfare Requirements of Husbandry Systems." In *Alternatives to Intensive Husbandry Systems: Proceedings of a Symposium Held at Wye College, University of London, Ashford, Kent, July 13–15, 1981*. Potters Bar, Hertfordshire, Eng.: Univ. Federation for Animal Welfare, 1981.

Havala, Suzanne, and Johanna Dwyer. "Position of the American Dietetic Association: Vegetarian Diets." *Journal of the American Dietetic Association* 88.3 (Mar. 1988): 351–55.

"Henry Bergh Coalition Demands ASPCA Reform." *International Society of Animal Rights Report*, spring 1994, 4.

Herzog, H. "The Ethical Ideology of Animal Rights Activists." Paper presented at the annual meeting of the Southeastern Psychological Association, New Orleans, Mar. 1991.

Hill and Knowlton, Inc. *Special Interest Group Profiles*. A report prepared for National Cattlemen's Association, Washington, D.C. Mar. 1990.

Hill, J. R., and D. W. B. Sainsbury. *Farm Animal Welfare, Who Cares? How?* Cambridge, Eng.: Dept. of Clinical Veterinary Medicine, 1990.

Hitt, Jack, Arthur Caplan, Gary Francione, Roger Goldman, and Ingrid Newkirk. "Just Like Us?" *Harper's*, Aug. 1988, 43–52.

Holden, Constance. "Animal Regulations: So Far, So Good." *Science* 238 (Nov. 1987): 880–82.
———. "Universities Fight Animal Activists." *Science* 243.4887 (Jan. 6, 1989): 17–19.
Horton, Larry. "The Enduring Animal Issue." *Journal of the National Cancer Institute* 81.10 (May 1989): 736–43.
———. "Physicians and the Politics of Animal Research in the 1990s." *Cancer Bulletin* 42.4 (1990): 218.
Houghton, Dean. "He Fights for Animal Rights." *Farm Journal, Hog Extra* 3.3 (Mar. 1987): 22–24.
Hoyt, John A. "Report of the President, 1990." HSUS membership meeting, San Francisco, Calif., Oct. 27, 1990.
———. "Tilling a Common Ground." Address presented by the president of HSUS at the California Farm Bureau Federation Conference, "Animal Agriculture: Conflict or Compromise?" Sacramento, Calif., Dec. 2, 1990.
Hubbell, John G. "The 'Animal Rights' War on Medicine." *Reader's Digest*, June 1990, 70–76.
Humane Farming Association. *HFA Blows Whistle on False Advertising: Federal Review Launched.* Special report. San Francisco, 1991.
Humane Society of the United States. *Making a Difference for Animals.* Washington, D.C., 1996.
———. *Statements of Policy.* Washington, D.C., 1984.
Hurnik, J. F. "Animal Welfare: Ethical Aspects and Practical Considerations." World Poultry Science Association Invited Lecture for the 79th annual meeting of the Poultry Science Association, Virginia Polytechnic Institute and State University, Blacksburg, Va., Aug. 9, 1990. *Poultry Science* 69 (1990): 1827–34.
In Defense of Animals. *Fur: A Dying Fashion, A Dead Investment?* San Rafael, Calif., n.d.
———. *Performers or Prisoners?* San Rafael, Calif., n.d.
———. *Twelve Things You Can Do.* San Rafael, Calif., n.d.
Irwin, Paul G. "The Eating with Conscience Fire Storm." *HSUS News*, spring 1994, inside front cover.
"ISAR to Work with IARL." *International Society of Animal Rights Report*, spring 1992, 4.
Jamieson, Dale. "Against Zoos." In *In Defence of Animals*, edited by Peter Singer, 108–117.
Jamison, Wesley, and William Lunch. "Results from Demographic, Attitudinal, and Behavioral Analysis of the Animal Rights Movement: A Preliminary Report." College of Agricultural Sciences and Dept. of Political Science, Oregon State Univ. 1991.
Jasper, James M., and Dorothy Nelkin. *The Animal Rights Crusade: The Growth of a Moral Protest.* New York: Free Press, 1992.
Johnson, Hugh. *Meeting the Animal Rights Challenge.* Park Ridge, Ill.: American Farm Bureau Federation, 1991.
Johnson, Kirk. "Arrest Points Up Split in Animal Rights Movement." *New York Times*, Nov. 13, 1988, sec. A40.
Jolma, Dena Jones. "Henry Salt and 100 Years of Animal Rights." *Animals' Agenda* 12.8 (Nov.–Dec. 1992): 30–32.
Katz, Elliot M. *Action in Defense of Animals.* IDA brochure, n.d.
Kelley, B. G. "The First Word: Rights and Respect." *AV Magazine* 98.8 (Sept. 1990): 1.
Klauber, Bridget. "See No Evil, Hear No Evil: The Federal Courts and the Silver Spring Monkeys." *University of Colorado Law Review* 63.2 (1992): 501–20.
Kopkey, Randie. "The Veal Industry View." In *Farm Animal Welfare in Indiana*, 7.
Krasney, John A. "Some Thoughts on the Value of Life." *Buffalo Physician* 18.3 (Sept. 1984): 6–13.
Kullberg, John. "Progress for Companion Animals." Abstract from the Decade for Animals Conference, Rockville, Md., Nov. 9, 1991.

Lambert, Charles. "Killed by 'Friendly Fire,' 'Beyond Beef' Campaign Threatens Family Farms and Ranches." National Cattlemen's Association statement, Denver, Colo., 1993.

Lansbury, C. *The Old Brown Dog: Women, Workers, and Vivisection in Edwardian England.* Madison, Wis.: Univ. of Wisconsin Press, 1985.

LaRochelle, Mark. "Brainwashing America's Children." *People's Agenda*, July 1991, 6.

———. "Will Fund For Animals Ban Pets?" *People's Agenda*, Oct. 1991, 4.

Leader, Robert W., and Dennis Stark. "The Importance of Animals in Biomedical Research." *Prospectives in Biology and Medicine* 30.4 (summer 1987): 470–84.

Leahy, Michael P. T. *Against Liberation: Putting Animals in Perspective.* London: Routledge, 1991.

———. "Animals and the Ethics of Slaughter." Paper presented at the Bioethics Institute, Univ. of Illinois at Urbana-Champaign, May 20, 1994.

Lichter, R., and S. Rothman. "What Interests the Public and What Interests the Public Interests." *Public Opinion* 6 (Apr.–May 1983): 44–48.

Linzey, Andrew. *Animal Theology.* Urbana: Univ. of Illinois Press, 1995.

———. *Christianity and the Rights of Animals.* London: SPCL; New York: Crossroads, 1987.

Loew, Franklin M. "Reductions in Animal Use in Veterinary Medical Education." *Animal Welfare Information Center Newsletter* (National Agricultural Library) 2.2 (Apr.–June 1991).

Lunch, William. *Midwives of Democracy: The Active Public in American Politics.* Ann Arbor: University Microfilms, 1976.

———. *The Nationalization of American Politics.* Berkeley: Univ. of California Press, 1984.

Luther, Lorenz Otto, and Margaret Sheffield Simon. *Targeted: The Anatomy of an Animal Rights Attack.* Norman: Univ. of Oklahoma Press, 1992.

Maggitti, Phil. "The AMA Makes Us Sick." *Animals' Agenda* 9.9 (Nov. 1991): 41–43.

———. "See How They Run: A Look at the Hidden Side of Greyhound Racing." *Animal's Agenda* 12.2 (Oct. 1991): 12–18.

Mandrell, T. D. "Alternatives and the Animal Welfare Act." *Animal Welfare Information Center Newsletter* (National Agricultural Library) 2.1 (Jan.–Mar. 1991): 1–2.

Mark, Diana A. "All Animals Are Equal, But Some Are Better Than Others: Patenting Transgenic Animals." *Columbus School of Law Review* (Catholic Univ. of America) 7JCHLP245 (spring 1991): 1–64.

Marquardt, Kathleen, Herbert M. Levine, and Mark LaRochelle. *Animal Scam.* Washington, D.C.: Regnery Gateway, 1993.

Martin, Phillip W. D. *The Animal Rights Movement in the United States: Its Composition, Funding Sources, Goals, Strategies and Potential Impact on Research.* Cambridge, Mass.: Harvard Univ., Office of Government and Community Affairs, 1982. Reprint, Clarks Summit, Penn.: Society for Animal Rights, 1982.

Mason, Jim, and Peter Singer. *Animal Factories.* New York: Harmony Books, 1990.

Masta, Robert I. Letter to the editor. *New England Journal of Medicine* 316.9 (Feb. 26, 1987): 55.

McCabe, Katie. "Beyond Cruelty." *Washingtonian* 25.2 (Feb. 1990): 72–77, 185–87, 189–95.

———. "Who Will Live, Who Will Die?" *Washingtonian* 21.11 (Aug. 1986): 112–18.

McCarthy, Coleman. "Our Outreach Director Speaks Out from a Cell." *Fund for Animals* 23.2 (n.d.): 2.

McCartney, Paul, and Linda McCartney. "The Art of Vegetarianism." *PETA News* 6.4 (fall 1991): 6–7.

McKeown, Thomas. *The Role of Medicine: Dream, Mirage or Nemesis?* Princeton, N.J.: Princeton Univ. Press, 1979.

Mench, Joy A., and Ari van Tienhoven. "Farm Animal Welfare." *American Scientist* 74 (Nov.–Dec. 1986):598–603.

Midgley, Mary. *Animals and Why They Matter*. Harmondsworth, Eng.: Penguin Books, 1983.

———. "Persons and Non-Persons." In *In Defence of Animals*, edited by Peter Singer, 52–62.

Moretti, Daniel S. *Animal Rights and the Law*. New York: Oceana Publications, 1984.

Morrison, Adrian R. "Biomedical Research and the Animal Rights Movement: A Contrast in Values." *American Biology Teacher* 55.4 (Apr. 1993): 204–8.

Muskin, Alies. "AAALAC: Promoting Quality Animal Care and Use." *Animal Welfare Information Center Newsletter* (National Agricultural Library) 2.3/4 (July–Dec. 1991): 1, 2, 7, 8.

National Academy of Sciences. Institute of Medicine. *Science, Medicine, and Animals*. Washington, D.C.: National Academy Press, 1991.

National Animal Interest Alliance. *Alliance Alert*. Portland, Ore., 1993.

National Farmers Union (UK). *Animal Welfare, An Outline of Policy*. London: National Farmers Union, 1991.

National Livestock and Meat Board. Beef Industry Council Veal Committee. *Building Stable Market Growth for Veal, 1993–97*. Chicago: National Livestock and Meat Board, 1992.

National Pork Producers Council. *The Pork Producer's Handbook on Animal Welfare/Animal Rights*. Des Moines, n.d.

National Rifle Association. *Animal Rights Terrorists and Their War Against Mainstream America*. Washington, D.C., 1990.

———. *The NRA and Hunting*. Washington, D.C., 1990.

National Wildlife Federation. *Trapping and Conservation*. Washington, D.C., 1979.

Newkirk, Ingrid. *Free the Animals!* Chicago: Noble Press, 1992.

———. *Save the Animals*. New York: Warner Books, 1990.

Nie, N., S. Verba, and J. Petrocik. *The Changing American Voter*. Cambridge, Mass.: Harvard Univ. Press, 1979.

"NIH: Science or Public Relations?" *PCRM Update*, Mar.–Apr. 1990, 1–9.

North American Vegetarian Society. *Vegetarianism: Answers to the Most Commonly Asked Questions*. Dodgeville, N.Y., n.d.

Ogden, Daniel M. "How National Policy Is Made." In *Increasing Understanding of Public Problems and Policies 1971*, 5–10. Chicago: Farm Foundation, 1971.

Oliver, Charles. "Liberation Zoology." *Reason* 22.2 (June 1990): 22–27.

Ornish, Dean. *Stress, Diet, and Your Heart*. New York: Holt, Rinehart and Winston, 1982.

Pacelle, Wayne. "Wildlife Mismanagement." *Animals' Agenda* 11.7 (Sept. 1991): 12–18.

Pacheco, Alex. "Dear *Animal Times* Reader." *PETA's Animal Times*, fall 1996, 2.

People for the Ethical Treatment of Animals. *Annual Review*. Rockville, Md., 1993

"Petitions to Congress Support Responsible Use of Laboratory Animals." *SCAW Newsletter* 12.3 (fall 1990): 16.

Petricciana, John C., and Ethel Thurston. "Regulation, Abolition or Alternative Research." *California Veterinarian*, Jan. 1983, 81–82.

Phillips, M. T., and J. A. Sechzer. *Animal Research and Ethical Conflict*. New York: Springer-Verlag, 1989.

Physicians Committee for Responsible Medicine. "Beyond the Draize Test." Washington, D.C., n.d.

———. "Declaration of Concern and Support." Membership solicitation letter. N.p, n.d.

Quaife, Thomas. "Exactly What Is Animal Welfare?" *Swine Practitioner*, May 1990, 19–20.

Ranney, A. *Channels of Power*. Washington, D.C.: American Enterprise Institute, 1983.

Reed, Susan, and Sue Carswell. "Animal Passion." *People*, Jan. 18, 1993, 35–39.

Regan, Tom. *The Case for Animal Rights*. Berkeley: Univ. of California Press, 1983.

———. *The Philosophy of Animal Rights*. Raleigh, N.C.: Culture and Animal Foundation, n.d.

————. *The Struggle for Animal Rights*. Clarks Summit, Penn.: International Society for Animal Rights, 1987.

————, ed. *Animal Sacrifices: Religious Perspectives on the Use of Animals in Science*. Philadelphia: Temple Univ. Press, 1986.

Regan, Tom, Gary Francione, and Ingrid Newkirk. "A Movement's Means Create Its Ends." *Animals' Agenda* 12.10 (Jan.–Feb. 1992): 40–45.

Reines, Brandon. "March 1993: The Beginning of the End for Animal Testing?" *International Society for Animal Rights Report*, summer 1993, 7.

Richards, Rebecca T., and Richard S. Krannich. "The Ideology of the Animal Rights Movement." Unpublished manuscript, Dept. of Sociology, California State Univ. and Dept. of Sociology, Utah State Univ., 1991.

Ricketts, Gary. "Humane Care for Animal Projects: An Overview." Teleconference materials, prepared for the Univ. of Illinois Cooperative Extension Service, Nov. 21, 1995.

Rifkin, Jeremy. *Beyond Beef: The Rise and Fall of the Cattle Culture*. New York: Dutton, 1992.

Robbins, John. *Diet for a New America*. Walpole, N.H.: Stillpoint Publishing, 1987.

————. "A Vegetarian Direction Can Help Alleviate the Current Energy Crisis." A Special Earth-Save Report. N.p., n.d.

Roberts, Catherine. "Science, Animal Abuse and Sacred Things." *NAVS Bulletin*, spring 1991, 26–27.

Rollin, Bernard. "Animal Production and the New Social Ethic for Animals." In *Food Animal Well-Being, 1993 Conference Proceedings and Deliberations*, 3–14. West Lafayette, Ind.: US Dept. of Agriculture and Purdue University, 1993.

————. *Animal Rights and Human Morality*. Buffalo, N.Y.: Prometheus Books, 1992.

————. "Animal Welfare, Animal Rights and Agriculture." *Journal of Animal Science* 68 (1990): 3456–61.

————. "The Ethics of Livestock Showing." In *Official Proceedings, National Youth Livestock Ethics Symposium, Las Vegas, Nevada, December 1–2, 1995*, 17–24. Bowling Green, Ky.: Livestock Conservation Institute, n.d.

————. *Farm Animal Welfare*. Ames: Iowa State Univ. Press, 1995.

————. *The Unheeded Cry*. Oxford, Eng.: Oxford Univ. Press, 1989.

Rowan, Andrew. "The Alternatives Concept." *Animal Welfare Information Center Newsletter* (National Agricultural Library) 2.2 (Apr.–June 1991): 1–2, 8.

————. "Animal Rights, Animal Welfare and Animal Protection." *SCAW Newsletter* 12.4 (winter 1990–91): 5–6.

————. "Animal Well-Being: Key Philosophical, Ethical, Political, and Public Issues Affecting Food Animal Agriculture." In *Food Animal Well-Being, 1993 Conference Proceedings and Deliberations*, 23–35. West Lafayette, Ind.: US Dept. of Agriculture and Purdue Univ., 1993.

————. Letter to the editor. *Animals' Agenda*, Sept. 1991, 7.

————. Letter to the editor. *Journal of the American Medical Association* 269.9 (Mar. 3, 1993): 1113–14.

————. *Of Mice, Models, and Men: A Critical Evaluation of Animal Research*. Albany: State Univ. of New York Press, 1984.

Rowan, Andrew N., Franklin M. Loew, and Joan C. Weer. *The Animal Research Controversy, Protest, Process and Public Policy*. Medford, Mass.: Center for Animals and Public Policy, Tufts Univ. School of Veterinary Medicine, 1995.

Ryder, Richard D. Address before the 7th International Animal Rights Symposium, Washington, D.C., July 9, 1994.

————. *Animal Revolution, Changing Attitudes Towards Speciesism*. Oxford: Basil Blackwell, 1989.

————. *Victims of Science: The Use of Animals in Research*. London: National Anti-Vivisection Society, 1983.

Sapontzis, S. F. *Morals, Reason, and Animals*. Philadelphia: Temple Univ. Press, 1987.

Scarce, Rik. *Eco-Warriors*. Chicago: Noble Press, 1990.

Screaming Wolf. *A Declaration of War: Killing People to Save Animals and the Environment*. Grass Valley, Calif.: Patrick Henry Press, 1991.

Shapiro, Kenneth J. Address before the 7th International Animal Rights Symposium, Washington, D.C., July 9, 1994.

————. "The Psychology of Dissection." *Animals' Agenda* 11.9 (Nov. 1991): 20–21.

Sharpe, Robert. *The Cruel Deception: The Use of Animals in Medical Research*. Wellington, Northamptonshire, Eng.: Thorsons Publishers, 1988.

Singer, Peter. *Animal Liberation: A New Ethics for Our Treatment of Animals*. New York: Random House, 1975.

————. *Animal Liberation: A New Ethics for Our Treatment of Animals*. 2d ed. New York: Random House, 1990.

————. "A Conversation with Peter Singer." *Animals' Agenda* 14.2 (Mar.–Apr. 1994): 25–29.

————. *Practical Ethics*. Cambridge: Cambridge Univ. Press, 1993.

————, ed. *In Defence of Animals*. Oxford: Basil Blackwell, 1985.

Smith, Rod. "Putting People First: New Organization Taking Up the Call to Challenge Animal Extremists' Agenda." *Feedstuffs* (Minneapolis, Minn.), Dec. 17, 1990, 5.

Southeastern Poultry and Egg Association. "A Discussion of the Economic Significance to the Producers and the Consumer of Converting to Less Intensive Commercial Egg Production in the United States," by D. D. King, F. A. Lasley, K. A. Holleman, and D. J. Bray. A report to Terry B. Kinney, administrator, Agricultural Research Service, US Dept. of Agriculture, Aug. 1983.

————. "An Economic Impact Analysis of Converting to Less Intensive Confinement of Poultry." Atlanta, Ga., n.d.

Sperling, S. *Animal Liberators: Research and Morality*. Berkeley: Univ. of California Press, 1988.

Spira, Henry. "Animal Rights." *Fellowship of Reconciliation* 57.9 (Sept. 1991): 13–15.

Strand, Rod, and Patti Strand. *The Hijacking of the Humane Movement*. Wilsonville, Ore.: Doral Publishing, 1993.

Stull, Carolyn L., and Duncan A. McMartin. *Welfare Parameters in Veal Calf Production Facilities*. Davis, Calif.: Veterinary Medicine Cooperative Extension, Univ. of California, Davis, 1992.

"Survey Shows Medical Students Find Dog Labs Valuable." *National Association for Biomedical Research News* 12.3 (May–June 1995): 2.

Swanson, Janice C. *Animal Welfare Legislation and Regulations, January 1979–February 1991*. QB 91-63. US Dept. of Agriculture, National Agricultural Library, Mar. 1991.

————. "Welfare Concerns for Farm Animals Used in Agricultural and Biomedical Research and Teaching." *Animal Welfare Information Center Newsletter* (National Agricultural Library) 5.1 (spring 1994): 3.

Swedish Ministry of Agriculture. *The Animal Protection Act. Swedish Code of Statutes*. SFS 1988:534, June 2, 1988.

Tester, Keith. *Animals and Society: The Humanity of Animal Rights*. London: Routledge, 1991.

Thomas, Keith. *Man and the Natural World*. New York: Pantheon Books, 1983.

Tiger, Steven. "Anti-Vivisectionism as Public Health Advocacy." *NAVS Bulletin*, spring 1991, 12–13.

————. "Is There Really a Conflict Between Concern for Animals and Concern for Human Health?" *NAVS Bulletin* 4 (1990): 10–11.

Todd, David. "Wolves: Predator Control and Endangered Species Protection: Thoughts on Politics and Law." *South Texas College of Law Review* 33 (July 1992): 459–92.

"Traffic in Misery." *HSUS News* 36.4 (fall 1991): 14–18.

Tweeten, Luther. "Public Policy Decisions for Farm Animal Welfare." Paper presented to International Conference on Farm Animal Welfare, Aspen Institute, Wye Center, Md., June 10, 1991.

UK Ministry of Agriculture, Fisheries and Food. *Animal Health 1990*. Report of the Chief Veterinary Officer. London: MAFF, 1991.

———. *Code of Practice, on the Care of Farm Animals and Horses During Their Transport on Roll-on/Roll/off Ferries; for the Care and Feeding of Animals in Government Approved Export Lairages; the Welfare of Horses, Ponies and Donkeys at Markets, Sales and Fairs*. London: MAFF, 1990.

———. *Codes of Recommendations for the Welfare of Livestock: Pigs, Cattle*. Reprint, London: MAFF, 1991.

———. *Operations on Farm Animals: A Guide to Legislation*. London: MAFF, 1991.

———. *Summary of the Law Relating to Farm Animal Welfare*. London: MAFF, 1992.

United Egg Producers. *Healthy Productive Management Practices of the U.S. Industry*. Atlanta, Ga., n.d.

———. "Recommended Guidelines of Husbandry Practices for Laying Chickens." N.p., n.d.

United Poultry Concerns. *Chickens*. Potomac, Md., n.d.

Universities Federation for Animal Welfare. *Guidelines on the Care of Laboratory Animals and Their Use for Scientific Purposes*. Potters Bar, Herts, Eng.: RSPCA and UFAW, 1987.

"USDA Report Shows Further Decline in Lab Animal Numbers." *Foundation for Biomedical Research News* 12.4 (July–Aug. 1995): 2.

US Dept. of Agriculture. Human Nutrition Information Service. *The Food Guide Pyramid*. Home and Garden Bulletin no. 252. Washington, D.C., n.d.

———. *USDA's Food Guide: Background and Development*. Administrative Report no. 389. Human Nutrition Information Service. Washington, D.C., Oct. 1992.

US Dept. of Commerce. *Census of Agriculture, 1992*. Washington, D.C., 1992.

US Dept. of Justice. *Report to Congress on the Extent and Effects of Domestic and International Terrorism on Animal Enterprises*. Washington, D.C., Aug. 1993.

"The Use of Pound/Shelter Animals in Research and Education." *NABR Issue Update*. Washington, D.C., n.d.

US House of Representatives. House Conference Report No. 99-447, 99th Cong. 1st sess. In *U.S. Code Cong. and Ad. News* 1985, 1676, 2518.

———. Committee on Agriculture. Subcommittee on Department Operations, Research, and Foreign Agriculture. *Review of US Department of Agriculture's Enforcement of the Animal Welfare Act, Specifically of Animals Used in Exhibitions*. Serial No. 102-75. Washington D.C., July 8, 1992.

———. Committee on Agriculture. Subcommittee on Livestock, Dairy and Poultry and the Subcommittee on Department Operations, Research, and Foreign Agriculture. Joint Hearing, *Veal Calf Protection Act*. Serial no. 101-18, H.R. 84. Washington, D.C., June 6, 1989.

US National Park Service. *Administrative Policies for Natural Areas of the National Park Service*. Washington, D.C., 1968.

Vance, Richard F. "An Introduction to the Philosophical Presuppositions of the Animal Liberation/Rights Movement." *Journal of the American Medical Association* 268.13 (Oct. 17, 1992): 1715–19.

Vansickle, Joe. "Swelling Rights Effort Grows More Radical." *National Hog Farmer*, Jan. 15, 1991, 10.

"Vegetarian Campaign." *PETA News* 8.1 (winter 1992): 16.

Warren, Mary Anne. "The Rights of the Nonhuman World." In *The Animal Rights Environmental Ethics Debate*, edited by Eugene C. Hargrove, 185–210. Albany: State Univ. of New York Press, 1992.,

Watson, Paul. "Reject, Isolate, Abandon Undisciplined ALF." *Animal People*, Mar. 1994, 6–7.

Weibers, David O. "Healing Society's Relationship with Animals: A Physician's View." *HSUS News* 36.4 (fall 1991): 27.

———. "Vision of a New Era." *HSUS News* 37.1 (winter 1992): 9–11.

"What Sort of Person Reads *Agenda?*" *Animals' Agenda* 4.2 (May–June 1983): 26.

White, Kenneth, and Kenneth Shapiro. "The Culture of Violence: The Animal Connection." *Animals' Agenda* 14.2 (Mar.–Apr. 1994): 18–22.

White, L. "The Historical Roots of Our Ecological Crisis". *Science* 155.3767 (Mar. 1967): 203–7.

"Who Gets the Money?" Parts 1–2. *Animals' Agenda* 11.2 (Mar. 1991): 33–34; 11.6 (July–Aug. 1991): 34–35.

Wiley, Carol. "Why It's Impossible to Be a Vegetarian." *Vegetarian Times* No. 165 (May 1991): 59–60, 89.

Wilson, J. *Political Organizations*. Berkeley: Univ. of California Press, 1976.

Windhorst, Hand-Wilhelm. "The Situation of German Intensive Animal Production." *Misset-World Poultry* 7.4 (1991): 41.

Winikoff, Michael. "Lota: The Battle Goes On—Successful Appeal Could Protect Circus Animals." *HSUS News* 38.1 (winter 1993) 9–10.

Wolf, Zoe. "Teaching Animal Issues." *Animals' Agenda* 12.2 (Mar. 1992): 20–22.

Woodier, Olwen. "Milk: Neither Natural Nor Wholesome." *Animals' Agenda* 14.3 (1994): 16–17.

Wunderlich, Gene. "The Ethics of Animal Agriculture." *Food Review* (USDA), Oct.–Dec. 1991, 24–27.

Wyant, Sara. "What Agriculture Pays Its Top Guns." *Prairie Farmer* 165.4 (Feb. 1993): 14–15, 25.

Zierer, Tita. "The Perils of Puppy Mills: From the Canadian Side." *Animals' Agenda* 13.2 (Mar.–Apr. 1993): 30–33.

Index

Brzoznowski, Julius, 169
Buddhists Concerned for Animals, 53, 208
budgets of animal rights organizations, 177
Bullington, Allan, 204
Burnett, Nancy, 174
Buyukmihci, Nedim C., 128, 204

cage system for laying hens, 3, 28, 30, 93, 127
California Cattlemen's Association, 226
California condor, 105, 146
California Farm Bureau, 42
Californians for Responsible Research, 52
California Political Action Committee for Animals, 208, 210
California Primate Research Center, 222
California State University, 222
California Wool Growers Association, 226
Campbell, Tom, 149
canned hunts, 102
Caras, Roger A., 36, 204
castration, 29, 94; of cattle, 127
cats: breeding, 194; in research, 73
Cave, Eleanor, 204
Cave, George P., 204
Cave, William, 204
Cedars-Sinai Medical Center, 223, 227
Center for Animals and Public Policy, 209
Center for Animal Welfare, 209
Center for Expansion of Fundamental Rights, 210
Center for Food and Animal Research, 205
Center for Health Science Policy, 209
Center for Respect for Life, 205
Chapman, Pamela, 217
Charles River Laboratories, 153
Charlton, Anna, 130, 187
Charrow, Robert, 12
Chicago Animal Rights Coalition, 206
Chicago Anti-Cruelty Society, 204
Christianity, 21
circuses, 102, 104
Citizens for Animals, 175
City of Hope Research Institute and Medical Center, 222
Clark, James A., 204
Clark, Stephen, 17
classroom, crusade in the, 109; indoctrination, 111
clenbuterol, 54

Clifton, Merritt, 8, 47, 56, 178, 204
Close, Doreene, 204
Coalition Against Fur Farms, 204
Coalition for Non-Violent Food, 91
Coalition to Abolish Classroom Dissection, 209
Coalition to Abolish the LD-50, 203
Coalition to End Animal Suffering and Exploitation (CEASE), 76, 135, 204–5
Coalition to End the Wild Bird Trade, 57
cock fighting, 44
Code of Practice for the Welfare of Horses, Ponies, and Donkeys, 214
Cohen, Carl, 81
Cohen, Murry, 204
Colorado State University, 206, 209
Columbia University, 158
Commission on Farm Animal Care, 133
Committee for Humane Legislation, 44, 205
companion animals, 125, 146, 194
Congressional Friends of Animals, 144, 148
Congressional Sportsmen's Caucus (CSC), 150–51
Convention on International Trade in Endangered Species (CITES), 101
Corbin, James, 119
Cornell University, 51, 158
Coronado, Rodney, 157, 204
Culture and Animals Foundation, 110, 208–9
Cunniff, Kenneth L., 205
Cunniff, Mary Margaret, 205
Curtis, Stanley L., 205
Cutler, Rupert, 205

Dailey, Tim, 159
Dairygold Distribution Center, 230
Davies, Brian, 178
Davies, Sarah, 105
Davis, Karen, 56, 149, 205
Davis Egg Ranch, 225
Dawkins, Marian, 91
Day, Doris, 45, 55, 90, 205
DeBakey, Michael, 76, 205
debeaking of chickens, 3, 92, 128
declawing of cats, 125, 128
deer: guidelines for transport of, 214; hunting, 171
Defenders of Wildlife, 57, 59, 169, 170, 173, 205
dehorning of cattle, 127

Medlock, Aaron, 43, 208
membership dues of animal rights organizations, 179
Mench, Joy, 92, 208
Mendes, Chico, 160
mice: under *Animal Welfare Act*, 167; for biomedical research, 220
Michaels, Gil, 208
Michigan State University, 157, 205
Midgley, Mary, 18
milk replacers for veal calves, 95
Miller, Bonnie, 208
Miller, Bradley, 178, 208
Millsaps, Reed, 208
mink production, 106
molting, induced, 127
Monkey Business (Guillermo), 206
Montavalli, Jim, 48, 208
Montgomery Fur Co., 232
Morgan, Richard, 208
Mouras, Belton, 208
movies, animals in, 104
Mrazek, Bob, 149

Natelson, Nina, 208
National Academy of Science (NAS), 76, 97
National Aeronautics and Space Administration, 231
National Alliance for Animals, 11, 206
National Animal Interest Alliance (NAIA), 140, 208, 210
National Anti-Vivisection Society (NAVS), 40, 76, 154, 185, 187, 203, 205, 208, 210
National Association for Biomedical Research (NABR), 76, 78, 139, 203, 210
National Association for the Advancement of Humane and Environmental Education, 206
National Association of Biology Teachers, 79
National Association of Humane and Environmental Education, 109
National Association of Nurses Against Vivisection, 210
National Association of People with AIDS, 78
National Broiler Council, 133, 134
National Cancer Institute, 222
National Cattlemen's Beef Association (NCBA), 133, 134, 137, 229

National Charities Information Bureau (NCIB), 50, 184
National Farmers Union (NFU), 207
National Hearing Dog Project, 37
National Humane Education Society (NHES), 40, 204
National Institute for Neurological and Communicative Disorders and Stroke, 223
National Institutes of Health (NIH), 53, 82, 148, 158, 165, 192, 205, 217, 223, 226
National Institutes of Mental Health, 208, 225
National Lamb Feeders Association, 133
National Livestock and Meat Board, 96, 133
National Livestock Producers Association, 133
National Marine Fisheries Service, 103, 149
National Milk Producers Federation, 134
National Pork Producers Council (NPPC), 97, 133, 134
National Rifle Association (NRA), 102, 140
National Science Teachers Association, 79
National Turkey Federation, 133, 134, 229
National Wool Growers Association, 133
Nature Conservancy, 229
Naval Medical Research Institute, 221
Nelkin, Dorothy, 193
Nelson, Tina, 208
New England Anti-Vivisection Society (NEAVS), 4, 8, 38, 39, 76, 149, 155, 159, 187, 203, 206, 207, 208
New Jersey Animal Rights Alliance, 175
Newkirk, Ingrid, 9, 39, 48, 54, 61, 107, 142, 159, 177, 208
New York University, 51
Nitabell Rabbitry, 225
North American Game Bird Association, 101
North American Vegetarian Society, 116
North Carolina State University, 110
North Shore Animal League, 177
Northwestern University, 40, 226

O'Barry, Richard, 208
Ogden, Daniel, 8
Ohio State University, 222
Olivers Egg Farm, 225
orangutans case, 233
Oregon State University (OSU), 60, 63
Orem, John M., 144, 158, 208
Ornish, Dean, 119
Owens, Major, 149

Pacelle, Wayne, 43, 102, 208
Pacheco, Alex, 9, 39, 48–49, 54, 142, 164, 165, 178, 216, 221, 229
Pallone, Frank, Jr., 142, 149
Paramount studios, 142
Parkinson Foundation, 53
patents on animals, 175
Patterson, Simone, 48
Paulhus, Marc S., 208
Pennsylvania State University, 205
People for the Ethical Treatment of Animals (PETA), 9, 33, 39, 48–50, 54, 58, 59, 76, 101, 103–6, 110, 111, 115, 142, 154, 157, 158, 164, 174, 175, 177–79, 183–85, 205, 206, 208, 209, 216, 230, 233, 234
People's Agenda, 141
Perdue, Frank, 46, 90
Performing Animal Welfare Society (PAWS), 104, 174, 175, 205, 233
PETA Kids, 50, 110
pets, 68, 107, 125; adoption, 108; vegetarian diets for, 119
philosophy, defined, 13
physicians, 122
Physicians Committee for Responsible Medicine (PCRM), 8, 39, 54, 76, 118, 123, 124, 180, 187, 203, 205, 217, 218
pigeon shoot, 102
Plutarch, 113
Political Action Committee for Animal Welfare and Protection, 208
Pork Producer's Handbook (NPPC), 136
pork production, 94
poultry production, 92
Poultry Science Association, 133
power clusters within animal industries, 191
predators, 164
Prescott, Heidi, 45, 208
Procter and Gamble, 53, 81
Producers Livestock Marketing Association, 231
Provimi, 133
psychologists, 130
Psychologists for the Ethical Treatment of Animals (PsyETA), 130, 204, 209
puppy mills, 108
Purdue University, 196, 203
Purina Mills, 134
Putting People First (PPF), 105, 141, 207, 210

rabbits in research, 73
Race Street Fish and Poultry, 225
Rancho Slaughterhouse, 232
rats, under *Animal Welfare Act*, 167
ravens, 172
Red Rock Canyon National Conservation Area 1990, 220
reduction of animals in research, 82
Reeve, Christopher, 208
refinement of animal research, 82
reformists, 10, 35
Regan, Susan, 208
Regan, Tom, 9, 15, 17, 19, 22, 29, 55, 61, 110, 194, 208
Reines, Brandon, 209
religion, 20–21
religious practices, 164; rituals, 174
research, animals in, 73, 81, 126, 146; alternatives to, 79
Revlon, 40
Richards, Rebecca, 63
Richey, Charles, 167
Rifkin, Jeremy, 52, 91, 97, 207, 209
Rinaldo, Matther, 149
Ringling Brothers Barnum and Bailey Circus, 105, 221
Robbins, John, 52, 76, 209
Roberti, David, 209
Roberts' Furs, 224
Rocky Mountain Humane Society, 205
rodeos, 102
Roe, Robert, 149
Rollin, Bernard, 12, 18, 24, 34, 73, 87, 99, 189, 209
Roman Catholic theology, 21
Rose, Naomi, 209
Ros-Lehtinen, Ileana, 149
Ross, Claudia, 160
Roush, Jeanne, 178, 209, 233, 234
Rowan, Andrew, 10, 22, 73, 80, 185, 193, 209
Rus Dun Egg Farm, 230
Rush, Robert, 174
Rutgers University, 110; Animal Rights Law Clinic, 160, 205; School of Law, 129
Ryder, Richard, 6, 17, 152, 160, 209

salaries: animal rights organizations, 186; opposition organizations, 186

Harold D. Guither is a professor of agricultural policy, emeritus, at the University of Illinois at Urbana-Champaign. He has taught courses in the economic history of agriculture and agricultural policy, organized state and national extension programs on agricultural and food policy issues, and conducted research on other public policy matters. During his thirty-nine years on the university faculty, he also served two years on a USAID assignment in Jordan and worked as a staff member in the US House of Representatives and in the US Department of Agriculture.